Working with English Grammar

An Introduction

This clear and concise introduction offers students of linguistics and English language a comprehensive overview of English grammar, including word structure, major and minor word classes, phrases, clauses and sentences. Based on twenty years' teaching practice, Louise Cummings adopts a unique approach of using three real-world contexts – first language acquisition, language disorders and non-standard dialects – as a pedagogical tool to make grammatical concepts meaningful to students and to improve engagement and understanding. In seven accessible chapters, students are encouraged to develop the analytical skills they require to give a comprehensive description of the grammar of the English language. A range of supportive learning aids is used, including:

- Learning objectives and section 'key points' summaries.
- Varied examples from world Englishes and print media.
- Homework assignments, exercises and revision questions.
- Targeted further reading suggestions and 'special topics' boxes.
- A glossary of 300 entries.
- An extensive range of online resources for instructors and students, including a test bank of 140 multiple-choice questions, useful links and an answer key.

LOUISE CUMMINGS is Professor in the Department of English at The Hong Kong Polytechnic University. She is the author or editor of over ten books, most recently *Communication Disorders* (2014), *Pragmatic Disorders* (2014), *The Cambridge Handbook of Communication Disorders* (Cambridge, 2014), *Case Studies in Communication Disorders* (Cambridge, 2016) and *Research in Clinical Pragmatics* (2017).

Working with English Grammar

An Introduction

Louise Cummings

Hong Kong Polytechnic University

CAMBRIDGE
UNIVERSITY PRESS

CAMBRIDGE
UNIVERSITY PRESS

University Printing House, Cambridge CB2 8BS, United Kingdom

One Liberty Plaza, 20th Floor, New York, NY 10006, USA

477 Williamstown Road, Port Melbourne, VIC 3207, Australia

314–321, 3rd Floor, Plot 3, Splendor Forum, Jasola District Centre, New Delhi – 110025, India

79 Anson Road, #06–04/06, Singapore 079906

Cambridge University Press is part of the University of Cambridge.

It furthers the University's mission by disseminating knowledge in the pursuit of education, learning and research at the highest international levels of excellence.

www.cambridge.org
Information on this title: www.cambridge.org/9781108415774
DOI: 10.1017/9781108235150

First published 2018

Printed in the United Kingdom by Clays Ltd, Elcograf S.p.A

A catalogue record for this publication is available from the British Library.

ISBN 978-1-108-41577-4 Hardback
ISBN 978-1-108-40207-1 Paperback

CONTENTS

FIGURES AND TABLES

EXERCISES

SPECIAL TOPICS

PREFACE

This book aims to give students a comprehensive introduction to the grammar of English. It is designed primarily for students with little or no prior knowledge of English grammar, many of whom will be studying grammar as part of a Linguistics, English Language or TEFL/TESOL degree. The text is also suitable for students who are preparing themselves for AS and A-Level English Language qualifications. Other readers of the volume include individuals who wish to increase their knowledge of English grammar for professional or personal reasons. Speech and language therapists, school teachers and translators are just some of the many individuals who must have a sound working knowledge of grammar in order to conduct their professional roles. This book will make an important contribution to the development of that knowledge.

Approach of this Text

This volume examines the grammatical features of Standard English. However, the emphasis throughout is on a descriptive approach to the study of grammar rather than on the grammatical forms that prescriptive grammarians believe speakers and writers should use. Many other grammar textbooks also claim to pursue a descriptive approach to the study of grammar but include only devised examples for the purposes of explanation and illustration. These examples have their place in the study of grammar. But that study is all the richer and more revealing when an examination of the actual grammatical forms that speakers and writers use is conducted alongside it. It is for this reason that the grammar of speakers of non-standard dialects of English, of typically developing children who are acquiring their native language and of individuals with language disorders will be discussed throughout this book. Not only are the grammatical forms used by these speakers worthy of academic study, but they are also an engaging route into an examination of the grammar of Standard English.

As well as taking a descriptive approach to the study of grammar seriously, these three applications of grammar serve another important purpose for student readers. When they are first exposed to the study of grammar, students are often 'switched off' by a subject that they consider to have little relevance to the real world and to issues that are of interest to them in their lives. I believe there is much that linguists can do to dispel this impression of grammar among students. When students come to university for the first time, they are often exposed to a range of non-standard dialects. Each of these dialects has its own grammatical features which sets it apart from Standard English. Students are often interested in these differences even if they do not know how to describe them. The language of young developing children is inherently interesting to students, particularly to those who are considering careers where they will work directly with children. They may note the grammatical errors that young children make and even wish to know how to characterise them. Finally, most students are concerned about family members and friends who have some disruption of their language skills on account of illness, disease or injury. They may be keen to learn more about the grammatical impairments that occur in children and adults with language disorders but may have no means of initiating this type of inquiry. By integrating these three examples of 'grammar in action' throughout this book, it is hoped that students can see the relevance to their lives of this most important branch of linguistics.

Features of this Text

The book has been written in clear, accessible language which will be readily understood by students of all levels. It also contains several educational features which will facilitate student learning. For clarity, these features are listed below:

Learning aids for students
- Learning objectives at the start of each chapter.
- Key points boxes at the end of each section which summarise main points.

Enrichment material
- Special topics boxes which allow students to explore aspects of grammar in further detail.
- Real-world examples from children and adults with language disorders, children who are acquiring English as a first language and speakers of non-standard dialects and World Englishes.

Applications
- Exercises with answers for use in the classroom and independent study. These exercises occur at the end of each section and allow students to apply their knowledge of concepts as soon as they are introduced.
- Over 80 revision questions with answers. These questions appear at the end of each chapter and provide students with further practice for course assessments.
- Homework assignments for each chapter provide students with structured activities to be completed between classes.

- End-of-chapter exercises allow instructors and students to establish if there has been sufficient learning for progression to the next chapter to occur.
- A website (www.cambridge.org/eng-grammar) with 140 self-test questions and answers. These questions can be used as a test bank for instructors or as a self-test resource by students.

Useful tools
- A glossary with 300 entries.
- Bold terms throughout the text which relate to entries in the glossary.
- Annotated suggestions for further reading.
- A detailed index.
- Figures and tables.
- Website with links to grammar resources.

Each of these features has been included to ensure that students have a self-contained resource which does not require supplementation with other texts and material. The combination of these features sets this volume apart from other textbooks in grammar. Many of these textbooks omit one or more of the features of this volume (e.g. a glossary) or include less well-developed versions of these features (e.g. questions with no answers). The decision to include each pedagogical feature has been motivated by my experience of teaching grammar to undergraduate students over the past 15 years. This experience has taught me that these features can play an important role in encouraging students to engage actively in their learning. They can also overcome several challenges that instructors confront in the teaching of grammar to university-level students. These challenges include the need to address a wide range of material in compressed, semester-long courses, and the requirement to support student learning outside of the classroom. The pedagogical features of this book provide students with maximum exposure to grammatical points and the scaffolding that is necessary to support independent study. Students who use this book can be confident that this wide range of features has something to offer their particular style of learning.

A Flexible Organisation

Instructors and students who use this book are not compelled to follow the chapters in the order in which they have been presented. Many instructors have a preference to begin the study of grammar at the level of sentences and work through progressively smaller units of grammatical analysis. Also, some students may find it easier to study grammar and understand its concepts when these are first presented in the context of sentences. The book has been written with these teaching and learning preferences in mind. Each chapter is sufficiently self-contained that there will be no detriment to an instructor's course or a student's learning if the chapters are taught and read in an order other than the one adopted. To derive maximal benefit for students from the book's pedagogical features, instructors may find it helpful to embed tasks and other activities within seminars, or to make the completion of these exercises a requirement on obtaining course credit. For their part, students will more readily develop an understanding of grammar when all tasks are attempted in full before consulting answers and when home-work assignments are seriously addressed. When used in the ways suggested, this book will reward the investment of time and effort.

A Final Note

Finally, I want to convey in this book not only the importance and relevance of grammar to different aspects of life, but also the passion and interest that gram-mar can generate in those who commit to studying it. I hope I have succeeded in both aims. If students hear a child's grammatical error with a new level of understanding, or become more inquisitive about the grammatical features of a non-standard dialect of English as a result of reading this book, then I believe these aims will have been achieved.

ACKNOWLEDGEMENTS

There are a number of people whose assistance I wish to acknowledge. I particularly want to thank Dr Andrew Winnard, Executive Publisher in Language and Linguistics at Cambridge University Press, for responding positively to the proposal for this book. Rosemary Crawley, Development Editor in the Higher Education Team at the Press, has provided excellent advice and support. I am grateful to Brian MacWhinney and Davida Fromm for their permission to use data from CHILDES and AphasiaBank, both components of the TalkBank system. I also wish to acknowledge the assistance of Judith Heaney who collated the manuscript. Finally, I have been assisted by several individuals during the preparation of this book, particularly Clementine Bowles, Robert Compton, Liz Morrish, Kathleen O'Mara and Ashley Ross. I am grateful to them for their helpful advice and grammatical insights during my many months of work on this volume.

1 The Study of Grammar

LEARNING OBJECTIVES

By the end of this chapter you will be able to do the following:

- Give a comprehensive definition of grammar.
- Understand the difference between a prescriptive and a descriptive approach to the study of grammar.
- Appreciate that, if taken seriously, a descriptive approach to the study of grammar requires us to look at grammatical features beyond those associated with Standard English.
- Understand that the grammatical features of young developing children, of children and adults with language disorders and of speakers of non-standard dialects are as worthy of study as the grammatical features of Standard English, and can be used as a pedagogical tool to illuminate the grammatical features of Standard English.

1.1 What is Grammar?

As with most questions in linguistics, the answer to this question varies depending on who you ask. For most linguists, **grammar** is the study of two main disciplines: **morphology** and **syntax**. Morphologists study the internal structure of words and the organising principles that govern this structure. In morphology, words are analysed in terms of their smallest meaningful parts known as **morphemes**. For example, it is of interest to morphologists that while *daughter* is a single morpheme, the word *teacher* contains two morphemes (the verb *teach* and the nominalising **suffix** *–er*). Morphologists are also interested in the different **prefixes** that can express negative meanings in English. The following prefixes serve to convey the opposite meaning of the **adjectives** and **verbs** to which they are added: <u>un</u>happy, <u>dis</u>similar, <u>de</u>mystify, <u>in</u>digestible, <u>a</u>synchronous, <u>non</u>compliant, <u>mis</u>understand, <u>im</u>moral. Morphologists examine why a prefix like *a–* conveys a negative meaning in only some of the words to which it is added. So while *a–* in <u>a</u>synchronous has the meaning 'not', the same prefix in words such as <u>a</u>theist and <u>a</u>moral has the meaning 'without'. The distribution of morphemes in a language, the meanings they express and the morphological processes that generate new words and word-forms are integral to the study of morphology. This aspect of grammar will be addressed in detail in Chapter 2.

For most linguists, grammar includes the study of syntax in addition to morphology. In no language in the world can words appear in sentences in a random or unpredictable order. With some exceptions (e.g. the location of **adverbs** in sentences in English), there is always a particular order on the occurrence of words. This order is examined in syntax. Linguists who work in syntax are interested in why *She appreciates all his many talents* is a grammatical sentence in English, while the sentence *She appreciates his many all talents* is not. Clearly, the difference relates to the order of the **determiners** *all, his* and *many* that appear before the **noun** *talents*. The reason why one order of these determiners is acceptable in English while another order is not is an issue of fundamental importance to the study of syntax. Also, as native speakers of English we know intuitively that adjectives must precede nouns in **noun phrases** (<u>old</u> house, <u>empty</u> space). However, a different syntactic pattern is found in French, where certain adjectives can precede nouns in noun phrases (<u>jolie</u> femme 'pretty woman') while other adjectives follow nouns in noun phrases (chat <u>noir</u> 'black cat'). These differences in word order between languages are revealing for workers in syntax who want to understand the syntactic principles that motivate them. Most of the chapters in this volume are concerned with the study of syntax.

Thus far, I have used the expression 'most linguists' when describing how linguists define the field of grammar. This is because one prominent linguist, **Noam Chomsky**, adopts a very different definition of grammar. It is Chomsky's aim to characterise the body of knowledge which speakers have about their **native language** and which allows them to produce any of its infinitely many well-formed sentences. According to Chomsky, this knowledge takes the form of a **generative grammar** which is divisible into three linguistic components: **phonology**, syntax and **semantics**. This is how Chomsky defines a generative grammar in his book *Aspects of the Theory of Syntax*:

> [A] generative grammar must be a system of rules that can iterate to generate an indefinitely large number of structures. This system of rules can be analysed into the three major components of a generative grammar: the syntactic, phonological, and semantic components. (Chomsky, 1965: 15–16)

Chomsky's primary concern is with the syntactic component of the grammar. This component specifies in an abstract way the different structures that can be sentences in a language. Certain structures are permissible by the syntactic rules of the language and could be sentences of the language in principle – even if no-one has ever used these sentences – while other structures violate these rules and cannot be sentences of the language. Each permissible sentence structure has a corresponding phonetic form – after all, most sentences must be expressed in spoken communication at some point. It is the phonological component of the grammar that determines the phonetic form of a sentence. Finally, each permissible sentence structure must be capable of expressing meaning and being understood and interpreted by hearers. It is the semantic component of the grammar that determines the semantic interpretation of a sentence. Chomsky's proposals for a generative grammar are beyond the scope of this volume. However, an excellent examination of generative grammar can be found in Carnie (2013) to which interested readers are referred.

It is also worthwhile to consider the responses of people other than academic linguists to the question at the start of this section. For many people, grammar conjures up memories of lessons at school during which teachers introduced **word classes** like nouns, verbs, adjectives and adverbs and pupils were taught how to identify **prepositions** and **conjunctions** in sentences. More often than not, these lessons also encouraged the use of correct grammar and emphasised the need to avoid bad, 'sloppy' or incorrect grammar. This **prescriptive approach** to the study of grammar is still very much alive today. It is evident, for example, in the responses of students who study **linguistics** for the first time at university and discover that they will not be taught rules for the correct use of grammar. It is also evident in complaints that are made to newspapers and broadcasters about the use of grammar by reporters, journalists and presenters. These prescriptive attitudes to grammar will be examined further in the next section. For school-age learners of foreign languages, the study of grammar might mean the rote learning of verbs which have irregular **past tense** forms and which may cause problems in a written exam if they are not committed to memory. For adult learners of foreign languages, grammar may mean acquaintance with a few simple grammatical forms that may facilitate ordering food in restaurants during a holiday. For individuals with **language disorders**, grammar may mean the loss of 'small words' like *the, he* and *of* – linguists call these words **function words** – which link parts of a sentence together and which permit the expression of comprehensible utterances. For each of these groups of people, grammar raises different, but equally important, issues and concerns. Some of these uses of grammar will be addressed further throughout the book.

The main points in this section are summarised below.

KEY POINTS WHAT IS GRAMMAR?

- Most linguists define grammar as the study of morphology and syntax. An influential linguist called Noam Chomsky adopts a different definition of grammar. Chomsky's generative grammar contains phonology and semantics in addition to syntax.
- Morphology is the study of the internal structure of words. Morphologists analyse words in terms of their smallest meaningful parts known as morphemes.
- Syntax is the study of sentence structure. In all natural languages, words occur in a certain order within sentences. For example, in English a subject noun or pronoun occurs before the verb in a declarative sentence (e.g. *The boy likes chocolate*).

- Grammar is not just of interest to academic linguists. It is a feature of almost every pupil's formal education either through English grammar lessons or the learning of foreign languages. These early experiences of grammar are often couched in prescriptive terms about correct and incorrect uses of grammar. Grammar is also significant to people with language disorders where its impairment represents a significant barrier to effective communication.

1.2 Prescriptive and Descriptive Approaches to Grammar

It is not just the content or scope of grammar that elicits different responses from linguists to the question at the start of this chapter. Linguists are also divided on the approach that should be taken to the study of this content. For some linguists, grammar should be studied from within a prescriptive perspective. The goals of a prescriptive approach to grammar are to institute standards of good or correct grammar and to legislate against bad or incorrect grammar. These standards stipulate norms which all speakers of the language should strive to uphold both in their own linguistic practices and through censorship of grammatical forms which deviate from these standards. **Prescriptive grammarians** can often be strong advocates for grammatical correctness in media organisations such as the British Broadcasting Corporation (BBC), in schools and universities, and in a range of other public institutions. Their calls for certain standards of grammar to be upheld are often accompanied by laments about how language and society in general are in a state of deterioration. The solution to this deterioration as far as grammar is concerned is to establish 'grammar departments' in media organisations and to increase monitoring of the use of grammar. All these elements of a prescriptive approach to grammar (as well as **pronunciation** and word meaning) are evident in the following articles from two British newspapers, the *Mail Online* and *The Guardian*:

Don't rely on us for good grammar, says the BBC: Broadcaster is no longer the bastion of correct English, its 'style chief' admits
The BBC is no longer the 'bastion' of correct English on radio and television, one of its editors has admitted. Thousands of viewers and listeners now complain to the corporation every year saying its once-high standards of grammar and pronunciation have slipped.

Ian Jolly, who is the BBC newsroom's 'style editor', conceded his presenters and reporters repeatedly make basic errors, such as confusing the word 'historic' with 'historical' and using the term 'chair' when they mean 'chairman' or 'chairwoman'. Following recent criticisms that presenters are also mispronouncing the letter 'H', he called on the BBC's senior management to prioritise efforts to make the corporation a linguistic 'standard bearer' once more.

Appearing on Radio 4's Feedback, he said: 'There are thousands of people who get in touch with us every year because of our output on radio and television and on the internet. So they do care. And the thing that people often point out is that they look to the BBC to uphold standards. So I do think that we used to be a standard bearer in these matters. Whether that's the case now I'm not so sure. I would love to see someone at the top of the BBC take up the challenge and put the emphasis back on the quality of our language so we can once again be a leader for the people who look to us. They think the BBC is the bastion and I would like to see us back at that position.'

Mr Jolly was asked to respond to a string of complaints received in the past week by Feedback. One listener, Stuart Grist, contacted the programme to complain about BBC reports into the resignations of Fiona Woolf and Baroness Butler-Sloss from the Government's sex abuse inquiry. He said: 'The other day it was reported that the child abuse enquiry had lost two chairs. Today we were told that two chairs had stepped down. Whatever next, "chairs found legless"? Or worse, "two chairs table motions"?'

Mr Jolly agreed it was incorrect to describe somebody as a 'chair' rather than a 'chairman' or 'chairwoman'. He added: 'I think it's one of the side effects of what we like to call political correctness. But I don't really see the need for it and we don't advocate using it. We think if a man's a chairman, he's a chairman. A woman's a chairwoman. If you know the gender of a person then there are quite good options there.'

Another listener complained about the repeated confusion of the word 'historic', which should be used to describe an important event, and 'historical', which simply means an event took place in the past. He said newspapers, police forces and even the judiciary have also made the same error, adding: 'So it is one of those phrases that has seeped into our consciousness. We never used to use it and now we are not sure which it should be and tend to get it wrong.'

Mr Jolly said he 'occasionally' tells off presenters for making grammatical mistakes, but said listeners and viewers should be more understanding of errors that creep into live broadcasts. He said: 'The BBC produces hundreds of hours of broadcasting every day, much of it live. Not every word is perfect. We would be concerned if writers were getting things wrong. I think we have to allow staff a little bit of leeway in the live broadcasting that makes up so much of our output.'

Last month, the BBC was criticised by the Queen's English Society for allowing presenters including Sara Cox and Radio 1 DJ Nick Grimshaw to say 'haitch' instead of 'aitch' when referring to the letter 'H'. It said such mistakes marked the beginning of a 'slippery slope', but the BBC said it was proud of the 'range of voices' across its programmes.

(Alasdair Glennie, *Mail Online*, 10 November 2014)

Daily Mail

Mind your language, critics warn BBC: Mistakes prompt a demand for grammar to be policed

The BBC is being urged to appoint a language chief by critics who claim that its reputation as a bastion of the Queen's English is fading fast. They claim that presenters and correspondents on both television and radio routinely misuse words, make grammatical mistakes and use colloquialisms in place of standard English.

Sir Michael Lyons, chair of the BBC Trust, will receive an open letter tomorrow calling for a 'democratic airing' of the proposals, which advocate the creation of a new post to scrutinise 'the syntax, vocabulary and style' of thousands of staff heard on the air. Although the BBC has a department dedicated to pronunciation, it has no equivalent for vocabulary or grammar.

Among the signatories are Professor Chris Woodhead, the former chief inspector of schools, Lord Charles Guthrie, the former chief of the defence staff, and MP Ann Widdecombe. 'We do so because language deeply affects all branches of society,' says the letter. Widdecombe argued that the way in which language was used by broadcasters had a huge impact on society. 'I think promoting the proper use of language is important. Whereas the BBC is better than most, even it is starting to get a bit slack,' she said. 'Mass communication has a tremendous effect.'

She and others want managers at the BBC to consider the suggestion by Ian Bruton-Simmonds, a member of the Queen's English Society, that it appoint a head of grammar. Under the proposals, 100 unpaid 'monitors' working from home would note grammatical slips or badly chosen vocabulary. The checkers would then report to a central adviser, who would write to broadcasters outlining what was said and what should have been said. ...

It is likely to be a tough battle. A BBC spokeswoman admitted there was no regular monitoring of correspondents. 'Grammar guidance is currently available to our staff on the corporation's intranet,' she said. 'It is only there for guidance; there are no set rules on grammar.' ...

(Anushka Asthana and Vanessa Thorpe, *The Guardian*, 28 October 2007)
Copyright Guardian News & Media Ltd 2017

A prescriptive stance to grammar is often motivated by a range of attitudes about language users. Many of these attitudes are negative, and even pernicious, in nature. Prescriptivism may mask an intolerance of **dialects** other than **Standard English**. The speakers of these dialects often belong to social classes and ethnic groups or live in geographical areas which are negatively evaluated by the defenders of Standard English. A prescriptive approach to grammar may also stem from a sense of nostalgia about the past and a refusal to accept that language evolves and changes over time. The authors of the above article in *The Guardian* reflect this concern when they describe the view of individuals who oppose the policing of grammar:

> 'Language evolves and we should evolve with it,' said Adam Jacot de Boinod, author of The Meaning of Tingo, which highlights the weaknesses of English by listing foreign words for which there is no English equivalent. He said once people reached 40, they often felt nostalgic for what they were taught as children – and if the call for a language adviser was simply 'to be pedantic and yesteryear', he would oppose it. (Anushka Asthana and Vanessa Thorpe, *The Guardian*, 28 October 2007)

The roots of prescriptivism can also be traced to attitudes about the educational background of speakers, with correct grammatical usage associated with well-educated speakers (and, by implication, incorrect grammatical usage associated with a lack of education). That this association is a central motivation for a prescriptivist stance towards grammar is also evident in *The Guardian* article. The extract below from this article reports the comments of one of the signatories of the open letter to the chairman of the BBC Trust:

> According to signatory James Cochrane, whose book Between You and I, A Little Book of Bad English has an introduction by the broadcaster John Humphrys, one man who never makes mistakes. 'You do not hear them on the Terry Wogan show because he is a well-educated man of a certain age,' argued Cochrane. He said he was supporting the campaign because 'the BBC ought to be a defender of good English'. (Anushka Asthana and Vanessa Thorpe, *The Guardian*, 28 October 2007)

The title of Cochrane's book – *Between You and I, A Little Book of Bad English* – invites an examination of one further motivation for a prescriptive approach to the study of grammar. This is an intolerance of the influence of other languages on English or, more precisely, all other languages with the exception of **Latin**. The title of Cochrane's book contains a grammatical form that is unacceptable to prescriptive grammarians. This is the use of the **subject pronoun** 'I' instead of the **object pronoun** 'me' after the preposition 'between'. The so-called prescriptively correct form – 'Between you and me' – is based on a Latin grammatical rule which requires the use of the **accusative case** after the Latin preposition *inter* ('between'). For prescriptive grammarians, it is the failure to comply with this grammatical rule in Latin which marks out 'Between you and I' as incorrect. Latin represents a linguistic gold standard which English must attempt to emulate. It is the same deference to Latin which leads to the rejection of *stadiums* and *funguses* as plural forms of the nouns *stadium* and *fungus*. The somewhat arbitrary application to English of Latin grammatical rules for the formation of plural nouns leads prescriptive grammarians to prohibit forms which many speakers of English consider to be acceptable and use routinely in both spoken and written language:

Nouns ending in –a
formula → formulae (prescriptively correct)
formula → formulas (prescriptively incorrect)

Nouns ending in –us
cactus → cacti (prescriptively correct)
cactus → cactuses (prescriptively incorrect)

Nouns ending in –um
curriculum → curricula (prescriptively correct)
curriculum → curriculums (prescriptively incorrect)

It should be noted that the rejection of a prescriptive approach to the study of grammar does not thereby commit one to the claim that there are not more or less appropriate grammatical forms to use in certain **contexts**. Clearly, formal writing in an academic assignment, for example, requires the use of grammatical forms in Standard English. So while speakers may say 'I seen him last week' in a conversation with friends, they are generally well advised to write 'I saw him last week' in the context of an essay. The context-appropriate use of grammar should not be confused with a prescriptive approach to grammar – linguists can subscribe to the former *at the same time* as they reject the latter. Prescriptivism in grammar transcends the context-appropriate use of grammar in that a prescriptivist would reject the use of a form like 'I seen him last week' even in spoken language. Such a form, prescriptivists argue, uses the **past participle** (*seen*) rather than the past tense (*saw*) and is unacceptable in all linguistic contexts, including spoken and written language. It will be assumed throughout this book that grammar can be used more or less context-appropriately even as a prescriptive approach to the study of grammar should be rejected.

The consequences of a prescriptive stance to language and grammar will now be illustrated in the case of African American Vernacular English.

SPECIAL TOPIC 1.1 AFRICAN AMERICAN VERNACULAR ENGLISH

A prescriptive attitude to grammar, and language in general, can have particularly serious consequences for certain groups of speakers. This is nowhere more clearly demonstrated than in the pervasive, negative attitudes that have surrounded, and in many cases continue to surround, the use of African American Vernacular English (AAVE). The extent of the marginalisation and disadvantage that speakers of AAVE experience is vividly articulated by Annie Blair, the mother of two children who attended the Martin Luther King Jr. Elementary School in a prosperous, mostly white suburb of Ann Arbor, Michigan. Annie recalls:

> "Um my kids was tested and was tested and was put into special ed classes and I felt like that they were not getting educated and was not treated equally and – I felt like that shouldn't be a barrier because of the language to stop them from being educated." (Source: *'Do you speak American?'*, Public Broadcasting Service, 2005)

Asheen was one of the black boys who attended the school. Some 25 years later, he recalls how teachers perceived the use of AAVE:

> "They sort of felt like we were unteachable in a sense, I would feel. So it kind of made them go towards other students more and gave them a little bit more help than they would give us." (Source: *'Do you speak American?'*, Public Broadcasting Service, 2005)

Ruth Zweifler, coordinator of the Student Advocacy Center, a non-profit community organisation, was unable to get school administrators to acknowledge the detriment that these children were experiencing on account of their use of AAVE. She recalls:

> "There were maybe twenty-four black, poor black children in a sea of affluent white families. And they really were having a very hard time." (Source: *'Do you speak American?'*, Public Broadcasting Service, 2005)

Zweifler's organisation filed a lawsuit. During the trial that followed in June 1979, a federal judge, Judge Joiner, acknowledged formally that AAVE represented a significant barrier to academic achievement and success, and that the school district had been insensitive to the linguistic background of the vast majority of African American students in the district. In his decision, Judge Joiner remarked: 'A language barrier develops when teachers, in helping the child switch from the home (black English) language to standard English, refuse to admit the existence of a language that is the acceptable way of talking in his local community'. The judge also defined 'black English' as a 'language system' that contained 'aspects of Southern dialect' and was 'used largely by black people in casual conversation and informal talk'. This landmark ruling was influential in changing many of the negative perceptions of AAVE that existed among educators and school administrators. Some of the grammatical features of AAVE will be examined in Chapter 3.

The alternative to a prescriptive approach to the study of grammar is a **descriptive approach**. **Descriptive grammarians** examine the grammatical forms that speakers *actually* use, rather than the grammatical forms which prescriptivists believe speakers *should* or *ought to* use. It is of interest to descriptive grammarians, for example, that the sentence 'I seen him last week' is used by speakers of **Belfast English** as well as by speakers of other dialects. The variation in grammatical forms in accordance with the social class, ethnic background, geographical region, age and gender of speakers is an important phenomenon requiring explanation according to descriptive grammarians, and should not be viewed as a subversion of prescriptive rules of correct grammar. For descriptive grammarians, Standard English is merely one dialect among many dialects of English, and its grammatical features have no stronger claim to correctness than the grammatical features of other dialects. Normative concepts such as 'correct' and 'incorrect' grammar have no place in the study of grammar where the aim is to give account of grammatical forms in actual use. The following examples of grammatical usage are of interest to descriptive grammarians:

(1) Who are you going to the party with?
(2) I done my homework last night.
(3) He wanted to really annoy her.
(4) Are youse going to the pub later?
(5) I couldn't get none nowhere.
(6) He's just gotten married.
(7) We as adults, as mainstream society, as Americans have really done bad by these little kids.
(8) He's going to the shop for to buy some milk.
(9) You was there, wasn't you?
(10) I've already chose my meal.

According to prescriptive grammarians, each of the above sentences contains a prohibited grammatical form. The sentence in (1) violates the prescriptive dictum that a sentence should never end in a preposition. The past participle (*done*) is used instead of the past tense (*did*) in the sentence in (2). The sentence in (3) splits the **infinitive** with the adverb *really*. The non-standard **pronoun** *youse* in the sentence in (4) is used of more than one addressee, while the sentence in (5) employs **multiple negation** (*not ... none nowhere*). The sentence in (6) uses a non-standard past participle, while the sentence in (7) does not use the suffix *–ly* on the adverb *bad*. The sentence in (8) is noteworthy on account of the use of the 'for–to' infinitive. In (9), a singular verb (*was*) is used in place of the plural form *were*. Finally, the sentence in (10) uses a past tense verb (*chose*) in place of a past participle (*chosen*).

Descriptive grammarians take a quite different view of the sentences in (1) to (10) above. These sentences are not examples of bad or incorrect grammar. Rather, they exemplify the wide variation in grammar that exists in varieties and dialects other than Standard British English. The sentences in (6) and (7) are examples of **American English**, while the 'for–to' infinitive in (8) is a feature of **Northern Irish English**. Many of the grammatical features in (1) to (10) can be justified on linguistic grounds even as they are judged to be inadequate in prescriptive terms. For example, the **split infinitive** in sentence (3) is able to achieve emphasis that is missing in the prescriptively correct forms *He wanted really to annoy her* and *He wanted to annoy her really*. Also, the speaker who uses the sentence in (4) is employing sound logic. In the same way that languages like French and German use different pronouns when there is one addressee (*tu* in French and *du* in German) and more than one addressee (*vous* in French and *Sie* in German), the speaker in (4) is using a plural pronoun (*youse*) to indicate the presence of more than one addressee where no such distinction between singular and plural pronouns exists in Standard English. The multiple negation in sentence (5) is a socially stigmatised form that is rejected by prescriptive grammarians more for its association with adolescent speakers in urban communities than on account of any objective linguistic inadequacy of this construction. In fact, the use of more than one negative form may be seen to achieve emphasis that is not apparent in the sentence *I couldn't get any anywhere*. In each case, where the prescriptive grammarian perceives grammatical error, the descriptive grammarian sees a rich and resourceful use of grammar by a range of socially situated speakers. In the chapters to follow, a descriptive approach to the study of grammar will be pursued.

The main points in this section are summarised below.

KEY POINTS PRESCRIPTIVE AND DESCRIPTIVE APPROACHES TO GRAMMAR

- A prescriptive approach to the study of grammar proceeds by instituting rules for the correct use of grammar. These rules, which include dictums such as 'a sentence should never end in a preposition' and 'an infinitive should not be split', are strongly advocated by prescriptive grammarians for use in schools, media organisations and other institutions.
- There are many factors motivating a prescriptive stance on grammar. In some cases, prescriptivism masks intolerance of speakers from certain social classes, ethnic backgrounds and geographical regions. Nostalgia for the past, negative attitudes about the educational background of speakers, and a refusal to accept language change, are other factors that motivate a prescriptive stance on grammar.
- Descriptive grammarians examine the grammatical forms that speakers actually use, and not the forms that prescriptivists think speakers should use or ought to use. These forms are often found in non-standard dialects of English and in other varieties of English (e.g. American English).
- Grammatical forms such as multiple negation, the use of the past participle instead of the past tense, and the use of the 'for-to' infinitive are of interest to descriptive grammarians. Many of these forms can be justified on linguistic grounds (e.g. they may allow speakers to achieve emphasis). Their rejection by prescriptivists is often for no other reason than that they are socially stigmatised forms (e.g. multiple negation).

1.3 Grammar in Real-World Contexts

A descriptive approach to the study of grammar brings grammarians into contact with the real-world contexts in which grammar is used. Descriptive grammarians examine grammatical features in the specific social and regional dialects in which they occur. Grammatical forms used by young and old speakers, and by urban and rural dwellers are also relevant to the study of grammar. Men and women use different grammatical forms as do speakers from a range of ethnic groups. All these forms are of interest to descriptive grammarians. In short, a commitment to describe the actual use of grammar entails a detailed characterisation of grammatical forms wherever these forms exist. This includes grammar in spoken and written language, in formal and informal settings, in different types of **discourse** (e.g. conversation and **narrative**) and in structured and spontaneous verbal interactions. This is a very different type of grammatical study to the one adopted by prescriptive grammarians who base their views on grammar not on evidence ('actual use') but on opinions. When they do look beyond their opinions, it is merely with the aim of rationalising their judgements of correctness. The real world influences grammar in interesting and often unexpected ways. In refusing to countenance this influence, prescriptive grammarians do a disservice to the rich complexity of grammar.

Most grammar textbooks undertake an examination of the grammatical features of a standard **variety** of English such as British Standard English. This textbook also has such an examination as one of its aims. But if we are to take a descriptive approach to grammar seriously, it should also be possible alongside this examination to consider some of the many other ways in which speakers use grammar. Standard English is a native dialect of only 15 per cent of the population in the UK (Trudgill, 1999). Moreover, its distribution throughout the population is not random. The grammatical forms of Standard English which are examined in textbooks are produced for the most part by well-educated adults who have intact language skills and belong to certain social classes and ethnic groups. If it is our aim to capture the actual use of grammar, then the grammatical forms of a range of other speakers must also be considered. Alongside mature grammatical forms produced by adult speakers, it should also be possible to examine immature grammatical forms used by children. There are many children and adults who, on account of **developmental disorders**, illness and injury, do not produce the grammatical forms found in textbooks. Yet, these forms are as much part of the actual use of grammar as are the grammatical forms of Standard English. Given that a minority of the population even uses Standard English, there are compelling grounds for examining the grammatical features of other, **non-standard dialects** in a descriptive study of grammar. All three uses of grammar will feature prominently in this volume.

Thus far, it has been argued that **grammatical development** in children, **grammatical disorders** in children and adults, and the grammars of non-standard dialects have as much relevance to a descriptive study of grammar as the grammatical features of Standard English which dominate grammar textbooks. However, it is important to be clear from the outside about the role that these other uses of grammar will play in this volume. They are not intended to be topics of study in themselves. That is, this book will not set out to describe and explain how grammar can be impaired in a range of developmental and acquired language disorders, for example. Nor will it undertake a comprehensive examination of grammatical development in children or a detailed discussion of the grammatical features of non-standard dialects of English. Rather, these other uses of grammar serve as a pedagogical tool by illustrating, exemplifying and illuminating particular grammatical features. Their role is to provide a window onto these features through which readers can appreciate more fully the nature and significance of different grammatical structures. It is often remarked by linguists, for example, that an aspect of normal language can be best understood by examining how it is impaired or disrupted in an individual with language disorder. In the same way, it is contended that students can more readily assimilate grammatical concepts and structures when they see how these structures are impaired in children and adults with language disorders. A similar pedagogical point can be made in relation to grammatical development in children and the grammars of non-standard dialects.

As well as illustrating key grammatical features, these applications of grammar have other pedagogical benefits. When grammar is taught as an academic discipline at school or university, many students query its relevance to their own lives and its value as an area of learning and knowledge. Questions about the relevance and value of grammar can be effectively addressed by introducing students to a number of applications of grammar from the outset of a module or course. The grammatical features of language disorders, grammatical development in children and the grammars of dialects other than Standard English are three such applications. Contrary to popular belief, language disorders are not rare occurrences. According to one commonly cited study, **specific language impairment** alone has an estimated overall prevalence rate of 7.4 per cent in monolingual English-speaking kindergarten children (Tomblin et al., 1997). Most people encounter individuals with language disorders at some point in their lives. This may take the form of language difficulties (e.g. **dyslexia**) in a sibling, friend or peer at school. Alternatively, a grandparent or other relative may develop language disorder (e.g. **aphasia**) following a **stroke** or **head injury**. Many students who study linguistics at university later pursue careers as teachers in mainstream and special educational settings. Even in mainstream schools, teachers routinely encounter children who have language disorders which compromise their academic work and social relationships. Language disorders are not confined to **speech and language therapy** clinics. They have relevance to all of us, including students of grammar.

The immature grammatical structures used by young, normally developing children are also of interest to students of grammar. Either through their own children or through various childcare roles, students are often brought into contact with the early grammatical forms that young children use. As well as studying grammar, students of linguistics often enrol in modules on **child language acquisition** where grammatical forms are examined alongside aspects of phonological, semantic and pragmatic development. For these personal and academic reasons, students often display an interest in the grammatical errors that young children make as they grapple with the complexities of the grammar of their native language. Finally, university is often the first exposure for many students to a range of dialects other than their own. Also at university, students may come into contact with varieties of English (e.g. American English) which have been previously experienced only through the media. Students may study grammar at university with a view to pursuing careers in Teaching English as a Foreign Language (TEFL) or Teaching English to Speakers of Other Languages (TESOL). Sensitivity to grammatical variation among different dialects and varieties of English is a key concern for such students. For all these reasons, the grammatical features of non-standard dialects may hold more than a fleeting appeal for students of grammar. In short, where a purely academic presentation of grammar may have difficulty satisfying students' expectations of relevance, it is hoped that grammar infused with real-world applications will elicit greater awareness among students of the importance of this linguistic discipline.

This book will adopt the following strategy as it examines a wide range of grammatical terms, concepts and structures. Firstly, grammatical features will be introduced and illustrated apart from the wider real-world contexts in which they occur. This will ensure that readers attend to key aspects of the feature under consideration. This might be the order of determiners in a noun phrase or the difference between the attributive and predicative uses of adjectives. Then, depending on the grammatical feature under examination, instances of its use in one or more of the real-world applications of grammar will be considered. For example, young children display a number of difficulties with the use of determiners during language development. By discussing these errors, many of which are highly creative in nature, another important form of illustration of the grammatical category of determiners is achieved. On other occasions, a particular grammatical feature may be best illustrated by the use of data from children or adults with language disorders or through examples of grammatical usage in a non-standard dialect of English. A combined approach that examines each grammatical feature, firstly on its own terms and then in a real-world context, results in a well-rounded treatment of grammar that is of relevance to student readers.

The main points in this section are summarised below.

> ### KEY POINTS GRAMMAR IN REAL-WORLD CONTEXTS
>
> * A commitment to a descriptive approach to the study of grammar requires that linguists examine all grammatical forms regardless of where they exist.
> * The grammar of British Standard English that is examined in textbooks is the grammar of one dialect only. This dialect dominates formal education, print and broadcast media, the criminal justice system and many other public institutions, even though it is the native dialect of only 15 per cent of the population in the UK.
> * British Standard English is not uniformly distributed throughout the population. Rather, it is a dialect associated with well-educated adults who belong to certain social classes and ethnic groups. Its dominance and prestige serve to diminish the significance of a range of other social and regional dialects which also have grammatical systems that warrant examination.
> * Grammar textbooks also exclusively examine the grammatical forms used by adults with intact language skills. Immature grammatical forms used by normally developing children are overlooked, as are grammatical errors produced by children and adults with language disorders. Grammatical immaturities and errors are interesting in their own terms and are revealing about grammar in general.
> * Grammatical development, grammatical disorders and grammatical usage in non-standard dialects may be used as a pedagogical tool to illustrate a range of terms, concepts and structures in grammar. In highlighting uses of grammar in the real world, these applications address concerns that grammar is an academic discipline with little relevance or value.

1.4 The Study of Grammars

It may appear strange to conclude a chapter entitled 'The Study of Grammar' with a section that refers to the study of *grammars*. After all, the chapter title treats grammar as a generic notion while the use of 'grammars' in the heading of this section implies the existence of multiple grammars. Any inconsistency or paradox is in appearance only, however. This is because there is no contradiction in treating grammar as a universal concept that can be applied to all languages, varieties and dialects – Chomsky does exactly that – and in simultaneously recognising that languages, varieties and dialects can and do have very different grammars. This is because grammatical patterns vary between languages (e.g. Russian, English), between different varieties of a single language (e.g. American English, **Australian English**) and between different dialects of a single variety (e.g. northern and southern dialects of British English). In addition to these grammars, it has been argued in this chapter that a range of other grammars also exist. Normally developing children display grammatical immaturities on their way to acquiring the adult, mature grammatical system of their native language. Also, children and adults with language disorders display impaired grammar on account of illness, injury and developmental disorders. The impaired grammar of these children and adults deviates from the grammatical features of intact language. But in neither case would we want to deny that what we have is a grammar, albeit one which is not fully formed or which has been impaired in some respect. In preparation for later chapters, where 'other grammars' are used as a pedagogical tool, this final section makes some preliminary remarks about the features of non-standard, immature and impaired grammars.

Some of the grammatical differences between American English and British English are explored in the following Special Topic.

SPECIAL TOPIC 1.2 AMERICAN AND BRITISH ENGLISH

Most people are aware that speakers of American and British English use different pronunciation (e.g. *schedule*: word-initial 'sh' in American English and 'sk' in British English) and vocabulary (e.g. *pavement–sidewalk*). However, people are less aware of the significant grammatical differences that also exist between these two varieties of English. In this book, a number of these differences will be examined. They include the use of the past tense in American English and bare infinitive in British English in sentences such as the following:

American English: *past tense*
They're going to fool around and let her lay there and die. (Lexington Herald Leader, Kentucky, 2017)

British English: *bare infinitive*
They're going to fool around and let her lie there and die.

American English uses prepositions in contexts where they are not used in British English, and vice versa, as illustrated by the following examples:

But those years of eating so many vegetables turned Brown off to them when she reached adulthood. (Daily Journal, Tupelo, Mississippi, 2017)
Cynthia Rodriguez filed a lawsuit [on] Tuesday in Cook County Circuit Court on behalf of her son. (Chicago Sun-Times, 2017)
The district continued to retain the aide to ride [on] the bus with the boy. (Chicago Sun-Times, 2017)

Collective nouns are also used differently in American and British English. In British English, these nouns can be treated as singular or plural nouns, so that sentences such as the following are possible:

The team is ecstatic about the new appointment.
The team are ecstatic about the new appointment.

In American English, collective nouns are treated as singular nouns, as illustrated by the verbs in these examples:

This small team in Freetown was responsible for overseeing $23.7 million of hazard payments. (Newsweek Global, 2015)

    Our fans are as loyal as any in sports and the team is deeply embedded in the community. (Washington Post, 2004)

    His staff responds to him because he's not afraid to get his hands dirty and do what needs to be done. (American Craft, 2004)

Grammatical differences between American and British English also extend to the internal structure or morphology of words. In the following example of American English, *winningest* is used to express the meaning 'most winning'. The superlative suffix *–est* cannot be added to the adjective *winning* in British English, which uses the form *most winning* instead:

> *"It's a little bit different because you're not hitting anybody, there's no rush on the quarterback and your wide receivers run undefeated," the state's co-winningest high school football coach, Lou Marinelli, said prior to this weekend's festivities at Dunning Field. (Connecticut Post, 2017)*

There are many other grammatical differences between British and American English. It is on account of these differences that the grammar of the English language is both interesting and perplexing. In this book, you will be equipped with the terms and concepts that are needed to characterise these differences wherever they occur.

1.4.1 Grammar of Non-Standard Dialects

Non-standard dialects of English are a rich repository of grammatical forms which, on account of historical accident, have not achieved the **prestige** of grammatical forms in Standard English. The contents of this repository can provide students of grammar with valuable practice in working with grammar. Through this practice, key skills are developed including the accurate identification of grammatical parts and increased facility in the use of a range of grammatical terms and concepts. To appreciate the contribution that non-standard grammatical forms can make to learning, consider the following examples of grammatical variation in dialects from across the UK. Audio-recordings of some of these utterances are available through the British Library (2016a):

(11) 'we went out last night, didn't us?'
    (SE: 'we went out last night, didn't we?')
(12) 'that's going to rain'
    (SE: 'it's going to rain')
(13) 'I had to rush off to meetings when I come home from work'
    (SE: 'I had to rush off to meetings when I came home from work')

(14) 'there's not that sort of employment in Penrith for them'
     (SE: 'there isn't that sort of employment in Penrith for them')
(15) 'she were wearing a mask'
     (SE: 'she was wearing a mask')
(16) 'you know yourself, if you've give something to a good cause, you feel good
     about it'
     (SE: 'you know yourself, if you've given something to a good cause, you feel
          good about it')

In each of these utterances, a specific grammatical feature differs from the corresponding form used in Standard English (SE). In (11), the use of the **object** pronoun 'us' as a subject is typical of the traditional dialect of the West Midlands and
the West Country. The utterance in (12) is from the **East Anglia dialect**. In this
case, the speaker uses 'that' for a neuter pronoun in subject position while 'it' is
used in object position (e.g. 'I heard it on the radio'). The use of 'come' as a simple
past tense in (13) is a feature of dialects across the UK, and is an older form than
the use of 'came' in Standard English. The utterance in (14) contains an unreduced
negative particle 'not' and is in widespread use in Scotland and Northern England.
Other negative particles used in Scottish dialects include 'I cannae believe it' and
'it's no possible'. The non-standard auxiliary in (15) is a feature of some dialects in
northern England and the Midlands. The auxiliary is unmarked for **person**, with
'were' used in *I were* and *he/she/it were* as well as in *we were, you were* and *they were*
as in Standard English. Finally, the non-standard past participle 'give' in (16) is a
feature of the Geordie dialect that is typical of Tyneside.

So what value do these forms have for the study of grammar? In order to describe
the grammatical features of each of these non-standard utterances, a wide range
of terms and concepts must be employed. We must know how to identify word
classes such as pronouns and verbs. Within each of these word classes, a grasp of
further terms and concepts is required. For example, no sense can be made of the
grammatical form in (11) if we cannot distinguish subject pronouns from object
pronouns. Similarly, an understanding of the neuter pronoun in (12) only makes
sense in a context where there are also masculine pronouns (*he/him*) and feminine pronouns (*she/her*). In relation to verbs, in order to appreciate the concept
of an **auxiliary verb**, we must also understand that there are main or **lexical
verbs** in language and the grammatical functions of these verbs. One function
of auxiliary verbs is to express negation. As the utterance in (14) demonstrates,
negation is also a source of grammatical variation across dialects. Negative particles of various types attach to the auxiliary verbs of sentences, with some of these
particles reduced (e.g. *She isn't cooking tonight*) while others are unreduced (e.g.
We cannae arrive late; You cannot play loud music). Also in relation to verbs, the
grammatical forms in (15) and (16) require an understanding of the difference
between the simple past tense (e.g. *They woke up late*) and the past participle (e.g.
They have woken up late). For the student of grammar, the description of just six

non-standard utterances has provided a valuable context in which to rehearse a range of grammatical terms and concepts.

1.4.2 Grammar in First Language Acquisition

The development of language across all of its levels (phonology, syntax, etc.) is the focus of **first language acquisition**. Grammatical development describes the stages that normally developing children pass through on their way to acquiring the mature grammatical system of their native language. Children experience a number of errors en route to acquiring this system. More often than not, these errors resolve spontaneously with further grammatical maturation. However, when they do occur, they provide a valuable, naturalistic context in which students can gain practice in working with grammatical forms. Some of the grammatical errors that young children make involve the application of internalised grammatical rules in contexts where they do not apply. Other errors occur as children attempt to mark a grammatical feature in an utterance in more than one way. Grammatical immaturities are interesting in that they can reveal emergent knowledge of the grammar of language on the part of children even as they are unable to produce adult grammatical forms. In demonstration of the practice in working with grammar that students can gain from describing grammatical immaturities, consider the following utterances produced by young children:

(17) 'We eated it all up'
(18) 'Him falled over'
(19) 'My cat eating a mouse'
(20) 'He do falling over'
(21) 'What did you bought?'
(22) 'My hand's the biggest than Ben's'
(23) 'My sore's worser now'
(24) 'It's furnitures'
(25) 'My's daddy is gone'
(26) 'This is him's car'

For the most part, the utterances in (17) to (21) involve verb errors. The utterances in (17) and (18) contain **overregularisation errors**. The children who produced these utterances have acquired a grammatical rule about the formation of the past tense in English, namely, that the suffix –*ed* should be added to the base form of the verb. However, they have mistakenly applied this rule to two verbs in English which have irregular past tense forms: *eat* – *ate* and *fall* – *fell*. The child in (18) has additionally used an object pronoun (*him*) in place of a subject pronoun (*he*). The utterances in (19) and (20) illustrate some of the problems with auxiliary verbs that young children can experience. The auxiliary verb is omitted in (19). The child who produces the utterance in (20) is aware that some auxiliary verb is required, but uses the wrong form. Past tense is marked on both the auxiliary verb and the main verb in (21), when it should only be marked on the auxiliary verb.

A range of other grammatical immaturities are illustrated by the utterances in (22) to (26). The utterances in (22) and (23) reveal common childhood errors in the use of comparative adjectives. The utterance in (22) contains elements of both the **comparative** and **superlative** forms of the adjective 'big'. The use of 'than' (comparative) alongside 'the biggest' (superlative) is a blend of these two forms of the adjective. A different comparative adjective error occurs in (23). In English, the adjective 'bad' has an irregular comparative form (*worse*). It is to this form that the child has added the regular comparative suffix *–er*. In (24), the child treats a **non-count noun** (*furniture*) as a **count noun** and adds the suffix *–s* to make it plural. The utterances in (25) and (26) contain errors in the use of **possessive determiners**. As well as an incorrect auxiliary verb (*is*), the utterance in (25) contains two markers of possession. There is correct use of the possessive determiner 'my' to which the **genitive** (*–'s*) has been incorrectly added. In (26), the genitive has been added to the object pronoun (*him*) to indicate possession or ownership instead of correct use of the possessive determiner *his*. Like the verb errors discussed previously, the characterisation of each of these immaturities provides students with valuable practice in applying grammatical terms and concepts to actual language use.

1.4.3 Grammar in Language Disorders

For many children, grammar does not develop along normal lines. For many adults also, previously intact grammar can become impaired on account of illness, injury or disease. When grammar is not acquired normally during the **developmental period** or breaks down in adulthood, a grammatical disorder is the result. Individuals with these disorders are assessed and treated by **speech and language therapists**, who must have sound knowledge of the grammar of language in order to manage these clients effectively. Students must also have a sound grasp of grammatical terms and concepts in order to characterise grammatical impairments in children and adults with accuracy. By way of illustration, consider the utterances in (27) to (32) below. The utterances in (27) to (29) have been produced by children with language disorders, while those in (30) to (32) have been produced by adults with language disorders:

(27) 'Her's painting a flower' (Moore, 2001)
(28) 'Yeah, he sleeping right here' (Moore, 2001)
(29) 'I go sleep uncle room, I sleep uncle bed' (McCardle and Wilson, 1993)
(30) 'I am being help with the food and medicate' (Chaika, 1982)
(31) 'um right (1.7) girl, (3.4) girl, (11.6) kick, (1.7) snake' (Beeke et al., 2007)
(32) 'O.K. cookie jar, cookin-fallin' water trees. To interpret what he's doing? He's falling ... to get the cookies I don't know if he's trying to say and ofring? The

water the sink. I told you about the she's claimin? the glass. I don't know if he's asking him to drink or what the girl I don't know if I can figure out if he's a girl I mean a boy that's about all the wh ... ' (Smith Doody et al., 1992)

The characterisation of each of these utterances draws on a range of grammatical concepts and terms. The utterances in (27) and (28) are produced by children with specific language impairment (SLI) who are aged 4;10 and 4;1 years, respectively. In (27), the child with SLI recognises the need to use an auxiliary verb, but attaches it to an object pronoun (*her*) instead of the subject pronoun (*she*). In (28), the child with SLI uses the correct subject pronoun (*he*) but omits the auxiliary verb (*is*). The utterance in (29) is produced by a child who has **FG syndrome** and **intellectual disability**. Several grammatical forms are omitted including the locative preposition (*in*), the possessive determiner (*my*), and the genitive (*uncle's room*). In fact, this child produces only one function word, the personal pronoun 'I'. He is somewhat more successful in using **content words** including verbs (*sleep, go*) and nouns (*uncle, bed, room*).

The utterance in (30) is produced by an adult with **schizophrenia**. In this case, the speaker's errors are morphological in nature in that he fails to use an inflectional suffix (*helped*) and a derivational suffix (*medication*). The speaker of the utterance in (31) is a man who sustained a left-hemisphere stroke in his forties. The damage caused by his stroke has resulted in **agrammatic aphasia**. In (31), he is attempting to describe a picture in which a girl is kicking a snake. His laboured, dysfluent output exhibits all the hallmarks of **agrammatism** including the presence of lengthy pauses and the omission of **articles** (*the*), an auxiliary verb (*is*), and the inflectional suffix *–ing* in 'kicking'. Also typical of agrammatism is the retention of the content words 'girl', 'kick', and 'snake'. Finally, the utterances in (32) are produced by a 47-year-old man who developed seizures following **encephalitis**. Although this speaker is able to produce a range of grammatical forms, it is the incompleteness of several of his syntactic constructions which is particularly disruptive to communication. This can be seen in the incomplete **prepositional phrase** in '*I told you about the ...* '. Also, this utterance is abandoned before a **verb phrase** is produced: *I don't know if he's asking him to drink or what the girl ...*. Each of these deficiencies cannot be adequately characterised in the absence of a number of grammatical concepts and terms. Like the other applications of grammar, the study of grammar in language disorders provides an invaluable opportunity for students to work directly with grammar.

The main points in this section are summarised below.

KEY POINTS THE STUDY OF GRAMMARS

- Grammar textbooks typically describe the features of only one grammar, namely, the grammar of Standard English. There are many other grammars which are not examined by textbooks for no other reason than that they lack the prestige of Standard English.

- Grammar textbooks are also only concerned with mature, intact grammatical forms. The grammatical forms used by normally developing children or by children and adults with disorders of grammar are overlooked by textbooks.
- The grammars of non-standard dialects, of immature language and of disordered language are still grammars, notwithstanding their failure to conform to some normative concept of grammar. These other grammars warrant examination within the mainstream study of grammar. They should not be investigated solely in specialised areas of study (e.g. language pathology).
- Students can obtain considerable practice in working with grammar by characterising grammatical forms used in non-standard dialects, the grammatical immaturities of young children and grammatical errors in individuals with language disorders. Knowledge of a wide range of grammatical terms and concepts is required in order to characterise these forms with accuracy.

1.5 Final Comments

This chapter has introduced a range of issues which are relevant to the study of grammar that is presented in this book. The first of these issues concerns the scope of grammar. Like most linguistic disciplines, grammar has no single definition which is accepted by all linguists. For most linguists, grammar is the study of two areas: morphology and syntax. But even this definition does not throw the net of grammar widely enough for one prominent linguist, Noam Chomsky. For Chomsky, grammar also contains phonological and semantic aspects. If the scope of grammar creates disagreement among linguists, then so too does the approach that should be taken to its study. The earliest recollections of grammar for most language users are school lessons in which pupils receive instruction in correct and incorrect forms of grammar. Often, these lessons impart rules to pupils to assist them in using 'good grammar' and avoiding 'bad grammar'. This prescriptive approach to grammar, it was argued, is motivated by a range of factors including linguistic prejudices about speakers of non-standard dialects. Prescriptive grammarians are also motivated by a desire to uphold Latin as a linguistic gold standard which English should attempt to emulate, whilst simultaneously rejecting any influence from modern foreign languages. By contrast, a descriptive approach examines the actual use of grammar by socially situated speakers. The grammatical variation that exists across dialects, for example, is not a sign of linguistic deficiency for a descriptive grammarian, but an interesting linguistic fact that requires explanation. Modern linguistics adopts a descriptive approach to grammar and language in general.

It was also argued in this chapter that if we are to take a descriptive approach to grammar seriously, then linguists should seek to describe grammatical forms wherever they exist. Most textbook treatments of grammar examine the grammatical features of only one dialect of English. That dialect is British Standard

English which has prestige by virtue of its association with official institutions and formal education. However, as the grammars of different dialects demonstrate, there are many different grammars and no individual grammar has a greater claim to legitimacy than any other grammar. The standard treatment of grammar in textbooks also reflects the fully mature grammatical forms of adults who have intact language skills. The grammatical immaturities of normally developing children and the grammatical errors of individuals with language disorders are still grammars, notwithstanding their deviation from fully mature, 'normal' grammar. The existence of these different grammars is never acknowledged in textbooks even though they are as much part of the rich complexity of grammar as are the grammatical features of Standard English. These 'other grammars' are significant in another respect. Whereas a straightforward academic presentation of grammar is perceived by many students to have little relevance to their lives and limited value as an area of knowledge and learning, the study of grammar in children undergoing language acquisition, in individuals with language disorders, and in speakers of non-standard dialects is better able to satisfy expectations of relevance. For all these reasons, these real-world uses of grammar will be adopted throughout the book as a pedagogical tool with which to illustrate, exemplify and illuminate grammatical concepts, terms and structures.

SUMMARY

In this chapter you have seen the following:

- Grammar has been defined as the study of morphology (word structure) and syntax (sentence structure). For Chomsky, grammar is a broader concept which involves phonology, syntax and semantics.
- Prescriptive grammarians stipulate the grammatical forms that speakers and writers *should* use while descriptive grammarians examine the grammatical forms that speakers and writers *actually* use.
- A descriptive approach to the study of grammar encourages us to look beyond the grammatical forms of Standard English and consider the grammar of speakers who are not traditionally examined in grammar textbooks. These speakers include young children who are acquiring language, children and adults with language disorders, and speakers of a range of non-standard dialects.
- These real-world applications of the study of grammar serve an important pedagogical purpose. In order to characterise the grammatical errors of young children, the grammatical impairments of children and adults with language disorders, and the grammatical features of non-standard dialects, an extensive repertoire of concepts and terms is required. These applications of grammar can therefore provide an effective pedagogical route into the study of the grammar of Standard English.

WEBSITE THE STUDY OF GRAMMAR

After reading the chapter, visit the website and test your knowledge of the study of grammar by answering the multiple-choice questions for this topic.

HOMEWORK ASSIGNMENT

American English shares many grammatical features with British English. However, it also has some features which are not used in British English. This exercise is designed to get you thinking about some of the differences between these two varieties. The following extracts are taken from an article in a newspaper called *Leader-Telegram* which is circulated in Eau Claire and the wider Wisconsin area in the United States. The article describes a research collaboration that has been established between the University of Wisconsin–Eau Claire and the Mayo Clinic Health System. The extracts in (A) and (C) are direct reported speech in the article, while the extract in (B) forms part of the commentary in the article. For extracts (A) and (B), you should describe *one* grammatical feature which sets these examples of American English apart from British English. Extract (C) clearly demonstrates that a certain prescriptive rule should have no place in the study of grammar. What is that rule?

(A) "But most important, it will better the lives of residents of the Chippewa Valley community."
(B) For the university, the agreement announced Wednesday furthers the commitment to faculty–student collaborative research.
(C) "The master collaborative research agreement that we're announcing today signifies our commitment to creating new opportunities for UW-Eau Claire to work more closely with Mayo Clinic as we seek to better prepare the next generation of scientists, innovators, health care providers and health care leaders."

SUGGESTIONS FOR FURTHER READING

(1) Berry, R. (2015) 'Grammar', in N. Braber, L. Cummings and L. Morrish (eds.), *Exploring Language and Linguistics*. Cambridge: Cambridge University Press, 111–36.

This chapter is an accessible introduction to grammar for those studying the discipline for the first time. Berry attempts a definition of grammar and examines the difference between a prescriptive and descriptive approach to grammar. He also considers two further distinctions: primary versus secondary grammar, and pedagogic versus scientific grammar. Other topics include the grammatical hierarchy from morphemes to sentences, word classes, phrases, clause elements and clause combination. Grammatical variation over time, across dialects and according to situations is also addressed. The chapter concludes by addressing the question 'Why does grammar matter?'.

(2) Börjars, K. and Burridge, K. (2010) *Introducing English Grammar*, Second Edition. Abingdon and New York: Routledge.

Chapter 1 in this book examines Standard English and variation and explores prescriptive and descriptive approaches to grammar. The chapter asks 'Why study English grammar?' and responds with the following reasons: to compare English to other languages; to study language acquisition by children; to assess and treat individuals with language disorders; to learn a foreign language; and to undertake analyses of literary and other texts. Grammar in a real-world context, the workplace, is examined. The chapter concludes with a discussion of the place of grammar among other branches of linguistics.

(3) Crystal, D. (2004) *Rediscover Grammar*, Third Edition. Harlow: Pearson Education.

Crystal provides a well-rounded introduction to the study of grammar in pages 10 to 34 of this highly readable book. There are similarities in coverage to the present chapter – Crystal asks 'What is grammar?' and discusses Standard English and varieties of English. Additionally, he discusses grammar in speech and writing, grammar in the electronic medium, and grammar and other areas.

QUESTIONS THE STUDY OF GRAMMAR

(1) Each of the following sentences is ungrammatical. For each sentence, state whether its ungrammaticality is related to *syntax* or *morphology*:
   (a) She complained about bitterly her boss.
   (b) He became unheartened after his poor test result.
   (c) She remained dispersuaded by his argument.
   (d) Pete lived with his elderly two aunts.
   (e) The actress derobed on stage.
   (f) John played again the record.

(2) The following article, which appeared in *The Telegraph*, describes the reactions of viewers to a BBC children's programme about a Rastafarian mouse. Read the article and consider to what extent prescriptive attitudes about language in general, and grammar in particular, are influencing the reactions of viewers.

Rastamouse provokes complaints of racism and teaching bad language

He is an animated reggae-singing mouse who has become a hit for the BBC, entertaining children with his attempts to fight crime and spread love and respect. Yet dreadlocked Rastamouse has provoked more than a hundred complaints to the corporation with parents expressing fears the show is racist and encouraging the use of slang.

Mothers on online parenting forums have even raised fears that the programme could result in playground fights if children try to copy the mouse. One mother on the Mumsnet forum, using the name TinyD4ncer, says she is concerned her child will be attacked for repeating some of the Jamaican Patois phrases used by the mouse. "The thing I'm most worried about is her saying the words like 'Rasta' and going up to a child and saying (these) things … my child is white and I feel if she was to say this to another child who was not white that it would be seen as her insulting the other child." Another parent, on Bumpandbaby.com, says: "just watched a couple videos … I'm going to say it is racist," while a blogger on musicmagazine website describes the show as "a mildly racist take on Rastafarians in the form of a cute mouse".

The BBC has received complaints from six viewers that the animated show stereotypes black people, while another 95 have complained about the language used in the show. The Rastafarian mouse, who leads a band called the Easy Crew and speaks in Jamaican Patois, uses phrases such as "me wan go" ("I want to go"), "irie" ("happy"), "wagwan" ("what's going on?"). His mission is to "make a bad ting good".

The show has proved to be very popular since it was launched on CBeebies last month, and has been praised for being funny and educational at the same time. "We wanted to create something contemporary, colourful and fun that would appeal not just to black children, but to other children as well," said Genevieve Webster, who co-authored the books that the show is based on. "I want children and grown-ups to watch it and enjoy it, be uplifted by the message and the seriously cool music."

A BBC spokesman said: "The Rastamouse books are written in Afro-Caribbean Patois rhyme and this authentic voice has been transferred to the TV series to retain its heart, integrity and distinctive quality. Rastamouse is part of a rich and varied CBeebies schedule, which is dedicated to reflecting the lives of all children in this country. Although Rastamouse has a particular appeal to young Afro-Caribbean children, its entertaining stories and positive messages – about friendship, respect and community – are intended to be enjoyed by all our young viewers, regardless of their backgrounds." (Jonathan Wynne-Jones and Jasper Copping, *The Telegraph*, 12 February 2011) © Telegraph Media Group Limited 2011

(3) Students often challenge the relevance of the study of grammar to their lives and its value as an area of learning and knowledge. One response to this challenge is to examine the different real-world contexts to which grammar may be seen to make a contribution. Identify <u>five</u> contexts in which knowledge of grammar may be judged to be beneficial.

(4) Each of the following utterances contains a grammatical form which deviates from the grammar of Standard English. Identify the form in question as belonging to (i) a non-standard dialect, (ii) immature language or (iii)

disordered language. Using grammatical terms, characterise the form in question.

(a) 'We wented to town, and we did have a haircut'

(b) 'I've rang them and they've come out'

(c) 'would be just 30 year ago'

(d) 'You drinked it'

(e) 'Girl, (2.8) she, (4.2) skipping'

(f) 'That's much more better'

(g) 'He need catched up'

(h) 'father had three brothers lived round the next street'

REVISION THE STUDY OF GRAMMAR

(1) Which of the following statements characterises how most linguists define the study of grammar?

(a) Grammar is the study of phonology, syntax and semantics.

(b) Grammar is the study of morphology and syntax.

(c) Grammar is the study of morphology and semantics.

(d) Grammar is the study of phonology and syntax.

(e) Grammar is the study of phonology and morphology.

(2) Which of the following statements are *true* claims about Chomsky's view of grammar?

(a) Grammar is a set of rules on the correct use of grammatical forms.

(b) Grammar is a body of knowledge which is only found in the adult speakers of a language.

(c) Grammar is a body of knowledge which generates the well-formed sentences in a language.

(d) Grammar has syntactic, phonological and semantic components.

(e) Grammar is a body of knowledge which only generates the well-formed sentences in the English language.

(3) What language do prescriptivist grammarians defer to when establishing rules for the correct use of grammar?

(4) Speaker identity is often behind the prescriptivist's intolerance of grammatical forms which are not used in Standard English. Name *five* aspects of speaker identity which motivate the prescriptivist's negative attitude towards these forms.

(5) Name a British public institution where there are calls for grammar to be policed.

(6) A true commitment to descriptive grammar implies that we examine the grammatical forms of speakers with disordered as well as intact language skills. Name *three* language disorders.

(7) Speakers of Belfast English and other non-standard dialects of English use forms such as *I seen him last week* and *I done it myself*. How do these forms deviate from their counterparts in Standard English?

(8) A young, normally developing child says *Daddy want car* and *Mummy drop dolly*. What two aspects of mature grammar are omitted from this child's utterances?

(9) *True or false:* The present-day dominance of British Standard English can be explained in large part by its long-standing association with official institutions and formal education.

(10) What grammatical feature of the following sentence is unacceptable to a prescriptive grammarian? *We don't want nothing.*

(11) Each of the following sentences is ungrammatical. For each sentence, state whether its ungrammaticality is related to *syntax* or *morphology*:

(a) He called up him.

(b) Tim went to the circus and Max so went to the zoo.

(c) He continued to listen even though he found the story disinteresting.

(d) I insist it.

(e) His explanation unmystified many things for her.

(f) The inspector decided that the car lacked road worthship.

(12) Prescriptive grammarians argue that each of the following sentences is a form of 'bad grammar'. For each sentence, state the grammatical rule that prescriptive grammarians use to justify this stance:

(a) He wants to really please his parents.

(b) After her many disappointments she didn't hope for nothing.

(c) Is this the knife that the girl was killed with?

(d) Let this be a secret between you and I.

(e) When did youse leave?

2   Word Structure

LEARNING OBJECTIVES

By the end of this chapter you will be able to do the following:

- Understand that words have an internal structure which is studied in the branch of linguistics known as morphology.
- Apply morphological concepts such as root, affix and lexical stem in an analysis of word structure.
- Understand the major and minor sub-divisions which exist within morphology. The major sub-division is between inflectional morphology and word-formation.
- Accurately identify morphemic word-formation processes such as derivational morphology (prefixation and suffixation), compounding and conversion.
- Accurately identify non-morphemic word-formation processes such as clipping, blending, acronym-formation and reduplication.

2.1 Introduction to Word Structure

For most grammarians, morphology is included in the study of grammar. It is the branch of linguistics that investigates words, how they are formed and their internal structure. Even to the untrained observer it is clear that words like *books*, *hopeful* and *walking* contain two parts. There is the main part of the word (*book*, *hope*, *walk*) and an ending (*–s*, *–ful*, *–ing*). Morphologists call these elements morphemes. Morphemes are the smallest meaningful units of language. The terms used to describe the morphemes *book* and *–s* are 'lexical stem' and 'suffix', respectively. These are just two of the terms that morphologists use to capture the internal structure of words. There will be many more introduced in this chapter. In opening up the internal structure of words to examination, we will see that this structure is at once interesting and puzzling. For example, the prefix in *unkind* allows a language user to express the opposite meaning of *kind*. Yet, to express the opposite meaning of the adjectives *discrete* and *honest*, two quite different prefixes are required: <u>in</u>*discrete* and <u>dis</u>*honest*. For still other adjectives, it is not prefixes that convey an opposite meaning but suffixes. This can be seen in *power<u>ful</u>* and *powerless*. Similar observations can be made of other word classes such as verbs. While *unkind* expresses the opposite meaning of *kind*, the same prefix in *unwind* does not express the opposite meaning of *wind* (i.e. *unwind* does not have the meaning 'not wind' but 'to slacken, undo or unravel'). If these different aspects of the morphology of words are challenging for linguists to explain, it is little wonder that children who are acquiring language can display a number of morphological errors or that morphology can be disrupted in children and adults with language disorders. In keeping with the approach to the study of grammar outlined in Chapter 1, some of these morphological features will also be examined in this chapter.

Returning to the words *books, hopeful* and *walking*, we identified *book, hope* and *walk* as the **lexical stems** of these words. A stem is a base morpheme to which other morphemes are attached. A stem is simple when it consists of only one part, as it does in the case of these words. It can also be complex when it contains more than one part. For example, in the word *unhelpful*, the part of the word to which the prefix *un–* is added is a complex stem because it contains two parts: *help* and *–ful*. Morphologists also use the term 'root'. A **root** is like a stem in that it is the core of the word to which other morphemes are added, but it is a morphologically simple unit. So in the word *books*, the simple stem *book* is also the root of the word. However, in the word *unhelpful*, it is *help* and not the stem *helpful* which is the root of the word as it is a morphologically simple unit. The stems and roots of several words are shown in Table 2.1.

The parts that attach to the stems of the words in Table 2.1 are called **affixes**. They include the affixes *im–* and *in–* which are attached to the front of the stem, and *–ness, –ful, –ly, –ation* and *–ion* which are attached to the end of the stem. The former affixes are known as prefixes, and the latter affixes are suffixes. You may query the need for the two suffixes *–ion* and *–ation*. The suffix *–ation* in *personifica-tion* must be treated as a separate morpheme because there is no form **personificate*

TABLE 2.1 The stems and roots of words

Word	Stem	Root
imperfect	perfect	perfect
mindlessness	mindless	mind
hospitalisation	hospitalise	hospital
infamous	famous	fame
mistrustful	mistrust	trust
hopefully	hopeful	hope
joyfulness	joyful	joy
imperishable	perishable	perish
personification	personify	person
domestication	domesticate	domestic

in English (as indicated by the asterisk) to which *–ion* can be attached in the way there is for *domesticate*. Also noteworthy is that what appears to be a single morpheme *–ly* is in fact two morphemes. In Table 2.1, the morpheme *–ly* turned the adjective *hopeful* into the adverb *hopefully*. But in the words *lovely* and *wily*, the morpheme *–ly* creates adjectives from nouns. It is the different grammatical functions of *–ly* in words like *hopefully* and *lovely* which leads us to treat this suffix as two distinct morphemes. At the same time as *–ly* is two distinct morphemes, a single morpheme may have a number of different **phonological realisations**. These variants of a morpheme – so-called **allomorphs** – arise on account of the different phonetic contexts in which a morpheme is used. Phonetic features of the sounds that immediately precede the morpheme effectively determine the particular form that the morpheme will take. For example, the morpheme for the past tense in English *–ed* is realised as [t] when it is preceded by the **voiceless consonant** [p] (e.g. *limped*), as [d] when it is preceded by the **voiced consonant** [g] (e.g. *dragged*), and as [ɪd] when it is preceded by the voiceless consonant [t] and the voiced consonant [d] (e.g. *lifted, welded*). Two further morphological terms – **bound morphemes** versus **free morphemes** – can be illustrated using the words in Table 2.1. Morphemes such as *fame* and *perish* are known as free morphemes as they can exist on their own. However, morphemes like *–able, –ous, im–* and *mis–* are bound morphemes as they cannot occur in isolation.

You can now get practice in working with allomorphs by attempting Exercise 2.1.

There will be many other terms in morphology introduced throughout the chapter. But in the meantime, we need to say something about the organisation of the chapter. It will follow the main branches in the study of morphology. The first major area to be examined is **inflectional morphology**. This is the branch of morphology that examines markers of grammatical categories such as tense, **case**, number and **aspect**. Inflectional morphemes such as *–s, –ed* and *–ing* create new word-forms (not new words) when they are attached to lexical stems, e.g. *walks; walked; walking*. The second main branch of morphology is **word-formation**. It includes **derivational morphology** along with a number of other word-formation processes. Where inflectional morphemes generate new word-forms of existing words, derivational morphemes generate new words. It is derivational

---

EXERCISE 2.1 ALLOMORPHS OF THE PAST TENSE MORPHEME

Each of the following verbs is a regular verb in English. To form the past tense of these verbs, the morpheme *–ed* is added to the base form of the verb. However, the phonological realisation of this morpheme is not the same in each case. For each verb, indicate which allomorph of the past tense morpheme is used and explain why this is the case:

walk   pretend   believe   strip   plant   apply

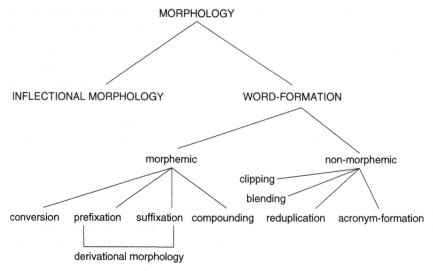

Figure 2.1 Branches of morphology

morphemes that permit the formation of the following words: _disengage; irrespon-sible; frightful; calmness_. The formation of these words involves **prefixation** and/or **suffixation**. However, word-formation goes beyond derivational morphology to include other processes such as **compounding** (e.g. _council estate_), **blending** (e.g. _breakfast + lunch → brunch_) and **clipping** (e.g. _(tele)phone → phone_). Blending and clipping differ from other word-formation processes in that they do not use morphemes to generate words, e.g. the parts of _breakfast_ and _lunch_ which come together to form _brunch_ are not morphemes. The diagram in Figure 2.1 illustrates the morphological processes that will be examined in this chapter.

The main points in this section are summarised below.

KEY POINTS INTRODUCTION TO WORD STRUCTURE

- Morphology is the branch of linguistics that investigates words, how they are formed and their internal structure. The discipline consists of two main areas: inflectional morphology and word-formation. Word-formation is further divided into derivational morphology (prefixation and suffixation), conversion and compounding and the non-morphemic word-formation processes of clipping, blending, acronym-formation and reduplication.
- Morphologists examine the individual morphemes that make up words. Morphemes are the smallest meaningful units of language.
- Morphologists use terms such as 'lexical stem', 'root' and 'affix' to describe the morphemes in words. A lexical stem is a base morpheme to which other morphemes are attached. The stem may be simple or complex. A simple lexical stem cannot be divided into other parts (e.g. _tree_ in _trees_). A complex lexical stem can be divided into other parts (e.g. _constitution_ in _constitutions_ can be divided into _constitute_ and _–ion_).

- The root is a stem that is a morphologically simple unit. In the word *helplessness*, the lexical stem is *helpless* as this is the base morpheme to which *–ness* is added. However, *help* is the root as it is morphologically simple.
- Morphemes can be added to the front and the end of a lexical stem. So-called affixes include prefixes like *im–* and *mis–* (*impossible* and *misunderstand*) and suffixes like *–ful* and *–ment* (*hopeful* and *agreement*).
- A single morpheme can have a number of variants or allomorphs. For example, the past tense morpheme *–ed* can be realised as [t] in *jumped*, as [d] in *banged* and as [ɪd] as in *pasted*.
- Bound morphemes cannot stand alone and must be attached to another morpheme, while free morphemes can exist on their own. So in the word *hopeful*, *–ful* is a bound morpheme while *hope* is a free morpheme.

2.2 Inflectional Morphology

In Section 2.1, inflectional morphemes were described as markers of grammatical categories such as tense, case, number and aspect. To these categories we can add person and **gradation**. Tense, aspect and person are grammatical features of verbs. Case and number are grammatical attributes of nouns, while gradation is a grammatical feature of adjectives. In Table 2.2, the different inflectional morphemes in English which mark these grammatical categories are given along with examples.

These morphemes are not as straightforward as they might at first appear. If we turn to the different allomorphs of the plural morpheme *–s* in English, we can see that this is the case. Like the different phonological realisations of the past tense morpheme *–ed* in English, the regular plural morpheme *–s* has three allomorphs which vary depending on the final sound of the stem to which the morpheme is added. The allomorph [s] is used when the preceding sound is voiceless like [t] is *cats*. When the preceding sound is a voiced consonant such as [g] in *dogs* or a vowel like [aɪ] in *eyes*, the allomorph [z] occurs. When the plural morpheme comes after a **sibilant sound** such as [s] in *houses* the allomorph [ɪz] is used. So far, we have only addressed regular allomorphs of the plural morpheme. There are also several irregular realisations of the plural morpheme, a number of which are shown in Table 2.2. In words like *teeth*, *geese* and *mice*, there is a vowel change to form the plural. In *teeth* and *geese*, [uː] is substituted by [iː] while in *mice* [aʊ] is substituted by [aɪ]. To form the plural of *sheep* there is no change in form (i.e. a zero form). In *oxen* the suffix [ən] is added while in *children* there is a vowel change ([aɪ] is replaced by [ɪ]) and the use of the suffix [ɹən]. We can also add the plural forms of a group of words in English of Latin origin. Here we include *octopus – octopi*, *curriculum – curricula* and *formula – formulae*.

It is important to point out that the bound inflectional morphemes in Table 2.2 relate to Standard English. There are non-standard dialects of English where these morphemes are not used or they are used in ways which differ from their

TABLE 2.2 Grammatical functions of bound inflectional morphemes in English

Nouns		Verbs			Adjectives
number	case	person	tense	aspect	gradation
Regular and irregular realisations of the plural morpheme in English, e.g. *cats; dogs; houses; teeth; geese; mice; sheep; oxen; children*	The genitive in English indicates possession or ownership or that something is part of something else, e.g. *man's car; girls' party; house's living room*	In English the morpheme *–s* marks the third person singular present tense in regular verbs, e.g. *He walks every day; She likes chocolate; It brings hope.* Irregular verbs have different third person forms, e.g. *Mary is at home; He goes to school*	The simple past tense in English is marked by *–ed* (*They walked home*) which may also be used for the past participle (*She had departed early*) and the passive voice (*The van was followed by the lorry*)	The morpheme *–ing* in English is used to mark present progressive aspect (*They are crossing the road*) and past progressive aspect (*She was travelling home*)	The morphemes *–er* and *–est* are used to form the comparative and superlative forms of regular adjectives in English, e.g. *faster* and *fastest*. Several adjectives in English have irregular comparative and superlative forms, e.g. the adjective *bad* has the comparative *worse* and the superlative *worst*. Other adjectives do not inflect for grade but use the lexical morphemes *more* and *most*, e.g. *more horrible* and *most horrible*

use in Standard English. A regional dialect which is associated with the city of Newcastle-upon-Tyne in England and the surrounding urban area of Tyneside is the Geordie dialect. Speakers of this dialect do not use the plural suffix *–s* on certain count nouns like *week, month, year* and *mile*. Also, the suffix *–s* is used on third person plural present tense verbs, a form which is not seen in Standard English. Both non-standard uses are illustrated below. Examples are from the British Library (2016b):

Zero plural marker
'would be just over 30 **year** ago, yes, aye'

Historic present
'the bairns [children] now, they **says**, 'Dad, we thought you were hard and you were hard then and we were frightened to talk to you.'

These are not the only non-standard uses of suffixes to be found in the Geordie dialect. Another feature will be described in Section 2.3. In the meantime, you can get further practice of working with some of the features described in this section by examining the Special Topic below.

SPECIAL TOPIC 2.1 ZERO PLURAL AND PAST TENSE MARKERS IN ASIAN AND CARIBBEAN ENGLISH

Speakers of the Geordie dialect are not alone in omitting the plural suffix *–s* on nouns. A zero plural marker is also a grammatical feature of **Caribbean British English**, as the following example illustrates:

'my **relative**, they were involve in the Community Association business'

Speakers of Caribbean British English also omit a further suffix introduced in Table 2.2. It is the past tense suffix *–ed* as in *work* in the following example:

'I **work** on that job for a few months'

This same grammatical feature occurs in Asian English. In the following example, the speaker does not use a past tense marker on the verbs *send* and *like*:

'so they **send** me photograph, which I approved and m, m, my wife, uh, pinched, uh, one photograph from the album, so obviously she **like**, uh, the photograph'

It is also worth noting that the inflectional morphology of English is altogether less complex than the inflectional morphology of languages such as German. In total, there are fewer than ten bound grammatical morphemes in Table 2.2, whereas German uses more inflectional morphemes than this for nouns alone. Nevertheless, young, English-speaking children make some interesting errors in

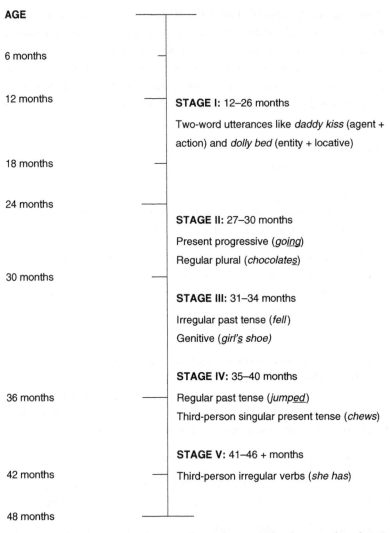

AGE

6 months

12 months

STAGE I: 12–26 months

Two-word utterances like *daddy kiss* (agent + action) and *dolly bed* (entity + locative)

18 months

24 months

STAGE II: 27–30 months

Present progressive (*going*)

Regular plural (*chocolates*)

30 months

STAGE III: 31–34 months

Irregular past tense (*fell*)

Genitive (*girl's shoe*)

STAGE IV: 35–40 months

36 months   Regular past tense (*jumped*)

Third-person singular present tense (*chews*)

STAGE V: 41–46 + months

42 months   Third-person irregular verbs (*she has*)

48 months

Figure 2.2 Morphological milestones during language development based on Brown (1973)

the use of inflectional morphemes during language development. Roger Brown (1973) was the first linguist to study the acquisition of inflectional morphemes by typically developing children. He charted the emergence of inflectional morphemes in accordance with children's **mean length of utterance** (MLU). Brown reported that the inflectional suffix for **progressive aspect** *–ing* is typically acquired between 27 and 30 months when children's mean length of utterance in morphemes (MLUm) is 2.25 (Stage II). At around the same stage, the suffix for plural nouns *–s* also emerges. Irregular past tense verb forms emerge between 31 and 34 months when mean MLUm is 2.75 (Stage III). The genitive form in *woman's dress* emerges at this same stage in development. At 35 to 40 months, when typically developing children have a mean MLUm of 3.5, the regular past tense suffix *–ed* is acquired (Stage IV). This is also the stage when children begin to use the suffix *–s* to mark agreement with a third-person singular subject. Third person irregular verbs such as *she does* and *he has* emerge in Stage V when children have a mean MLUm of 4.0. Children are typically 41–46+ months of age at this stage. These morphological milestones are illustrated in Figure 2.2.

The chronological ages at which these morphemes appear is somewhat less important than the order in which they occur. This is because there is considerable variation in the age of acquisition in even typically developing children. The order of acquisition and the errors that young children make on their way to full mastery of each major type of morpheme reveal something of a developing child's morphological knowledge. It is instructive to consider these errors as an exercise in extending your knowledge of the inflectional morphemes of English. Some of the morphological errors produced by a young girl called Lara between 22 and 34 months of age are displayed in Table 2.3. Lara was recorded in her home in conversation with her caregivers once or twice a week between the ages of 1 year 9 months and 3 years 3 months (Rowland and Fletcher, 2006). Her utterances are organised according to the type of morpheme they may be taken to exemplify. Lara's age in years and months is shown in brackets after each utterance.

Most errors in Lara's use of the progressive *–ing* morpheme involve omission of the morpheme. This occurs on the verbs *sleep, hide, do, make, swim* and *play*. In one utterance, Lara uses the morpheme when it is not required (*Let me doing that big pond*) while in a further utterance (*Is it gets dark?*) the morpheme *–s* is used in place of *–ing*. A number of Lara's errors in the use of plural *–s* involve omission of the morpheme (*animal, sausage, jigsaw*). She also uses plural *–s* when it is not required (*onions, babies*) and makes errors on two nouns that involve a vowel change to form the plural (*man, feets*). The error on *feets* is particularly interesting as Lara has marked the noun twice for plural, once through a vowel change and then by adding *–s*. Lara displayed considerable difficulty with irregular past tense verbs. More often than not, she produced overregularisation errors where she added the past tense morpheme *–ed* to the base form of the verb to produce forms such as *throwed* and *goed*. The base form without a suffix was also used in place of the past tense (*drink – drank*). On one occasion, Lara used a variant of the past tense morpheme *–ed* (*drawded*). Regular past tense verbs were less problematic for Lara. When errors did occur, they usually involved omission of the past tense morpheme *–ed*. An interesting morphological error occurs in the utterance *I pick it uped* again. Lara is aware that the past tense morpheme *–ed* is required. However, the morpheme is attached to the adverb *up* rather than the verb *pick*. The genitive (*'s*) was frequently omitted in Lara's utterances. Lara used the genitive in *Abi mum's poorly mummy?* but attached it to the wrong noun (*mum's* instead of *Abi's*).

Lara's rich use of inflectional morphemes extends to regular and irregular third-person singular verb forms. For the most part, Lara simply omitted the third-person singular *–s* morpheme. In the utterance *He's eat pencils*, Lara appears to be aware that the *–s* morpheme is required but attaches it to the pronoun *he* rather than the verb *eat*. On one further occasion, Lara uses the *–s* morpheme

TABLE 2.3 One child's morphological errors between 22 and 34 months

Morpheme	Utterance
Progressive –ing	Everybody's sleep (1;11)
	Because daddy's coming down and we're hide (2;05)
	Let me doing that big pond (2;08)
	Is it gets dark? (2;08)
	What [are] you do? (2;08)
	What are you make? (2;09)
	I'm do it for him (2;09)
	And now I'm swim (2;09)
	Is he play with the toys? (2;09)
Plural –s	More animal (1;10)
	I done two sausage (2;00)
	Three little man sitting on the wall (2;01)
	Put the feets down (2;01)
	Shall we do one of these jigsaw? (2;07)
	I need another onions (2;07)
	That's a babies (2;07)
Irregular past tense	Lara doed it (1;10)
	Look I drawed (2;06)
	I drawded a fish (2;06)
	Who drink my tea? (2;08)
	Winnie The Pooh goed to the woods (2;08)
	I throwed it (2;09)
	I falled over (2;09)
	I lied down (2;09)
Genitive – 's	That mummy car (1;11)
	Where's mummy poorly knee gone? (2;02)
	Abi mum's poorly mummy? (2;10)
Regular past tense –ed	I pick it uped again (2;06)
	I nick Amy's seat (2;09)
Third-person singular present tense –s	He just stay there (2;00)
	Mummy want some money (2;02)
	It come apart (2;03)
	This one doesn't hurts (2;06)
	He's eat pencils (2;07)
	He eat them up hisself (2;08)
	And Tigger sit on his chair there (2;08)
	It look like daddy's (2;08)
	Who want to go up the ladder? (2;08)
	When Amy get bigger she will do this (2;09)
	Grandad say pooey (2;09)
	We show what Elsie Grandma want to do (2;09)
Third-person singular present tense, irregular	That one go there (2;02)
	Mummy have (2;02)
Past participle –ed	I [have] nearly finish this (2;00)
	I've maked it (2;00)
	Have you pour them out? (2;08)
Past participle, irregular	I [have] broked it now (2;07)
	I've throwned it (2;08)
	I've leaved some space for you (2;08)
	I've donned another bird and you've done that bird (2;09)

even when the presence of the auxiliary verb renders it redundant (*This one doesn't hurts*). In place of irregular third-person singular verbs like *goes* and *has*, Lara uses the base form of the verb. These errors are predictable given what we know about Lara's use of morphology. Lara treats verbs like *go* and *have* as regular verbs. On regular verbs, she omits the third-person morpheme –*s*. She replicates this pattern when she produces *go* and *have*. In terms of the past participle, Lara omits the morpheme –*ed* in *finish* and *pour*. In the utterance *I've maked it*, Lara has treated an irregular verb as a regular verb and proceeded to attach the morpheme –*ed* to the base form of the verb to form the past participle. Irregular past participles pose considerable difficulties for Lara. In *leaved*, Lara has attempted to form the past participle by adding the regular past participle morpheme –*ed* onto the base form of the verb. A quite different error occurs in *throwned* and *donned*. Here, Lara has added the past participle morpheme –*ed* to what is already the past participle form of the verb. That Lara succeeds in using *done* in the same utterance as *donned* is a sign that she has knowledge of the correct morphological form even if that knowledge is not always expressed. A different error again occurs in *broked*. In this case, Lara has attached the past participle morpheme –*ed* to the past tense form of the verb.

You can get further practice in working with noun morphology by attempting Exercise 2.2.

EXERCISE 2.2 LARA'S NOUN MORPHOLOGY

Now that you have seen some of the morphological errors that Lara makes, it is time for you to describe these errors for yourself. Twelve of Lara's noun errors are shown below. Characterise the type of error that Lara has committed in each case. Also, for nouns where the morpheme –*s* is normally used to form the plural, indicate if it is realised as [s], [z] or [ɪz]. For example, if Lara used *dog* in place of *dogs*, she would have omitted the morpheme –*s* which would be realised as [z] if it were present.

(a) I write lots of name (2;09)
(b) We haven't got sheeps (2;10)
(c) I don't like fishes (2;10)
(d) Where have your marble gone? (2;11)
(e) I don't like mans (2;11)
(f) Two foot came out (2;11)
(g) And we're going to get some knife and forks (2;11)
(h) Can I make the cup of teas and you make the dinner? (3;00)
(i) Can you open their mouthses? (3;01)
(j) You're not a children (3;01)
(k) Is she getting more tooth? (3;02)
(l) I haven't had any go (3;03)

It is important to point out that as well as inflectional morphemes, Lara is able to use a range of free grammatical morphemes. These morphemes are function words like articles (*a, the*), prepositions (*in, beside*) and conjunctions (*and, because*). Like bound inflectional morphemes, these words have grammatical functions. But unlike inflectional morphemes, they can stand alone in the absence of other morphemes. Function words will be described further in Chapter 3. In the meantime, we turn our attention to another group of morphemes in the study of word structure. So-called derivational morphemes create new words rather than word-forms. They can generate words in a range of grammatical classes, e.g. *discover* (verb), *discovery* (noun), *discoverable* (adjective). However, derivational morphemes do not have the grammatical function of inflectional morphemes. Whereas inflectional morphemes can be applied to most or all members of a class (e.g. *–s* can be attached to the third-person form of all regular verbs in English), derivational morphemes have a much more limited scope of application. For example, the suffix *–ness* cannot be applied to all adjectives to form nouns (*kindness* is acceptable while *wiseness* is not). Another difference between inflectional and derivational morphemes is that derivational morphemes are closer to the stem of the word. In the word *constitutions*, the derivational morpheme *–ion* attaches directly to the stem while the inflectional morpheme *–s* appears at the end of the word. Inflectional morphemes are a closed, small class of items. The class of derivational morphemes is altogether larger, with morphemes finding new applications all the time. For example, with the emergence of Facebook the class of derivational morphemes that can be used with *friend* (*befriend, friendship, friendly, unfriendly*) has expanded to include *unfriend* and *defriend*.

The main points in this section are summarised below.

KEY POINTS INFLECTIONAL MORPHOLOGY

- Bound inflectional morphemes serve as markers of grammatical categories like tense (past tense *–ed*), case (genitive *–'s*), number (plural *–s*), aspect (progressive *–ing*), person (third-person singular *–s*) and gradation (comparative *–er* and superlative *–est*).
- The plural morpheme *–s* in English has three variants or allomorphs which are determined by the sound at the end of the stem to which the morpheme attaches. These allomorphs are [s] as in *cats*, [z] as in *dogs* and [ɪz] as in *matches*.
- There are also several irregular realisations of the plural morpheme in English. They include vowel change (*tooth – teeth*), no change in form (*sheep – sheep*), addition of suffix *–en* (*oxen*), vowel change and use of suffix [ɹən] (*child – children*) and forms of Latin origin (*fungus – fungi*).
- The system of inflectional morphemes in English is considerably simpler than that of languages like German. Nevertheless, typically developing children produce a range of errors as they acquire the morphology of English. They may omit morphemes, add them to the wrong word in an utterance, add an incorrect morpheme, or 'double up' on morpheme use.

- Aside from bound grammatical morphemes, there are also free grammatical morphemes. These so-called function words include articles (*a, the*), prepositions (*under, next to*) and conjunctions (*but, since*).
- Inflectional morphemes differ from derivational morphemes in that they create word-forms rather than words, are further away from the stem of the word, are a closed, small class of morphemes and have a wider scope of application than derivational morphemes.

2.3 Derivational Morphology

The second main branch of morphology is called word-formation. It examines derivational morphology as well as other word-formation processes such as compounding. In this section, the derivational processes of prefixation and suffixation will be addressed.

2.3.1 Prefixation

In prefixation, a bound lexical morpheme is added to the front of the base. The result is a new word (rather than a word-form) which more often than not belongs to the same word class. For example, when *dis–* is added to the verb *connect*, another verb *disconnect* is created. And when *re–* is added to the noun *birth*, another noun *rebirth* is derived. In each case, the grammatical class of the word has been maintained but the prefix has changed the word's meaning. The addition of *dis–* has changed the meaning of the verb to become 'take something apart' while *re–* added to *birth* means 'the birth of something or someone again'. The effect of the prefixes in each case is semantic (changing word meaning) rather than grammatical (changing word class). A small number of prefixes do not adhere to this general pattern and change the class of the words to which they are added (along with meaning). These prefixes are shown below along with examples:

> *a–*: avow (noun *vow* → verb *avow*)
> *be–*: besiege (noun *siege* → verb *besiege*)
> *en–*: entrust (noun *trust* → verb *entrust*)
> *de–*: defame (noun *fame* → verb *defame*)
> *dis–*: dismantle (noun *mantle* → verb *dismantle*)
> *un–*: unread (verb *read* → adjective *unread*)

To the extent that prefixes are contributing to the semantics of words, some general semantic types can be identified. We have already encountered the meanings of two prefixes: *dis–* means 'to reverse an action' and *re–* means 'to do something again'. Further examples of the use of these prefixes with these meanings are shown below:

> prefix *dis–*: dismount; disengage; disinherit
> prefix *re–*: redraw; reinstate; reinvigorate

Beyond verbs, the prefix *dis–* has a quite different meaning when it is used in nouns and adjectives. The use of *dis–* in these words has the meaning 'the opposite or converse of'. Examples include:

> nouns: *dishonour; dissatisfaction; disunity*
> adjectives: *dishonest; disloyal; dissimilar*

What is the meaning of the prefixes in the underlined words in the following sentence?

> A Downtown neighbourhood of low-income, elderly and <u>disabled</u> residents borne amid controversial "urban renewal" a half-century ago may be <u>reshaped</u> again. (*Wisconsin State Journal*, 2017)

The same pattern of prefixes changing their meaning across different word classes is also observed in *un–*. When this prefix is used in verbs, it has the meaning 'reversing the action'. But when it is attached to adjectives, its meaning is 'the converse of':

> verbs: *unlock; unplug; unwind*
> adjectives: *unreasonable; unclear; unacceptable*

The meanings of some other, commonly used prefixes are shown below along with examples:

> *a–*: ('lack of') – *amoral; aseptic; asocial* (adjectives)
> *in–*: ('the converse of') – *inactive; inexcusable; insatiable* (adjectives)
> *non–*: ('not') – *non-member; non-practising; non-scientific* (nouns and adjectives)
> *de–*: ('reverse the action') – *destabilise; decentralise; dehydrogenisation* (verbs and nouns)

Some prefixes convey pejorative meanings and numerical information. Others express meanings such as extent and size or time, order and location. Still other prefixes express stance and attitude. Examples of each of these prefixes are shown below:

> *mal–*: ('bad') – *maladjustment; malnourished; maladminister*
> *poly–*: ('many') – *polytechnic; polymorphous; polymerise*
> *hyper–*: ('extreme') – *hypermarket; hyperglycaemic; hyperventilate*
> *mini–*: ('little') – *minicab; minicomputer; minibus*
> *fore–*: ('before') – *forerunner; foregoing; foresee*
> *post–*: ('after') – *postimpressionism; postoperative; postdate*
> *inter–*: ('between') – *intersex; interspecific; interrelate*
> *anti–*: ('against') – *antifreeze; antimalarial; antimagnetic*
> *pro–*: ('for') – *pro-Protestant; prorevolutionary; pro-Israel*

When a word contains a prefix and a suffix, one of these affixes is more closely associated with the base of the word than the other affix. Consider the following words. These words appear to have the same morphological structure, that is, a prefix followed by a noun, verb or adjective and then a suffix.

mistrustful: prefix + noun + suffix
disfigurement: prefix + noun + suffix
reusableness: prefix + adjective + suffix
infamous: prefix + noun + suffix
imperishable: prefix + verb + suffix
unhelpful: prefix + noun + suffix

However, this apparent similarity of structure belies the fact that these words have different internal constituent structures. In the first three words, the prefix is more closely identified with the base of the word than the suffix. This is indicated, as previously, by the fact that the forms marked by an asterisk do not exist in English:

mistrustful (*trustful)
disfigurement (*figurement)
reusableness (*usableness)

Because the prefix is more closely associated with the base than the suffix in these words, their internal morphological structure is represented as follows. The diagram in (A) shows that the suffix is added to a prior morphological unit that consists of the prefix and a noun.

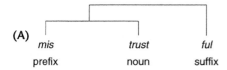

(A)
   mis   *trust*   *ful*
   prefix   noun   suffix

In the words *infamous*, *imperishable* and *unhelpful*, the opposite pattern obtains. This time, the suffix is more closely associated with the base than the prefix. Once again, we know this is the case because the forms indicated by an asterisk do not exist in English:

infamous (*infame)
imperishable (*imperish)
unhelpful (*unhelp)

As before, this internal morphological structure can be illustrated in a diagram in (B) which shows that the prefix is attached to a prior morphological unit that consists of a noun or a verb and a suffix.

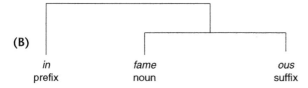

(B)
   in   *fame*   *ous*
   prefix   noun   suffix

Knowledge of the different morphological structures of these words allows us to say that the derivation of the words *mistrustful* and *infamous* proceeds as indicated in (C) and not as indicated in (D):

(C) *trust → mistrust → mistrustful*
     fame → famous → infamous
(D) *trust → trustful → mistrustful*
     fame → infame → infamous

Now it is your turn to get practice in analysing the morphological structure of words by attempting Exercise 2.3.

EXERCISE 2.3 MORPHOLOGICAL STRUCTURE

Draw diagrams like those in (A) and (B) above to reveal the morphological structure of the following words. Beside each diagram, illustrate the formation history of the word using the format in (C) above:

    unreasonable   dethronement   inflexible   disguisable

2.3.2 Suffixation

The other word-formation process in derivational morphology is suffixation. Like prefixation, suffixation is a word-formation process in which a bound lexical morpheme is added to a base that consists of at least one free lexical morpheme. Unlike prefixation, the morpheme is attached at the end rather than the front of the base. Also unlike prefixation, suffixation involves a change in word class (with some exceptions, e.g. the nominal suffix in *professorship*). Some of these word-class changes are shown below:

(E) *waste – wastage* (noun–noun)
    improve – improvement (verb–noun)
    fragile – fragility (adjective–noun)
(F) *hope – hopeless* (noun–adjective)
    mind – mindful (noun–adjective)
    dispute –disputable (verb–adjective)
(G) *passive – passively* (adjective–adverb)
    sky – skywards (noun–adverb)
    crab – crabwise (noun–adverb)
(H) *incentive – incentivise* (noun–verb)
    formal – formalise (adjective–verb)
    soft – soften (adjective–verb)

Each type of suffixation assumes the name of the word class that the process acts on and the word class that the process results in. For example, the suffixations in

(E) all result in nouns and are called 'nominalisations'. The type of nominalisation depends on whether suffixation acts on a noun (de-nominal nominalisation), a verb (de-verbal nominalisation), or an adjective (de-adjectival nominalisation). So the suffixation in *improve – improvement* is a de-verbal nominalisation. The suffixations in (F) are all adjective formations. Some adjective formations involve nouns and are de-nominal adjective formations like *hope – hopeless*. Others involve verbs and are de-verbal adjective formations like *dispute – disputable*. The suffixations in (G) are all adverb formations. Where an adjective is involved as in *passive – passively*, it is a de-adjectival adverb formation. The suffixation in *sky – skywards* is a de-nominal adverb formation. Finally, the suffixations in (H) are verb formations of two types: de-nominal verb formations (*incentive – incentivise*) and de-adjectival verb formations (*soft – soften*).

In Section 2.2, it was stated that inflectional morphemes like plural *–s* in Standard English are not necessarily a feature of non-standard dialects like the Geordie dialect. The same is true of the derivational suffixes which have just been described. In Standard English, suffixation generates adverbs from adjectives as in *automatic + ly → automatically*. However, the suffix *–ly* is not a consistent feature of adverb use in the Geordie dialect, as the following example from the British Library (2016b) demonstrates:

Zero adverbial marker
'didn't know you were doing it, yeah, you used to just do it **automatic**'

Forms such as the zero adverbial marker should reinforce the fact that the morphological features of Standard English are not always shared by non-standard dialects.

The semantics of noun-, adjective- and verb-forming suffixes is noteworthy. The noun-forming suffixes in (E) generate abstract nouns. But other noun-forming suffixes give rise to concrete nouns that refer to people and objects (e.g. *employer, housing*). The adjective-forming suffixes in (F) capture qualities and characteristics of people and situations (e.g. *The war was hopeless; She was mindful of his difficulties*). Other suffixes in this category express meanings such as ability (e.g. *washable* 'able to be washed'). Verb-forming suffixes often produce **transitive verbs** that convey the meaning 'to make something X'. So, *formalise* means to make something (plans, etc.) formal while *soften* means to make something (leather, etc.) soft. The semantic properties of bases also influence the suffixes which can be added to them. For example, the suffix *–ee* can generally only be added to bases which express the role of patient in a **paraphrase** (e.g. *trustee* 'someone who is entrusted with legal authority to be exercised for another's benefit').

Suffixation often involves changes to the base which are not seen in prefixation. Phonetic changes to the base can occur. They include changes to vowel sounds such as the stressed vowels in *sane, mobile* and *obscene*. Consonant sounds may also change during suffixation. In *race, please* and *permit*, **alveolar consonants** are substituted with **palatal consonants** of the same voicing. In some cases, suffixation may bring about vowel and consonant changes simultaneously. In *divide*, **palatalisation** of [d] is accompanied by a **laxing** of the stressed vowel [aɪ]. In some types of suffixation there is a shift in the location of stress in the word. The change in stress pattern also affects vowel pronunciation. This can be seen in *psychopath, professor* and *satan*. Finally, suffixation may bring about changes in **vowel quality**, a change of consonant and **stress migration**. This occurs in the suffixation that results in *impugnation*:

Vowel sounds
sane – sanity: [e] → [æ]
mobile – mobility: [aɪ] → [ɪ]
obscene – obscenity: [i] → [ɛ]

Consonant sounds
race – racial: [s] → [ʃ]
please – pleasure: [z] →[ʒ]
permit – permission: [t] → [ʃ]

Vowel and consonant sounds
divide – division: [d] → [ʒ] [aɪ] → [ɪ]

Stress
ˈpsychopath → psyˈchopathy
proˈfessor → profesˈsorial
ˈsatan → saˈtanic

Vowel and consonant sounds and stress
imˈpugn – impugˈnation [u] → [ʌ] [pj] → [p]

As well as changing the base of the word, suffixation differs from prefixation in a further respect. Unlike prefixes, several suffixes can occur together. Examples include *hopelessness, desirability* and *industrialisation* in which the word class changes with the addition of each new suffix:

hopelessness
–less (adjective-forming suffix)
–ness (noun-forming suffix)

desirability
–able (adjective-forming suffix)
–ity (noun-forming suffix)

industrialisation
–ial (adjective-forming suffix)
–ise (verb-forming suffix)
–ation (noun-forming suffix)

Many children and adults with language disorders experience difficulties in using derivational suffixes. An examination of some of the errors that these individuals make can help you get practice in accurately identifying derivational suffixes. The

TABLE 2.4 The morphological errors of a man with deep dyslexia

Target	Response	Target	Response
option	opting	partly	parted
computer	computed	worthless	worthily/worthery
goodness	goodly	crabby	crabbing
wordy	words	teaser	tears/tea
brainless	brainly	sickish	sickering/sickly
thickly	thickening/thickens	stockist	stocking
sexist	sexy	illness	illy/illery
washer	washing	sweetie	sweeties
scabby	scabs	goddess	godistest/godery
buzzer	buzz/buzzing	tourist	tourists

morphological errors in Table 2.4 were produced by a man known as 'DE' who was 45 years of age at the time of testing. DE was studied by Rastle et al. (2006). When he was 16 years old, he was involved in a motor scooter accident which was followed within 24 hours by a stroke. Since this time, he has experienced language difficulties and a condition called deep dyslexia (the individual with deep dyslexia can read words with concrete meanings more easily than words with abstract meanings). DE was asked to read aloud lists of suffixed words.

Many of DE's morphological errors involve the substitution of a derivational suffix with an inflectional suffix. This can be seen in the following words:

Inflectional suffix for progressive (–ing)
option → opting
crabby → crabbing
buzzer → buzzing
washer → washing (–ing may also be a derivational suffix)
stockist → stocking

Inflectional suffix for past tense (–ed)
partly → parted
computer → computed

Inflectional suffix for plural (–s)
wordy → words
tourist → tourists
scabby → scabs
sweetie → sweeties

Three other errors produced by DE also involve the use of inflectional suffixes. But in these cases, the base to which the suffix is added has also been changed. In *teaser*, the base changes to *tear* and the inflectional suffix –s is added. In *sickish*, two suffixes are added to the base *sick*. The derivational suffix –er is first to be added and is followed by the inflectional suffix *–ing*. In *goddess*, DE adds the inflectional suffix *–est* to the derivational suffix *–ess*. Also, the vowel in the derivational suffix has changed from [ɛ] to [ɪ].

> teaser → tears
> sickish → sickering
> goddess → godistest

DE's remaining morphological errors are of two types. Some errors involve the omission of the derivational suffix (buzzer → buzz) or the derivational suffix and part of the base (teaser → tea). Other errors involve the substitution of the target derivational suffix by another derivational suffix. This can be seen in the following words:

> sex<u>ist</u> → sex<u>y</u>
> ill<u>ness</u> → ill<u>y</u>/ill<u>ery</u>
> good<u>ness</u> → good<u>ly</u>
> brain<u>less</u> → brain<u>ly</u>
> sick<u>ish</u> → sick<u>ly</u>
> god<u>dess</u> → god<u>ery</u>
> worth<u>less</u> → worth<u>ily</u>/worth<u>ery</u>
> thick<u>ly</u> → thick<u>en</u>

The word *thickly* is interesting in a further respect. DE uses the derived form *thicken* as the basis of inflectional suffixation in *thickening* (progressive suffix *–ing*) and *thickens* (third-person singular *–s*). DE certainly has access to a wide range of derivational suffixes. However, these suffixes are attached to the wrong bases and are used inconsistently.

You can now extend your knowledge of derivational suffixes by attempting Exercise 2.4.

EXERCISE 2.4 DERIVATIONAL SUFFIXES IN LANGUAGE DISORDER

Now that you have seen some of the errors that DE makes in his use of derivational suffixes, it is time for you to attempt an analysis of these errors for yourself. The forms below were also produced by DE in the study by Rastle et al. (2006). Examine these forms in detail. Individually or in a group, analyse the types of errors made by DE as he reads these words aloud:

(a) cabbie → cab
(b) zipper → zip
(c) swimmer → swimming
(d) election → elect
(e) blandly → blankly
(f) grower → grown

(g) meanness → meaning/mean

(h) madly → madness

(i) smoothly → smootly/smoother

(j) swiftly → swifty

(k) willowy → willows

(l) buffer → bluff

(m) childish → child/childly

(n) arsonist → arsoner/arson

(o) chilly → chills

(p) killer → kill

(q) tallish → tall/taller

(r) talker → talking

The main points in this section are summarised below.

KEY POINTS DERIVATIONAL MORPHOLOGY

- Word-formation is the second main branch of morphology. It includes derivational morphology which is the study of prefixation and suffixation.
- In prefixation a bound lexical morpheme is added to the front of a base to create a new word (e.g. *obey* – <u>dis</u>*obey*).
- Prefixation changes the meanings of words but maintains the word class (*disobey* is another verb, for example). A small number of prefixes change word class as well as meaning (e.g. *vow*: noun → *avow*: verb).
- The semantics of prefixes can vary with word class. For example, the prefix *un-* has the meaning 'to reverse the action' when used in verbs (e.g. *uncover*) but means 'the converse of' when used in adjectives (e.g. *unattractive*).
- In some words where prefixes and suffixes are used, the prefix is more closely associated with the base than the suffix (e.g. *mistrust-ful*). In other words, the suffix is more closely associated with the base than the prefix (e.g. *ir-responsible*).
- Suffixation is a word-formation process in which a bound lexical morpheme is added to the end of a base that consists of at least one free lexical morpheme. For the most part, suffixation changes the class of a word (e.g. *kind*: adjective → *kindness*: noun). The particular suffixation that results in *kindness* is called a de-adjectival nominalisation.
- Like prefixes, suffixes convey a range of meanings. For example, the adjective-forming suffix *–able* expresses ability such as *likeable* ('able to be liked') and *doable* ('able to be done').
- Unlike prefixation, suffixation can bring about phonetic changes to the base of the word. Vowel and consonant sounds may change as a result of suffixation. The location of stress in the word may also shift as a result of suffixation.
- Also unlike prefixes, several suffixes may occur simultaneously in a word, with each one changing the class of the word, e.g. industrialisation: *–ial* (adjective-forming suffix), *–ise* (verb-forming suffix) and *–ation* (noun-forming suffix).

2.4 Compounding

Another word-formation process is called compounding. A compound is formed when two or more roots come together. These roots may be bound morphemes as in *autoplasty* or free morphemes as in *wellhead*. Consider the compounds in italics in the following sentences:

(1) The *warship* sank with all on board.
(2) The *black economy* is a risk to the country's stability.
(3) She bought the *spinning wheel* at an auction.
(4) The *playroom* was beautifully decorated.
(5) The inexperienced waiter muddled up the *place settings*.
(6) Her *pearl-grey* shoes stole the show.
(7) The university had become a *career-ending* institution.
(8) Jack wanted to see a *fast-moving* film.
(9) The violinist *fine-tuned* her instrument.
(10) Paul was *sky-diving* when the accident happened.

These compounds can be used to illustrate several features of compounds in general. In terms of spelling, some compounds are written as single words (e.g. *warship*). Others are written as two words (e.g. *spinning wheel*) or have two parts which are connected by a hyphen (e.g. *career-ending*). Some of the compounds in (1) to (10) are nominal compounds (e.g. *black economy*) while others are adjectival compounds (e.g. *pearl-grey*) or verbal compounds (e.g. *fine-tune*). Some are **root compounds** in which the component parts are simple lexemes (e.g. *playroom*). However, others are **synthetic compounds** because they contain bound morphemes in addition to free morphemes (e.g. *sky-diving*). Compounds typically contain a **modifier** and a **head**. For example, in *warship* the head of the compound is *ship* and its modifier is *war*. In this case, both the head and modifier are nouns. However, in other nominal compounds the modifier can be an adjective (*black* economy) or a verb (*play*room). Heads and modifiers are important to a number of other distinctions relating to compounds. In an **endocentric compound** (also known as a determinative compound), the modifier represents a subtype of whatever the head represents. So a *warship* is a type of ship and a *playroom* is a type of room. In an **exocentric compound** (also known as a bahuvrihi compound), the compound is a subtype of a category that is represented by a word outside of the compound. In the compound *bluebottle*, the word outside the compound is *insect* so that a *bluebottle* is a type of insect. In a **coordinative compound** (also known as a dvandva compound), both elements are heads and contribute equally to the meaning of the compound. This can be seen in the compounds in italics in (11) to (13):

(11) John was the *owner-occupier* of the flat.
(12) The dress was a *blue-green* colour.
(13) *Owner-trainer-breeder* Gail Temperton can't fault the horse heading into Hastings this week. (*Waikato Times*, New Zealand, 2017)

Underline the words in the following sentences which are generated by means of compounding.

> "We really wanted to create a landmark with something that is really impactful from the outside", Andreas said. (*Milwaukee Journal Sentinel*, 2017)
>   They exited the bus, slapped on some sunscreen, and headed for the back of the line, hoping to reach the doors before closing. (*Wausau Daily Herald, Wisconsin*, 2017)

You can now get further practice of working with compounds by attempting Exercise 2.5.

EXERCISE 2.5 COMPOUNDING

Part A: Examine the following compounds. For each compound, indicate if it is (1) a root compound or a synthetic compound and (2) a nominal, adjectival or verbal compound:

(a) dogleg
(b) angelfish
(c) gun-shy
(d) housing benefit
(e) lone-wolf
(f) loose-leaf
(g) make believe
(h) oil painting

Part B: Examine the following compounds. For each compound, indicate if it is an endocentric, exocentric or coordinative compound:

(a) fighter-bomber
(b) foxglove
(c) lovebird
(d) folk-rock
(e) newcomer
(f) nightingale
(g) playtime
(h) nursery school

A question of some interest to morphologists is how a compound like *redhead* differs from a syntactic phrase like *red head*. There are several ways in which a compound can be distinguished from a phrase. The first concerns the location of stress. In a true compound the main stress most often occurs on the first constituent (ˈredhead) while in a phrase it is found on the second constituent (red ˈhead).

In a compound the first constituent cannot be inflected or modified. So forms such as *redshead* and *really redhead* are not acceptable while *redheads* (inflected second constituent of compound) and *really red head* (modified noun phrase) are acceptable. The meaning of a compound is more than the meaning of its parts. This is why compounds have separate entries in dictionaries. This is not the case in a phrase where the meaning can be gleaned from the individual constituents. So, *redhead* is a person who has red hair while *red head* is a head which is red possibly on account of sunburn, make-up and so on. In a phrase the head can be replaced by *one* in **coordination** (e.g. *At the carnival John had a blue head and Mary had a red one*). This is not the case in a compound (e.g. *John loves redheads and Bill dislikes redones*). Even when one of these criteria does not apply in a particular case (e.g. stress occurs on the second constituent in the compound head¹quarter), the combination of these criteria ensures that compounds and phrases can be reliably distinguished.

Finally, compounds can express a large range of semantic relations. Some of these relations include {function} as in *exercise bike* ('a bike that is used for

TABLE 2.5 Semantic relations in noun–noun compounds expressed by children with specific language impairment

Compound	Explanation
car door	it's a car and a door
book shelf	books go on shelves
grapefruit juice	we make juice from grapes
hospital bed	it's a bed in a hospital
fruit basket	it holds fruit
step ladder	ladders have steps
cardboard box	cards go in it
baby book	it's a book for babies
snow fort	you make it out of snow
apron string	aprons are made of string
duck feet	duck have feet
chocolate cake	it's a cake made of chocolate
peanut butter	I like peanut butter
crayon box	it's a box for crayons
roof rack	your roof gets racked
cheese sandwich	it's a sandwich with cheese in it
paper napkin	you have to wipe your mouth
heat rash	it's a rash made of heat
apple core	it's the core of an apple
power tools	the tools are made of power
breakfast cereal	you eat cereal at breakfast time
corn bread	it's bread made of corn

exercise'), {location} as in *field study* ('a study that is conducted in the field'), {comparison} as in *forked lightning* ('lightning that has the shape of a fork'), {part–whole} as in *windowpane* ('the sheet of glass that is part of a window'), {material} as in *crystal ball* ('a ball made of glass or crystal that is used for predicting the future'), {containment} as in *cheesecake* ('a tart that contains cream cheese'), {source} as in *seaweed* ('an algae that originates in the sea') and {time} as in *daydream* ('a dream-like fantasy experienced while awake during the day').

Semantic relations between modifiers and heads in noun–noun compounds pose considerable difficulties for children with specific language impairment (SLI). The ability of children with SLI to explain these relations was examined by McGregor et al. (2010). The responses of these children to a number of noun–noun compounds are shown in Table 2.5.

The semantic relations between modifier and head are correctly explained in several of these compounds. These relations are displayed below:

Location
hospital bed: it's a bed in a hospital

Function
fruit basket: it holds fruit
baby book: it's a book for babies
crayon box: it's a box for crayons

Material
snow fort: you make it out of snow

Part-whole
step ladder: ladders have steps
apple core: it's the core of an apple

Time
breakfast cereal: you eat cereal at breakfast time

Containment
chocolate cake: it's a cake made of chocolate
cheese sandwich: it's a sandwich with cheese in it
corn bread: it's bread made of corn

In addition to these semantic relations, which were adequately explained, children with SLI in this study were unable to give an account of the semantic relations expressed by a number of other compounds. Three responses failed to express any semantic relation between the modifier and head of the compound:

car door: it's a car and a door
peanut butter: I like peanut butter
roof rack: your roof gets racked

What is more interesting are the responses which indicate a misunderstanding of the semantic relation expressed by the compound. On three occasions, the semantic relation is incorrectly understood to be one of {material}:

> apron strings: aprons are made of string
> power tools: the tools are made of power
> heat rash: it's a rash made of heat

In *apron strings*, the actual semantic relation is {part–whole}. In *heat rash* and *power tools*, it is {causation: 'rash caused by heat'} and {means: 'tools which work by means of power'}, respectively. Other compounds in which the semantic relation is misrepresented include the following:

> duck feet: duck have feet {comparison} → {part–whole}
> cardboard box: cards go in it {material} → {function}
> paper napkin: you have to wipe your mouth {material} → {function}

In *grapefruit juice*, the semantic relation is correctly understood to be one of {source} but the source in this case is incorrectly identified as grapes rather than grapefruit. In *book shelf*, there is some appreciation of the {function} relation of the compound even if this is not explicitly expressed as such.

The main points in this section are summarised below.

KEY POINTS COMPOUNDING

- Compounding occurs when two or more roots come together. The roots may be bound morphemes (e.g. *autocrat*) or free morphemes (e.g. *job centre*).
- Some compounds take the form of a single word (e.g. *heartache*), some are two words (e.g. *fruit fly*) and some are hyphenated (e.g. *singer-songwriter*).
- Compounding results in nominal, adjectival and verbal compounds. These compounds can have various constituents. For example, nominal compounds may contain two nouns (e.g. *milk chocolate*) or an adjective and a noun (e.g. *slowcoach*).
- Some compounds contain only simple lexemes and are root compounds (e.g. *doghouse*) while others contain bound and free morphemes and are synthetic compounds (e.g. *driving licence*).
- Compounds contain heads and modifiers. If the modifier is a subtype of whatever is expressed by the head, the compound is an endocentric compound (e.g. an *earthworm* is a type of worm that lives in the soil). If the compound is a subtype of something outside of the compound, then it is an exocentric compound (e.g. a *pickpocket* is a type of person who steals from other people). In a coordinative compound, there are two heads (no modifier) with neither subordinate to the other (e.g. *singer-songwriter*).
- Several criteria can be used to distinguish compounds from phrases. These criteria include stress which occurs in the first constituent of a compound (e.g. 'redhead) and the second word in a phrase (e.g. red 'head).
- Compounds express a range of meanings including {time} as in *nightclub*, {function} as in *bathing cap* and {location} as in *street theatre*.

2.5 Conversion and Back-Formation

The word-formation processes which have been described so far all involve a visible change in the form of a **lexeme**. But there is a word-formation process which changes the word class of a lexeme but which does not involve the addition of affixes as in prefixation and suffixation or the use of two or more roots as in compounding. Known as **conversion** or zero derivation, it is a significant source of new words in English. Conversion is responsible for generating verbs from nouns as in the following examples:

Nouns → verbs
torch: *They torched the building*
access: *The analyst accessed the files*
hammer: *The joiner hammered the nail into the wall*

English has many de-nominal verbs which can be identified through the use of semantic paraphrases. These paraphrases often contain the noun from which the verb is derived. So, *to torch* is 'to apply a torch to property or an object' and *to hammer* is 'to use a hammer to drive a nail into something'. Some verbs which are derived from nouns by means of conversion are found in certain varieties or dialects or English but not in other varieties or dialects of English. For example, *contract* may be used as a verb in American English, as the following example illustrates:

> *The jail's medical services must be provided by <u>contracting</u> with a health care provider licensed in Kentucky, but each jailer decides who to <u>contract</u> with.*
> (*Lexington Herald Leader*, Kentucky, 2017)

In British English, nominal *contract* is used in place of verbal *contract* in this context (e.g. *The jail's medical services must be provided by establishing a* <u>contract</u> *with ...*). The conversion which generates the verb *repurpose* from the noun *purpose* is a feature of both British and American English. The use of *repurposing* in the following example of American English involves not only the conversion of the noun *purpose* into a verb, but also prefixation (<u>re</u>*purpose*) and the addition of an inflectional suffix (*repurpos<u>ing</u>*):

> *Lindsey and Paule said they hope to keep <u>repurposing</u> vacant land for beekeeping and hosting events with their bees. (The Detroit News, 2017)*

As well as de-nominal verbs, conversion results in de-verbal nouns and de-adjectival verbs:

Verbs → nouns
to look: *She gave him a nasty look*
to call: *Sally made a long-distance call to her mother*
to crack: *The crack in the vase reduced its value*

Adjectives → verbs
slow: *They slowed the pace of the walk*
cool: *Jack cooled the wine in time for the meal*
busy: *Mary busied herself to take her mind off work*

It should be emphasised that while the derivation itself does not involve a visible change to the word in terms of the addition of affixes, once the word joins a new word class it assumes all the inflectional suffixes of that new class. So the adjective *cool* undergoes conversion to the verb *to cool* and then inflectional suffixation to become *cools* (present tense *–s*), *cooled* (past tense *–ed*) and *cooling* (progressive *–ing*).

What type of conversion do you think occurs in the underlined word in the following sentence?

The city's Community Development Authority and a non-profit are <u>eyeing</u> a major redevelopment of more than 400 dated and deteriorating housing units. (*Wisconsin State Journal*, 2017)

To get further practice of working with conversion, you should now attempt Exercise 2.6.

While the **orthographic form** of words for the most part does not change with conversion, the base of the word can undergo phonetic changes as a result of conversion. The location of stress in the word can change as in the following examples:

com'pound (verb) – 'compound (noun)

EXERCISE 2.6 CONVERSION
Each of the following sentences contains a word which has been generated by means of conversion. Identify the word and indicate if it is a de-verbal noun, a de-nominal verb or a de-adjectival verb:

(a) He buttered the bread on both sides.
(b) Fran emptied the cupboard in her search for flour.
(c) The dog's cry was disturbing to the neighbours.
(d) The film star jetted around the world.
(e) The student e-mailed questions to her lecturer.
(f) The walk was too long for the elderly man.
(g) Maureen carpeted the dining room in time for the wedding.
(h) The deaf student signed to her friend.
(i) The entire experience had humbled her.
(j) She blossomed under a new dance teacher.
(k) The protester bared himself to the crowd.

con'flict (verb) – 'conflict (noun)

pro'test (verb) – 'protest (noun)

Other phonetic changes can occur in the voicing of consonant sounds. In the following conversions the voiceless consonants [f] and [s] in the nouns *shelf, house* and *advice* become voiced consonants [v] and [z] in the verbs *to shelve, to house* and *to advise*:

noun: shelf [f] → verb: to shelve [v]

noun: house [s] → verb: to house [z]

noun: advice [s] → verb: to advise [z]

As well as a phonetic change, the verbs *shelve* and *advise* exhibit an orthographic change. The questions at the end of the chapter will give you practice in identifying these base changes in conversion.

Conversion can be used in some interesting ways by young, typically developing children. Consider the following examples from Peccei (1999). For each utterance, the child's age is indicated in years and months:

2;4:   You have to scale it (weigh cheese)

3;11: I'm going to earth this (bury)

2;4:   I'm souping (eating soup)

2;6:   I'm darking the sky (colouring a picture)

3;0:   How do you sharp this? (holding a pencil)

3;0:   Full this up (holding out a cup)

In the first three utterances, children are erroneously using noun–verb conversion. In each case, a noun (*scale, earth* and *soup*) undergoes conversion to a verb. In the case of *souping*, a verbal inflectional suffix for the progressive *–ing* is used after conversion has occurred. The last three utterances exemplify the use of a different type of conversion. In these utterances, the adjectives *dark, sharp* and *full* undergo conversion to verbs. Once again, the verbal inflectional suffix for the progressive is used in *darking*. Although these words are, strictly speaking, errors of conversion, they nonetheless reveal that these children have some understanding of this word-formation process.

A word-formation process which does not sit clearly under either morphemic or non-morphemic word-formation in Figure 2.1 is **back-formation**. This process involves the **elision** of morphemes or morpheme-like elements and changes the word class of a lexeme. It is quite unlike the word-formation processes that we have seen so far which have either resulted in the addition of morphemes (prefixation and suffixation) or left the form of a word unchanged (conversion). The derivation of *baby-sit* from *baby-sitter* can be used to demonstrate back-formation. Back-formation occurs when a root compound like *baby-sitter* is treated as a synthetic compound consisting of a base *baby-sit* to which the suffix *–er* has been added. However, the base *baby-sit* did not exist in English prior to the emergence of *baby-sitter*. It has, in fact, only been coined as a verb after *baby-sitter* came into widespread use. Other examples of back-formation include the following:

> *self-destruction* → *to self-destruct*
> *editor* → *to edit*
> *television* → *to televise*
> *burglar* → *to burgle*
> *lazy* → *to laze*
> *type-writer* → *to type-write*
> *sculptor* → *to sculpt*
> *pre-emption* → *to pre-empt*
> *scavenger* → *to scavenge*
> *swindler* → *to swindle*
> *resurrection* → *to resurrect*

In each of the words to the left of the arrow, it appears that a suffix (*–ion, –or, –ar, –y*) has been added to a base. But what seems to be a base has, in fact, only been coined as a verb after the noun from which it was derived was already established in English. With each derivation resulting in a verb, back-formation is similar to conversion in that it is a productive source of new verbs in language. Because they do not involve the addition of morphological material, back-formations are more difficult to identify than other word-formation processes. For example, some morphologists argue that verbal compounds like *sky-dive* (see Section 2.4) are not compounds at all but back-formations from *sky-diver*.

The main points in this section are summarised below.

KEY POINTS CONVERSION AND BACK-FORMATION

- Conversion or zero derivation is a word-formation process in which there is a change of word class but no visible change in word form such as occurs in affixation.
- Conversion can generate de-nominal verbs (e.g. $brush_N$ → $brush_V$), de-verbal nouns (e.g. $walk_V$ → $walk_N$) and de-adjectival verbs (e.g. $clean_A$ → $clean_V$).
- Although the process of conversion does not involve overt suffixes, a word which has been derived by means of conversion can then undergo inflectional suffixation (e.g. $brush_V$ → *brushing*).
- Conversion can result in stress modification (e.g. $'reject_N$ → $re'ject_V$), and voicing and orthographic modification (e.g. $wreath_N$ [θ] → $wreathe_V$ [ð]).
- Back-formation is another source of new verbs in language. It occurs when forms like *editor* are treated as bases (*edit*) to which a suffix (*-or*) is added. The apparent base is then coined as a verb (*to edit*).

2.6 Non-Morphemic Word-Formation Processes

Morphologists are also interested in examining a number of other word-formation processes which do not involve the use of morphemes. These processes are
called clipping, blending, **acronym-formation** and **reduplication**.

2.6.1 Clipping

Clipping involves a shortening of a word through the deletion of some of its
phonological material. The deleted material can include morphemes but is not
limited to them. For example, the clipping in *professor* → *prof* removes the derivational suffix *–or* (a morpheme) but also the non-morphemic material (*ess*). Unlike
other word-formation processes, clipping does not change the meaning or the
word class of a lexeme. The following derivations are examples of clipping:

> hamburger → burger
> omnibus → bus
> Vietnam → nam
> doctor → doc
> laboratory → lab
> prefabricated → prefab

In *hamburger, omnibus* and *Vietnam*, the front of each word has been clipped.
Clipping occurs at the end of *doctor, laboratory* and *prefabricated*. As *hamburger*
illustrates, clipping can occur in compound nouns. Other examples of clipped
compound nouns include the following:

> motor car → car
> Rolling Stones → Stones
> public house → pub
> zoological garden → zoo

In *motor car* and *Rolling Stones* entire words are clipped, while in *public house* and
zoological garden words and word-parts are clipped. Other patterns of clipping
occur in the compound nouns *situation comedy* and *detoxification centre*:

> situation comedy → sit com
> detoxification centre → detox centre

In *situation comedy* the end of each word in the compound is clipped, while in
detoxification centre the end of the first word is clipped. In some cases, clipping
removes the front and end of the word. This can be seen in *influenza*:

> influenza → flu

What type of clipping do you think occurs in the underlined word in the following sentence?

The non-profit Bayview Foundation envisions a $4 million investment to <u>rehab</u> existing housing. (*Wisconsin State Journal*, 2017)

2.6.2 Blending

Another non-morphemic word-formation process is blending. This is where words are merged based on their sound structure rather than their morpheme structure. In a typical blend, each word contributes equally to the blend, as can be seen in the following examples:

stagnation + inflation → stagflation
smoke + fog → smog
motor + hotel → motel
spoon + fork → spork
information + entertainment → infotainment
breakfast + lunch → brunch
electric + execute → electrocute

In some blends, one word appears in its entirety in the blend. This occurs in the following examples:

winter + entertainment → wintertainment
Reagan + economics → Reaganomics
car + hijacking → carjacking
cheese + hamburger → cheeseburger
mock + documentary → mockumentary
glitter + literati → glitterati
sex + texting → sexting
guess + estimate → guesstimate

In other blends, both words appear in their entirety in the blend. This occurs in *sexploitation* which is a blend of *sex* and *exploitation*. In the same way that the form of the word is blended, the meaning is also a blend of its constituent parts. So *brunch* is a meal which is eaten late in the morning and combines breakfast with lunch, and *sexting* is the texting of sexually-based material.

Blending is a very productive word-formation process, with new blends continually appearing in language. Broadcast and print media generate a large number of blends such as the use of *Brexit* to mean the British exit from the European Union and *Brangelina* to refer to the Hollywood couple Brad Pitt and Angelina Jolie. Part of the appeal to children of stories by the author Roald Dahl is Dahl's extensive use of blending. One well-known blend used by Dahl is *gloriumptious* from *glorious* and *scrumptious*. Another is *churgle* which is a blend of *chuckle* and *gurgle*. Before Dahl, Lewis Carroll also used blending in his nonsense poem 'The Jabberwocky'. The *slithy toves* in the first line of this poem contains two blends:

slimy + lithe → slithy
toads + doves → toves

The form *slithy* is known as an **intercalative blend**. This is where the two source words are so tightly integrated that the sounds of one word (*slimy*) are interspersed with the sounds of the other word (*lithe*).

As well as creative uses of blending in the media and literature, individuals with language disorders can use this word-formation process in interesting ways. Consider the following data from a study of **confrontation naming** in 15 adults with chronic schizophrenia which was conducted by Barr et al. (1989). The words to the left of the arrows are the target words, and the words to the right of the arrows are the subjects' responses:

raft → 'raft'
wreath → 'Christman rath ... no, wreath'
nozzle → 'nozzle'
noose → 'noosle ... no, rope ... a noose'
octopus → 'octopus'
cactus → 'octatoos ... no, octopus ... no ... the thing you find in Mexico ... (phonemic cue) ... captus'

There is a recurring pattern in these responses. The first word in each pair – raft, nozzle and octopus – is correctly produced. However, these correct responses are then carried over into the naming of the second word in each pair where they form a number of interesting blends with these words. The attempt to name 'wreath' results in *rath* which is a blend of *raft* and *wreath*. The response to 'noose' is *noosle* which is a blend of *noose* and *nozzle*. Finally, two blends are produced during the attempt to name 'cactus'. First, *octatoos* is produced which is a blend of *octopus* and *cactus*. Second, *captus* is produced which is a blend of *cactus* and *octopus*. There is additional complexity in this second blend in that /p/ of *captus* is from 'octopus' while /t/ is from 'cactus'. Even as they reveal disruption in the morphology of language, the errors of these adults with schizophrenia are creative and fascinating.

To get further practice of working with blending, you should now attempt Exercise 2.7.

2.6.3 Acronym-Formation

Acronym-formation has produced a large number of words in English. In this word-formation process, a word is formed from the initial letters of the words in a compound or phrase. These letters may be pronounced as a word as in AIDS

EXERCISE 2.7 BLENDING

Each of the following words is a blend in English. Examine each word and indicate the source words from which it is derived:

(a) nutriceutical
(b) blizzaster
(c) affluenza
(d) Chunnel
(e) kitchenalia
(f) motormobilia
(g) gaydar
(h) skyjacking
(i) mankini
(j) Britpoperati

(Acquired Immune Deficiency Syndrome) and NATO (North Atlantic Treaty Organization). Other acronyms which are pronounced as words include:

UNICEF	United Nations International Children's Emergency Fund
RAM	Random access memory
WHO	World Health Organization
radar	radio detection and ranging
laser	light amplification by stimulated emission of radiation
moodle	modular object-oriented dynamic learning environment

Alternatively, the letters may be pronounced separately as in BBC (British Broadcasting Corporation). These forms are known as **initialisms**. They include the following examples:

tlc	tender loving care
cd	compact disc
lol	laughing out loud
brb	be right back
SUV	sport/suburban utility vehicle
PLO	Palestinian Liberation Organization
FAQs	frequently asked questions
TV	television
UK	United Kingdom

As the examples listed above illustrate, acronyms and initialisms are often associated with agencies and organisations (e.g. WHO), commercial products (e.g.

SUV), digital language (e.g. lol, OMG), and computing and information technology (e.g. RAM, moodle).

2.6.4 Reduplication

Finally, reduplication is a word-formation process in which a word or part of a word is repeated. It is a feature of the **onomatopoeic forms** which are used by young children, e.g. *choo-choo* and *woof-woof*. In some reduplications, the entire word is repeated, e.g. *hush-hush* and *bye-bye*. A vowel change occurs in other reduplications. This can be seen in the following examples:

hip-hop
chit-chat
criss-cross
pitter-patter
splish-splash

In other reduplications, the vowels remain constant but a consonant sound changes with the result that the words rhyme:

walkie-talkie
lovey-dovey
super-duper
boogie-woogie
teeny-weeny

Less often, there may be a vowel change and deletion of a syllable in reduplication, e.g. *kitty-cat*.

The main points in this section are summarised below.

KEY POINTS NON-MORPHEMIC WORD-FORMATION PROCESSES

- Several word-formation processes do not involve the addition or deletion of morphemes. These non-morphemic processes include clipping, blending, acronym-formation and reduplication.
- Clipping involves a shortening of a word through the deletion of some of its phonological material. The deleted material can include morphemes but is not limited to them. In *advertisement* → *advert*, two derivational suffixes (*–ise* and *–ment*) are clipped, but in *professor* → *prof* non-morphemic material alongside a morpheme (*–or*) is clipped.
- Different parts of words can be clipped. The front is clipped in *bicycle* → *cycle*. The back is clipped in *examination* → *exam*. The front and back are clipped in *refrigerator* → *fridge*.
- In blending source words are merged based on their sound structure rather than their morpheme structure. In some blends, source words contribute equally to the blend, e.g. *breakfast* + *lunch* → *brunch*. In other blends, one of the source words appears in its entirety in the blend, e.g. *stay* + *vacation* → *staycation*.

- Acronym-formation generates a large number of new words in English. Every letter in an acronym is the initial letter of a word in a compound or phrase. Often, the resulting letter string can be pronounced as a word, e.g. *UNICEF*. Where the individual letters are spelled out, it is called an initialism, e.g. *BBC*.
- Reduplication is a feature of the onomatopoeic forms that are used by young children, e.g. *choo-choo*. In some reduplications a vowel sound changes (e.g. *wishy-washy*) while in others a consonant sound changes (e.g. *super-duper*).

The morphological processes examined in this chapter are often reinvented in interesting ways by different groups of speakers. In the following Special Topic, we examine the use made of morphology by one such group, Australian teenagers.

SPECIAL TOPIC 2.2 MORPHOLOGY IN AUSTRALIAN YOUTH LANGUAGE

Deviation from a linguistic standard is one way in which teenagers can establish an identity for themselves. This is as true of morphology as it is of grammar in general. To appreciate some of these non-standard uses of morphology, we examine how morphology is used in *Dolly*, a popular magazine read by Australian youth. The following sentences appeared in the online magazine in July 2017.

(a) Either way, we are officially <u>shook</u>.
(b) We totally <u>ship</u> these two, mostly 'cos they're so <u>freaking</u> adorable together.
(c) And while the four <u>mains</u> are total <u>besties</u>, we love how each has their own distinguishable style.
(d) Not content with being way more skilled with a makeup brush than us <u>normies</u>, some beauty gurus have taken things next level.
(e) We're betting these latest snaps of Bells getting '<u>handsy</u>' with her other ex Blackbear will have her <u>legit</u> fuming.

Several morphological processes are illustrated by the underlined words in these sentences. Novel uses of clipping occur in (b) and (e). In (b), *ship* is derived by means of clipping of the word *(relation)ship*, while *legit* in (e) is a clipping of the word *legit(imate)*. In Australian youth language, *ship* means to affirm a romantic relationship between two people (usually celebrities) or to hope that such a relationship will develop. The word *legit* is used to mean 'literally' in utterances like 'I am legit going to fail this test'. *Ship* and *legit* are used as a verb and an adverb, respectively. This differs from the grammatical categories of the words from which they are derived (*relationship* is a noun and *legitimate* is an adjective). So conversion occurs alongside clipping in the derivation of these words. Conversion also occurs in sentences (c) and (d). Each of the underlined words in these sentences is a noun. These nouns are derived from adjectives in the following phrases:

> *main* characters → *mains*
> *best* friends → *besties*
> *normal* people → *normies*

These de-adjectival nouns assume the plural ending of the nouns that they modify in the noun phrases on the left. In (a), *shook* is used in place of standard *shaken*. In Standard English, the verb *to shake* displays irregular morphology, with *shook* (not *shaked*) the past tense of the verb and *shaken* the past participle. The speaker in this case is using a past tense verb where a past participle would be required in Standard English. In (b), the word *freaking* is used as a euphemism for the word 'fucking'. The addition of the suffix *–ing* to *freak* is not part of standard usage which includes words like *freaky*, *freakish* and *freakier*. Finally, in (e) *handsy* is used to describe Bells and her ex 'making out' or letting their hands roam. This word is derived from the addition of the suffix *–y* to the noun *hands* in much the same way that *matey* is derived from the noun *mate*. Quite apart from achieving a deterioration of language, as prescriptive linguists would have us believe, the language used by Australian youth is making inventive use of a range of morphological processes.

SUMMARY

In this chapter you have seen the following:

- Words like *hopeless* and *unpredictable* have an internal structure built on morphemes such as *–less, un–, –able* and *hope*.
- Morphemes can be variously categorised as roots, affixes and lexical stems. In the word *unpredictable*, the root is *predict*, the affixes are *un–* and *–able* (a prefix and suffix, respectively) and the lexical stem is *predictable*.
- Inflectional morphology is a major sub-division in morphology. Inflectional morphemes are markers of grammatical categories such as tense (past tense: *played*), case (genitive: *Mike's bike*), number (plural: *dogs*), aspect (progressive: *walking*), person (third person: *sings*) and gradation (comparative: *smaller*).
- Word-formation is the second major sub-division in morphology. It can be further sub-divided into morphemic and non-morphemic word-formation processes. Morphemic word-formation processes include conversion (*torch* → *torched*), compounding (*council estate*) and prefixation (*unreal*) and suffixation (*delightful*), both types of derivational morphology.
- Non-morphemic processes include clipping (*influenza* → *flu*), blending (*breakfast + lunch* → *brunch*), acronym-formation (*UNESCO*) and reduplication (*bye-bye*).

WEBSITE WORD STRUCTURE

After reading the chapter, visit the website and test your knowledge of word structure by answering the multiple-choice questions for this topic.

HOMEWORK ASSIGNMENT

Morphological features can vary considerably between different varieties and dialects of English. The following utterances are produced by American English speakers. Each utterance contains a morphological feature which differs from an equivalent feature in British English. The British English equivalent is shown in parentheses. Using your knowledge of inflectional morphology, characterise the morphological features that occur in these examples of American English:

(a) "I knew we'd broken open the game, but I couldn't believe I'd gotten [got] that close and didn't get in." (*USA TODAY Sports*, 2015)

(b) "Fate shined [shone] upon him", Simms says. (*USA TODAY Sports*, 2015)

(c) He knows shooting won't come easy [easily] for all great athletes. (*USA TODAY Sports*, 2015)

(d) "I said a cah! She said what is a cah? I says [said] what's a cah – I said you know automobile, vehicle, thing you get in and drive." (Massachusetts speaker featured in *'Do you speak American?'*, Public Broadcasting Service, 2005)

(e) "His pants were so tight if he'd have farted it would have blowed [blown] his boots off." (Texas speaker featured in *'Do you speak American?'*, Public Broadcasting Service, 2005)

(f) Neighbours say they can scarce [scarcely] afford the legal bills they have racked up in the dispute. (*Denver Post*, 2015)

SUGGESTIONS FOR FURTHER READING

(1) Aronoff, M. and Fudeman, K. (2011) *What is Morphology?*, Second Edition. Malden, MA: Wiley-Blackwell.

Chapter 1 of this book introduces many of the basic morphological concepts (allomorphs, prefixes, etc.) examined in this chapter. However, it goes further in examining the morphology of languages other than English and in discussing some of the principles which are integral to morphological analysis.

(2) Haspelmath, M. and Sims, A. D. (2010) *Understanding Morphology*, Second Edition. Abingdon and New York: Routledge.

Chapter 1 in this volume introduces morphology and compares the morphology of English with the morphology of other languages. Later chapters address basic concepts such as morphemes and allomorphs (chapter 2) and morphological processes like affixation and compounding (chapter 3).

(3) Lieber, R. (2010) *Introducing Morphology.* New York: Cambridge University Press.

You can usefully extend your knowledge of morphology by pursuing sections in several chapters of this book. Processes of lexeme formation such as affixation, compounding and conversion are examined in chapter 3, while types of inflection are addressed in chapter 6.

QUESTIONS WORD STRUCTURE

(1) When prefixes and suffixes are added to certain adjectives, a negative or opposite meaning is expressed. Think of as many prefixes and suffixes as you can that may be used for this purpose. Give two examples of each prefix or suffix that you identify.

(2) In Appendix 1, there are four sets of data from Lara. Data set 1 contains Lara's errors in the use of the progressive morpheme *–ing*. Data set 2 contains her errors in the use of irregular past tense verbs. In data set 3, her errors in the use of irregular past participles are shown. Finally, data set 4 contains Lara's errors in the use of the third-person singular morpheme *–s*. Examine these data sets and then answer the questions that follow:

   (a) In data set 1, Lara omits the *–ing* morpheme in several verbs. Give three examples of where this occurs.

   (b) In data set 1, Lara attaches *–ing* to an adjective instead of a verb. Where does this occur?

   (c) On another occasion in data set 1, Lara uses *–ing* but then attaches a further morpheme to it. Where does this occur in the data?

   (d) In data set 2, Lara often adds the past tense morpheme *–ed* to the infinitive form of irregular verbs. Give three examples where this occurs. What name is given to this error?

   (e) On three occasions in data set 2, Lara adds the past tense morpheme *–ed* to the past tense form of the verb. Identify the three utterances where this occurs. How would you characterise this type of error?

   (f) In data set 3, Lara uses the past tense for the past participle. Identify the three instances where this occurs.

   (g) How would you characterise the morphological errors in these utterances? *He's fallened over; Because it's eatened all up*

   (h) How would you characterise the morphological error in *Now she's aten it all up*? How does the error that you have identified differ from the error identified in response to question (g)?

   (i) Lara displays four different types of error in the use of the third-person singular morpheme *–s*. The two most common errors involve the use of *–s* on the third-person plural form of the verb and the omission of *–s* on the third-person singular form of the verb. Give one example of each type of error.

(j) Two other errors in Lara's use of the third-person singular morpheme –*s* are exemplified by the utterances below. Characterise each of these errors:

Can you makes her talk?

She's want to toddle round

(3) In Section 2.3, DE's morphological errors were described as being inconsistent. This means that DE used different suffixes on different occasions in place of a target suffix. Return to Section 2.3 and examine DE's data again. List the different suffixes that take the place of the following target suffixes: –*less*, –*ness*, –*ist* and –*ly*.

(4) Examine the following root compounds. For each compound, identify the semantic relation expressed by the compound:

(a) garden centre

(b) nail bomb

(c) night nurse

(d) roadblock

(e) wolfhound

(f) ponytail

(g) fruitcake

(h) straw man

(i) earthquake

(j) farmyard

(5) Conversion of nouns and adjectives to verbs is a common word-formation process in English. Some of these conversions can result in modifications to stress and the voicing of consonants. For each noun–verb conversion below, indicate if a stress modification, voicing modification or no modification occurs:

(a) bath → to bathe

(b) insult → to insult

(c) plant → to plant

(d) half → to halve

(e) torment → to torment

(f) breath → to breathe

(g) man → to man

(h) belief → to believe

(i) decrease → to decrease

(j) grief → to grieve

(6) The following verbs have all been derived by means of back-formation. State the forms from which they are derived:

(a) liaise

(b) enthuse

(c) fundraise

(d) emote

(e) combust

(f) benchpress

(g) redact

(h) vacuum-clean

(i) aircondition

(j) copy-edit

(7) Identify the type of non-morphemic word-formation process which generates the italicised words in the following sentences:

(a) The castle was declared a cultural heritage site by *UNESCO*.

(b) Her plans for the company were very *wishy-washy*.

(c) The *exam* was not as difficult as he had predicted.

(d) Libby and Frances were self-confessed *chocoholics*.

(e) Jack left his *camcorder* at the hotel.

(f) Tom had been secretary-general of the *WTO* for ten years.

(g) Mary forced herself to go to the *gym* every day.

(h) She listened to the *tick-tock* of the clock and longed for the exam to be over.

(i) The departure lounge at the airport showed endless *infomercials*.

(j) The *IMF* produced a gloomy economic forecast in its annual report.

REVISION WORD STRUCTURE

(1) Identify the stems and roots of the following words: *domestication – mistrustful – joyfulness*.

(2) How is the past tense suffix for regular verbs in English (*–ed*) realised in each of the following examples: *walked – played – trusted – blinded – smoked – longed – relayed?*

(3) Inflectional morphemes are markers of tense, case, number, aspect, person and gradation. Match each of the following words and phrases to one of these grammatical categories: *houses – travels – managed – Bill's boat – friendliest – sleeping*.

(4) The plural morpheme in English has several irregular realisations. Using examples, describe *five* ways in which this morpheme is realised.

(5) Add the following prefixes and suffixes to the words in the box below to form new words. Identify the grammatical class of the new word that has been formed by means of prefixation and/or suffixation. Prefixes: *un–, mis–, dis–*; suffixes: *–able, –ful; –ness*.

sustain	pity	distract	play	communication
wish	engage	loyal	manage	wise

(6) Identify the classes (noun, verb or adjective) to which the component words of the following compounds belong.

country club	windbreak	killjoy	fishpond
ashtray	make-believe		waterwheel
redhot	greenhouse		sea breeze

(7) *True or false:* Conversion is a word-formation process which changes the word class of a lexeme but does not involve a visible change in the form of a word.

(8) What word-formation process describes the derivation of the verb *to type-write* from the noun *typewriter*?

(9) The field of medicine makes extensive use of acronyms and initialisms. Several of these are shown in the box below. State whether each form is an acronym or an initialism. Also, state what each form stands for.

CAT scan	AIDS	MRI	HIV	ECG
HRT	STI	TBI	PET scan	ICU

(10) *True or false:* The onomatopoeic form *bow-wow* is derived by means of clipping.

(11) What word-formation process leads to the derivation of the words *Brexit* and *Brangelina*?

(12) *True or false:* Clipping is a non-morphemic word-formation process.

3 Major Word Classes

3.1 Introduction to Major Word Classes

In the previous chapter, the morphological features of words in English were examined. These features have direct relevance to the topic of this chapter. This is because the morphological form of many words is a guide to their lexical category. In this way, we know when we see a word which ends in *–ed* that it is likely to be a verb, or a word which ends in *–ly* that it is likely to be an adverb. Of course, the English language contains exceptions to these patterns. We saw in the last chapter that there are certain adjectives in English which can also end in *–ly* (e.g. *lovely*), and there are adjectives and nouns in English that end in *–ed* (e.g. *hard-wired, deed*). Nevertheless, these morphological patterns apply in a sufficiently large number of cases to be a reliable guide to the lexical categories of words. But there are other criteria which are also used to identify the categories or classes of words. When teachers introduce word classes to pupils at school for the first time, it is semantic criteria that are used to aid word class identification. So verbs are described as 'doing words', adjectives are characterised as 'describing words' and nouns are described as 'the names of people, places and things'. But you do not have to think hard about words in English to find exceptions to these criteria. The verb in the sentence *She has a cold* involves no 'doing' whatsoever. And *honour* is a noun but it is not the name of a person, place or thing. In short, semantic features provide an even less reliable guide to word category than morphological features. Word class identification which proceeds on the basis of semantic criteria alone will lead us into many erroneous categorisations.

There is another set of features which can assist us in identifying the class of words. They are syntactic features and they relate to the distribution of words in phrases and sentences. To help us understand these features, consider the following sentences:

> The builder's *plan* was to lay the foundations in a fortnight.
> They *plan* to visit Paris next spring.

Both sentences contain the word *plan*. But in the first sentence, *plan* is a noun while in the second sentence it is a verb. How can we tell this when the morphological form of the word is identical in both cases? We can obtain important information which will help us with word class identification by looking at the position of the word in the sentence. In the first sentence *plan* is preceded by the genitive noun *builder's* which suggests that the plan is part of the noun phrase which contains *builder*. Also, the main verb *was* follows the word *plan* which suggests that *plan* must be part of a noun phrase that is serving as the subject of the sentence. The location and syntactic category of *plan* in the second sentence is quite different. In this sentence, *plan* is preceded by the subject pronoun *they* which indicates that it must be a verb. Clues to the different syntactic categories of *plan* thus lie in the position of this word within the sentence. The same is true of phrases. Consider the word *following* in the phrases below:

> Phrase 1: a large *following*
> Phrase 2: *following* the accident

The word *following* is a noun in the first phrase and a preposition in the second phrase. But, once again, how can we tell this when the word has the same morphological form in both phrases? In the first phrase, *following* is preceded by the adjective *large* which is a modifier in a noun phrase which has *following* as its head. In the second phrase, *following* precedes a noun phrase from which position it must be a preposition. As with the position of words in a sentence, the position of words in a phrase provides vital clues as to their syntactic category.

This chapter will begin the examination of the following word classes: nouns (including pronouns); verbs; adjectives; adverbs; determiners; prepositions; and conjunctions. The first four classes are major word categories and are addressed in this chapter. They contain the content words of language. Importantly, membership of these classes is open which means that new words can join these categories as the language changes over time. This can be seen in the addition of words like *internet, blog* and *Twitter* to the word class of nouns in recent years. The three remaining word classes – determiners, prepositions and conjunctions – are examined in Chapter 4. They contain the function words of language and are minor word classes. These words are grammatical rather than lexical in nature, and they belong to classes which have a closed membership. So the class of prepositions, for example, cannot be expanded in the way that the word class of nouns can be expanded. The semantic, morphological and syntactic features of these word classes will be examined. Word classes can pose challenges to young children who are acquiring language and to children and adults with language disorders. Speakers of non-standard dialects of English can also deviate from the word classes of Standard English in interesting ways. To help you understand the relevance of the study of word classes to real-world language use, examples from these different types of speaker will be examined throughout this chapter and Chapter 4.

3.2 Nouns and Pronouns

To begin our discussion of the word class of nouns, consider the following list of nouns in English:

castle   trust   woman   Rome   tables   kindness   trader Sally
industrialisation dog oxen agreement responsibility water

These nouns exemplify the type of people and entities (concrete and abstract) that nouns may be used to denote. Nouns can be used to name physical objects such as *castle* and *tables* as well as abstract entities like *trust* and *kindness*. They can also name people like *Sally* and *woman* and animals such as *oxen* and *dog*. They may also be the names of natural kinds such as *water* and cities like *Rome*. Processes like *industrialisation* are also named by means of nouns as are occupational roles such as *trader*. In fact, there is no part of human existence or experience which cannot be captured by nouns. It is unsurprising, therefore, that nouns should constitute one of the largest lexical categories in any language. That said, we have already seen how the ability of nouns to denote certain people, objects and places (i.e. semantic criteria) does not get us very far in a grammatical characterisation of nouns. For as soon as we consider words like *crown* which may refer to a physical object (a crown), a person (the monarch) or a notion or idea (monarchy or kingship), there is some blurring between semantic criteria. To these criteria, we must add morphological features of nouns. We saw in Chapter 2 that most nouns in English mark plural **number** through the addition of the **inflectional suffix**

–s as in *tables*. But there are also many nouns (the noun *oxen* is but one example) which do not follow this pattern and must be individually acquired by young children. Indeed, the use of a rule for the formation of plural nouns in English leads to errors in children's language such as *fishes* and *sheeps*. You are referred to Section 2.2 for discussion of the different plural allomorphs in English.

But even the number of nouns is more complicated than it might at first appear. Not every use of *–s* at the end of a noun indicates plural number as the nouns *aesthetics* and *minibus* illustrate. Also, a noun like *crowd* refers to a group of people and yet it is a singular noun as indicated by the use of the verb *was* in the sentence *the crowd was rebellious*. Some nouns exemplify the opposite pattern in that a plural noun refers to a single object or thing. This occurs in the nouns *jeans* and *minutes* as in the sentence *The minutes of the meeting were inaccurate*. Some nouns are grammatical plurals even though they appear to be singular nouns. This is true of the noun *police* as in the sentence *The police were under attack*. Still other nouns only have a plural form. This occurs in *clothes*, a singular equivalent of which does not exist. With so many possibilities to consider in relation to the number of nouns, it is unsurprising that young children should find this aspect of grammatical development challenging. Some plural noun errors are displayed in Table 2.3. To these errors we might add forms such as *it's furnitures* which will be discussed subsequently. In the meantime, two further morphological features of nouns are noteworthy. Nouns can also be identified by their ability to take the genitive (*'s*) form as in *child's book*. And aside from inflectional suffixes, words such as *agreement* and *responsibility* illustrate that nouns can also take a range of derivational suffixes (e.g. *–ment, –ity*). The combination of these different morphological features provides a reliable means of identifying most nouns in English.

In terms of their syntactic features, nouns can be phrases in sentences. They can occupy the role of a phrase either on their own or with other words preceding and following them (in Chapter 5, we will use the terms '**pre-modifier**' and '**post-modifier**' to describe these words). Some examples of nouns in the role of phrase in a sentence are shown below:

> <u>Tim</u> smiled.
> <u>The train</u> crashed.
> She bought <u>the blue dress</u>.
> <u>The man in the taxi</u> laughed.

The nouns in these sentences allow us to explore two important grammatical distinctions.

3.2.1 Common and Proper Nouns

The first distinction is between **common nouns** and **proper nouns**. The words *train, dress* and *man* are common nouns. These nouns are general names for people and things. A proper noun refers to a unique person, place or thing. While common nouns may be thought of as referring to a set with many members, proper nouns refer to a set with just one member. So the noun *train* is a common noun while *Flying Scotsman* (a famous British locomotive) is a proper noun. Proper nouns are spelled with a capital letter such as in *Tim*. However, a number of proper nouns have lost this feature and are treated as common nouns (e.g. *aspirin* was originally a brand name of the pharmaceutical company Bayer). Aside from capitalisation, proper nouns differ from common nouns in other ways. Because they name a unique person or thing, proper nouns do not have a plural form unless under special circumstances (e.g. *The Tims of this world are hard to find*). Also, where common nouns can take modifiers such as the **definite article** (*the*), adjectives (*blue*) and prepositional phrases (*in the taxi*), proper nouns can only be modified under certain circumstances. So while the first sentence below is grammatical, the second sentence is clearly not:

> It was her dream to travel on <u>the historic Flying Scotsman</u>.
> *She did her best to help <u>the depressed Tim</u>.

To see some common nouns and proper nouns in action, let us return to Lara and examine how she uses these different types of noun. Some of Lara's utterances are shown in Table 3.1. Lara's age in years and months is indicated in brackets after each utterance. As one might expect, most of Lara's proper nouns are the names of people in her wider environment. Occasionally, she uses proper nouns as brand names (e.g. *Maltesers*). Lara uses the genitive –*'s* correctly in some proper nouns (*Elsie Grandma's bottle*). On other occasions, she omits the genitive (*Rosie mouth*) or uses it when it is not required (*Amy's*). We described above how proper nouns, unlike common nouns, can only be preceded by the definite article in certain circumstances. Lara's utterance *Not <u>the Emily</u> comes to my nursery* suggests she has some understanding of these circumstances.

Lara also makes extensive use of common nouns. Unlike proper nouns, common nouns permit modification. Lara uses a range of modifiers with these nouns, including **cardinal numerals** (*two*), demonstrative and possessive determiners (*these, my*) and adjectives (*blue*). However, she can also omit the definite article (*in box*). Her use of the plural suffix –*s* in common nouns is somewhat inconsistent.

TABLE 3.1 Lara's use of proper and common nouns

Proper noun	Common noun
Where's Rosie mouth gone? (2;02)	I'm getting in box (2;04)
I got Elsie Grandma's bottle (2;04)	Shall we do one of these jigsaw? (2;07)
Think Amy's wants a toy (2;06)	That's a babies (2;07)
Maltesers in that shop (3;01)	Where my blue jumper? (2;08)
Mother: Which Emily? Lara: Not the Emily comes to my nursery (3;03)	Can you make two towers? (2;09)

Lara can use this suffix correctly (*towers*), omit it when it is required (*these jigsaw*), and use it when it is not required (*a babies*).

3.2.2 Count and Non-Count Nouns

Common nouns can be further subdivided into count nouns and non-count nouns. A count noun denotes an entity which has a clear boundary and can be individuated. As the name suggests, these nouns refer to people and things which can be counted. Count nouns can be pluralised and preceded by a cardinal numeral (*two boys*) and the **indefinite article** (*a boy, an* egg). A non-count or **mass noun** denotes entities which lack a clear boundary and exist as an indivis-ible mass (*grass, water*). They cannot be used with cardinal numerals (**two waters*) or the indefinite article (**a grass*). There are, of course, uses such as the following:

> *The geneticist developed three grasses.*
> *The restaurant had a water from the south of France.*

These uses of the nouns *grass* and *water* are no longer with their mass meanings. In the first sentence, *grass* means 'strains or breeds of grass'. In the second sentence, *water* refers to different types of water, possibly from several natural sources around the world. It is not unusual for non-count nouns to be used as count nouns. When this occurs, they can be pluralised and used with the indefinite article and cardinal numerals. But you need to be aware that these uses represent a change in the meaning of the word, as the following examples illustrate:

> *Non-count noun:* The production of cheese dropped by 12 per cent last year.
> *Count noun:* The hostess offered her guests a selection of Italian cheeses.
>   [Plural –s]
> *Non-count noun:* The supermarket ran out of butter early on Christmas Eve.
> *Count noun:* A salted butter is best for making shortcrust pastry. [Indefinite article]
> *Non-count noun:* An inspection of the car showed that it needed oil.
> *Count noun:* She was shown the prices of five oils in the garage. [Cardinal numeral]

Let us return to the example *it's furnitures*. The child who produced this utterance is treating the non-count noun *furniture* like a count noun and has proceeded to add the plural suffix *–s* to it. During language acquisition, children produce a range of errors when they begin to use non-count nouns for the first time. Some of these errors are shown in Table 3.2. These utterances were produced by a young girl called Ella who was recorded at home in conversation with her par-ents between the ages of 1;0 and 3;6 years (a late recording of Ella was conducted when she was 5;00 years)(Forrester, 2002). Ella's interactions with her parents were video-recorded and audio-recorded. The latter recordings were transcribed in detail. As well as errors, Ella also produced utterances which showed that she

TABLE 3.2 Count and non-count nouns used by a typically developing child called Ella

Count noun	Non-count noun
One horsey I liked (2;07)	I don't want bread on mine (2;05)
Have some more biscuit (2;09)	I'm had some juice in my cup (2;05)
Why cows make milk? (2;09)	An toasted cheese by hisself (2;06)
I've put these bits on it (2;10)	That's a filing paper (2;10)
I'm cutting a pear (2;11)	A honey from a bees (3;03)
And two months (3;00)	Can I put a bit of rice in? (3;05)
He's looking at a cards (3;03)	I got a little bit of salt look (3;05)
Melanie's got those cards (3;03)	I think her thinks it is a real food (5;00)

had a developing understanding of the conceptual distinction at issue in count and non-count nouns.

For the most part, Ella uses count nouns correctly. She is aware that count nouns, unlike non-count nouns, can be preceded by an indefinite article (e.g. *a pear*), cardinal numerals (e.g. *one horsey, two months*), and **demonstrative determiners** like *these* and *those* (e.g. *these bits, those cards*). In the utterance *Why cows make milk?*, Ella correctly pluralises the count noun *cows* but not the non-count noun *milk*. Her knowledge of the distinction between count nouns and non-count nouns meant that she was able to avoid the ungrammatical utterance **Why cows make milks?*. Nevertheless, she also displays some errors in her use of count nouns. She treats *biscuit* in the utterance *have some more biscuit* as a non-count noun. Also, the indefinite article can only occur with a singular count noun so the form *a cards* is incorrect. Ella is also able to use some non-count nouns correctly (e.g. *bread*). She is aware that non-count nouns can be preceded by quantity words (e.g. *some juice*) and expressions like *a bit of* (e.g. *a bit of rice*). However, she also treats a number of non-count nouns like count nouns. This can be seen in the utterances which contain the nouns *food, cheese, honey* and *paper*. Each of these nouns is preceded by the indefinite article, leading to ungrammatical phrases like **a real food*.

3.2.3 Abstract and Concrete Nouns

To conclude this discussion of nouns, two further features will be examined. The first is the distinction between **abstract nouns** and **concrete nouns**. An abstract noun refers to an intangible entity. It may be a concept or idea, a virtue, value or an emotion. Words like *patience, anger* and *honour* are all abstract nouns. Concrete nouns describe tangible entities such as people, physical objects and events. Words like *boy, vase* and *wedding* are all concrete nouns. To classify a noun as abstract or concrete, we must think about its meaning or what it refers to (in other words, its semantics). This semantic distinction is, however, relevant to a discussion of the grammatical features of nouns. This is because some abstract nouns are restricted in the determiners that can be used with them. So while the use of the indefinite article with concrete nouns like *a house* and *an elephant* is grammatical, it is not grammatical to use the indefinite article with certain abstract nouns. This can be seen in the first sentence below. But you should also note the second sentence below where the abstract noun *belief* can be used with the indefinite article:

> **Mary displays <u>a</u> tremendous <u>patience</u> at work.*
> *Mary displays <u>a</u> strong <u>belief</u> in God.*

This difference in grammatical usage is related to the fact that *patience* is a non-count noun and *belief* is a count noun. The distinction between abstract and concrete nouns cuts across the distinction between count and non-count nouns. That is, some abstract nouns are count nouns while others are non-count nouns. The same is true of concrete nouns.

The distinction between abstract and concrete nouns in language is very powerfully illustrated in clients with language disorder. In some of these clients, one of these categories of nouns can be impaired while the other category is intact. This occurred in a patient known as S.B.Y. who was studied by Warrington and Shallice (1984). S.B.Y. had made a partial recovery from **herpes simplex encephalitis**. He was asked to define a number of abstract and concrete nouns. Some of his definitions are shown below:

Abstract nouns
Debate – discussion between people, open discussions between groups
Malice – to show bad will against somebody
Caution – to be careful how you do something

Concrete nouns
Ink – food – you put on top of food you are eating – a liquid
Frog – an animal – not trained
Cabbage – use for eating, material it's usually made from an animal
Tobacco – one of your foods you eat

While S.B.Y. was able to give accurate, detailed definitions of abstract nouns, his definitions of concrete nouns were largely erroneous. Although S.B.Y.'s difficulties were related to a semantic impairment, the manifestation of this impairment as a marked inability on the part of this client to comprehend concrete nouns is quite striking.

3.2.4 Collective Nouns

Finally, there is a group of nouns in English which have a singular and plural form, but where the singular form as well as the plural form can be used with plural verbs. So-called **collective nouns** include words such as *jury, crowd* and *class*. These nouns can all be conceived of in two ways: either as a single group or as a number of individuals. It is this semantic feature of these nouns which permits them to take a plural verb even when they have a singular form:

> *The jury has considered the evidence.* [Singular noun + singular verb]
> *The jury have considered the evidence.* [Singular noun + plural verb]
> *The juries have considered the evidence.* [Plural noun + plural verb]

To get practice of working with collective nouns, you should now attempt Exercise 3.1.

Because they can take the place of noun phrases in a sentence, pronouns will be examined in this section. However, they can also be classed as determiners and so we will consider them again in Chapter 4.

3.2.5 Personal Pronouns

Pronouns are very common indeed in language where one of their functions is to avoid the repetition of noun phrases. This can be seen in the following sentences:

> *The girl bought the red dress and mailed the red dress to her friend.* [Without pronoun]
> *The girl bought the red dress and mailed it to her friend.* [With pronoun]
> *The policeman stopped the man. The policeman questioned the man.* [Without pronoun]
> *The policeman stopped the man. He questioned him.* [With pronoun]

The second sentence in each of these pairs of sentences uses the **personal pronouns** *he, him* and *it* to achieve **anaphoric reference** to a preceding noun phrase known as the **antecedent**. Through the use of pronouns, these sentences avoid considerable repetition. *He* is a subject personal pronoun and *him* and *it* are object personal pronouns. The terms 'subject' and 'object' describe the case of pronouns, a distinction which is not reflected in nouns in English. But pronouns in English do not change their morphological form to reflect case alone. They also have different forms for person and number. Most native English-speaking students first become aware of how pronouns vary for person and number when they learn a

EXERCISE 3.1 COLLECTIVE NOUNS

Which of the following nouns are collective nouns? For those nouns that you identify to be collective nouns, devise sentences in which the singular form of the noun is used with singular and plural verbs:

herd   ship   tent   staff   hospital   team

crew   field   illness   government   holiday

foreign language like French and are encouraged to commit forms like *je marche* (I walk), *tu marches* (you walk) and *il marche* (he walks) to memory. These forms are first, second and third person pronouns. To these singular pronouns we can add plural pronouns: we walk, you walk and they walk. The full personal pronoun system in English with its case, person and number properties is shown in Table 3.3.

Several features of these pronouns are noteworthy. First person pronouns refer to the speaker and, in the case of the plural pronouns *we* and *us*, other people as well as the speaker. Second person pronouns address either a single person or more than one person. Third person pronouns refer to one or more people who are not the speaker or hearer. Third person singular pronouns have masculine, feminine and non-personal forms. For masculine and feminine forms, the selection of pronouns is determined by the biological sex of the **referent**. So in the sentence *he is smiling*, the pronoun 'he' may refer to Paul, the policeman and so on. This differs from a language like German where the choice of third person singular pronouns is determined by the **gender** of the nouns that they replace. This can be seen in the following sentences.

Masculine
Der Tisch ist schön, weil er neu ist.
The table is nice, because it is new.

Feminine
Die Katze schläft, weil sie müde ist.
The cat is sleeping, because it is tired.

Neuter
Das Mädchen ist traurig, weil es ins Bett gehen muss.
The girl is sad, because she has to go to bed.

The clearest possible demonstration that German pronouns are not governed by biological sex but by the gender of nouns they replace can be seen in the noun *Mädchen* ('girl'). This noun and the corresponding pronoun *es* ('she') have a neuter gender in German even though a girl is a person who is biologically female.

TABLE 3.3 Personal pronouns in English

Person/number	Subject case	Object case
1st person singular	**I** like French wine.	The boys chased **me**.
2nd person singular	**You** look depressed.	The children trust **you**.
3rd person singular	**He** is smiling. **She** is crossing the road. **It** is raining.	Sally likes **him**. The story amused **her**. The teacher recited **it**.
1st person plural	**We** are going home.	The car pursued **us**.
2nd person plural	**You** must clean the room.	Jack saw **you** yesterday.
3rd person plural	**They** are leaving early.	The audience applauded **them**.

The pronoun *it* can have a semantically empty referent as in the sentence *it is raining*. Alternatively, in a sentence like *the teacher recited it*, the pronoun *it* refers to inanimate things like a poem or a song. The third person pronoun does not vary with case but it does change with number. The pronoun which stays the same regardless of both case and number is *you*. The pronoun system of present-day English has no way of distinguishing between a single hearer and more than one hearer in either subject or object case. This has not always been the way the English language has operated. In **Old English**, for example, nominative (subject) pronouns were *þu* (singular) and *ge* (plural) while accusative (object) pronouns were *þe/þec* (singular) and *eow* (plural). Also, there are non-standard dialects of **Modern English** which use different second person pronouns to indicate when a single person or more than one person is addressed. Speakers of Belfast English, for example, use the forms *youse (yous)* or *youse-uns* when more than one person is addressed:

> *Are you going to the pub?* [Second person singular]
> *Are youse going to the pub?* [Second person plural]

This non-standard second person plural pronoun is also a grammatical feature of the **Geordie dialect**, as the following examples illustrate:

> *He says, 'I'll see youse in the woods!'*
> *I'll see yous later, folks* [Lara's father, a speaker of Durham dialect]

Aside from the second person plural pronoun, non-standard usages of other English pronouns are also very common. Here are two further examples from the Geordie dialect. In the first example, the first person plural object pronoun *us* is used in place of its singular counterpart *me*. In the second example, the first person plural subject pronoun *we* is used in place of its object counterpart *us*:

> 'used to get dropped off, off the bus in the mornings and, uhm, they picked **us** up on the way back'
> 'she took **we**, she wouldn't let **we** go, I mean, she, she did, she'd always took **we** on these trips'

Even within Standard English, the form of pronoun use may seem to be counter-intuitive on some occasions. For example, a parent may use *we* instead of *you* to say to a child *Are we going to be good today?*, a form which reflects the more powerful status of the parent in a caregiver–child relationship. When addressing a guest, a hotelier may use *she* instead of *you* in *Would Madam prefer if she could order dinner later?* as a means of achieving politeness in a service encounter. These forms are quite common in English and should be treated as context-specific uses of the standard system of pronouns.

To help you develop further your understanding of personal pronouns, you should now attempt Exercise 3.2.

EXERCISE 3.2 LARA AND PERSONAL PRONOUNS

During language acquisition, young children can make some interesting errors in their use of personal pronouns. Several of Lara's attempts at using personal pronouns are shown below. For each utterance, describe the type of error she has made:

(a) It's shuts now (2;02)
(b) Me do it (2;02)
(c) Don't kiss it because hurts (2;03)
(d) I'm going to mend (2;06)
(e) Mum is sitting there and me me's sitting there (2;07)
(f) He's eat pencils (2;07)
(g) Her's going in the baby bouncer? (2;08)
(h) Why are you all by himself? (2;08)
(i) Me have a box? (2;08)
(j) He's wants his dummy? (2;08)

3.2.6 Possessive, Demonstrative and Reflexive Pronouns

As well as personal pronouns, there are several other categories of pronouns in English. Possessive, demonstrative and **reflexive pronouns** are displayed along with examples in Table 3.4.

There are two main types of **possessive pronoun**. There are possessive pronouns which are determiners in a noun phrase such as *my castle* and *our swimming pool*. There are also possessive pronouns which exist on their own as a noun phrase in a sentence. For example, in the sentence *Mary liked ours best of all*, the possessive pronoun *ours* could be replaced by a possessive noun phrase like *our oil paintings*. There are four **demonstrative pronouns** in English. Like possessive pronouns, demonstrative pronouns can be determiners in noun phrases like *this mat* and *those apples*. These pronouns convey information about the position of people and things relative to the speaker. So *this mat* suggests that the mat is close to the speaker, while *those apples* indicates that the apples are at a distance from the speaker. Demonstrative pronouns can also stand alone in a sentence. When they do, they refer to or point to different things. For example, in the sentence *the girl wants this*, the demonstrative *this* may refer to a dress that the speaker is holding up (non-linguistic context). In the sentence *that is unbelievable*, the demonstrative *that* may refer to a story the speaker has just been told (linguistic context). Because *that* is referring to prior linguistic context in this case, the pronoun is described as anaphoric. Independent demonstratives like independent possessives can be full noun phrases:

> These [the ancient vases] are too expensive.
> The boy lost those [the car keys].

TABLE 3.4 Possessive, demonstrative and reflexive pronouns in English

Pronoun	Singular	Plural

Possessive	Determiner possessives:
	My, your, his, her, its
	e.g. **My** car is expensive
	     Your dog is ferocious.
		Determiner possessives:
		Our, your, their
		e.g. **Their** house is for sale.
		     Our luck has changed.

	Independent possessives:
	Mine, yours, his, hers, its
	e.g. This book is **mine**.
	     I want **yours**.
		Independent possessives:
		Ours, yours, theirs
		e.g. The plan was **ours**.
		     They left **theirs** at home.

Demonstrative	Determiner demonstratives:
	This, that
	e.g. **This** book is boring.
	     I believe **that** man.
		Determiner demonstratives:
		These, those
		e.g. **These** flowers are dead.
		     Those kids are noisy.

	Independent demonstratives:
	This, that
	e.g. The girl wants **this**.
	     That is unbelievable.
		Independent demonstratives:
		These, those
		e.g. **These** are too expensive.
		     The boy lost **those**.

Reflexive	*Myself, yourself, himself, herself, itself*
	e.g. I washed **myself** today.
	     She hurt **herself** outside.
		Ourselves, yourselves, themselves
		e.g. We lost **ourselves**.
		     They love **themselves**.

Reflexive pronouns are readily identified by their –*self* and –*selves* endings. These pronouns must have an antecedent noun phrase in the same clause. In the sentence *Jack exhausted himself,* the reflexive pronoun *himself* refers to the noun phrase *Jack*. In this case, the reflexive pronoun occurs at a distance from the noun phrase. There are other uses of reflexive pronouns where they immediately follow the noun phrase to which they refer. This emphatic use of reflexive pronouns is illustrated by the sentences below:

> <u>I myself</u> checked the locks before leaving the house.
> <u>The oncologist himself</u> confirmed the patient's diagnosis.

Speakers of non-standard dialects can deviate from these pronouns in interesting ways. In the Geordie dialect and Northern Irish English, object pronouns can be used in place of demonstrative pronouns:

> **'them** days you didn't, you didn't live with lasses'
> ''ve got flat-irons here, haven't you? Yes, there they are, **them** are my mothers, look at the candlestick are these the same ones?'

Non-standard reflexive pronouns are also a grammatical feature of the Geordie dialect. The Standard English pronouns *myself* and *ourselves* give way to forms like *mysell* and *oursells*:

> 'so, I used to sit in the, in the st, the bus stop, in the shelter, you know, just on the, on the ground and have my bait, by **mysell**'
> 'I think I, we had the best years, you know, for entertaining **oursells**'

As well as non-standard uses of these different pronouns, young children can make a number of errors when they begin to use possessive, demonstrative and reflexive pronouns for the first time. To help you gain practice in identifying these pronouns, we will examine several of Lara's pronoun errors. These are displayed in Table 3.5.

Lara's possessive pronoun errors are of several kinds. She often uses subject pronouns (*they dinner*) and object pronouns (*me book*) in place of possessive determiners (*their dinner, my book*). Lara also uses independent possessives where a possessive determiner is required (*mine chair* for *my chair*). When possessives are used, Lara often selects the wrong one (*he brushed her teeth*). Sometimes, Lara uses a possessive determiner when an independent possessive is required (*Is this your or mine?*). Occasionally, genitive 's is attached to a subject pronoun to take the place of a possessive determiner (*He's leg's broken*). This error reveals that Lara is at least aware of the notion of ownership that is integral to the meaning of possessive pronouns. The genitive can also be added to an independent possessive (*Mine's is just in there*) or a possessive determiner (*It's not her's bedtime now*). Lara has achieved a 'doubling up' of the meaning of possession or ownership in these errors. Errors of this type suggest that Lara has a developing conceptual knowledge of possessive pronouns even as she has difficulty using possessive pronouns correctly.

TABLE 3.5 Lara's use of possessive, demonstrative and reflexive pronouns

Pronoun	Lara's utterances
Possessive	Mine chair (2;02) Mine's is just in there (2;06) Can I make your bigger (2;07) Mine turn (2;08) I turn (2;08) You wash you back (2;08) He brushed her teeth (2;08) What he's [is his] bed? (2;08) Where's they dinner gone? (2;09) They going to they daddy (2;09) He's leg's broken (2;09) A giant coming to get me book (2;09) I have to have me wheels (2;09) It's not her's [your] bedtime now (2;09) Eating them dinner (2;10) Is this your or mine? (2;10)
Demonstrative	This animals (2;00) You haven't got any of this [these] (2;09) You have them all marbles (2;11)
Reflexive	Is she all by himself (2;08) Are we all by ourself? (2;08) He eat them up hisself (2;08) Where has he hurt hisself, Georgy? (2;10) He hurt herself (3;00) So they tried to make theyselves into a tower (3;01)

Lara also makes a number of interesting errors when she uses demonstrative and reflexive pronouns. She uses singular demonstrative pronouns when plural forms are required (*this animals*). She also uses the third person plural object pronoun *them* in place of the plural demonstrative *those* (but she below for a different interpretation of this usage). Lara uses reflexive pronouns which do not agree with the antecedent to which they refer. This occurs in *Is <u>she</u> all by <u>himself</u>?* and *<u>He</u> hurt <u>herself</u>.* Lara's other reflexive pronoun errors are of one of two types. On occasion, she uses *–self* in place of *–selves* as in *Are we all by ourself?* The other type of error involves an incorrect base to which *–self* or *–selves* is added. This results in forms like *hisself* and *theyselves*.

It should also be noted that Lara's grandmother produced utterances such as *Them's the Christmas presents* and *I'll have to move me feet, won't I?* In the first utterance, Lara's grandmother uses the plural object pronoun *them* plus *–s* for the plural demonstrative *those*. In the second utterance, she uses the first person singular object pronoun *me* in place of the possessive determiner *my*. Both of these forms are grammatical features of Durham dialect which Lara's father also uses. Further examples are shown below:

Lara's grandmother
'You do **them**.'
'**Them**'s fish with with lady's heads, aren't they?'
'I'm gonna have five minutes sit now because **them** other ones are not very nice'
'You forgot **them** two, didn't you?'
'Don't touch **them** ones yet'
'Do you want to look at **them** pictures before we turn over?'

Lara's father
'I seem to have lost **me** head'

Lara uses these pronoun forms also (e.g. 'I've got **me** umbrella'). It is likely that some of Lara's 'errors' in the use of these pronouns are, in fact, dialectal patterns acquired from listening to her father and grandmother.

3.2.7 Reciprocal, Indefinite, Interrogative and Relative Pronouns

The final four categories of pronouns in English are reciprocal, indefinite, interrogative and **relative pronouns**. These pronouns are displayed in Table 3.6 along with examples.

Reciprocal pronouns are similar to reflexive pronouns in that they must have an antecedent in the same clause. As their name suggests, they express a two-way (reciprocal) relationship. **Indefinite pronouns** are a large class of pronouns. They express meanings such as quantity and definiteness. They do not take the place of a noun phrase and have no antecedent as the example *Somebody left the lights on* illustrates. It is exactly because it is not possible to identify an individual to occupy the role of noun phrase that the pronoun *somebody* is used.

TABLE 3.6 Reciprocal, indefinite, interrogative and relative pronouns in English

Pronoun	Examples
Reciprocal	*Each other, one another* e.g. Charles and Mary phoned **each other** every day. The sisters never wrote to **one another**.
Indefinite	*Something, someone, somebody, anything, anyone, anybody,* *everything, everyone, everybody, nothing, no-one, nobody* e.g. **Somebody** left the lights on. They invited **everyone** to the party.
	Many, more, both, most, some, neither e.g. **Neither** of the plans was feasible. **Most** of her story was unbelievable.
Interrogative	*Who, whom, whose, which, what* e.g. **Who** arrived late for the meeting? **Whose** swimming pool did you use?
Relative	*Who, whom, whose, what, which, that* e.g. The woman **who** sings in the choir is ill. The person to **whom** this letter is addressed no longer lives here.

Interrogative pronouns are used to ask questions. The form of these pronouns reflects the case of the person who is identified by means of the question. In the question *Who hid the chocolate?*, the pronoun *who* indicates a subject case (*Mary hid the chocolate*). In the question *Whose jacket is this?*, the pronoun *whose* indicates a genitive (*It's Mary's jacket*). There is no such variation in form for the pronouns *what* and *which*. The pronoun *what* identifies something non-personal (*What did she say?*), while the pronoun *which* may be non-personal (*Which is your car?*) or personal (*Which is your child?*). Finally, relative pronouns occur in **relative clauses** where they relate to a preceding noun phrase. This can be seen in the sentence *The judge who sentenced the man was criticised for his leniency*, where the relative pronoun *who* relates to the noun phrase *the judge*.

Identify the noun phrases related to the underlined relative clauses in the following (very long!) sentence:

> Sara Eskrich, <u>who represents the area and sits on the Community Development</u> <u>Authority's board,</u> is offering a resolution to create a neighbourhood plan for the Triangle and adjacent Monona Bay neighbourhood <u>that would guide</u> <u>coming investment in housing, more retail and services, and improvements for</u> <u>traffic including pedestrians and cyclists.</u> (*Wisconsin State Journal*, 2017)

Of course, what we have just described is the use of these pronouns in Standard English. Non-standard dialects of English often use different pronouns or may even omit certain of these pronouns. This occurs in the Geordie dialect which we have been describing. Speakers of this dialect omit the relative pronoun *who* and use a non-standard pronoun *what* in place of *that* in relative clauses. These uses are illustrated below:

Zero relative pronoun
'father had three brothers [**who**] lived round the next street'

Relative pronoun 'what'
'know, you know you pray on a mat or something clean, that somebody, you
know, **what** nobody's walked over'

It was described above how Lara's grandmother and father use non-standard demonstrative, possessive and personal pronouns. Lara's grandmother also uses the non-standard relative pronoun *what* as the following utterance illustrates:

'Grandma's got a box of cars at home **what** your daddy used to play with'

Utterances like this are a salient reminder that not every deviation from Standard English in Lara's language should be taken to be an error. Some are simply grammatical features of the particular dialect to which Lara is exposed.

The main points in this section are summarised below.

KEY POINTS NOUNS AND PRONOUNS

- Nouns can be identified by using semantic, morphological and syntactic criteria. Not all of these criteria are equally reliable. There are many nouns, for example, which do not refer to people and objects (the standard semantic characterisation of nouns). They include *wedding* (an event) and *mechanisation* (a process).
- Nouns can be categorised according to a number of distinctions. There are common nouns (*boy, chair*) and proper nouns (*Mark, Paris*). There are also count nouns (*pencil, car*) and non-count nouns (*milk, honey*). This latter distinction can cause confusion for young children who may treat a non-count noun as if it were a count noun, and pluralise it accordingly (*It's furnitures*).
- There is a further (semantic) distinction between abstract and concrete nouns. Abstract nouns refer to intangible entities such as *justice* and *love*, while concrete nouns refer to tangible entities like *table* and *glass*.
- Collective nouns are somewhat unique in that they can take a plural verb even in singular form (e.g. *The committee have made a decision*). This is possible because these nouns can refer to a group or the individuals which make up a group. Collective nouns include words like *staff, crew* and *team*.
- Pronouns are often studied alongside nouns as they can take the place of noun phrases in sentences. In the sentence *Jack is smiling because he won a car*, the personal pronoun *he* replaces the proper noun *Jack*. Grammarians also classify pronouns as determiners.
- With the exception of *you* and *it*, personal pronouns change their form with case (subject and object) and number (singular and plural). They also have masculine, feminine and non-personal third person singular forms (*he, she, it*).
- Possessive and demonstrative pronouns may be determiners in noun phrases (*my car, this hat*) or they may exist independently (*mine is red, this is too hot*). Reflexive pronouns have distinctive –*self* or –*selves* endings (*myself, ourselves*) and have an antecedent in the same clause.

- Reciprocal pronouns (*each other, one another*) also have an antecedent in the same clause. Interrogative pronouns like *who* and *which* are used to ask questions. Indefinite pronouns like *someone* and *everything* express quantity and definiteness. Relative pronouns like *who* and *which* introduce a relative clause and relate to a preceding noun phrase (*The child who can run to school will always be fit*).

3.3 Verbs

Another major word class is verbs. Verbs denote actions, mental and physical processes, states and events, as illustrated by the following examples:

> Jack <u>ran</u> to the shop (physical action)
> She <u>reflected</u> on her situation (mental process)
> Her teeth <u>decayed</u> at a young age (physical process)
> Sally <u>has</u> a bad cold (state)
> It <u>is</u> very warm in here (state)
> The vicar <u>baptised</u> the child (event)
> The detective <u>interrogated</u> the suspect (event)

3.3.1 Morphological Features of Verbs

The inflectional morphology of main or lexical verbs in English was examined in Section 2.2. To the base form of the verb, the following inflectional suffixes can be added (the base form is the part of the verb that follows the infinitival marker *to*):

> Base form: walk
> Present tense (third person singular): walk<u>s</u> (e.g. Billy walks to school)
> Past tense: walk<u>ed</u> (e.g. Billy walked to school)
> Past participle: walk<u>ed</u> (e.g. Billy has walked to school)
> –ing form: walk<u>ing</u> (e.g. Billy is walking to school)

Of course, this pattern of inflectional morphemes only applies to regular verbs in English. There are many verbs in English which do not follow this pattern. While there are some similarities between the different forms of these so-called irregular verbs, they do require special attention by all language learners. It is unsurprising, therefore, that it is irregular verbs that pose the greatest challenge to young children acquiring English as their native language and to people learning English as a foreign language. Several irregular verbs are shown in Table 3.7.

The following Special Topic will help you develop your knowledge of the past tense and past participle in English.

TABLE 3.7 Some irregular verbs in English

Infinitive	Base form	Present tense (third person singular)	Past tense	Past participle	–ing form
to be	be	is	was, were	been	being
to throw	throw	throws	threw	thrown	throwing
to eat	eat	eats	ate	eaten	eating
to have	have	has	had	had	having
to run	run	runs	ran	run	running
to do	do	does	did	done	doing

SPECIAL TOPIC 3.1 PAST TENSE AND PAST PARTICIPLE IN NON-STANDARD DIALECTS

There are many dialects in English where speakers use non-standard forms for the past tense and past participle parts of verbs. These dialects include Geordie speakers and speakers of Belfast English. Speakers of these dialects often use the past participle of verbs as the past tense:

'bought our house and, uh, it's the best thing we **done**, like'

The opposite grammatical pattern also occurs – the past tense form of the verb is used as a past participle:

'I've **rang** them and they've come out'
'was big baskets **took** with food and'

The bare infinitive form of the verb is also often used as the past tense, as these examples illustrate:

'the water **come** out the mouth – it was like a lion's face, but it, the water **come** out the mouth'
'vegetables was straight out the soil and we **eat** them'
'theory used to be if you chewed your fingernails or ate a grape pip or something it went straight to your appendix and **give** you appendicitis'
'the club would put a trip on for we, but if we had to go down to Swalwell to get the train; so that was all right – we **run** down'

The bare infinitive form of the verb may also be used as a past participle, as this example illustrates:

'now you know yourself, if you've **give** something to a good cause, you feel good about it'

These non-standard usages of the past tense and past participle should serve to remind you that the grammatical forms we are studying in this book represent only one possibility – other grammatical patterns are not just possible but actually occur in non-standard dialects of English.

TABLE 3.8 Errors in the inflectional morphology of verbs in a typically developing child (Lara) and children with specific language impairment

Type of error	Typically developing child	Children with SLI
Overregularisation	Lara doed it (1;10) I've maked it (2;00)	The giraffe never runned (8;10) And the elephant comed (7;08)
Omission of –ing	Everybody's sleep (1;11) And now I'm swim (2;09)	Is do it (4;07) Is hurt ears (4;07)
Omission of present tense (third person)	He just stay there (2;00) Grandad do that (2;00)	The guy hurt him knees (4;06) He want the balloon (4;07)
Omission of –ed past tense	I pick it uped again (2;06) I nick Amy's seat (2;09)	Giraffe call her dad (8;10) The dog fix it up (8;10)
Omission of –ed past participle	I [have] nearly finish this (2;00) Have you pour them out? (2;08)	They have help her (5;09) Have you ask them? (6;02)

We saw in Section 2.2 how young, typically developing children can struggle with the inflectional morphology of verbs. Lara committed overregularisation errors in which an irregular verb was treated as a regular verb and the suffix –ed was added to form the past tense (e.g. *Lara doed it; I've maked it*). Lara also omitted the progressive –ing suffix (e.g. *Everybody's sleep*) and the third person singular present tense suffix –s (e.g. *He just stay there*). Many of these same morphological errors are found in the verb productions of children with specific language impairment (SLI). However, because these children have a specific and severe deficit in language, these errors tend to persist in children with SLI for much longer than they do in typically developing children. This can be seen in Table 3.8 if we compare the ages at which Lara made certain verb errors and the ages at which these same types of error occur in children with SLI.

Aside from inflectional morphology, verbs also exhibit certain derivational morphological features. Verbal endings such as –ate and –en in *orchestrate* and *broaden* tell us something about a verb's derivation, namely, that it is derived from a noun (*orchestra*) and an adjective (*broad*), respectively. Also, it is only verbs which can take suffixes like –able and –ment to generate adjectives (*washable*) and nouns (*agreement*), respectively.

3.3.2 Tense, Finite and Non-Finite Verbs

The remainder of this section will address the syntactic properties of verbs. When we described the inflectional morphology of verbs, we used terms like 'present tense' and 'past tense'. The **tense** of a verb describes its morphological marking. Any verb which carries tense, that is, is morphologically marked as present or past is described as a **finite verb**. It is important when describing finite verbs that we understand that not every present tense verb refers to an event that is currently taking place. Also, not every past tense verb captures an event that occurred in the past. The tense of verbs only corresponds with the actual time of events in certain circumstances. Each of the following sentences contains a verb in the simple present tense (i.e. a single verb in the present tense). These sentences describe habitual actions which need not relate to present time:

> Mary *sees* her therapist every week.
> He *moans* all the time about work.
> John *visits* Rome every summer.

For example, Mary may only have a consultation with her therapist every Thursday afternoon, while it may be several months before John's trip to Rome is an event in present time. Apart from habitual actions, the simple present tense may be used to describe events which will take place in the future and states which endure over time:

> Tom *becomes* the director of the company next year. [Future event]
> Being a parent *is* expensive. [Enduring state]

There is one group of verbs where the simple present tense relates directly to real time. In fact, the mere act of speaking utterances which contain these verbs constitutes an action in present time (a **speech act**). So-called **performative verbs** are illustrated by the following examples:

> I *baptise* this child John Brown.
> I *name* this ship the Queen Elizabeth 2.
> I *promise* to come to the party.

Like the simple present tense, the simple past test involves a single verb with no auxiliaries. It relates to past time much more than the present tense does to present time. So in sentences like the following, it is clear that the verbs are describing actions and events which took place in the past:

> Jan *left* Spain yesterday.
> Billy *washed* his car last week.
> The teenagers *made* terrible noise last night.

Present and past are the only tenses in English. Unlike other languages, English does not have a specific verb form for future tense. What appears to be that verb form – the auxiliary *will* or the contracted form in *I'll* – is in fact only one of several ways of referring to future events in English. Some of these different ways are shown below:

> I *will* arrive around 8 o'clock. [Auxiliary *will*]
> I *am going to* write a book on bee keeping. [Verb *be* + *going to*]
> Oscar *might* arrive a bit late. [Auxiliary *might*]
> The class *graduates* next week. [Simple present tense]
> They *are about to* leave their jobs. [Verb *be* + *about to*]
> The new smart phone *is coming* to a store near you. [Verb *be* + *coming*]

To recap, verbs in present or past tense are tensed verb forms. These verbs are called finite verbs. But there are also verbs which are not marked for tense. These verbs are called **non-finite verbs**. They include four types of verb: the **present participle**, the past participle, the infinitive and the **bare infinitive**. Examples of each of these non-finite verbs are shown below:

> *Leaving* home is a very stressful experience. [Present participle]
> *Postponed* for the second time, the match was about to take place. [Past participle]
> They wanted *to visit* Beijing. [Infinitive]
> The walker saw the woman *enter* the park. [Bare infinitive]

3.3.3 Lexical and Auxiliary Verbs

The distinction between finite and non-finite verbs leads us into the distinction between lexical and auxiliary verbs in English. This is because there are many sentences which do not contain a single verb in either the simple present tense or the simple past tense. These sentences contain a verb string. A verb string has a main or lexical verb and one or more auxiliaries. To decide if a verb string is finite or non-finite, we must look at the first verb in the string and ask if it is tensed. If it is tensed, the entire verb string is finite even though the verb which comes next in the string is non-finite. Consider the following examples:

> Jack *has decided* to leave university.
> *has*: present tense
> *has decided*: finite verb string
> Paula *can play* the piano.
> *can*: present tense
> *can play:* finite verb string
> The teacher *had asked* for assistance.
> *had*: past tense
> *had asked:* finite verb string

In order for a verb string to be non-finite, all the verbs in the string must be non-finite, as the following example illustrates:

> *Having announced* his retirement, the boxer decided to return to the ring.
> *having:* present participle
> *announced:* past participle
> *having announced:* non-finite verb string

The main or lexical verbs in the above sentences – words like *decided, play* and *asked* – not only convey considerable meaning but also determine what other elements can occur in the sentence. The verbs which precede these lexical verbs – *has, can* and *had* – are called auxiliary verbs. Auxiliary verbs 'help' lexical verbs to convey meaning in a sentence. It is for this reason that they must always occur with a lexical verb, either explicit or understood, whereas a lexical verb can occur on its own. In the pair of sentences below, the lexical verb *ordered* in parentheses is understood. Accordingly, the auxiliary verb *had* does not occur without a lexical verb and the second sentence is grammatical, initial appearance notwithstanding:

> The waitress asked if anyone had ordered pizza. Sally replied that she had [*ordered pizza*].

To give you further practice in working with auxiliary and lexical verbs, you should attempt Exercise 3.3.

EXERCISE 3.3 LEXICAL AND AUXILIARY VERBS

Young children often omit lexical and auxiliary verbs from their early utterances. To give you practice in identifying these verbs, this exercise asks you to examine a number of Lara's utterances in which either an auxiliary verb or a lexical verb has been omitted. For each utterance, state what type of verb Lara has omitted. Also, indicate in each case what the omitted lexical or auxiliary verb is likely to be:

(a) I done more table (1;10)
(b) And daddy crying (2;00)
(c) That Lara keys (1;10)
(d) It got hole in it (2;01)
(e) I good girl (1;10)
(f) I done two sausage (2;00)
(g) Where my car? (1;11)
(h) That blue (1;11)
(i) I running (2;01)
(j) Where daddy going? (2;01)
(k) I being crocodile (2;01)
(l) That daddy jumper (1;11)
(m) Mummy done it that one (2;01)
(n) That a green book (1;11)
(o) They cooking (2;01)
(p) I building tower as well (2;01)

3.3.4 Modality, Aspect and Voice

Auxiliary verbs help lexical verbs convey meaning by contributing three types of information: modality, aspect and voice. The **modality** of auxiliary verbs can change the meaning of a sentence from one which is a prediction or strongly held conviction that the events in the sentence will happen to one which is little more than conjecture or supposition on the part of the speaker that the events in question will occur. This can be seen in the following examples where the **modal auxiliary verbs** express different degrees of certainty by the speaker:

> Mary *will* be an Olympic champion. [High certainty]
> Pauline *may* visit us next year. [Low certainty]

It is a sign of the semantic versatility of modal auxiliary verbs that these same verbs can express different meanings in other sentences. In the first sentence below, the modal auxiliary *will* lacks the meaning of prediction that it had above and is expressing instead a commitment or promise. Similarly, the modal auxiliary *may* which expressed tentativeness above is conveying permission to do something in the second sentence below:

> I *will* arrive at the party on time. [Promise]
> You *may* use my car at the weekend. [Permission]

Other meanings expressed by modal auxiliary verbs include obligation, necessity, desire, and threat. The following sentences illustrate each of these meanings:

> Visitors *should* respect the rules of the club. [Obligation]
> You *must* not operate machinery when taking this drug. [Necessity]
> I *would* love to see Meatloaf in concert. [Desire]
> You *may* conclude that it is unwise to testify in this court case. [Threat]

Aside from modality, auxiliary verbs can also convey information about the aspect and voice of a sentence. Aspect indicates that the action of a verb is either completed (perfect aspect) or is continuing (progressive aspect). To form the perfect aspect in English, the auxiliary verb *have* is used followed by the past participle. If the auxiliary verb is in the present tense (*has* or *have*), the aspect is called present perfect. If the auxiliary verb is in the past tense (*had*), the aspect is called past perfect. To form the progressive aspect, the auxiliary verb *be* is used followed by the present participle. If the auxiliary verb is in the present tense (*am, are, is*), the aspect is called present progressive. If the auxiliary verb is in the past tense (*was* or *were*), the aspect is called past progressive. There are two further aspects shown below called the present perfect progressive and the past perfect progressive. They are formed from the present and past tense of the auxiliary *have*, the past participle of the auxiliary *be* and the present participle. These different forms of the perfect and progressive aspect are illustrated below, and will be described again when we come to discuss verb phrases in Chapter 5:

> They *have been* on holiday. [Present perfect]
> She *had been* on holiday. [Past perfect]
> John *is repairing* the fence. [Present progressive]
> Jill *was driving* at the time of the accident. [Past progressive]
> They *have been eating* breakfast. [Present perfect progressive]
> Frank *had been stealing* cars. [Past perfect progressive]

The final feature of auxiliary verbs to be addressed here is **voice**. In English, an **active sentence** can be changed into a **passive sentence** by introducing the auxiliary verb *be*, adding a prepositional phrase (*by* ...), changing the verb into its passive participle (PPART) form, and reversing the position of the subject and object noun phrases. This is illustrated below.

Active voice: The dog chased the man down the street.

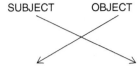

Passive voice: The man was chased by the dog down the street.

         Be PPART Prep. phrase

In the passive, what was the object noun phrase (*the man*) in the active sentence occupies a position in front of the verb and is called a grammatical subject. The subject noun phrase (*the dog*) in the active sentence is the object of the preposition *by* in the passive sentence. Because it still has the function of a subject in that it performs an action (in this case, chasing), it is called a logical subject. The prepositional phrase in the passive is optional. The passive sentence above could just as easily read *The man was chased down the street*. There are occasions when speakers consider it preferable not to identify the **agent** of the action, for example, when the identity of the agent is unknown or when a speaker wishes to avoid attributing blame to an individual (e.g. in the passive sentence *The priceless Ming vase was dropped*). The optional prepositional phrase allows the speaker not to identify the agent of the action under these circumstances.

The use and understanding of passive sentences by adults with aphasia is particularly interesting. You can read about it in this Special Topic.

SPECIAL TOPIC 3.2 PASSIVE SENTENCES IN APHASIA

Adults with the language disorder aphasia can have difficulty producing and comprehending sentences in the passive voice. When given a choice of four pictures and asked to point to the picture that corresponds to a spoken sentence, a correct selection is made in response to the first sentence below but an incorrect picture is chosen in response to the second sentence (clients with aphasia often point incorrectly to the picture that shows the girl chasing the boy):

> Sentence 1: *The mouse was chased by the cat.*
> Sentence 2: *The girl was chased by the boy.*

Why does this difference in response occur when both sentences are grammatical passives? Comprehension of grammatical structures such as the passive is often compromised in aphasia. When this occurs, clients with aphasia rely on their world knowledge to help them decode sentences. That world knowledge leads to a correct interpretation of the passive construction in sentence 1 – it is normally the case that mice are chased by cats. However, world knowledge cannot facilitate the comprehension of the passive construction in sentence 2 – we can have no expectations about whether girls are more likely to chase, or be chased by, boys.

In this latter scenario, clients with aphasia adopt a linear processing strategy in which the first noun phrase (*the girl*) is treated as the agent in the sentence and the second noun phrase (*the boy*) is treated as the object. As a result, the picture that shows the girl giving chase to the boy is normally selected.

In Exercise 3.3, Lara was observed to omit a number of auxiliary verbs. However, beyond identifying these verbs, there was no attempt made to comment on their contribution to the modality and aspect of Lara's utterances. In Table 3.9, more of Lara's utterances are presented. Once again, an auxiliary verb is omitted from each utterance. The missing auxiliary verb is indicated in parentheses. Each utterance was produced when Lara was 3 years 3 months old.

The two aspects which are consistently compromised by Lara's omission of auxiliary verbs are the present progressive and present perfect as in (16) and (4) below:

Present progressive: We [are] sitting down in back.
Present perfect: I [have] got nobody in the house.

The one auxiliary verb that Lara does use is the modal auxiliary *can*. This occurs in an **interrogative** (question) in (5) and in a **declarative** (statement) in (12). In (5), Lara is aware that to form an interrogative the modal auxiliary *can* and subject *Amy* must undergo **inversion** to become *Can Amy move away ... ?*. The modal auxiliary in this utterance has the meaning of 'is it possible to'. Lara seems to be saying that because Amy is not willing to share with others, it should be possible to move her away. The modal auxiliary *can* in (12) has a different meaning. In this utterance, *can* suggests that the addressee is required, or obliged, to hoover 'this bit'. In (2), Lara omits a form called the **dummy auxiliary**. The presence of *does* is necessitated by the use of **negation** *not*. Some auxiliary must be introduced to function as the operator when negation is used, and the semantically empty

TABLE 3.9 Lara's utterances with omitted auxiliary verbs

1	You [are] not putting your shoes on.	10	I [have] got lots of cards now.
2	The Emily that [does] not comes to my nursery.	11	You [have] only got a few.
3	What [is] Amy doing?	12	You [have] got to hoover that bit and then you can hoover this bit.
4	I [have] got nobody in the house.	13	You [are] not getting me any.
5	Can Amy move away because she [is] not sharing?	14	We [are] putting the marbles in here.
6	We [have] got a dice.	15	Monkey [is] swinging.
7	I [have] turned it on now.	16	We [are] sitting down in back.
8	You [are] taking the things off me.	17	We [are] not going in the boot.
9	You [are] going to have them all.	18	You [are] not having a picnic.

dummy auxiliary *does* fits the bill perfectly. As well as omitting the dummy auxiliary, Lara omits other auxiliaries in the presence of negation. These auxiliaries include *are* in utterances (1), (13), (17) and (18), and *is* in utterance (5). Because Lara has omitted the auxiliary *have* in utterance (4), she has no option but to use the indefinite pronoun *nobody*. However, in Standard English negation is marked on the auxiliary verb in which case the form *anybody* is used instead: I *haven't* got anybody in the house. Knowledge of the form and function of auxiliary verbs has allowed us to give a detailed characterisation of the auxiliaries that Lara is omitting from her utterances at 3 years of age.

3.3.5 Verbs *Have*, *Be* and *Do*

Each of the auxiliary verbs that Lara omitted was some part of the verbs *have, be* or *do*. These verbs can be main or lexical verbs as well as auxiliary verbs in English. Consider the following sentences:

Mary *has* a birthday next week.
She *is* certain that the stock market will crash.
The woman *does* all her own painting.

The verbs *has, is* and *does* in these sentences are lexical verbs. We know that they cannot be auxiliary verbs because they exist on their own and so they cannot 'help' a lexical verb. Another sign that they are lexical verbs is that, for *has* and *does* at least, the dummy auxiliary *do* must be introduced to achieve negation and to form an interrogative. We saw how Lara omitted the dummy auxiliary *do* for negation in utterance (2) above when the lexical verb *come* was used. The need for this same auxiliary in the sentences below is a test that the underlined verbs have lexical rather than auxiliary status:

Mary *doesn't* <u>have</u> a birthday next week. [Negation]
Does the woman <u>do</u> all her own painting? [Interrogative]

Lexical *be* is an exception to *have* and *do* in that it does not require the dummy auxiliary *do* to achieve negation or to form an interrogative:

She *isn't* certain that the stock market will crash. [Negation]
Is she certain that the stock market will crash? [Interrogative]

Lexical and auxiliary uses of *be* are examined further in this Special Topic.

SPECIAL TOPIC 3.3 LEXICAL AND AUXILIARY *BE* IN A NON-STANDARD DIALECT

In Standard English, a verb agrees with the number of the subject. This is known as subject–verb agreement or concord. It is illustrated by the following sentences which contain lexical and auxiliary *be*. In the first sentence, the singular auxiliary verb *is* agrees with the singular noun phrase *the boy*. In the second sentence, the plural lexical verb *are* agrees with the plural noun phrase *the boys*:

> **Standard English**
> The boy **is** crossing the road. [Auxiliary *be*]
> The boys **are** very unhappy. [Lexical *be*]

In Durham dialect, there is often a lack of concord between the subject and verb. Accordingly, we find sentences like the following produced by Lara's grandmother in which a singular verb (auxiliary *is* and lexical *is*) is used with a plural subject (*the plants* and *your books*, respectively). Standard English requires the use of lexical and auxiliary *are* in both these sentences:

> **Durham dialect**
> 'I think a lot of the plants **is** growing very well' [Auxiliary *be*]
> 'Some of your books **is** over there, aren't they?' [Lexical *be*]

Lack of subject–verb concord is also a grammatical feature of Asian English, as the following example illustrates:

> 'my marriages **was** typical arranged marriages'

3.3.6 Classes of Lexical Verbs

There is much more to be said about lexical verbs. Lexical verbs can be grouped according to the elements that must appear alongside them in order to form a grammatical sentence. The first thing we can say is that all lexical verbs must have a subject as forms such as **Chases* and **Climbs* are ungrammatical as sentences. To the extent that all lexical verbs must have a subject, the presence of a subject does not serve to distinguish different classes of lexical verbs. However, lexical verbs are distinguished by the presence or absence of other elements. Consider the following sentences:

> Tim *smiled* throughout the concert.
> The man *hit* the table with full force.
> Jack *gave* the book to his friend.

In the first sentence, the verb *smiled* is followed by the **adverbial** *throughout the concert*. The adverbial answers the question *When?* and is an optional **adjunct**. What this means is that we can leave the adjunct out of the sentence and still end up with a grammatical sentence: *Tim smiled*. Because the verb *smiled* can occur alone, even if on occasion it is followed by optional elements, it is called an **intransitive verb**. In the second sentence, the lexical verb *hit* is followed by two elements. One of these two elements *with full force* is another optional adjunct.

It certainly adds information to the sentence but its presence is not obligatory. However, the other element *the table* is the object of the verb and is a necessary element in the sentence (**The man hit* is clearly ungrammatical). Lexical verbs which must have a single object after them are called **mono-transitive verbs**. In the third sentence above, there are two obligatory elements which come after the lexical verb *gave*. One is a direct object (*the book*) and the other is an indirect object (*to his friend*). If either of these object elements is missing, an ungrammatical sentence is the result: **Jack gave the book* and **Jack gave to his friend*. A lexical verb which must be followed by a direct and an indirect object is called a **di-transitive verb**. As well as intransitive, mono-transitive and di-transitive verbs, this section will also examine intensive and complex transitive verbs.

To give you further practice of working with lexical verbs, you should now attempt Exercise 3.4.

EXERCISE 3.4 LARA AND LEXICAL VERBS

It was described above how all lexical verbs require a subject but that other elements in the sentence like direct object and indirect object may be optional or obligatory. Several utterances that Lara produced when she was 3 years 3 months old are shown below. Part A: For each utterance, indicate if the underlined elements are optional or obligatory. Part B: Indicate if the following verbs are intransitive, mono-transitive or di-transitive: *throwed; gave; see; holded; sit.*

(a) I throwed <u>him</u>.
(b) I didn't broke <u>it</u>.
(c) I gave <u>mine the tea on the afternoon</u>.
(d) We got <u>a dice</u>.
(e) I turned <u>it</u> on <u>now</u>.
(f) You holded <u>something</u>.
(g) Can you open <u>door for me</u>?
(h) Do you want to see <u>over gate</u>?
(i) We putting <u>the marbles in here</u>.
(j) He can sit <u>in back</u>.

It was stated above that intransitive verbs can be followed by adjuncts such as *throughout the concert*. However, such elements are optional and are, therefore, overlooked when we say that an intransitive verb occurs on its own (with the exception of an obligatory subject, of course). The optional adjuncts which occur with intransitive verbs are adverbials of time, manner and reason and address the questions *When?, How?* and *Why?*, respectively. This can be seen in the sentences below:

The visitors arrived <u>at midday</u>. [Adverbial of time: *When?*]
John travels <u>by train</u>. [Adverbial of manner: *How?*]
She resigned <u>because of illness</u>. [Adverbial of reason: *Why?*]

Intransitive verbs can occur with words like *in, up* and *down*. So-called particles in combinations such as *shut up* and *sit down* are part of the verb they accompany. These verb–particle combinations are known as **intransitive phrasal verbs**. Several of these verbs were used by Lara, as the following examples illustrate:

He *fallen over* (3;01)
My bobble's *comed off* (3;01)
You got to *lie down* (3;01)
Is it Amy *falling off* the bed? (3;01)
I already *sit down* (3;03)

Particles can also occur with transitive verbs, as these examples from Lara illustrate:

Throw ball *up* like that (3;02)
I *turned* it *on* now (3;03)

The noun *ball* and pronoun *it* are direct objects of the transitive verbs *throw* and *turned*. These verbs are called **transitive phrasal verbs**. It will be observed that the direct object noun or pronoun occurs between the lexical verb and particle and not after the particle as in **Throw up ball like that*.

Some interesting differences in the use of verbs in Australian English and British English are explored in the following Special Topic.

SPECIAL TOPIC 3.4 INTRANSITIVE VERBS IN AUSTRALIAN ENGLISH

You might think that a transitive verb or an intransitive verb in one dialect or variety of English will be a transitive verb or an intransitive verb in all other dialects or varieties of English. This is not the case, however. Australian English treats as intransitive verbs a number of verbs which are used transitively in British English. These verbs include *nominate* and *contest* which are used as transitive verbs in the following sentences:

British English
They <u>nominated the actor</u> for an award.
He <u>contested the decision</u> to close the bank account.

These same verbs are used intransitively in the following sentences which are taken from an article in *The Sydney Morning Herald*.[1] These uses of these verbs will be unfamiliar to British English speakers, but are a routine feature of spoken and written English for Australian English speakers:

Australian English

(a) 'Five men have **nominated** to fill the West Australian Senate vacancy, including two former state MPs, official nomination papers leaked to Fairfax Media reveal.'

(b) 'Erin Watson-Lynn, a director at Asia Link and a single mother, had considered **nominating** and had recently met delegates but on Friday ruled out throwing her hat in the ring for now.'

(c) 'Asked why he was **nominating**, 55-year-old company director and pro-life advocate Gabi Ghasseb said it was "to keep Australia great and secure, in these uncertain times in our world with global maneuvering, I believe that the wisdom of God is required." '

(d) 'Her decision not to **contest** will reopen the debate about the Liberal party's poor representation of women in Parliament.'

These examples demonstrate the importance of not adhering to pre-determined grammatical categories (for example, that *nominate* is a transitive verb) when studying grammar. There will always be instances when these categories are shown not to be true!

1. *Source:* 'Not a woman in sight: Leaked nomination papers reveal five male nominees to fill Liberal Senate role', *The Sydney Morning Herald*, 7 July 2017.

Turning to mono-transitive verbs, they take only a single object which must be a direct object. In each of the following sentences, the underlined word(s) is the direct object of the mono-transitive verb in italics:

Paul *bought* <u>a red Mini</u>.
The dressmaker *cut* <u>the expensive fabric</u>.

A test of a transitive verb is that it should be able to participate in a passive sentence. This is because a passive is formed when the object of an active sentence becomes a subject. The verbs *bought* and *cut* can both be used in passive sentences and are transitive verbs as a result:

<u>A red Mini</u> was bought by Paul.
<u>The expensive fabric</u> was cut by the dressmaker.

As well as transitive phrasal verbs, there are other sub-categories of mono-transitive verbs. When we discussed transitive phrasal verbs, we said that the object occurred between the lexical verb and particle in sentences such as *He turned the television on*. In so-called **prepositional verbs** this pattern is not possible – the direct object must appear after the preposition or particle. This can be observed in the following sentence:

The grandparents looked after the children all day.

We know that *looked after* is a transitive verb as it can occur in a passive sentence: *The children were looked after by the grandparents all day*. However, it must be a prepositional verb rather than a transitive phrasal verb as the direct object *the children* cannot appear between the verb *looked* and the preposition or particle *after*:

*The grandparents looked the children after all day.

Other mono-transitive verbs take an entire clause rather than a noun or a pronoun as the object. The underlined elements in the sentences below are object clauses of the mono-transitive verbs in italics:

Jan *hoped* the plane would be on time.
Michael *believed* the fridge was empty.

Lara produced many utterances which contain object clauses. A number of these utterances are shown below, with the object clause underlined and the mono-transitive verb in italics. In the first three utterances, the object clause contains a *to*-infinitive (**infinitive clause**). The object in the last three utterances is a *that*-clause. Both of these clauses are **subordinate clauses** which will be discussed further in Chapter 6:

To-infinitive
Are you *trying* to keep in the lines? (3;02)
Do you *want* to give the other baby a cuddle? (3;02)
I *want* to borrow them (3;03)

That-clause
I *think* it's a train set (3;02)
Do you *think* they want to go to bed now? (3;02)
I *wished* I wanted the rolling pin (3;02)

It is worth adding a cautionary note about mono-transitive verbs. We have said that these verbs must take an object such as a noun, a pronoun or a clause. But consider the following utterances:

The man was attacked.
A: Do you want to come into town with me?
B: I don't want to.

The first utterance is a passive sentence with the object deleted in the *by*-phrase (e.g. The man was attacked *by the escaped prisoner*). The second example is an exchange between two people, A and B. Person A asks Person B a question. B's response uses **ellipsis** in that the object clause *to come into town with you* has been largely omitted. Do we want to say in these cases that the verbs *attack* and *want* are not mono-transitive verbs after all and that in these cases they are actually intransitive verbs? The answer is 'of course not'. Just because an object no longer appears with a verb in a passive sentence or is omitted by a speaker in a response to a question does not mean that the verb in question is no longer a transitive verb.

Turning to di-transitive verbs, they take two objects, one direct and the other indirect. The indirect object comes before the direct object, as the following sentences illustrate:

John *gave* me the money.
[Indirect object – *me*; direct object – *the money*]
She *told* him a really good story.
[Indirect object – *him*; direct object – *a really good story*]
The lawyer *offered* us poor advice.
[Indirect object – *us*; direct object – *poor advice*]
Their patents *gave* people the confidence to drive places they didn't think
   possible. (*Wausau Daily Herald,* Wisconsin, 2017)
[Indirect object – *people*; direct object – *the confidence*]
We were fortunate enough that the Newcastle Falcons *granted* me early
   release. (*Bay of Plenty Times,* New Zealand, 2017)
[Indirect object – *me*; direct object – *early release*]

This order of objects is reversed, however, when a preposition such as *to* or *for* is used to introduce the indirect object. In this case, it is the direct object which appears before the indirect object:

The teacher *gave* the homework <u>to</u> the class.
[Indirect object – *the class*; direct object – *the homework*]

The passive test can be used to show that the objects used with di-transitive verbs really are objects. The following passive sentence finds the indirect object of *John gave me the money* move into the position of the subject in the sentence. Of course, the pronoun must be changed from *me* to *I* in order to reflect the change from object case to subject case:

I was given the money by John.

In order for the direct object of a di-transitive verb to become the subject of a passive sentence, the indirect object must become a prepositional phrase. This can be seen in the use of *to me* in the following passive sentence:

The money was given to me by John.

The objects used with di-transitive verbs thus far have all been noun phrases (*the money, poor advice*) and pronouns (*me, us*). However, the direct object of a di-transitive verb may also take the form of a clause, as the underlined parts of the following sentences illustrate:

They told him that <u>the problem would take some time to be resolved</u>.
He asked her if <u>the price of the item reflected the discount</u>.

It is also perfectly grammatical for speakers to delete the indirect object in certain di-transitive verbs so that we have a sentence like the following:

He asked if the price of the item reflected the discount.

But in the same way that the absence of an object in certain uses of mono-transitive verbs was not reason to say they were not transitive, the deletion of the indirect object should not lead us to say that *asked* is not a di-transitive verb.

To give you practice in identifying and describing di-transitive verbs, several utterances that contain these verbs are displayed in Table 3.10. The utterances were produced by Lara and by children with specific language impairment (SLI). Three of Lara's utterances contain the di-transitive verb *tell*. In the utterance in (4) the verb *told* is used in the absence of both a direct object and an indirect object. In the utterance in (1) the indirect object *her* is used but there is no direct object. In most di-transitive verbs the indirect object can be deleted. However, the verb *tell* permits the deletion of either the indirect object or the direct object. This explains why Lara's utterance *I told her* is grammatical notwithstanding the deletion of the direct object. In utterance (5) Lara uses an indirect object (*you*) and a direct object with the verb *told*. However, this time the direct object is a clause (*I've got one of these*). Utterances (2) and (3) both use the pronoun *me* as the indirect object and clauses as the direct object (*you want a road* and *you want to come in*). However, in (2) the direct object clause comes *after* the indirect object, while in (3) the direct object clause comes *before* the indirect object.

As expected, the children with SLI produce grammatical errors which are typical of this language disorder. These errors include a 'doubling up' of past tense (e.g. *gaved*), incorrect use of pronouns (e.g. object pronoun *her* instead of subject pronoun *she*), and incorrect use of the indefinite article with a non-count noun (e.g. *a money*). Additionally, there are deficits in how these children use di-transitive verbs. The utterance in (10) contains two indirect objects. One of these objects is a noun phrase (*the balloon carrier*) while the other indirect object is a pronoun (*them*). However, other di-transitive verbs are used correctly. For example, these children are clearly aware when an indirect object of a di-transitive verb must appear in a prepositional phrase, namely, when it is preceded by a direct object (e.g. *He gaved it* to her). When the direct object appears after the indirect object, as it does in utterances (7) and (9), the indirect object is not used in a prepositional

TABLE 3.10 Di-transitive verbs in utterances produced by a typically developing child (Lara) and children with specific language impairment

	Typically developing child		Children with SLI
1	I told her (3;03)	6	He gaved it to her (8;09)
2	You've got to ask me if you want a road (3;01)	7	Her give him a money (5;01)
3	If you want to come in you've got to ask me (3;01)	8	He asked if you can buy me a balloon (8;06)
4	Amy didn't told (2;08)	9	The lifeguard showed her the sign (8;11)
5	I told you I've got one of these (2;09)	10	The doctor gave them the money to the balloon carrier (8;11)

phrase. In utterance (8), the direct object is a clause (*you can buy me a balloon*). *Ask* is one of the di-transitive verbs which permits the indirect object to be deleted. The child with SLI who produces the utterance in (8) undertakes this deletion. The children with SLI who produced these utterances clearly have considerable knowledge of how to use di-transitive verbs. However, it should be emphasised that these children are much older than typically developing children before this knowledge is acquired.

Two further classes of lexical verbs are **intensive verbs** and **complex transitive verbs**. Intensive verbs are also called copular verbs and **complex intransitive verbs**. They take a **subject complement**. This is most often a noun phrase or an adjective that refers to the same person or thing referred to by the subject of the sentence. In the following sentences, the noun phrase *a cardiologist* and the adjective *fantastic* refer to the subjects *Frank* and *the music*, respectively:

Frank is a cardiologist.
The music sounds fantastic.

A clause may also be a subject complement as in the following sentence: *Her sincerest wish is that* <u>Bill makes a speedy and full recovery</u>. **Adverbial complements** may also be used with intensive verbs. These are prepositional phrases such as *in a fortunate position* and *under considerable pressure* in the sentences below:

Jack is <u>in a fortunate position</u>.
The teachers are <u>under considerable pressure</u>.

Unlike other prepositional phrases which are optional adjuncts in a sentence (e.g. *Paul travels home* <u>by car</u>), the prepositional phrases used with intensive verbs are obligatory.

Complex transitive verbs require a direct object and an **object complement**. The object complement refers to the same thing as the direct object. This can be seen in the following example:

They found <u>the boy friendly</u>.

The direct object *the boy* and the object complement *friendly* are co-referential expressions in that they both refer to the same person. In this case, the object complement is an adjective. However, it can also be a noun phrase or a prepositional phrase, as in the examples below:

The judge considered <u>him a fraudster</u>. [Noun phrase]
They named <u>their baby Tom</u>. [Noun phrase]
The verdict left <u>their hopes in pieces</u>. [Prepositional phrase]
Hunting is driving <u>species into extinction</u>. [Prepositional phrase]

Intensive verbs are examined further in Exercise 3.5, which you should now attempt.

EXERCISE 3.5 LARA AND INTENSIVE VERBS

The following utterances were produced by Lara when she was 3 years 3 months old. Each utterance contains an intensive verb. Identify the subject complement in each sentence. Also, indicate if the subject complement is a noun phrase, an adjective phrase or a prepositional phrase:

(a) Amy's horrid.
(b) You're in the sea.
(c) It's the helicopter.
(d) This is lovely water.
(e) I'm mummy's friend.
(f) Now it's ready.
(g) I'm a ghost.
(h) You're the elephant, mummy.
(i) Amy's in the rain.
(j) This is our bed.

To conclude this section on verbs, we return to a variety of English that was introduced in Chapter 1. So-called African American Vernacular English (AAVE) is a widely used variety of English by (mostly) African American speakers, particularly in large urban areas in the United States. In Chapter 1, we saw how negative attitudes about AAVE among educators and school administrators had limited the educational opportunities of young black children in the public education system in the USA. These attitudes were based on the widespread misconception that AAVE was a less sophisticated language variety than Standard American English. At least some of these negative attitudes had their origin in the use of non-standard grammatical features by speakers of AAVE. A full treatment of these features can be found in Rickford (1999). A few of them will be discussed here.

The grammatical features of AAVE cut across several of the concepts that we have examined in relation to verbs, including tense, aspect and the distinction between lexical and auxiliary verbs. In Standard American English, speakers use copula and auxiliary *is* and *are* to express states and actions in the present tense. So forms such as *He is tall* and *They are running* are typical of Standard American English. Speakers of AAVE do not use copula and auxiliary *is* and *are* in this context. Instead, grammatical forms such as *He tall* and *They running* are commonly used in this variety of English. There is no auxiliary *is* in the following examples:

> I tell him to be quiet because he don't know what <u>he talking</u> about.
> I mean, he may say something's out of place but <u>he cleaning up</u> behind it and you can't get mad at him.

To emphasise the completed nature of an action, AAVE speakers use *done* (e.g. *He done did it*). The completion of an action is effectively marked twice through the use of the verbs *done* and *did*. This pattern is not observed in Standard American English, where *done* is used as a past participle in sentences like *He has done the dishes*. Speakers of AAVE use invariant or habitual *be* to indicate actions and events that occur habitually or repeatedly. The following examples illustrate the use of habitual *be* in declarative and interrogative sentences:

> He <u>be</u> walkin.
> She <u>be</u> working all the time.
> Do they <u>be</u> playing all day?

Habitual actions in Standard American English may be expressed through the use of present tense as in *He visits his mother every Friday*. Another grammatical feature of AAVE is the use of *had* + V–*ed* to express the simple past. In Standard American English, this verb form expresses the past perfect:

> Then he <u>had called</u> his daddy.
> Then we <u>had went</u> outside.

The following examples of *had* + V–*ed* are taken from a corpus of narratives produced by pre-adolescent African-American students in East Palo Alto, California (Rickford and Théberge Rafal, 1996). This same grammatical feature is reported by these authors to occur in the speech of pre-adolescents and adolescents from East Harlem, New York and adolescents and young adults from Springville, Texas:

David, 10 years
...cause we was half wrestling, half boxing and he <u>had pushed</u> me down.

Cathy, 12 years
...and my brother he <u>had got</u> mad at me 'cause I was on the phone...

Jane, 13 years
...she drove cars, then she <u>had drove</u> some that looked like bubber cars...

The final grammatical feature of AAVE which we will examine is the use of unstressed *been* or *bin* for the present perfect in sentences such as the following:

> AAVE: *He been sick.*
> SAE: *He has been sick.*
> AAVE: *They been eating.*
> SAE: *They have been eating.*

This form does not connote remoteness, unlike stressed *BIN* in the following examples of AAVE, which indicates that the action happened or the state came into being long ago:

> She BIN married.
> He BIN ate it.

You should now attempt Exercise 3.6 which will encourage you to reflect further on American English.

EXERCISE 3.6 'GOT' AND 'GOTTEN' IN AMERICAN ENGLISH

This exercise is designed to get you thinking about the different ways in which 'got' and 'gotten' are used in American English. In British English, there is no form 'gotten', and 'got' is used as an irregular past tense verb (e.g. *They got some milk*) and as a past participle (e.g. *The Wilsons have got a reservation*). However, in American English, a quite different pattern applies. 'Gotten' is a past participle in American English. Meanwhile, 'got' can be a past participle, a past tense verb, and an auxiliary verb in American English. Identify the form of the underlined verbs in the following examples of American English:

(a) Whenever they got in an accident, they got fired, or didn't know who to call or where to call (*Idaho Statesman*, 2017)

(b) The same share also says that the "right to protest or criticize the government" has gotten out of hand (*San Antonio Express*, 2017)

(c) "Knowing that we got played or are victims of some sick person drugging is almost surreal", he said (*Milwaukee Journal Sentinel*, 2017)

(d) They have not gotten adequate funding to protect people's financial lives in the way that they should (*Washington Post*, 2015)

(e) We've got to do something about crazy people getting guns (*CNN*, 2015)

(f) Freud got mentioned once, barely in passing (*Newsweek Web Exclusives*, 2011)

(g) "The fact that you've got someone exfiltrating information doesn't mean you've got a technical problem", he said (*Washington Post*, 2010)

(h) "The church has gotten it wrong a few times on science", he said (*USA TODAY*, 2015)

(i) We've got flash flood watches and warnings going on as we zoom in here and show you (*NBC*, 2015)

(j) I know I've got skills. I've had maybe 15 almost opportunities, and then each time the project got pulled (*Atlanta Journal Constitution*, 2012)

The main points in this section are summarised below.

KEY POINTS VERBS

- The semantic features of verbs are very wide ranging. Verbs denote actions (*run, swim*), mental processes (*think, wonder*), physical processes (*grow, solidify*), states (*have, be*) and events (*marry, baptise*).
- Semantic features alone cannot be reliably used to identify verbs. To these features we must add morphological and syntactic properties of verbs.

- The morphological features of verbs include inflectional suffixes and derivational suffixes. Inflectional suffixes such as *–ing* (progressive) and *–ed* (past tense) are added to the base of the verb. Derivational suffixes such as *–ate* can be added to nouns to form verbs (*orchestra → orchestrate*), while suffixes like *–able* can be added to verbs to form adjectives (*believe → believable*).
- Syntactic properties of verbs include tense. Tense describes the morphological marking of verbs as present tense or past tense. Verbs which are marked for tense are finite verbs.
- Tense is not the same as time. For example, the simple present tense may be used to refer to future time (e.g. *Sally visits Prague next week*).
- English does not have a future tense. However, there are a number of ways of referring to events in future time in English (e.g. *I will leave tomorrow; Jack is going to visit her*).
- Verbs which are not marked for tense are non-finite verbs. They include the present participle, past participle, infinitive and the bare infinitive. Even if one of these forms appears in a verb string, the entire string is finite if the first verb in the string is finite.
- Auxiliary verbs 'help' the main or lexical verb to convey meaning in a sentence. Unlike lexical verbs, auxiliary verbs cannot occur on their own. They must always be accompanied by a lexical verb, either explicitly or understood. Auxiliary verbs contribute information about the modality, aspect and voice of the sentence.
- Modal auxiliary verbs like *may, will* and *can* express a range of meanings including permission (*You may use my flat*), prediction (*She will be a champion swimmer*) and uncertainty (*They might conclude the deal today*).
- Aspect indicates that the action of a verb is either completed (perfect aspect) or is continuing (progressive aspect). The perfect aspect uses the past participle of the verb (e.g. *She has visited the doctor*). The progressive aspect uses the present participle (e.g. *Mary is crossing the road*).
- A sentence may be active voice (*The dog bit the man*) or passive voice (*The man was bitten by the dog*). To form the passive, the verb *be* is followed by the passive participle and an optional *by*-phrase. The subject in the active sentence moves from pre-verbal position to post-verbal position in the passive sentence. The object in the active sentence moves from post-verbal position to pre-verbal position in the passive sentence.
- The auxiliary verbs *have, be* and *do* can also be lexical verbs. There are five classes of lexical verbs: intransitive; mono-transitive; di-transitive; intensive; and complex transitive.
- Intransitive verbs do not require an object. Mono-transitive verbs require a direct object. Di-transitive verbs require a direct object and an indirect object. Intensive verbs require a subject complement. Complex transitive verbs require a direct object and an object complement.

3.4 Adjectives

Another major word class is adjectives. Adjectives refer to attributes, qualities or characteristics of people and things. They can also convey evaluations or judgements about people and things. In the sentences below, the descriptive function of the adjective is indicated in parentheses:

The dog is *dirty*. [Physical state]
The meal was too *spicy*. [Taste]

The movie was really *good*. [Evaluation]
She found the *square* peg under the sofa. [Shape]
The *tall* building was on fire for hours. [Height]
The *large* parcel was delivered to her door. [Size]
Her *blue* dress went to the cleaners. [Colour]

For the other major word classes, we saw that semantic features alone were not a reliable guide to class membership. The same is true of adjectives. The adjective in the following sentence does not appear to fall under any of the descriptive functions that we have just identified: *She had a* <u>celestial</u> *presence*. Also, one and the same word can be an adjective and a noun. So as well as *She found the* <u>square</u> *peg under the sofa*, the word 'square' can be used as a noun in the sentence *He had four* <u>squares</u> *at the end of the game*. To the semantic features of adjectives we must add morphological features.

3.4.1 Absolute, Comparative and Superlative Adjectives

Most adjectives are gradable and can represent different degrees of a quality or state. So a girl can be *pretty*, or she can be *prettier* than her friend, or she can be the *prettiest* person in her class. The system of inflection for **gradable adjectives** in English is shown in Table 3.11.

To form the comparative and superlative of most adjectives in English, the suffixes *–er* and *–est* are added to the adjective stem. For a number of adjectives, the stem also undergoes some modification. The 'y' in adjectives like *lovely* and *grungy* is changed to 'i' before these endings are added. Other adjectives like *wet* and *big* take an additional consonant letter before the endings are added to the stem. For adjectives that end in 'e' in the **absolute** form, like *fine* and *ripe*, the endings *–r* and *–st* are added to the stem. Aside from regular adjectives, there are a number of irregular adjectives in English which change substantially to form the comparative and superlative. These irregular

TABLE 3.11 Inflection for grade in regular and irregular adjectives

	Absolute	Comparative	Superlative
Regular	poor	poorer	poorest
	lovely	lovelier	loveliest
	fine	finer	finest
	wet	wetter	wettest
Irregular	good	better	best
	bad	worse	worst
	far	farther/further	farthest/furthest
	well (healthy)	better	best

TABLE 3.12 Adjectives which do not inflect for grade

Absolute	Comparative	Superlative
honest (two syllables)	more honest	most honest
trustworthy (three syllables)	more trustworthy	most trustworthy
miraculous (four syllables)	more miraculous	most miraculous
perpendicular (five syllables)	more perpendicular	most perpendicular

adjectives include *good, bad* and *well* (meaning healthy) where there is no similarity between the absolute, comparative and superlative forms. In the irregular adjective *far*, stem modifications involve the addition of consonant letters in *farther/farthest* or a vowel change as well as addition of consonant letters in *further/furthest*.

There is a substantial group of adjectives in English which do not inflect for grade. These adjectives take the degree adverbs *more* and *most* to form the comparative and superlative, respectively. Most of these adjectives contain two or more syllables as the examples in Table 3.12 show. However, there are exceptions to this pattern, with some adjectives of two syllables inflecting for grade rather than using *more/most* (e.g. *luckier/luckiest* rather than *more lucky/most lucky*), although there may be disagreement among speakers about the adjectives where this applies.

The properties denoted by some adjectives in English do not admit of degrees. Accordingly, comparative and superlative forms of these adjectives do not exist. The following sentences contain adjectives of this type:

> *These angles are <u>equal</u>.*
> **This angle is more equal than that angle.*
> *Her actions were <u>illegal</u>.*
> **Her actions were more illegal than his actions.*

Aside from inflectional morphology, adjectives can also be identified on the basis of derivational morphological features. Adjectives are often derived from nouns by means of suffixes such as *–al, –ful* and *–ish* (e.g. *music<u>al</u>; hope<u>ful</u>; freak<u>ish</u>*). Adjectives may also be derived from verbs. Suffixes such as *–able* and *–ible* may be used to identify these adjectives (e.g. *like<u>able</u>; forc<u>ible</u>*).

As one might imagine, absolute, comparative and superlative forms of adjectives can be particularly challenging for young children who are acquiring English as a first language. To illustrate some of the difficulties that can arise during language acquisition, several of Lara's utterances are displayed in Table 3.13. Each utterance contains one of the forms of the adjective *big*. This adjective is used more than any other by young children. The utterances are arranged in chronological age order. The age at which each utterance is produced is indicated in years and months.

TABLE 3.13 Lara's use of the adjective *big*

Age	Lara's utterances
2;03	I've got a bigger poorly toe
2;06	It's much bigger
2;10	That's the biggest
2;10	Make it even more bigger
2;10	She can go up the steps when she's big, can't she?
3;00	You didn't make it very bigger, did you?
3;00	Josh is getting bigger
3;01	That one's bigger and that one's little

Lara is clearly able to use the comparative and superlative forms of the adjective *big* correctly on some occasions. At 3 years of age, she produced *Josh is getting bigger* (comparative) and at 2 years 10 months she uttered *That's the biggest* (superlative). However, there are also several errors in the use of these forms at this stage in Lara's language development. One of these errors is the use of the comparative adjective *bigger* when the absolute form of the adjective is required. This can be seen in the following utterances:

> You didn't make it very bigger [*big*], did you?
> That one's bigger [*big*] and that one's little

The converse error also occurs when Lara uses the absolute form of the adjective in place of the comparative form. This can be seen in the following utterance:

> She can go up the steps when she's big [*bigger*], can't she?

Lara also displays an error when she uses the degree adverb *more* in the utterance *Make it even more bigger*. This is because *big* is an adjective which inflects for grade. The suffix –*er* is alone sufficient to mark the comparative form of the adjective. Lara is aware, however, that the adverb *much* can appear before the comparative adjective in *It's much bigger*. In Lara's remaining utterance – *I've got a bigger poorly toe* – the comparative *bigger* has been used in place of the absolute form of the adjective *big*. If Lara had been attempting to say *I've got a poorly big toe*, we could add that the adjective has been used in the incorrect position in the noun phrase.

3.4.2 Attributive and Predicative Adjectives

The position of adjectives in a noun phrase leads us into a discussion of the syntactic properties of adjectives. Adjectives can be used attributively (**attributive adjective**) or predicatively (**predicative adjective**). When an adjective comes before the noun it modifies, it is used attributively. In *selfish person* and *incredible story*, the adjectives *selfish* and *incredible* are used attributively. Adjectives can also follow verbs in sentences. When this occurs, they are said to be used predicatively. In the following sentences, *selfish* and *incredible* are used predicatively:

> Tom and Mary are selfish.
> The story was truly incredible.

The large majority of adjectives in English are like *selfish* and *incredible* in that they can be used attributively and predicatively. However, there are some adjectives which can only be used attributively (e.g. *entire*) and others which can only be used predicatively (e.g. *aware*):

> His entire life was a disappointment.
> *His life was entire.
> The man was aware of his error.
> *The aware man made an error.

3.4.3 Words Before and After Adjectives

Certain words can precede and follow adjectives. Adjectives which denote properties that involve degrees can be preceded by **intensifying expressions**. Examples of these expressions are shown in the following sentences:

> He was <u>really</u> exhausted after the fight.
> Jan was <u>so</u> tired that she fell asleep.
> Michael was <u>very</u> pleased with the football result.
> The teacher was <u>extremely</u> frustrated by the pupil's progress.
> The situation was <u>too</u> unpleasant to contemplate.

Even adjectives which do not denote properties that involve degrees can take intensifying expressions under certain circumstances. Sentences like the following will be familiar to you from everyday language use:

> I was <u>really</u> dead on my feet after the interview.
> His version of events was <u>so</u> true.

As well as degree adverbs like *very* and *really*, a range of other adverbs can precede adjectives. Examples of these adverbs are used in the following sentences:

> His behaviour was <u>socially</u> unacceptable.
> The court judged his actions to be <u>legally</u> indefensible.
> His position on the issue was <u>logically</u> unsound.

Certain words and constructions can also follow adjectives. They include prepositional phrases, adverbs and clauses. Clauses may be introduced by a comparative adjective, contain a *to*-infinitive or take the form of a *that*-clause:

> Mary was very unwell <u>during her holiday.</u> [Prepositional phrase]
> Mark's exam result was good <u>enough</u> to get into college. [Adverb]

> *The oil painting was more expensive <u>than she had imagined</u>.* [Comparative adjective]
>
> *He was angry <u>that his shirt was stained</u>.* [*That*-clause]
>
> *She was too afraid <u>to leave the building</u>.* [*To*-infinitive]

What is the post-modifier of the adjective in the following sentence?

> "I am really keen to stay on board with New Zealand Rugby" (*The Dominion Post*, 2017)

3.4.4 Post-Positive Adjectives

Above, we said that an adjective stands in front of the noun that it modifies in a noun phrase (e.g. *old woman*). There are occasions, however, when an adjective can occur after the noun in a noun phrase. Examples of so-called **post-positive adjectives** include *princess <u>royal</u>, governor <u>general</u>* and *times <u>past</u>*. Post-positive adjectives must be used when it is a pronoun that is modified:

> *There is <u>something rotten</u> in British politics.*
>
> *<u>Someone more experienced</u> would have rejected that proposal.*

Post-positive adjectives are often used in the titles of films and books to achieve salience. Examples include *Mission Impossible*, an action spy film produced by and starring Tom Cruise, and *Murder Most Foul*, one of the Miss Marple detective stories written by Agatha Christie.

   To give you further practice of working with adjectives, you should now attempt Exercise 3.7.

EXERCISE 3.7 LARA AND THE ADJECTIVE *BIG*

This exercise will give you further practice in describing some of Lara's utterances which use the adjective *big*. Each utterance has been chosen because one or more words appear alongside *big*. In a group or individually, examine each utterance. Then characterise how Lara uses the adjective *big* in each case.

(a) Have the big plate (2;10)

(b) Lara's not very big enough (2;09)

(c) It's too big (3;02)

(d) You're a great big pain in the bum (3;03)

(e) Let me do a big really big (2;08)

(f) Can I have a big bouncy yet? (3;00)

(g) Shall I show you how I make a big long field? (3;03)

(h) Is the blue one bigger? (2;07)

(i) All the big bits go here (3;03)

(j) Nice big strong chair (3;02)

The main points in this section are summarised below.

KEY POINTS ADJECTIVES

- Adjectives denote a wide range of properties, attributes, qualities and judgements. The semantic properties of adjectives are not sufficient to determine class membership and must be supplemented by morphological and syntactic properties.
- Many adjectives are gradable in that they permit different degrees of a state or attribute. The inflectional suffixes –er and –est are used to form the comparative and superlative forms of most gradable adjectives in English. Irregular adjectives like *good* and *bad* do not follow this pattern (*gooder/goodest* and *badder/baddest*).
- Many gradable adjectives of two syllables or more do not inflect for grade. To form the comparative and superlative forms of these adjectives, the degree adverbs *more* and *most* are used (e.g. *more despicable/most despicable*).
- Adjectives like *dead* and *pregnant* do not denote states or properties which admit of degrees. Accordingly, there are no comparative and superlative forms of these adjectives.
- Derivational morphology can also be used to identify adjectives. Adjectives can be derived from verbs through the addition of suffixes like –able (*translatable*) and –ible (*suggestible*). Also, adjectives can be derived from nouns through the use of suffixes like –al (*maniacal*), –ful (*truthful*) and –ish (*hawkish*).
- Most adjectives can be used attributively and predicatively. An adjective used attributively precedes the noun it modifies (e.g. *the happy child*). An adjective used predicatively comes after a verb (e.g. *The child is happy*). Some *adjectives* can only be used either attributively or predicatively.
- Degree adjectives can have adverbs known as intensifiers as modifiers (e.g. *really sad; extremely unpopular*). Other adverbs can also modify adjectives (e.g. *sexually explicit; financially prohibitive*).
- Certain words and constructions can follow adjectives. They include prepositional phrases (*afraid of the dark*), adverbs (*good enough*) and clauses (*angry that the bus had departed*).
- Some adjectives follow the noun in noun phrases (e.g. *princess royal*). Post-positive adjectives must be used with pronouns (e.g. *something strange*).

3.5 Adverbs

3.5.1 Function and Meaning of Adverbs

The class of adverbs is difficult to define in terms of its semantic features. Many adverbs modify verbs and express information related to the time, place, direction, manner and frequency of an action. Examples include the underlined words in the following sentences:

> *Paul and Ellie arrived early.* [Time]
> *They went abroad last year.* [Place]
> *Mark visited his grandmother regularly.* [Frequency]
> *She skipped cheerfully down the street.* [Manner]
> *He went away this morning.* [Direction]

However, adverbs do more than modify verbs. We saw in Section 3.4 that they can also modify adjectives. Adverbs which modify adjectives are in some respects semantically empty. Their function is to intensify the particular property denoted by the adjective. Examples of these adverbs are shown below:

> She was _very_ upset about the decision.
> They were _extremely_ rude to the bus conductor.
> Mike was _too_ tired to play football.

Adverbs like _however, moreover_ and _nevertheless_ function as sentence connectors and express meanings such as 'in addition' and 'in spite of':

> She wanted the job. _However,_ she was not prepared to leave home.
> The plans were uneconomical. _Moreover,_ they violated state laws.
> He sprained his ankle. _Nevertheless,_ he won the race.

Other adverbs have an overtly grammatical function and express little in the way of meaning. These adverbs include words like _more_ and _most_ which are used to form the comparative and superlative forms of adjectives and adverbs. The following sentences illustrate the use of these adverbs:

> The exam was _more_ difficult than she had expected. [Comparative adjective]
> The exam was the _most_ difficult one she had ever done. [Superlative adjective]
> She ran _more_ quickly on the second day of the competition. [Comparative adverb]
> She ran _most_ quickly on the second day of the competition. [Superlative adverb]

Many adverbs can be used to express the attitude of a speaker or to achieve emphasis. This is demonstrated by the examples below:

> _Unbelievably_ he displayed no remorse for his crimes. [Attitude]
> _Foolishly_ she gave him the money. [Attitude]
> That is _definitely_ a mistake. [Emphasis]

3.5.2 Morphological Features of Adverbs

Morphological features are not as helpful in deciding class membership for adverbs as they are for other word classes. In terms of inflectional morphology, adverbs can inflect for grade, e.g. _quickly – quicklier – quickliest_. However, most adverbs use _more_ and _most_ to form comparative and superlative forms, e.g. _more slowly/most slowly_. Like adjectives, there are some adverbs in English which have irregular comparative and superlative forms, e.g. _badly – worse – worst_. In terms of derivational morphology, many adverbs are formed by adding the suffix _–ly_ to an adjective, e.g. _loving + –ly → lovingly_. However, there are many adverbs in English which cannot be identified by means of this suffix, e.g. _quite, often_ and _soon_. Also, if the presence of the suffix _–ly_ is somewhat blindly applied, there are a number of adjectives in English which will be incorrectly identified as adverbs, e.g. _lovely,_ *ghastly* and *wily*. Some other suffixes commonly used in adverbs are *–ways, –wise* and *–wards*. You should also be aware of some variation in the use of these suffixes in varieties of English other than British English. For example, the suffix *–ward* is used to form adverbs in the following sentences in American English:

> *If within five feet, a flyaway barrier would be required so honey bees fly upward and away from neighboring properties. (The Detroit News, 2017)*
> *Remember all the hand wringing afterward how he [Trump] had embraced a false equivalence? (Miami Herald, 2017)*

Now it is your turn to get practice of working with the derivational morphology of adverbs by attempting Exercise 3.8.

EXERCISE 3.8 DERIVATIONAL MORPHOLOGY OF ADVERBS

Turn each of the words below into an adverb, using one of the following derivational suffixes: *–ly; –wards; –ways; –wise*

(a) proper
(b) out
(c) other
(d) hopeful
(e) sky
(f) happy
(g) left
(h) south
(i) length
(j) like
(k) special
(l) end
(m) pleasant
(n) back
(o) edge
(p) ready
(q) clock
(r) front
(s) after
(t) crab

3.5.3 Words Before and After Adverbs

We have already described most of the syntactic properties of adverbs. Adverbs can modify verbs as in *run quickly* and *sing beautifully*. They can also modify adjectives as in *wonderfully eccentric* and *emotionally unstable*. The adverbs in these examples convey meaning. Other adverbs which modify adjectives convey little meaning and are used to intensify an adjective, e.g. _really_ _tired_. Certain adverbs may also modify other adverbs. In the following sentences, the underlined adverb modifies the adverb that immediately follows it:

> _Rather_ stupidly she left the children alone in the house.
> He was _very_ quickly removed from the guest list.
> He exited the room _too_ hurriedly.

However, not every adverb can be modified by an adverb. For example, sentence connectors like _however_ and _nevertheless_ cannot take any modifiers. Finally, a prepositional phrase may be used alongside certain adverbs, as in the following sentences:

> Bizarrely _on this occasion,_ the fusion of chilli and lime seemed to work.
> Dangerously _under the influence,_ he drove at top speed through the town.

3.5.4 Real-World Uses of Adverbs

To get practice in identifying adverbs, let us look at some of Lara's utterances. These utterances were produced in a 7-month period between 2;06 years and 3;01 years. The utterances are displayed in Table 3.14 in chronological age order. Where possible, the target form which Lara has not used is shown in parentheses.

Lara displays several types of errors in her use of adverbs. On two occasions, she omits an obligatory adverb. The adverb _away_ is omitted in _Because he's mummy a long way_. The degree adverb _more_ is omitted in _This is even wobbly_ where its function is to modify the adjective _wobbly_. On other occasions, Lara uses an adverb but selects the wrong one. In the question _Is that the wrong way out?_, Lara uses the adverb _out_ instead of _round_. Sometimes Lara uses adverbs when it is adjectives that are required. This can be seen in the utterances _We have to be quietly_ and _You need_

TABLE 3.14 Lara's use of utterances containing adverbs

Age	Lara's utterances
2;06	It's offed [off] already
2;09	Lara's not very big enough
2;10	We have to be quietly [quiet]
2;10	Daddy's just only got one
2;10	Because he's mummy's a long way [away]
2;10	This is even [more] wobbly
2;11	You done it not nice [You haven't done it nicely]
3;00	There wasn't any [very] much left
3;00	Is that the wrong way out [round]?
3;01	You need the normally [normal] bricks

the normally bricks where the adverbs *quietly* and *normally* are used in place of *quiet* and *normal*, respectively. The opposite error occurs in *You done it not nice*. In this utterance, Lara uses the adjective *nice* in place of the adverb *nicely*. On two further occasions, adverbs are used when they are not required. This occurs in *Daddy's just only got one* where one of the adverbs *just* and *only* can be omitted. It also occurs in the utterance *Lara's not very big enough* where the intensifying adverb *very* should be omitted, leaving only the post-modifying adverb *enough*. In *There wasn't any much left*, Lara uses the pronoun *any* which appears to take the place of the adverb *very*. Finally, there is the slightly strange use of the adverb *off* in the utterance *It's offed already*. Lara appears to add a past tense verb ending onto this adverb. This may occur because she is referring to an event in past time – the television is *already* off.

Like other major word classes, adverbs are often used in interesting ways by speakers of non-standard dialects. Speakers of the Geordie dialect, for example, may omit the suffix *–ly* in adverbs. These speakers do not use adverbs like *really* and *very* to modify adjectives either. These non-standard forms are illustrated by the examples below:

Zero adverbial marker
'didn't know you were doing it, yeah, you used to just do it **automatic**'

Non-standard modifiers of adjectives
'mean I'm lucky, I've been lucky – **dead** lucky!'
'she said she was **fair** sick of looking for these cows'
'and it was **real** nice in the woods'

The main points in this section are summarised below.

KEY POINTS ADVERBS

- Adverbs vary considerably in the type and amount of meaning that they convey. When used to modify verbs, adverbs can express meanings such as manner (*clap enthusiastically*), direction (*run away*), time (*leave now*) and place (*live here*). When used to modify adjectives, some adverbs convey little meaning and serve only to intensify an adjective (*really tired*), while other adverbs add meaning to the adjective (*morally repugnant*).
- In terms of inflectional morphology, the comparative and superlative forms of gradable adverbs can take the suffixes *–er* and *–est* (*quickly – quicklier – quickliest*). There is often modification of the stem to which these endings are added (e.g. 'y' changes to 'i'). Alternatively, *more* and *most* can be used to form the comparative and superlative forms of adverbs (*honestly – more honestly – most honestly*). Irregular adverbs follow neither of these patterns (*well – better – best*).
- In terms of derivational morphology, adverbs are often derived from adjectives through the addition of the suffix *–ly* (*productive – productively; restful – restfully*). Adverbs can also

be derived from nouns through the use of the suffixes –*wards* (*skywards*), –*wise* (*crabwise*) and –*ways* (*sideways*).

- In terms of their syntactic features, adverbs may modify verbs (*chanted repeatedly*), adjectives (*blissfully unaware*) and other adverbs (*very deliberately unpleasant*). Adverbs like *however* and *nevertheless*, which function as sentence connectors, cannot take modifiers.

SUMMARY

In this chapter you have seen the following:

- The class of a word can often be identified using a combination of morphological, semantic and syntactic criteria.
- Words can be distinguished on the basis of whether they contribute meaning to a sentence (content word) or have a grammatical role in a sentence (function word).
- Nouns can be common or proper (*boy* – *Mike*), count or non-count (*table* – *furniture*), concrete or abstract (*book* – *love*) and collective (*committee, staff*).
- Pronouns can take the place of noun phrases in sentences and can be possessive (*The car is his*), demonstrative (*This is filthy*), reflexive (*She bathed herself*), reciprocal (*They hate each other*), interrogative (*Who ate the cake?*), indefinite (*Somebody called the police*) and relative (*The book which you recommended was disappointing*).
- Verbs can be finite (*The prisoner escaped*) and non-finite (*Playing cards is boring*). There are also auxiliary verbs (*The man is cutting the cake*) and lexical verbs (*The man is cutting the cake*). Verbs can be distinguished according to the grammatical parts that follow them. For example, a di-transitive verb takes a direct object and an indirect object (*She gave him the keys*).
- Adjectives denote properties, qualities, attributes and judgements. They may inflect for grade (*taller* – *tallest*) or use *more* and *most* to form the comparative and superlative (*more horrible* – *most horrible*). Adjectives may be attributive (*The ferocious dog barked loudly*) or predicative (*The dog is ferocious*). There are a small number of post-positive adjectives in English (*The Surgeon General issued health advice*).
- Adverbs have several functions. They can modify verbs and express meanings such as time (*leaves today*), manner (*works hard*) and place (*lives here*). They can function as intensifiers (*very tired*). Some adverbs like *however* and *moreover* function as sentence connectors. Many adverbs inflect for grade (*quicklier* – *quickliest*) while some use *more* and *most* to form the comparative and superlative (*more recently* – *most recently*).

WEBSITE MAJOR WORD CLASSES

After reading the chapter, visit the website and test your knowledge of major word classes by answering the multiple-choice questions for this topic.

HOMEWORK ASSIGNMENT

This assignment has two parts and will require you to access the Electronic World Atlas of Varieties of English at: http://ewave-atlas.org

PART A: In this chapter, we have seen how in Standard English negation is marked on the auxiliary verb and the negative particle is reduced (e.g. *I* haven't *got anybody in the house*). A fully articulated negative particle is used in dialects in the North of England and in Scotland. Moreover, it is not attached to the auxiliary verb so that a form like *I've not* is used in place of *I haven't*. Find other examples of dialects which do not follow the pattern of Standard English.

PART B: We have also seen how in Standard English the dummy auxiliary *do* must be introduced to achieve negation and to form an interrogative of a clause that contains the lexical verb *have* (e.g. *He* doesn't *have any money;* Did *you have a party?*). However, outside of Standard English, the dummy auxiliary *do* is not always used to achieve negation of a clause which contains the lexical verb *have*. Speakers in northern England and Scotland do not use *do* in this context, as the following example illustrates: 'if you wanted to go to college or you wanted to go to university you couldn't if you **hadn't** the money'. Younger speakers particularly in Southern England are more likely to use the dummy auxiliary when the negative particle is used with *have*: 'if you **didn't have** the money'. Find other examples of dialects which do not follow the pattern of Standard English.

SUGGESTIONS FOR FURTHER READING

(1) Altenberg, E. P. and Vago, R. M. (2010) *English Grammar: Understanding the Basics*. New York: Cambridge University Press.
   This volume provides an accessible discussion of the major word classes in four units: unit 1 (Nouns), unit 2 (Verbs), unit 4 (Adjectives) and unit 8 (Adverbs). Each unit has a number of *Test Yourself* questions with answers which will give you further practice in working with these word classes.
(2) Payne, T. E. (2006) *Exploring Language Structure: A Student's Guide*. Cambridge: Cambridge University Press.
   Chapter 4 in this book examines nouns, verbs, adjectives and adverbs. The author defines the major word classes based on syntactic distribution and morphological form. There is also discussion of the semantic concepts expressed by each word class.
(3) Huddleston, R. and Pullum, G. K. (2005) *A Student's Introduction to English Grammar*. New York: Cambridge University Press.

The authors examine the major word classes in three accessible chapters: chapter 3 (verbs, tense, aspect and mood), chapter 5 (nouns and noun phrases), and chapter 6 (adjectives and adverbs).

QUESTIONS MAJOR WORD CLASSES

(1) For each of the following sentences (i) identify the italicised noun as *concrete* or *abstract* and *count* or *non-count*, and (ii) identify the underlined noun as *common* or *proper*.

(a) <u>John</u> has lots of *love*.

(b) The <u>horticulturalist</u> has produced a new *grass*.

(c) <u>France</u> produces a lot of *wines*.

(d) The *grass* was cut last <u>weekend</u>.

(e) *Bread* made by the <u>Smith</u> family is very high quality.

(f) The business <u>men</u> lacked *trust* in each other.

(g) In <u>Spain</u>, a lot of *wine* is produced.

(h) The market <u>stall</u> had a wide selection of *breads* for sale.

(i) <u>Bill</u> has lots of *loves*.

(j) The *trusts* were opened in her <u>name</u>.

(2) Lara produced a wide range of errors when she attempted to use possessive pronouns. These errors were described in detail in Section 3.2. Some more of Lara's utterances are shown below. Characterise the personal pronoun error in each utterance. Which of these 'errors' may actually be a feature of Lara's dialect?

(a) They had they dinner (2;10)

(b) My want to put it on (2;02)

(c) Where's me hat? (2;10)

(d) You turn (2;07)

(e) I getting me socks? (2;08)

(f) I broke me road (2;09)

(g) That's you car (2;01)

(h) Me turn (2;08)

(i) But he mouth rubbed off (2;09)

(j) They at they stables (2;09)

(3) The following utterances were produced by Lara when she was 3 years and 2 months old. Each utterance contains a mono-transitive verb which is followed by an object clause. Identify the clause in each utterance, and state if it is a *to*-infinitive or a *that*-clause.

(a) I don't think I will need these.

(b) I want to see some donkeys at the zoo.

(c) That bit says she can play with it.

(d) You've got to stay still.

(e) Do you think your baby's still hungry?

(f) I'll try to do a wee wee.

(g) She's got to have a hat on.

(h) I think that goes there.

(i) You remember you have to tell daddy.

(j) Do you want to come to our picnic one day?

(4) Part A: Add a suffix to each of the following words to form an adjective:

(a) road

(b) sheep

(c) poet

(d) loathe

(e) coward

(f) care

(g) shock

(h) professor

(i) curl

(j) harm

(k) sea

(l) psychology

Part B: For each of the following sentences, indicate if the adjective is *attributive* or *predicative*.

(a) The old house sold within a month.

(b) Dolphins are graceful.

(c) The picture was almost certainly from the classical period.

(d) At the time of its demolition, the bridge was unsafe.

(e) An opportunistic infection killed the patient.

(5) Identify the words in italics in the following sentences as either *adjectives* or *adverbs*. What do these sentences demonstrate?

(a) Chomsky's *early* writing is influential.

(b) Sally found the *round* peg under the sofa.

(c) He arrived *late* for dinner.

(d) He drives too *fast* in town.

(e) This is a *hard* module.

(f) He left *early* to catch the train.

(g) His *late* aunt was greatly missed.

(h) She looked *round* and saw the attacker.

(i) The *fast* car sped through the streets.

(j) He studies *hard* all year.

(6) At 3 years of age, Lara is using a wide range of adverbs in her expressive language. Several of Lara's utterances are shown below. Examine each utterance and identify the adverb(s) it contains. Using these utterances, give two examples of an adverb that expresses the following meanings: *direction; place; time* and *manner*.

(a) When he come home.

(b) I will put the ends together.

(c) Pick that bit up quickly.

(d) Monster hasn't gone yet.

(e) I'm just riding.

(f) Can we put that way round?

(g) Amy can play with my field now.

(h) Can you pick it up?

(i) It fell down there.

(j) Jigsaw in here.

REVISION MAJOR WORD CLASSES

(1) Identify the noun in the following sentences. Classify the noun in each case as (i) a thing, (ii) a person, (iii) a place or (iv) a concept.

(a) I have found a wallet.

(b) Who has seen my new pen?

(c) Children are not scary.

(d) There was happiness everywhere.

(e) I have been to town.

(f) They went home early.

(g) The problem is sure to go away.

(h) I can see the girls.

(i) He looked at me with horror.

(j) The house was abandoned.

(2) Identify the auxiliary verbs and main verbs in the following sentences.

(a) My watch has been running slowly.

(b) I won't be going to the party.

(c) I anticipate a very promising future.

(d) She must have left by now.

(e) I shall have a drink of milk.

(f) My glass is empty.

(g) They couldn't fix the boiler.

(h) I do wish you would stay.

(i) Do you know what he said?

(j) I have found the book.

(3) Identify the main (or lexical) verbs and auxiliary verbs in the parts in italics in the following extract.

The farmers *had known* for some days that the weather *could change*. They *had been working* frantically when suddenly the skies *opened*. Many days of hard labour *were disappearing* before their eyes. Their distress *was* all the greater given that last year's crop *had met* a similar fate. Surely now *was* the time for a change of tactic. If maize *had been* difficult to *cultivate*, perhaps barley *would improve* their fortunes.

(4) Using the terms *place, time, manner* and *direction*, describe the meaning expressed by the adverbs in italics in the following sentences.

(a) She yelled *frantically* at the intruder.

(b) John is leaving *now*.

(c) She lived *there* for many years.

(d) He shouted that he was going *home*.

(e) They wandered *aimlessly* through the forest.

(5) Using the following sentences, give *one* example of each of the grammatical categories in (a) to (e) below.

Bill was the smartest boy in the school.

She went abroad in search of love.

The students are always using her butter.

(a) lexical verb

(b) auxiliary verb

(c) proper noun

(d) common noun

(e) concrete noun

(6) Construct comparative and superlative forms of the following adjectives:

(a) tasty

(b) bad

(c) reliable

(d) small

(e) good

(7) For each of the following sentences, (i) identify the adverb used, and (ii) describe the meaning expressed by each adverb.

(a) The students are working most diligently this year.

(b) "Where is your exercise book?" shouted the teacher.

(c) The wedding guests have already arrived.

(d) "When should we leave?" asked Fran.

(e) She's living locally until she buys a car.

(f) "How did you sleep?" the nurse asked the patient.

(8) Each of the following sentences contains an adjective. For each sentence, (i) identify the adjective, and (ii) indicate if the adjective is attributive or predicative:

(a) He had endless admiration for her.

(b) This decision may have unforeseen consequences.

(c) The damage to the vase was irreparable.

(d) The excavation revealed items of historical significance.

(e) As a musician, he was particularly precocious.

(9) Each of the following sentences contains one or more pronouns. For each sentence, (i) identify the pronoun(s), and (ii) label each pronoun as *possessive, personal, demonstrative, reflexive, reciprocal, interrogative* or *indefinite*.

(a) My gift is more expensive than yours.

(b) This is not a good idea.

(c) She locked herself out of the house.

(d) Does anyone want more cake?

(e) Bill and Susie never trusted each other.

(f) Who left the dirty dishes in the sink?

(g) Mark found something under the stairs.

(h) The man who lives above the shop is a doctor.

(i) Nobody likes Jane.

(j) They saw one another for the last time.

(10) What types of lexical verbs are contained in the following sentences?

(a) Joyce gave Bill twenty pounds for the vase.

(b) Jack smiled menacingly.

(c) Nigel thumped the desk in rage.

(d) They elected Trump president.

(e) Max choked on a fish bone.

(11) Construct comparative and superlative forms of the following adverbs:

(a) quickly

(b) forcefully

(c) fast

(d) recently

(e) far

(12) Identify the aspect of the verbs in the sentences in Part A, and the voice of the verbs in the sentences in Part B.

Part A

(a) Sally is sewing the button onto the shirt.

(b) Mike had been ill for several months.

(c) Jane had been living alone.

(d) She has been absent from work.

(e) The scouts were building a camp fire.

(f) The boys have been threatening the elderly man.

(g) They have been camping for many weeks.

(h) Frank was watching a film.

(i) The boss has been unbearable all morning.

(j) He had crashed the car in France.

(k) Sarah is working in town.

(l) The children were planning their adventure all week.

(m) She has been misbehaving all day.

(n) Tom is flying abroad.

(o) The prisoner had escaped for the third time.

(p) She has bought too much.

Part B

(a) The girl is painting the wall.

(b) The pigeon was attacked by the cat.

(c) The police officer is being threatened.

(d) The child kicked the ball.

(e) The race was won by Fred.

(f) I brushed the path.

(g) The actor was roundly criticised by a critic.

(h) He is preparing a meal.

4 Minor Word Classes

LEARNING OBJECTIVES

By the end of this chapter you will be able to do the following:

- Identify members of the three minor word classes: determiner, preposition and conjunction.
- Understand that determiners, prepositions and conjunctions are function words which play a grammatical role in the sentence.
- Identify the determiners that come before the noun in a noun phrase and the order in which they occur. They include definite and indefinite articles, quantity words, cardinal and ordinal numerals, and possessive and demonstrative determiners.
- Recognise single-word, two-word and three-word prepositions and be able to identify the meanings they express.
- Recognise coordinating and subordinating conjunctions and the grammatical parts (clauses, nouns, etc.) that they link.

4.1 Introduction to Minor Word Classes

The major word classes of nouns, verbs, adjectives and adverbs can do little grammatical work in the absence of minor word classes. The three minor word classes are determiners, prepositions and conjunctions. The words in these classes convey less meaning than the content words in the major word classes. There are also fewer of them – you can exhaust the prepositions that you know much more quickly than the nouns that you know. Minor word classes have a closed membership. To demonstrate this, ask yourself how many new words have joined the class of prepositions in the time it has taken words like *sexting, blog* and *Twitter* to be added to the class of nouns. The answer is 'none'. Semantic, morphological and syntactic properties were called upon to identify words in the major word classes. These properties were not reliable guides to class membership in all cases, but they still worked for the most part. When it comes to minor word classes, some of these same properties do not get us very far at all. For example, prepositions do not display the inflectional and derivational morphological features that allowed us to identify adjectives and adverbs. And while prepositions such as *during* and *under* express meanings of time and place, respectively, so too do words like *now* and *here* which are adverbs. Semantic properties of the minor word classes will only take us part of the way to identifying class membership of a word. It will become evident that we must rely more than ever on syntactic properties to help us identify members of the minor word classes.

In Chapter 3, discussion of the major word classes was facilitated by examining grammatical features of non-standard dialects. We also considered the errors of two young, typically developing children (Lara and Ella) who were acquiring the nouns, verbs, adjectives and adverbs of English. Some errors of children with specific language impairment were also examined. We will return to these same language users during the discussion of determiners, prepositions and conjunctions in this chapter. The minor word classes can tax young children and children with language disorders on account of the grammatical complexity that they represent. Determiners, prepositions and conjunctions are the small function words of language that link words, phrases and clauses together. When these words are missing from a child's linguistic repertoire, the mean length of utterance is reduced and with it the complexity of the ideas that a child can communicate. The same is true of adults with language disorders. In adults with agrammatic aphasia, function words like determiners, prepositions and conjunctions are often lost. The retention of content words such as nouns and verbs allows these speakers to maintain some degree of meaningful communication notwithstanding the telegrammatic nature of their language. Still, the absence of function words places a significant burden on the hearer who must decide how grammatically isolated nouns and verbs are supposed to relate to each other. The language of clients with this type of aphasia very forcefully illustrates the grammatical significance of function words, and will be examined in this chapter.

4.2 Determiners

Determiners are a group of little function words which come before the noun in a noun phrase. Their function is to convey further information about the noun such as quantity and number. Some noun phrases with their determiners are underlined in the following sentences:

She locked <u>the door</u> behind her. [Definite article]
They watched <u>a burglar</u> enter the building. [Indefinite article]
The delay added <u>several hours</u> to her trip. [Quantity word]
Jane has <u>two dogs</u> at home. [Cardinal numeral]
Mike won <u>first prize</u> for his marigolds. [Ordinal numeral]
Jack sold <u>his swimming pool</u>. [Possessive determiner]
Frank wants <u>those pots</u> to be moved. [Demonstrative determiner]

4.2.1 Definite and Indefinite Articles

Let us take each determiner in turn. The definite article (*the*) and the indefinite article (*a/an*) signal a difference in the knowledge that is shared between speakers/writers and hearers/readers. Use of the definite article indicates that the person or object denoted by the noun is known to the hearer. In the utterance *The bus shelter was vandalised*, use of the definite noun phrase *the bus shelter* indicates that the hearer knows the particular shelter to which the speaker refers. However, if the speaker says *The teenager vandalised a bus shelter*, there is no expectation on the part of the speaker that the location and identity of the bus shelter will be known to the hearer. This lack of shared knowledge is expressed by the use of the indefinite article *a*. Once the bus shelter becomes part of shared discourse between the speaker and hearer, the speaker may refer to it subsequently using the definite article. For example, the speaker may go on to say *The teenager received community work for damage to the bus shelter*. We can say more about definite and indefinite articles. They can only be used with certain types of nouns. The definite article can be used with singular and plural count nouns as well as non-count nouns:

> She saw <u>the boy</u> on the bus. [Singular count noun]
> She counted <u>the boys</u> on the bus. [Plural count noun]
> She lifted <u>the litter</u> on the bus. [Non-count noun]

However, the indefinite article can only be used with one of these nouns, a singular count noun:

> She ordered *a pizza* in the restaurant. [Singular count noun]
> *She ordered *a pizzas* in the restaurant. [Plural count noun]
> *She ordered *a meat* in the restaurant. [Non-count noun]

The indefinite article in the last two sentences can be replaced by the quantity determiner *some*. Alternatively, the nouns can appear without any determiner:

> She ordered *some pizzas/pizzas* in the restaurant.
> She ordered *some meat/meat* in the restaurant.

In generic noun phrases, the definite article and indefinite article may be used with singular count nouns. However, neither article may appear before plural count nouns and non-count nouns:

> The programme was about the origins of the pizza. [Singular count noun]
> A pizza is a quick, filling meal. [Singular count noun]
> *The/a pizzas keep everyone happy. [Plural count noun]
> *The/a meat can increase your cholesterol. [Non-count noun]

The use of definite and indefinite articles in three varieties of English, Asian and Caribbean English and Hong Kong English, is examined in the following Special Topic.

SPECIAL TOPIC 4.1 ARTICLE USE IN DIFFERENT VARIETIES OF ENGLISH

In our discussion so far, we have described how definite and indefinite articles are used in Standard British English. Other varieties of English use these determiners differently. For example, speakers of Asian English can omit definite and indefinite articles, as the following example illustrates:

> 'and then, uh, there was, uh, no fear of going to an Indian restaurants and sending your suit for a dry-cleaning **[the]** next day, because they were well-ventilated etcetera and I'm, I'm very pleased that Indian food has come **[a]** long way'

Omission of the indefinite article is also a grammatical feature of Caribbean English, as this example illustrates:

> 'in **[a]** couple of days I foun, I got my own, I got a job'

In Hong Kong English, definite and indefinite articles may also not be used in contexts where we would expect to use them in Standard British English. The following examples are taken from an English language newspaper in Hong Kong:

> 'Sustaining multiple injuries, the middle-aged man was rushed to **[the]** Prince of Wales Hospital' (*The Standard*, Hong Kong, 2017)
>
> 'A former local newspaper reporter pleaded not guilty to three counts of access to **[a]** computer with dishonest intent at the Eastern Magistrates' Courts today' (*The Standard*, Hong Kong, 2017)

The use of zero articles in Asian and Caribbean English and Hong Kong English serves as a reminder that the 'rules' for use of the definite and indefinite articles in Standard British English do not apply to other varieties of English.

You have seen that Hong Kong English uses zero articles in contexts where a definite article or an indefinite article would be expected in British English. Where does this grammatical feature occur in the following sentences?

> 'Wang Bo, a 57-year-old woman, faced two charges – one of public servant soliciting an advantage and one of public servant accepting an advantage, the anti-graft agency said' (*The Standard*, Hong Kong, 2017)
>
> '"It is of utmost importance to maintain water security, especially in this age of fluctuating and changing climate", Lam said' (*The Standard*, Hong Kong, 2017)

4.2.2 Numerals and Quantity Words

Numerals are an important group of determiners. However, they can also stand on their own as nouns. Examples of both uses of numerals are shown below:

> *Judy bought the <u>first</u> house she saw.* [Determiner]
> *I have only <u>two</u> cigarettes left.* [Determiner]
> *The local hospital was the <u>first</u> to be closed.* [Noun]
> *The <u>five</u> of them were detained by the police.* [Noun]

When used as nouns, numerals can be preceded by the definite article. They can also be preceded by a numeral as a determiner and take a plural –*s* ending:

> *Three <u>tens</u> are thirty.*

When numerals are used as determiners, they express information about quantity (cardinal numerals) and sequence (**ordinal numerals**) in the noun phrase. Also expressing sequence is a sub-class of ordinals called **general ordinals**. These ordinals are not related to numbers and include words like *next, last* and *previous:*

> *Her <u>last</u> boyfriend was a complete disaster.*
> *A reference was requested of her <u>previous</u> employer.*

Quantity words are a significant group of determiners in the noun phrase. They include the following underlined expressions:

> *<u>Any</u> financial assistance would be welcome.*
> *<u>Both</u> children crossed the road.*
> *<u>Some</u> resistance is to be expected.*
> *<u>Few</u> soldiers wanted to recount their experiences.*
> *She had <u>enough</u> determination for the both of them.*
> *The stocks attracted <u>many</u> investors.*
> *Bill understood <u>all</u> aspects of the problem.*
> *The police encountered <u>several</u> angry protesters.*
> *They listened to <u>neither</u> side of the debate.*
> *She could see <u>no</u> resolution to their current difficulties.*
> *<u>Each</u> term brought a fresh set of challenges.*
> *<u>Every</u> lecturer opposed the new policy.*

4.2.3 Possessive and Demonstrative Determiners

The final determiners introduced above are possessive and demonstrative determiners. We saw in Chapter 3 that possessive pronouns can be determiners in a noun phrase or they can occur independently as full noun phrases:

> *She loves <u>our</u> Norwegian sauna.* [Possessive determiner]
> *We tried to sell <u>ours</u> earlier this year.* [Independent possessive]

The genitive marker (*'s*) which expresses possession or ownership may also be a determiner in a noun phrase. Examples include:

> *Fran's cakes were a gastronomic experience.*
> *The vet examined the dog's leg.*

Like possessives, demonstrative pronouns can be determiners in noun phrases or they can occur independently:

> *Those results are disgraceful.* [Demonstrative determiner]
> *Who left these on the floor?* [Independent demonstrative]

In the second sentence, the use of *these* involves pointing to a referent in the non-linguistic context of the utterance. Whether used independently or as determiners in a noun phrase, demonstratives locate people and objects as either close to the speaker (*this/these*) or at a distance from the speaker (*that/those*).

It is now your turn to get practice of working with determiners by attempting Exercise 4.1.

EXERCISE 4.1 DETERMINERS IN ALZHEIMER'S DEMENTIA

This exercise is designed to give you practice in identifying determiners. The text below is from a 77-year-old man with possible Alzheimer's dementia. He has been asked to describe the cookie theft picture from the Boston Diagnostic Aphasia Examination (Goodglass et al., 2001). Data are from the DementiaBank (Becker et al., 1994). Examine the extract and then answer the questions that follow.

> "The mother and her two children and the children are getting in the cookie jar and she's doing the dishes and spilling the water and she had the spigot on and she didn't know it perhaps and they're looking out into the garden from the kitchen window it's open and the uh cookies must be pretty good they're eating the tair uh the chair is uh tilting and he's gonna fall of and uh the mother's splashing her shoes and stockings all up overflowing the water and there's um uh a window and curtains on the window and I can see some trees outside there and and there's dishes that had been washed and she's drying them and there's some shrub out there and ... "

(a) Give one example of a noun phrase which contains two determiners.
(b) Identify the determiners in the noun phrase that you select in response to (a).
(c) Identify the determiner in the noun phrase *her shoes*.
(d) Which determiner does this client use more than any other in this extract?
(e) Identify two noun phrases which have quantifying expressions as determiners.

4.2.4 Lara's Use of Determiners

Now that the determiners have been introduced, let us see how Lara goes about using them. Several of her utterances that contain determiners are displayed in Table 4.1. Lara's age in years and months is shown in round brackets. Target determiners are indicated in square brackets.

When use of the definite article is required, Lara can make three types of error. She uses the indefinite article with the non-count noun *glue* when a definite article is required. Lara also uses the indefinite article with a plural count noun instead of the definite article. This occurs in *a woods*. Quite often, the definite article is omitted altogether as in the utterance *Got it [the] wrong way round*. Lara's use of the indefinite article can also be problematic. Sometimes, the indefinite article is simply omitted as in the utterance *Is Abi [a] big girl?* The quantity word *some* can take the place of the indefinite article in utterances such as *I want some [a] drink of that*. The opposite error also occurs. In the utterance *Would you like a [some] marble tea?*, the indefinite article is used in place of *some*. These errors are related and to understand them, we need to think about the type of nouns that can have *some* and *a/an* as a determiner. The quantity determiner *some* can be used with plural count nouns and non-count nouns. When Lara uses *some* with *drink*, she has mistakenly taken this noun to be a non-count noun, as it can be in certain sentences (e.g. <u>Drink</u> *completely dominates his life*). Similarly, when Lara uses the indefinite article with *tea*, she has mistakenly taken this noun to be a count noun, as it can be in certain sentences (e.g. *China produces many different* <u>teas</u>). In

TABLE 4.1 Lara's use of determiners

Determiner	Lara's utterances
Definite article	You have a [the] glue after me (2;07) Got it [the] wrong way round (2;08) Can you make a [the] woods? (2;08)
Indefinite article	Is Abi [a] big girl? (2;07) Here's some [a] little bit of yours for you (2;08) I want some [a] drink of that (2;10) Would you like a [some] marble tea? (2;11)
Numeral	Where is my two gloves? (2;07) Where has the two things gone? (2;08) Is it those two [two's] birthday? (2;10)
Quantity	I need more [another] jigsaw (2;08) Have you eaten your dinner all? (2;07) I'm gonna get some lots (2;10) You have them all [all those] marbles (2;11) You go on the another [other] bike (3;00)
Possessive	You wash you [your] back (2;08) He brushed her [his] teeth (2;08) But he [his] leg's come off and he [his] head's come off (2;09)
Demonstrative	We're gonna use these lot [that lot] in a minute (2;07) Are you going to have one of those grey? (3;01)

short, the determiner error in both of these cases is related to Lara's difficulties in distinguishing count from non-count nouns.

In terms of numerals, Lara is able to use cardinal numerals as nouns and as determiners. In the following utterances, Lara uses the cardinal numeral *two* as a noun. This is indicated by the presence of the demonstrative determiners *these* and *those* in front of the numeral:

> *What is these two called?* (2;07)
> *What are those two gonna do?* (2;08)

Numeral determiners are also used by Lara. In the utterance *Where is my two gloves?*, the numeral *two* is preceded by the possessive determiner *my*. In the utterance *Where has the two things gone?*, the numeral *two* is used with the definite article *the*. In both of these utterances, the determiners are correctly sequenced, a point we will return to subsequently. In the utterance *Is it those two [two's] birthday?*, the numeral *two* is a noun. So why is this utterance included in Table 4.1 which displays determiners? The noun *two* is used as a genitive (*two's*) in this utterance and has the function of a possessive determiner. It could as easily appear as a possessive determiner in Table 4.1.

Lara makes extensive use of quantity determiners, albeit not always successfully. The determiner *all* is used in utterances such as the following:

> *Have you eaten your dinner all?* (2;07)
> *You have them all [all those] marbles* (2;11)

In both of these utterances, *all* should appear at the beginning of the noun phrase (e.g. *all your dinner*). However, in *your dinner all* it appears after the head noun. In *them all [all those] marbles*, the quantity word *all* appears after the demonstrative determiner (or at least what should be a demonstrative determiner). Here we see for the first time that Lara is having difficulty in using determiners in the correct order in noun phrases. Occasionally, Lara uses quantity words when they are not required as in the utterance *I'm gonna get <u>some</u> lots*. The quantity word *another* poses some difficulties for Lara. In the utterance *You go on the another [other] bike*, she incorrectly uses *another* in place of the determiner *other*. An interesting error occurs in the utterance *I need more [another] jigsaw*. Lara uses *more* which is also a determiner that expresses quantity. However, this determiner should be followed by a non-count noun (e.g. *more juice*). It cannot be used with the count noun *jigsaw*.

Finally, Lara uses possessive and demonstrative determiners in noun phrases. We saw in Chapter 3 that Lara mistakenly uses subject pronouns in place of possessive determiners. This is again evident in the utterances in Table 4.1, where *you back* and *he leg* is used in place of *your back* and *his leg*, respectively. Even when a possessive determiner is used, it is often the wrong one, e.g. *He brushed her [his] teeth*. In terms of demonstrative determiners, Lara uses a plural demonstrative with a singular noun in *We're gonna use these lot*. In the interrogative *Are you going to have one of those grey?*, a demonstrative determiner is used in the absence of a head noun in the phrase.

4.2.5 Order of Determiners

We saw that when two or more determiners were used in a noun phrase, Lara displayed some difficulty in correctly sequencing these determiners. Determiners cannot occur in front of the noun in any order. There is a strict order on their occurrence as the following sentences illustrate:

> She visited _her two elderly aunts_ regularly.
> *She visited two her elderly aunts regularly.
> *She visited elderly her two aunts regularly.

Determiners are further categorised as pre-determiners, central determiners and post-determiners. **Pre-determiners** express information about quantity in the noun phrase. These determiners include **multiplying expressions** such as _twice_ and _three times_, **fractions** like _half_, and the words _all_ and _both_:

> She earns _three times_ his salary. [Multiplying expression]
> Mike ate _half_ the cake. [Fraction]
> Sally saw _both_ children in the park. [All/both]

There are four **central determiners**. The definite and indefinite articles are the most common central determiners. The other two types of central determiner are possessives and demonstratives. The final category of determiners is **post-determiners**. Here we include cardinal and ordinal numerals, general ordinals such as _previous_ and _next_ and **quantifying expressions** like _many_ and _several_. Central and post-determiners are underlined in the following sentences:

> He still remembered _his first_ love.
> She looked away for _a few_ minutes.

Post-determiners are the only determiners where two can be used together. Both post-determiners are underlined in these sentences:

> His _last two_ relationships ended badly.
> _Few other_ books have captured this sentiment so powerfully.

The different pre-determiners, central determiners and post-determiners are illustrated in Figure 4.1. In the sentence _All his previous proposals were unfeasible_, all three determiner slots are filled. It is much more common for only one or two slots to be filled.

4.2.6 Determiners in Children with Language Disorder

To examine the different categories of determiners in more detail, we will consider their use by young children with specific language impairment (SLI). In Table 4.2, the utterances of children with SLI of different ages are displayed. Some utterances

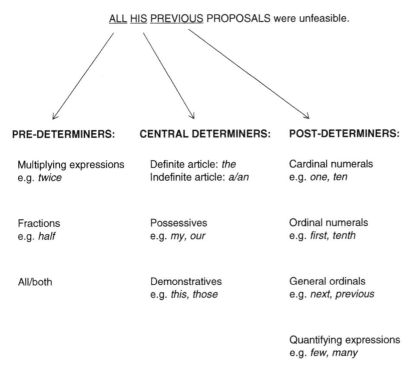

ALL HIS PREVIOUS PROPOSALS were unfeasible.

PRE-DETERMINERS:	CENTRAL DETERMINERS:	POST-DETERMINERS:
Multiplying expressions e.g. *twice*	Definite article: *the* Indefinite article: *a/an*	Cardinal numerals e.g. *one, ten*
Fractions e.g. *half*	Possessives e.g. *my, our*	Ordinal numerals e.g. *first, tenth*
All/both	Demonstratives e.g. *this, those*	General ordinals e.g. *next, previous*
		Quantifying expressions e.g. *few, many*

Figure 4.1 The order of determiners in the noun phrase

reveal considerable **linguistic competence** on the part of these children in the use of determiners. In other utterances, determiners are either omitted or assume an incorrect position in the noun phrase. The utterances are displayed in chronological age order.

Several of these children's utterances contain two determiners. In each case, the determiners are used in the correct order in the noun phrase. In the first sentence below, a central determiner – the definite article *the* – is followed by a post-determiner, the cardinal numeral *two*. The definite article is used with the pre-determiner *all* in the second sentence. In the third sentence, two post-determiners, the quantifying expressions *some* and *more*, are used together. This example illustrates the point made earlier, that post-determiners are the only category of determiner where two may be used alongside each other:

It is like the two guys.
It gots all the way there!
And here is some more balloons.

Several determiner errors are also evident in the utterances in Table 4.2. One of these errors involves placing the determiner after the noun that it modifies. This occurs in *And he grab airplane her*. Often, children with SLI use a single determiner when two determiners are necessary. This occurs in the following

TABLE 4.2 Use of determiners by children with specific language impairment

Gender (Age)	Utterances in SLI
Male (4;06)	And he grab airplane her
Female (4;08)	His tummy was hurting because he eat all food
Female (4;08)	The dog talked to other bunny
Female (5;04)	A more more balloon
Male (5;05)	It is like the two guys
Male (5;05)	It gots all the way there!
Female (5;07)	And here is some more balloons
Female (5;10)	He can do something about this the airplane

sentences where a central determiner, the definite article *the*, is required in each case:

> *His tummy was hurting because he eat all [the] food.*
> *The dog talked to [the] other bunny.*

Sometimes, two determiners are used together incorrectly, such as in the following examples. In the first example, two central determiners – the demonstrative determiner *this* and the definite article *the* – appear together. In the second example, a central determiner (the indefinite article *a*) and a post-determiner (the quantifying expression *more*) occur together:

> *He can do something about this the airplane.*
> *A more more balloon.*

Central and post-determiners can be used together as in the sentence *They located the error after a first inspection of the documents*. The reason the combination of the indefinite article and quantifying expression results in an ungrammatical noun phrase in this case is that *more* can only be used with plural count nouns which the word *balloon* should be in this phrase (*more balloons*). Clearly, the indefinite article cannot be used as a modifier in a noun phrase which has a plural count noun as its head.

You have already seen how different varieties of English use determiners, and particularly definite and indefinite articles, in ways other than those observed in Standard British English. One such variety is Hong Kong English. This is a good point at which to examine the grammatical features of Hong Kong English in more detail. In the following Special Topic, you will see that zero use of definite and indefinite articles in contexts where these articles would be expected to occur in British English is only one way in which the grammars of these two varieties differ from each other.

SPECIAL TOPIC 4.2 GRAMMATICAL FEATURES OF HONG KONG ENGLISH

Hong Kong English (HKE) has a well-established set of grammatical features which set this linguistic variety apart from other varieties of English. In Section 4.2.1, we saw one such feature. This was zero use of definite and indefinite articles in contexts where these articles would be used in Standard British English. An example of this feature is shown below:

'It isn't too late to pass those changes that will increase [the] patients' voice on the Medical Council' (*The Standard*, Hong Kong, 2017)

The converse pattern – use of a definite article where Standard British English would not use an article – is also a common feature of HKE:

'But when we talk about the express railway, it involves a lot of uncertainties like the economic cycle and <u>the</u> population growth and all kinds of stuff' (*The Standard*, Hong Kong, 2017)

Another grammatical feature of HKE is the deletion of 'to' before infinitives, as the following example illustrates:

'The group said although the Social Welfare Department had increased the allowance by 4.3 percent in February, it failed [to] match rent increases' (*The Standard*, Hong Kong, 2017)

Singular nouns in British English can assume a plural form in HKE:

'Lai should be upset, since he had pledged in his <u>heydays</u> he would never sell his media kingdom to anyone' (*The Standard*, Hong Kong, 2017)

Also, where British English uses plural nouns, the suffix -*s* may be omitted from these nouns in HKE. In the second example below, the suffix –*s* occurs in the first use of the noun *account* but is dropped in the second use of this noun:

'A university student claimed that Hong forcibly kissed him and touched his private <u>part</u>' (*The Standard*, Hong Kong, 2017)
  'Through seven local bank <u>accounts</u> and two betting <u>account</u>, the middle-aged man, who has a triad background, and woman allegedly laundered about HK$ 7 million between May 2011 and March 2017' (*The Standard*, Hong Kong, 2017)

Two grammatical features of HKE are illustrated by the following sentence. They are zero-relativisation in subject position (omission of a relative pronoun following a subject noun phrase) and deletion of auxiliary 'be' before a progressive verb:

'The railway [which is] costing a fortune to build is scheduled to be
operational in the third quarter next year' (*The Standard*, Hong Kong, 2017)

Finally, object pronoun drop – the omission of an object pronoun that is infera-
ble from context – is also a feature of HKE. In the following sentence, the object
pronoun 'it', which refers to Beijing's one country, two systems policy towards
Hong Kong, is omitted after the preposition 'about':

'Seizing the opportunity to focus on one country, two systems while Beijing
is still willing to talk about [it] is the wisest move at the end of the day' (*The
Standard*, Hong Kong, 2017)

Other grammatical features of Hong Kong English can be found in the Electronic
World Atlas of Varieties of English at: http://ewave-atlas.org

The main points in this section are summarised below.

KEY POINTS DETERMINERS

- A group of function words in English which come before the noun in a noun phrase and
  convey information such as quantity and number.
- Determiners include the definite and indefinite articles (*the*/*a*/*an*), possessive and
  demonstrative determiners (*my*/*your*/*this*/*those*), cardinal and ordinal numerals
  (*eight*/*tenth*), and quantifying expressions (*several*/*few*).
- Not all determiners can appear before a noun in a noun phrase. For example, the definite
  article can be used with singular and plural count nouns as well as non-count nouns.
  However, the indefinite article can only be used with singular count nouns.
- Numerals are an important group of determiners. Numerals can also be nouns. When
  used as nouns, numerals may take numeral determiners and a plural –s ending (e.g. *Five
  tens are fifty*).
- General ordinals are a sub-class of ordinal numerals. Like ordinal numerals, they convey
  information about sequence, e.g. *next* meeting; *previous* appointment.
- Possessive determiners such as *my* car and *your* house are not the only determiners
  which express possession or ownership. Genitive nouns may also function as possessive
  determiners, e.g. *girl's* party.
- Determiners can be further categorised as pre-determiners, central determiners and
  post-determiners. Pre-determiners include multiplying words like *twice* and fractions
  like *half*. Central determiners include definite and indefinite articles. Post-determiners
  include cardinal and ordinal numerals. Unlike other categories of determiner, two post-
  determiners can occur together, e.g. *She proposed the first two amendments at the meeting.*

4.3 Prepositions

Prepositions are small function words such as *in, during* and *under* which stand in front of nouns in noun phrases. Their function is to relate people, objects and events represented by these noun phrases to each other. For example, in the first sentence below the boys are in a spatial relationship to the road. In the second sentence the driver has a functional relationship to the match in that it is used to light the cigarette:

> The boys are running <u>across</u> the road.
> The lorry driver lit the cigarette <u>with</u> a match.

4.3.1 Meaning of Prepositions

Many prepositions are like *across* in that they are used to express spatial meanings. Other prepositions of this type include the underlined words in the following sentences:

> The vase is <u>on top of</u> the table.
> The dog is <u>under</u> the chair.
> The missing keys were <u>in</u> the box.
> The house is <u>next to</u> the lake.
> The church is <u>beside</u> the ancient burial ground.
> The teacher sat <u>between</u> the boy and the girl.
> The timer is <u>above</u> the cooker.
> They searched <u>below</u> the bed.
> The sign is <u>over</u> the shop door.
> They ran <u>through</u> the fields.
> Jack walked <u>along</u> the river.
> They live <u>near</u> their parents.
> He parked <u>at</u> the train station.

Alongside spatial meanings, prepositions can also convey temporal information. In each of the following sentences, the preposition serves to relate people, things and events in time:

> John lives in Madrid <u>during</u> the winter.
> She left <u>after</u> the main meal.
> Sam arrived <u>before</u> the summer holidays.
> The volcano erupted <u>for</u> a month.

Aside from space and time, prepositions can express a range of other meanings. Some of these meanings are illustrated by the sentences below:

> They travelled to their destination <u>by</u> plane. [Means]
> She broke the window <u>out of</u> badness. [Cause]

> *The house <u>with</u> the outdoor pool is for sale.* [Possession]
> *They walked at speed <u>towards</u> the exit.* [Direction]
> *The police opened the door <u>with force</u>.* [Manner]

It should be noted that the preposition *with* has been used so far with three different meanings: *with a match* (instrument), *with the outdoor pool* (possession) and *with force* (manner). It is not unusual for prepositions to have more than one meaning. For example, the preposition *by* has a different meaning in each of the following sentences. In the first three sentences, *by* has a spatial meaning:

> *They walked <u>by</u> the river on their way home.* [Space: 'along']
> *Heather lived <u>by</u> the sea.* [Space: 'next to']
> *The workmen entered the building <u>by</u> the back door.* [Space: 'through']
> *A ransom was demanded <u>by</u> the hijackers.*
> *The booking was made <u>by</u> telephone.*
> *She was troubled <u>by</u> the reports of violence.*
> *The vase was damaged <u>by</u> accident.*
> *The suppliers received the charter <u>by</u> royal appointment.*

Exercise 4.2 gives you further practice of working with prepositions. You should now attempt this exercise.

EXERCISE 4.2 PREPOSITIONS IN SPECIFIC LANGUAGE IMPAIRMENT

The following utterances are produced by children with specific language impairment (SLI) during a narrative production task. SLI can disrupt many aspects of grammar including the use of prepositions. Examine each utterance and identify the preposition error that it contains. The gender and age of each child is indicated in parentheses. The data are reproduced from the CHILDES database (MacWhinney, 2000).

(a) And he give the thing for the elephant (male: 5;05)
(b) And then that guy gets mad on the elephant (male: 5;05)
(c) They hanged on a balloon (male: 5;05)
(d) He is playing a plane (male: 4;8)
(e) He put it right back on his hands (male: 4;8)
(f) And the elephant slipped over the ground (female: 6;01)
(g) The elephant saw the airplane on the giraffe hand (female: 6;01)
(h) He give it the elephant (male: 5;05)
(i) It is going in the side the water (male: 5;05)
(j) The puppy and the kitty going in the sandbox (female: 5;05)

4.3.2 Simple and Complex Prepositions

Most of the prepositions examined so far are single words and are called **simple prepositions**. Some prepositions are two words (*next to*) and three words (*on top of*). These are called **complex prepositions**. Other two-word and three-word prepositions are underlined in the following sentences:

> *The show was cancelled <u>due to</u> illness.*
> *He felt excluded <u>because of</u> his disability.*
> *They ordered chips <u>in addition to</u> garlic bread.*
> *<u>In spite of</u> setbacks, he succeeded in achieving his goal.*

4.3.3 Words Before and After Prepositions

Prepositions combine with noun phrases to form prepositional phrases. These phrases have an adverbial function. A sentence can have one or more adverbials which answer questions such as *How? When?* and *Where?*:

> *James arrived <u>by car</u> [how?].*
> *James arrived <u>by car</u> [how?] <u>at midnight</u> [when?].*
> *James arrived <u>in Paris</u> [where?] <u>by car</u> [how?] <u>at midnight</u> [when?].*

Apart from noun phrases, prepositions can also be followed by other prepositions (e.g. *They appeared <u>from under the bridge</u>*). Only one modifier can stand in front of a preposition, and that is an adverb:

> *The man jumped <u>right</u> over the bar.*
> *It was <u>just</u> after midnight.*
> *The boys crept <u>back</u> along the tunnel.*

4.3.4 Prepositions in Lara and Ella

Now that we have seen different types of prepositions and the words that can occur with them in sentences, it is time for you to get practice in identifying and describing this word class. We turn once again to our two typically developing children, Lara and Ella, to see examples of prepositions at work. Table 4.3 displays the utterances of both these children. Age in years and months is shown in round brackets. The target or missing preposition in each utterance is indicated in square parentheses.

We will take each of these children's utterances in turn. Lara makes two types of error when she uses prepositions. She often omits prepositions as in *Go [to] bed* and *She can play [with] my blocks*. A range of meanings are expressed by the prepositions that Lara omits. In the following sentences, the prepositions *for* and *at* express meanings of time and space, respectively:

> *I want to play [for] five minutes.*
> *Is this what I got [at] Miranda's party?*

TABLE 4.3 Prepositions in two typically developing children

	Lara's utterances		Ella's utterances
1	I'll go on [under] table (3;00)	16	I wan go [to] park (2;03)
2	Were you cross to [with] Amy? (3;00)	17	Not go [to] nursery (2;04)
3	I'm very pleased at [with] you (3;00)	18	I wan a bit [of] daddy toast (2;04)
4	I want to play [for] five minutes (3;01)	19	I go in [on] the sofa (2;06)
5	I've got in [into] bed (3;01)	20	There's some in [on] my leg (2;06)
6	I can do it all on [by] myself (3;01)	21	When we lib [in] a house (2;07)
7	She can play [with] my blocks (3;01)	22	Not at too hot (2;07)
8	How can we get at [into] the attic? (3;01)	23	He wants to sit [on] top of saw (2;09)
9	You going to have it at [in] the morning (3;02)	24	Not fill it on [to] the top (2;09)
10	I gave mine the tea on [in] the afternoon (3;02)	25	Teena look out [out of/at] the house (2;10)
11	Is this what I got [at] Miranda's party? (3;03)	26	To the top [of] a hill (2;10)
12	Move out [of] the way because my horsey will go (3;03)	27	Cat out [outside] the door (3;03)
13	She's had it it [for] long time (3;03)	28	Inside [in] your flower beds (3;05)
14	Go [to] bed (3;03)	29	I'm putting the spoon in [between] my teeth (3;05)
15	There's Amy on [in] Elsie Grandma kitchen (2;11)	30	And then we going in [into] the library (3;07)

Lara uses incorrect prepositions more often than she omits prepositions. **Locative prepositions** such as *in* and *under* are frequently a source of error, as the following sentences illustrate:

> I'll go on [under] table.
> I've got in [into] bed.
> How can we get at [into] the attic?
> There's Amy on [in] Elsie Grandma kitchen.

Lara has particular difficulty when the preposition *in* is used with a temporal meaning. In both of the sentences below, the preposition *in* is used to refer to part of the day. Lara uses an incorrect preposition in both cases:

> You going to have it at [in] the morning.
> I gave mine the tea on [in] the afternoon.

In English, we get cross *with* someone and are pleased *with* someone. We also do things *by* ourselves. Lara has also not yet acquired the use of prepositions in constructions of this type:

Were you cross <u>to</u> [with] Amy?
I'm very pleased <u>at</u> [with] you.
I can do it all <u>on</u> [by] myself.

Like Lara, Ella also omits prepositions. Most of the prepositions that Ella omits express spatial meanings:

I wan go [to] park.
Not go [to] nursery.
When we lib [in] a house.

Ella produces three utterances which all contain the word *top*. However, each utterance contains a different type of preposition error. The three utterances are shown below:

He wants to sit [on] top of saw.
Not fill it <u>on</u> [to] the top.
To the top [of] a hill.

In the first sentence above, *top* is used as part of the three-word preposition *on top of*. The first word in this preposition is omitted. In the other two sentences, *top* is a noun and not a preposition. In the second sentence, Ella uses the wrong preposition with the noun – *on the top* instead of *to the top*. In the third sentence, Ella omits the preposition *of* and fails to relate *top* to *hill* as a result.

Also like Lara, Ella selects the wrong preposition on quite a number of occasions. In several utterances, she is close to the correct form but doesn't quite achieve it:

Teena look <u>out</u> [out of] the house.
Cat <u>out</u> [outside] the door.
<u>Inside</u> [in] your flower beds.
And then we going <u>in</u> [into] the library.

On other occasions, Ella replaces the correct spatial preposition with an incorrect spatial preposition (usually *in*). These errors suggest that Ella has a developing concept of space even if it is not yet fully formed:

I go <u>in</u> [on] the sofa.
There's some <u>in</u> [on] my leg.
I'm putting the spoon <u>in</u> [between] my teeth.

Not all of Ella's preposition errors concern the concept of space. For example, in the following sentence Ella omits the preposition *of* which expresses a part-whole relationship between *bit* and *daddy toast*:

I wan a bit [of] daddy toast.

The omission of the preposition *of* in the utterance above is a **grammatical immaturity** in the language of a typically developing child. However, it is interesting to note that this very same form is a feature of the Geordie dialect we have been examining in this book. Speakers of this dialect can produce utterances such as the following:

'do **a bit** part-time teaching sometimes, I get teaching and that'

4.3.5 Prepositions in British and American English

One of the most significant differences between British and American English involves the use of prepositions. In British English, the preposition *on* is used to locate actions and events within a particular day of the week. So sentences such as the following are commonplace in British English:

She plays badminton <u>on Mondays</u>.
Sally left Rome <u>on Thursday</u>.
The children found the cat <u>on Friday</u>.

In American English, the preposition *on* is often not used before days of the week. These examples are taken from newspapers in the USA:

"I can sell water to a well", Marshall jokingly tweeted <u>Sunday night</u>. (Denver Post, 2017)
   Protesters who last week staged a 57-hour sit-in at Sen. Cory Gardner's Denver office returned to the general vicinity <u>Thursday</u> with hundreds of allies. (Denver Post, 2017)
   An experienced skydiver died <u>Saturday</u> after a midair collision during a jump at a Brazoria County skydiving center. (The Houston Chronicle, 2017)

Sometimes, a preposition is used in American English where a different preposition is used in British English. British English speakers are likely to use the preposition *to* in the first example below and *in* or *from* in the second example below:

"I'm very happy to promote Gregory Eaton <u>into</u> this role", Miles said in a news release. (Lincoln Journal Star, Nebraska, 2017)
   There was little dissent <u>on</u> Council as to the need for stormwater improvements. (Casper Star Tribune, Wyoming, 2017)

Also, American English does not use prepositions after certain verbs where the use of these prepositions is obligatory in British English. For example, the verb *protest* in British English can be transitive and intransitive. When it is used as a transitive verb, it takes a clause as object. When it is used as an intransitive verb, it must be followed by a preposition such as *against* or *about*:

He protested <u>that the plans were too expensive</u>. (Transitive verb: clause as object)
They protested <u>against</u> the new employment laws. (Intransitive verb: preposition against)
We protested <u>about</u> the decision to withdraw funding. (Intransitive verb: preposition about)

Prepositions like *against* and *about*, which are obligatory in this context in British English, are not used in American English. In the following example from a US newspaper, *protest* is used as a transitive verb which has a noun phrase (*Intuit's decision*) as a direct object. The equivalent sentence in British English would require the intransitive use of *protest* followed by *against*:

> Among Intuit's critics are two former employees who said they <u>protested Intuit's decision</u> not to do more to halt seemingly fraudulent returns when they worked at the company. (*Washington Post*, 2015)

Another example is the use of the preposition *on* after the verb *impact*. In British English, this preposition is obligatory in sentences such as the following example:

> The decision to close the mine negatively impacted <u>on</u> everyone.

(It should be noted that many prescriptive grammarians would not accept the verbal form of *impact* in British English, preferring instead the use of *impact* as a noun: *The decision to close the mine had a negative impact on everyone.*) No preposition follows verbal *impact* in American English, as these examples illustrate:

> The Facebook group has given a forum for discussing problems, solutions, and what <u>impacts</u> students. (*The Huntsville Times*, Alabama, 2017)
>   The conversations we've had prompted me to recently ask my students ... what <u>impacted</u> their achievement and success. (*The Huntsville Times*, Alabama, 2017)

Finally, American English can use words as prepositions which do not have this use in British English. In the following examples, the adjective *absent* has the function of a preposition. Its meaning is equivalent to the meaning of the preposition *without*:

> <u>Absent</u> the federal bailout, those firms would have gone into bankruptcy, and their shareholders would have gotten nothing. (*Washington Post*, 2015)
>   <u>Absent</u> a dramatic change, we know for sure that any deal with Iran will include two major concessions to Iran. (*New York Times*, 2015)
>   But next year, even <u>absent</u> a vote, a whole lot of Coloradans are likely to pay significantly more in taxes. (*Denver Post*, 2015)

The main points in this section are summarised below.

KEY POINTS PREPOSITIONS

- A class of function words, the members of which relate people, objects and events represented by noun phrases in a sentence to each other. For example, the locative preposition *on* in the sentence *The medieval castle is on the hill* relates the medieval castle in space to the hill.

- Prepositions may be single words (*from, inside*), two words (*due to, next to*) or three words (*in front of, in addition to*).
- Prepositions express a wide range of meanings. Most commonly, prepositions relate people and objects in space (*on the table, in the fridge*) and time (*during summer, for ten minutes*). They may also convey meanings such as instrument (*with an axe*), manner (*with force*), direction (*towards the door*) and cause (*out of malice*).
- A single preposition can have multiple meanings. For example, *with* can express possession (*They bought a house with a conservatory*), means (*She sliced the turkey with a carving knife*) and manner (*She moved with speed through the shop*).
- When combined with noun phrases, prepositions form prepositional phrases. These phrases have an adverbial function in the sentence. The sentence *They travelled by train to York* has two adverbials, *by train* and *to York*, which address the questions *How?* and *Where?*, respectively.
- Nouns are not the only words which can follow prepositions. Other prepositions can also follow prepositions (e.g. *They emerged from behind the door*).
- The only words which can stand in front of prepositions are adverbs (e.g. *The accident happened just before his birthday*).

4.4 Conjunctions

Conjunctions are a class of words which links phrases and clauses together. There are two types of conjunctions: coordinating and subordinating (or complementisers, as they are also known).

4.4.1 Coordinating Conjunctions

Coordinating conjunctions are words like *and, or* and *but* that link units of the same syntactic category. These units may be nouns, adjectives, adverbs or clauses, as is shown in the following sentences:

> They like *cheese* and *wine*. [Nouns]
> The dog was *dirty* and *wet*. [Adjectives]
> Sally works *quickly* and *competently*. [Adverbs]
> *Jack washed the car* and *Mary mowed the lawn*. [Clauses]

The basic coordinating conjunctions *and, or* and *but* may be joined by other words such as *both…and, either…or, neither…nor* and *not only…but also*. These so-called **correlative conjunctions** are more emphatic than the basic coordinating conjunctions:

> They visited *both* Rome *and* Paris.
> She wants *either* ice cream *or* a brownie for dessert.
> *Neither* the original proposal *nor* its amendments were judged to be satisfactory.
> The art work was *not only* valuable *but also* irreplaceable.

That the units which are linked by coordinating conjunctions are of equal syntactic status is demonstrated by the fact that the order of the units can be reversed without altering the meaning of the sentence. The sentences *Jack is old and wise* and *Jack is wise and old* have the same propositional meaning. We will see that this does not occur in **subordinating conjunctions**, where reversal of the order of the units can change sentence meaning.

Coordinating conjunctions are examined further in Exercise 4.3, which you should now attempt.

EXERCISE 4.3 LARA AND COORDINATING CONJUNCTIONS

To give you practice in identifying coordinating conjunctions, we will examine how Lara uses this class of words. The following utterances were produced by Lara when she was just over 3 years old. For each utterance, (i) identify the coordinating conjunction, and (ii) describe the units that are linked by means of this conjunction:

(a) There's a space there but she's not sharing it with me.
(b) Is this a helicopter or aeroplane?
(c) This car is black and white.
(d) I'm the mummy and you're the daddy.
(e) You can help me do these or do you want to do the wheelbarrow?
(f) I had it for my birthday but I didn't want it.
(g) Shall I go round and round?
(h) This is my duvet and this is my pillow.
(i) Is it my jigsaw or your jigsaw?
(j) I want sausages and spaghetti.
(k) Does that go that way or does that go that way?
(l) Hoover my house and I'll hoover your house.
(m) Do you want coffee or tea?
(n) I'm doing that one but it doesn't fit in here.
(o) Do you want to make tea or shall I?

4.4.2 Subordinating Conjunctions

The much larger group of conjunctions is subordinating conjunctions. These conjunctions introduce subordinate clauses such as the underlined clause in the following sentence:

She believed <u>that he would return one day</u>.

The underlined clause in this sentence has a very different status from the clauses which are conjoined by coordinating conjunctions (e.g. <u>*Mike paints the walls*</u> *and* <u>*Sue cuts the grass*</u>). The latter clauses have equal syntactic status. However, in the sentence above, the underlined clause is subordinate to the main clause which is the full sentence. Because it is dependent on the main clause, the subordinate clause is a dependent clause. The clause it depends on – the main clause or full sentence – is an independent clause. The subordinate clause in each of the following sentences is underlined:

> The performance was cancelled <u>because the lead actor was unwell</u>.
> <u>Although he liked the film</u>, he would not recommend it to his friends.
> <u>If he leaves early</u>, he will get the best seat on the train.
> The building poses a fire risk <u>unless these precautions are considered</u>.
> He had not returned, <u>since the accident happened</u>.
> They left <u>after the show ended</u>.

Because the clauses which are linked by subordinating conjunctions do not have equal status, the order in which they appear does affect sentence meaning. Let us return to the last sentence above. This sentence means that the show had concluded by the time they left. In the following sentence, the order of the clauses is reversed. This has the effect of changing sentence meaning. Now the sentence means that the show had not concluded by the time they left:

> The show ended after they left.

The reversal of clauses is also responsible for the quite different meanings of the following sentences:

> I visited the dentist, because I had toothache.
> I had toothache, because I visited the dentist.

Subordinating conjunctions, and the clauses they introduce, express a range of meanings. Some of these meanings are illustrated by the sentences below:

> The match was cancelled <u>because it was raining</u>. [Reason]
> The bus broke down <u>so we decided to walk home</u>. [Result]
> <u>If you wash the car</u>, I will pay you £20. [Conditional]
> The situation got worse <u>before she was able to phone the police</u>. [Temporal]
> <u>Even though she locked the gate</u>, the dogs were able to escape. [Concessive]
> He wanted to leave earlier <u>than she wanted to get up</u>. [Comparative]

4.4.3 Subordinating Conjunctions in Children

Once again, we can gain practice in identifying and describing subordinating conjunctions by examining how they are used by typically developing children and by children with specific language impairment. Table 4.4 contains utterances produced by both types of children during a narrative production task. The gender and age of the children are indicated in brackets. The data are from the CHILDES database (MacWhinney, 2000).

TABLE 4.4 Use of subordinating conjunctions by typically developing children and children with specific language impairment

Typically developing children	Children with SLI
The daddy did not come because he was angry last time (female: 4;06)	When he was playing with it, it actually got stuck in the swimming pool (male: 9;04)
The little guy said you could go in the pool (female: 4;10)	The elephant say the ball is in the swimming pool (female: 9;07)
He could not get it out because it was too far away (female: 4;10)	The moose was swimming in the water so he can get the ball (female: 9;07)
He did not want to because he was crying (female: 4;10)	The guard said you cannot have a balloon so the kangaroo goed with the balloon (female: 9;07)
That one said fifty dollars so they got a different one (female: 4;10)	He had no money so they were very sad (male: 9;07)
The elephant closed her eyes while he put the bandaid on (female: 7;02)	He digged some sand and put it in a bucket while the other kid was making a sandcastle (male: 9;08)
The elephant explained I took a airplane from the giraffe (female: 7;02)	The zebra said the elephant was flying it (male: 9;08)
The giraffe started to cry because nobody could get it (female: 7;02)	When jelly was trying to catch it, peanut got very mad at her (female: 9;09)
The rabbit said he wants that one so the balloon man gave the balloon for five cents (female: 7;02)	Longnose wanted to try it so he grabbed it out of her hand (female: 9;09)
The rabbit went to ask her mom if she could have some money (female: 7;02)	Longneck was so sad that he was crying (female: 9;09)
The elephant was scared that he would drown (male: 7;06)	The rabbit got very mad because it broke (female: 9;09)
The giraffe guy is pretending that it is doing loopdeloops and stuff (male: 8;07)	Rabbit was getting so hungry that he ate the carrots (female: 9;09)
The rabbit eats too much so now he has a tummyache (male: 8;07)	She wondering if she could take it off (female: 9;09)
The bunny asks if he can get one (male: 8;07)	I think I am going to buy one for peanut (female: 9;09)
He frowns because he does not have any money (male: 8;07)	He ask if he could buy them a balloon (female: 9;09)

The utterances produced by the typically developing children contain five different subordinating conjunctions: *because, if, so, that* and *while*. For the most part, these conjunctions are linking two clauses, one dependent (subordinate clause) and the other independent (main clause or sentence). The dependent clause is underlined in each of the following sentences:

> He frowns *because he does not have any money.*
> The bunny asks *if he can get one.*
> That one said fifty dollars *so they got a different one.*
> The elephant was scared *that he would drown.*
> The elephant closed her eyes *while he put the bandaid on.*

In one utterance, two subordinating conjunctions, *that* and *so*, link three clauses: the main clause and two subordinate clauses. The subordinate clauses are both dependent on the main clause. The first subordinating conjunction (*that*) is implicit in the sentence and has been included in square parentheses below.

MAIN CLAUSE

The rabbit said [that] he wants that one so the balloon man gave the balloon for five cents.

SUBORDINATE CLAUSE 1

SUBORDINATE CLAUSE 2

It is quite common for *that* to be omitted by speakers on the assumption that it will be understood by hearers. This also occurs in the following sentences:

> *The little guy said [that] you could go in the pool.*
> *The elephant explained [that] I took a airplane from the giraffe.*

Through these subordinating conjunctions typically developing children are able to express a range of meanings, including reason, result and time (temporal):

> *The giraffe started to cry because nobody could get it.*
> [Why did the giraffe start to cry? **Reason:** Nobody could get it]
> *The rabbit eats too much so now he has a tummyache.*
> [What was the **result** of the rabbit eating too much? He has a tummyache]
> *The elephant closed her eyes while he put the bandaid on.*
> [When did the elephant close her eyes? **Temporal:** While a bandaid was being put on]

Turning to the children with SLI, they produced six different subordinating conjunctions: *that, so, while, when, because* and *if*. These conjunctions link two clauses for the most part as in the sentence *The rabbit got very mad because it broke.* However, the children with SLI also produced sentences with three clauses such as the following:

> *He digged some sand and put it in a bucket while the other kid was making a sandcastle.*
> *The guard said [that] you cannot have a balloon so the kangaroo goed with the balloon.*

In the first of these sentences, the three clauses are linked by means of a coordinating conjunction (*and*) and a subordinating conjunction (*while*). In the second sentence, two subordinating conjunctions, *that* and *so*, link the three clauses. As before, this sentence contains two subordinate clauses which are dependent on the main clause.

The subordinating conjunction *that* in the above sentence is not explicitly stated, but is nonetheless part of the grammatical structure of the sentence. Several other sentences used by the children with SLI also contain *that* implicitly:

```
┌─────────────────────────────────────────────────────────────────────┐
│                           MAIN CLAUSE                                 │
└─────────────────────────────────────────────────────────────────────┘
The guard said [that] you cannot have a balloon so the kangaroo goed with the balloon.
        ┌───────────────────────────────────────────────────────────┐
        │                  SUBORDINATE CLAUSE 1                      │
        └───────────────────────────────────────────────────────────┘
                            ┌──────────────────────────────────────────┐
                            │         SUBORDINATE CLAUSE 2              │
                            └──────────────────────────────────────────┘
```

> *The elephant say [that] the ball is in the swimming pool.*
> *The zebra said [that] the elephant was flying it.*
> *I think [that] I am going to buy one for peanut.*

Like typically developing children, the children with SLI are able to express a range of meanings through the use of subordinating conjunctions. The conjunctions *while* and *when* both express temporal meanings; *because* and *so* express reason and result, respectively:

> *He digged some sand and put it in a bucket <u>while the other kid was making a sandcastle</u>.*
> [When did he dig some sand and put it in a bucket? **Temporal:** While the other kid was making a sandcastle]
> <u>*When he was playing with it,*</u> *it actually got stuck in the swimming pool.*
> [When did it get stuck in the swimming pool? **Temporal:** When he was playing with it]
> *The rabbit got very mad <u>because it broke</u>.*
> [Why did the rabbit get very mad? **Reason:** Because it broke]
> *Longnose wanted to try it <u>so he grabbed it out of her hand</u>.*
> [What was the **result** of Longnose wanting to try it? He grabbed it out of her hand]

It may have occurred to you that the children with SLI are able to produce the same range of subordinating conjunctions as typically developing children. It might be argued that this is unexpected given that children with SLI have a language disorder. But it is important to note the greater chronological age of the children with SLI. These children are much older than typically developing children before the same range of subordinating conjunctions can be produced. Also, the children with SLI exhibit a number of other grammatical errors. Verb errors include the use of incorrect past tense forms (*goed – went, digged – dug*), omission of auxiliary verbs (*she wondering*), and use of **present tense** verbs instead of past tense verbs (*say – said, ask – asked*). The persistence of these grammatical immaturities in children over 9 years of age is a reminder that the use of subordinating conjunctions has been achieved by children with SLI after a much longer developmental course than in typically developing children.

To get further practice of working with subordinating conjunctions, you should now attempt Exercise 4.4.

EXERCISE 4.4 SUBORDINATING CONJUNCTIONS IN ALZHEIMER'S DEMENTIA

The following utterances were produced by adults with probable Alzheimer's dementia (AD) or mild cognitive impairment (an intermediate stage between normal cognitive decline of aging and AD). The utterances were recorded during the cookie theft picture description task in the Boston Diagnostic Aphasia Examination (Goodglass et al., 2001) and are taken from the DementiaBank (Becker et al., 1994). The gender and age of clients are indicated alongside each utterance. You should (i) identify the subordinating conjunction that links the clauses in these utterances, and (ii) underline the dependent clause in each utterance:

(a) The stool that the boy is standing on is tipping over (male: 77 years)

(b) She's standing in water if that's action (female: 64 years)

(c) She's asking him for one so he's handing one down to her (male: 68 years)

(d) The little girl's crying because he ain't giving her no cookies (female: 68 years)

(e) His sister is sushing so that the mother won't turn around (male: 79 years)

(f) She seems to be looking out the window while she's drying her dish (male: 68 years)

(g) The mother is washing the dishes as the sink is running over (male: 79 years)

(h) I did say she was letting the water run over the sink (male: 68 years)

(i) She is washing dishes while her sink is overflowing with water onto the floor (male: 64 years)

(j) The stool is turning over on him that he's standing on (female: 79 years)

The main points in this section are summarised below.

KEY POINTS CONJUNCTIONS

- Conjunctions are a class of words that link nouns, adjectives, adverbs and clauses together. There are two types of conjunction: coordinating conjunctions and subordinating conjunctions.
- Coordinating conjunctions are words like *and, but* and *or* which link units of the same category. These units may be nouns (*Fran likes cheese and wine*), adjectives (*She looked thin and unwell at the concert*), adverbs (*They work quickly and tirelessly*) and clauses (*Mike is a banker and his wife is a lawyer*). Coordinating conjunctions also include forms such as *not only ... but also* and *either ... or*. These so-called correlative conjunctions are more emphatic than basic coordinating conjunctions.
- The order of the units which are conjoined by coordinating conjunctions does not affect sentence meaning. For example, the sentences *She hates German wine but loves French cheese* and *She loves French cheese but hates German wine* have the same meaning.

- Subordinating conjunctions are a much larger group of conjunctions than coordinating conjunctions. They only link clauses which are not of equal status. One clause (the subordinate clause) is dependent on another clause (the main clause or sentence). For example, in the sentence *Jack left work early because he had finished his report*, the subordinating conjunction *because* introduces a subordinate clause (*he had finished his report*) that is dependent on the full sentence.
- The order of clauses that are linked by a subordinating conjunction does affect the meaning of a sentence. For example, the sentences *Mike sold the house because he had financial difficulties* and *Mike had financial difficulties because he sold the house* have different meanings.
- Subordinating conjunctions can express a range of meanings including reason (*She was crying because she cut her finger*), time (*When you arrive, you should give Judith a call*) and result (*A fight broke out so they left the pub*).

To extend your knowledge of the minor word classes examined in this chapter, you should read the following Special Topic on expressive language in adults with aphasia.

SPECIAL TOPIC 4.3 EXPRESSIVE LANGUAGE IN APHASIA

At the start of the chapter, we described how some speakers with aphasia struggle to produce function words such as determiners, conjunctions and prepositions. These speakers are able to produce content words such as nouns and verbs, although they do so with considerable struggle and effort. Expressive language assumes the appearance of a telegram. Clinicians call this language agrammatism. Below, a 57-year-old man is relating a story based on pictures to an examiner. This man has Broca's aphasia as a result of a stroke. His spoken output is slow and laboured, with many pauses between individual words and phrases (the pauses are not indicated in the transcription). These data are from AphasiaBank (MacWhinney et al., 2011):

> 'uh cat [traɪm] tree and stuck now and father is climbing up tree and now little kitty soon I don't know but see barking now why I don't know father and barking a lot I don't know yeah okay now a bicycle and ladder I don't know and now oh bird singing and fire chief now running and and uh engine? No fire chief and kitty soon uh fire and ladder and kitty soon'

This client is able to produce content words. He uses nouns (*father, engine*), lexical verbs (*barking, running*), adjectives (*little*) and adverbs (*now, soon*). However, there is only one auxiliary verb (*is climbing*) and one determiner (*a bicycle*) used during the story. (The dummy auxiliary *do* in *I don't know* does not count as this is a type of automatic speech for the client.) Also, only two conjunctions (*and, but*) are used, and there are no prepositions at all. In the absence of pictures, a hearer will struggle to follow the events in the story, notwithstanding the many content words that are used. The loss of function words in this client's expressive language leaves us struggling to integrate small pockets of information such as the father climbing up the tree and the fire chief running.

SUMMARY

In this chapter you have seen the following:

- Function words fall into one of three minor word classes: determiners; prepositions; and conjunctions. Unlike major word classes, membership of minor word classes is not as readily determined by morphological and semantic criteria.
- Determiners occur in front of nouns in noun phrases and convey information such as quantity and number. They include definite and indefinite articles (*the man, a chair*), cardinal and ordinal numerals (*six pints, first prize*) and quantity words (*many books*). Only certain determiners can be pre-determiners, central determiners and post-determiners.
- Prepositions relate noun phrases which represent people, places and things to each other in a sentence (*The child is on top of the cushion*). Prepositions may be single words (*beside, under*), two words (*next to, together with*) and three words (*in addition to, on top of*). They express a range of meanings including space (*beside the church*), time (*during winter*) and means (*with an axe*).
- There are two classes of conjunctions: coordinating (*and, or, but*) and subordinating (*since, because, although*). Coordinating conjunctions can link nouns, adjectives, adverbs and clauses. Subordinating conjunctions can only link clauses.

WEBSITE MINOR WORD CLASSES

After reading the chapter, visit the website and test your knowledge of minor word classes by answering the multiple-choice questions for this topic.

HOMEWORK ASSIGNMENT

The subordinating conjunction *if* may be used to introduce a clause that expresses a hypothetical situation (e.g. *If I were Prime Minister, I would raise taxes*). You will observe that the verb *were* instead of *was* follows this conjunction even though the subject pronoun *I* is singular. Here is an example of this feature in actual use:

> "If it <u>were</u> just my husband and I, we would go, because we'd love to see it, but the kids are hot and tired", she said. (*Wausau Daily Herald*, Wisconsin, 2017)

The Electronic World Atlas of Varieties of English states that the opposite grammatical pattern is pervasive or obligatory in Australian English and New Zealand
English – *was* is used in place of *were* in a hypothetical or conditional clause of this
type (e.g. *If I was you*). Consider the following extracts from *The Sydney Morning
Herald* and *The New Zealand Herald*. Do these extracts support what we would
expect to be the case based on the Electronic World Atlas of Varieties of English?
If not, why do you think this is the case?

> 'Fifty-nine-year-old Mark Lewis, who was the state agriculture minister until
> the Liberals defeat in the March state election, said if he were in the Senate he
> would add strength and diversity to the West Australian Liberal party team in
> Canberra.' (*The Sydney Morning Herald*, 2017).
>
> 'The models, for instance, suggest that if the carbon dioxide concentration in
> the atmosphere were to reach double its pre-industrial level, the planet would
> warm by anywhere from about 1.5C to 4.5C.' (*The New Zealand Herald*, 2017).

SUGGESTIONS FOR FURTHER READING

(1) Altenberg, E. P. and Vago, R. M. (2010) *English Grammar: Understanding the
Basics*. Cambridge: Cambridge University Press.
The minor word classes are examined in separate units in this volume: determiners (Unit 3), prepositions (Unit 5) and conjunctions (Unit 6). Information
is presented in a series of lessons. For example, in Unit 6 coordinating conjunctions, subordinating conjunctions and correlative conjunctions are examined
in lessons 18, 19 and 20, respectively. The *Test yourself* questions and answer
keys at the end of each unit will give you practice in identifying members of
these word classes.

(2) Crystal, D. (2004) *Rediscover Grammar*, Third Edition. Harlow: Pearson
Education.
Several sections in this book examine the minor word classes. In relation to
determiners, you should read: section 35 (types of determiner), section 36 (the
articles), section 37 (predeterminers) and section 38 (postdeterminers). For
further information on conjunctions, you should read: section 64 (types of
coordination), section 65 (types of subordination) and section 66 (the meanings of conjunctions). For discussion of prepositions, you should read: section
59 (the function of prepositions), section 60 (simple and complex prepositions) and section 61 (prepositional meanings).

(3) Hurford, J. R. (1994) *Grammar: A Student's Guide*. Cambridge: Cambridge
University Press.
The three word classes addressed in this chapter are examined further in several sections of Hurford's text. Conjunctions and prepositions can be found
on pages 46 and 190, respectively. The determiners are discussed in several

sections: article (18), cardinal numeral (23), demonstrative (59), numeral (145), ordinal numeral (146) and possessive (181).

QUESTIONS MINOR WORD CLASSES

(1) The following utterances are produced by children with specific language impairment. The gender and age of the children are shown in parentheses. For each utterance, (i) identify the type of determiners it contains (cardinal numeral, definite article, etc.), and (ii) indicate if the determiners you identify are pre-determiners, central determiners or post-determiners.

(a) The bunny put some more sand on the castle (female: 9;07)

(b) On the wall it says no running (female: 9;03)

(c) He only got one dollar (female: 9;03)

(d) She cut her knee (male: 9;07)

(e) He gave them the last two balloons (female: 9;09)

(f) Then all his food was gone (male: 9;07)

(g) He had no money (male: 9;07)

(h) Three bunnies are playing in the sandbox (female: 9;03)

(i) The giraffe was playing with his toy plane (male: 9;07)

(j) So they got the two balloons (male: 9;07)

(k) Cookie [a girl's name] took out all her food (female: 9;09)

(l) He had all kinds of stuff (male: 9;07)

(m) But there was no money (female: 9;09)

(n) The balloons is fifty cents (female: 9;03)

(o) And then another lady comes (female: 9;03)

(2) Identify the single-word, two-word and three-word prepositions in the following passage. To guide you, single-word prepositions are used twenty times. Two-word prepositions occur five times, and three-word prepositions occur three times.

> Ben's room was one of the best in the block. In addition to a wash-basin there was a wardrobe with two shelves and, next to that, a large cupboard. In front of the cupboard was a small table with a drawer, and inside the drawer was a booklet of information about the town, along with some notepaper. On top of the wardrobe there were some extra pillows and, underneath those, some extra blankets. At the other end of the room was a small fridge. He looked hopefully inside the fridge, but instead of the expected cans of juice he found only a piece of mouldy cheese, together with some stale bread. He drew the curtains and looked out of the window. Across the street was a café, with tables outside the door. A group of men were sitting around one of the tables, arguing intently about something.

(3) For each of the following sentences, (i) identify the conjunction(s) that is (are) present, and (ii) indicate if the conjunction is a coordinating conjunction or a subordinating conjunction:

(a) After the exams he was tired and depressed.
(b) Bill had been anxious and frightened since he was mugged.
(c) He couldn't decide if he wanted wine or whiskey.
(d) He went to bed after he watched the film.
(e) She wanted to confront the bully but she was too scared to do so.
(f) We left home early so that we could avoid the traffic.
(g) You can have either ice cream or chocolate brownies for dessert.
(h) Unless you pass your exams, you cannot continue your studies.
(i) He is not only attractive but also highly accomplished.
(j) When you leave the property, you must inform the landlord.

(4) Identify the structures (nouns, adjectives, adverbs and clauses) that are linked by conjunctions in the following sentences.

(a) He is driving dangerously and carelessly.
(b) Until you accept the situation, you cannot begin to deal with it.
(c) Jill wanted trust and commitment in her relationship.
(d) Difficult issues are never black or white.
(e) He broke his hand while he was playing cricket.
(f) John wanted red wine but Fran wanted white wine.
(g) He was happy in summer but sad in winter.
(h) His job was making him frustrated and depressed.
(i) Joan will travel to Spain or Portugal this summer.
(j) I can't remember if he likes coffee or tea.

REVISION MINOR WORD CLASSES

(1) Describe the determiners used in each of the italicised phrases in the following sentences.

(a) She earns *half the salary* of *her husband*.
(b) He travels abroad *twice a year*.
(c) *The doctor* calls with her *every day*.
(d) *This week* you can double *your chances* on *the lottery*.
(e) *All five children* were ill after *the party*.

(2) Classify the determiners in each of the examples below as (i) a definite article, (ii) an indefinite article, (iii) a possessive, (iv) a numeral, (v) a quantity word or (vi) a demonstrative.

(a) the shop
(b) this sweater
(c) many examinations
(d) my car

(e) few surprises

(f) an inhibition

(g) first place

(h) three weeks

(i) a difficulty   .

(j) ten months

(k) his expectations

(l) that boy

(3) For each of the following sentences, (i) identify the word in italics as being either a preposition or a verb, and (ii) think of a sentence that contains the preposition or verb counterpart of each of the words in italics.

(a) *Considering* his crazy behaviour, it was no surprise that he fell.

(b) He was *following* the car when the accident happened.

(c) "You're *regarding* this evidence in a superficial way", shouted the juror.

(d) *Including* Mike, there were ten players in the team.

(e) The teacher is *excluding* anyone who talks.

(4) Identify the words in italics in each of the following sentences as either a preposition or a subordinating conjunction.

(a) It will be the end *of* civilisation *as* we know it.

(b) *Although* he plays tennis, he doesn't watch it *on* the television.

(c) She will be angry *if* he leaves the dishes *in* the sink.

(d) He claims *that when* he arrived the discharged gun was *on* the ground.

(e) *Before* he contacted the police, he threw the knife *into* the river.

(f) *Even though* he knew better, he had a large whiskey *before* the exam.

(5) Insert an appropriate subordinating conjunction into the blank space in the following sentences (by 'appropriate' is meant a conjunction that makes sense in the particular context of the sentence):

(a) I asked _____ I could go to the cinema.

(b) _____ the bus had broken down, we all had to walk.

(c) The school will close early, _____ the children can get home before the snow.

(d) _____ you leave now, you'll miss the train.

(e) I hurt myself_____ I was playing cricket.

(f) Carry on along that road _____ you come to a church.

(6) Using the terms *place, time, cause* and *means*, describe the meaning expressed by the prepositions in italics in the following sentences.

(a) Birds migrate *during* the winter.

(b) *Because of* his illness, he remained indoors.

(c) He sat *beside* the teacher.

(d) She chopped the wood *with* an axe.

(e) The teenagers ran *through* the tunnel.

(7) For each of the following sentences, (i) identify the preposition used, and (ii) describe the meaning expressed by each preposition.

(a) The family lives above the shop.

(b) He was abroad for three weeks.

(c) The match was cancelled on account of bad weather.

(d) The nasty child hit the dog with a stick.

(e) She is buying a house between the park and the lake.

(8) Each of the following sentences contains a conjunction. For each sentence, (i) identify the type of conjunction used as either a coordinating conjunction or a subordinating conjunction, and (ii) describe the word classes or other constructions that are linked by means of these conjunctions.

(a) The plans were ambitious and progressive.

(b) He wanted to travel abroad but he had no money.

(c) The boy was taken to hospital after the doctor examined him.

(d) She wants chips or rice with her dinner.

(e) If we leave now, we will arrive on time.

(f) He had lived in France since he was young.

(9) Give *one* example of each of the following DETERMINER + NOUN combinations.

(a) indefinite article + noun

(b) demonstrative determiner + ordinal numeral + noun

(c) definite article + cardinal numeral + noun

(d) possessive determiner + noun

(e) fraction term + possessive determiner + noun

(10) Complete the sentences below by inserting the determiners indicated in parentheses into the blank spaces.

(a) Mary invited _____ guests to the dinner party [cardinal numeral].

(b) Sarah is very popular as indicated by her _____ friends [quantifying expression].

(c) We let _____ neighbours use the swimming pool [possessive].

(d) She sold _____ her shares in the company [fraction].

(e) Bobby was the _____ runner to cross the finish line [ordinal numeral].

(f) The business partners met _____ a week [multiplying expression].

(g) There were strong grounds on which to reject _____ proposal [definite article].

(h) She was _____ inspiration to those who knew her [indefinite article].

(i) Her _____ job lasted for only six months [general ordinal].

(j) Pam wants _____ dress rather than the dress in the window [demonstrative].

(11) Complete the sentences below by inserting either coordinating conjunctions or subordinating conjunctions into the blank spaces.

(a) Mary cut the grass _____ John washed the car [subordinating conjunction].

(b) She wanted to accept the offer _____ it was too low [coordinating conjunction].

(c) I was bored _____ frustrated by the end of the lecture [coordinating conjunction].

(d) _____ you do the laundry, I will make dinner [subordinating conjunction].

(e) Three weeks had elapsed _____ the child disappeared [subordinating conjunction].

(f) Are you coming with me _____ staying on your own? [coordinating conjunction].

(g) He was ill _____ he ate too much chocolate cake [subordinating conjunction].

(h) The weather is fine _____ it can change very quickly [subordinating conjunction].

(i) She is eager to help _____ lacks the necessary experience [coordinating conjunction].

(j) _____ you are a friend of Bill, you can stay with me [subordinating conjunction].

(12) What type of determiner is the word *my* in the noun phrase *all my suggestions*?

5 Phrases

LEARNING OBJECTIVES

By the end of this chapter you will be able to do the following:

- Identify noun, verb, adjective, adverb and prepositional phrases and characterise their internal structure using the terms 'head', 'pre-modifier' and 'post-modifier'.
- Recognise determiners, adjectives and nouns in the pre-modifier of noun phrases, and prepositional phrases, *to*-infinitives, past participles, present participles, relative clauses and adjective phrases in the post-modifier.
- Recognise auxiliary verbs and adverb phrases in the pre-modifier of verb phrases, and noun phrases, adjective phrases, clauses, prepositions and adverb phrases in the post-modifier.
- Recognise adverb phrases in the pre-modifier of adjective phrases, and adverbs, prepositional phrases, *to*-infinitives and *that*-clauses in the post-modifier. Understand that adjective phrases can be pre-modifiers and post-modifiers in other types of phrase.
- Recognise adverbs in the pre-modifier of adverb phrases, and prepositional phrases in the post-modifier. Understand that adverb phrases can be pre-modifiers and post-modifiers in other types of phrase.
- Recognise adverb phrases in the pre-modifier of prepositional phrases, and noun phrases, prepositional phrases, adjective phrases, adverb phrases and clauses in the post-modifier. Understand that prepositional phrases can be post-modifiers in other types of phrase.
- Apply functional labels such as 'adjunct', 'complement' and 'specifier' to the parts of a phrase.

5.1 Introduction to Phrases

Although this chapter is devoted to the topic of phrases, we have already discussed phrases in several places in earlier chapters. This is because it is impossible to characterise certain word classes without discussing the words that occur alongside them, and these words constitute phrases. For example, determiners like articles, **numerals** and quantity words have a particular location in a **sentence**, and it is in front of a head noun in a noun phrase. Similarly, prepositions do not stand in splendid isolation from other words in a sentence. They are found in front of noun phrases in a sentence, the combination of which forms a prepositional phrase. So discussion of phrases up to this point has been rightly unavoidable. However, until now, we have not needed to be able to pick out phrases within a sentence as the phrase has always been presented in isolation. When we examine sentences, we are immediately confronted with the difficulty of knowing where a phrase starts and ends. Let us try to identify the noun phrases in the following sentence:

The elderly man with the walking stick bought three tins of organic soup.

There is a noun phrase in front of the verb *bought*. But exactly which of the following combinations of words makes up this noun phrase?

(1)	(2)	(3)	(4)

the elderly man – the walking stick – the elderly man with the walking stick – elderly man

It can only be (3) as this is the only combination of words which can be replaced by a pronoun and still result in a grammatical sentence:

He bought three tins of organic soup.

Our pronoun test can also be applied to the noun phrase which follows the verb *bought*. There are five words which follow this verb. How many of these words constitute the noun phrase?

(1)	(2)	(3)	(4)

three tins – of organic soup – tins of organic soup – three tins of organic soup

As before, there is only one of these strings of words which can be replaced by a pronoun and still result in a grammatical sentence. That is the string in (4):

The elderly man with the walking stick bought them.

So the pronoun test has reliably helped us to identify all the words that make up the noun phrases before and after the verb *bought* in this sentence. However, the pronoun test can undertake further work for us. It can also help us to identify noun phrases *within* these noun phrases. In the noun phrase *the elderly man with the walking stick*, the pronoun *it* could replace *the walking stick: the elderly man with it*. So, clearly, *the walking stick* is another noun phrase. In the noun phrase *three tins of organic soup*, the pronoun *it* can replace *organic soup: three tins of it*. So, *organic soup* is also a noun phrase within a larger noun phrase. Even when we strip a sentence down to its most basic phrases, our work is not done. This is because each of these phrases has an internal structure. In this chapter, we will use terms like 'head', 'pre-modifier' and 'post-modifier' to identify the component parts of individual phrases.

So far, we have only talked about noun phrases. But sentences in English contain a number of phrases other than noun phrases. They also contain verb phrases, **adjective phrases, adverb phrases** and prepositional phrases. We must also learn how to identify these phrases in a sentence, and to navigate our way around their internal structure. Terms like 'noun phrase' and 'verb phrase' are formal labels which capture the shape or structure of parts of language. But we can also talk about the functions that these structures play in **clauses** and sentences. We will examine these functions, which include **subject** and **direct object**, in Chapter 6. In this chapter, we will briefly examine functions *within* phrases. To this end, we will use terms such as 'specifier', 'complement' and 'adjunct'. However, the emphasis throughout the chapter will be on a structural analysis of phrases. We will look at the types of pre-modification and post-modification used by young, typically developing children, as well as by children and adults with language disorders. We will also include examples of the use of phrases by speakers of non-standard dialects. Having acquainted ourselves with the internal structure and function of phrases, we will then be ready to examine their use in clauses in Chapter 6.

5.2 Noun Phrases

We have already described how it is possible to look at a sentence and decide which string of words within it is a noun phrase. The pronoun test allowed us to say with relative certainty which words in the following sentence constitute noun phrases and which words are definitely not noun phrases. For convenience and clarity, here is the sentence again, with the two noun phrases (NP) that we replaced with pronouns both underlined:

<u>The elderly man with the walking stick</u> bought <u>three tins of organic soup</u>.
          NP1   NP2

5.2.1 Heads in Noun Phrases

Each of these noun phrases contains two nouns. In the first noun phrase, these nouns are *man* and *stick*. In the second noun phrase, the nouns are *tins* and *soup*. How do we decide which of these nouns is the head of the phrase? We can begin by asking ourselves which of the nouns the phrase is about. For example, in NP1 the phrase is not really about a walking stick. Rather, it is about a man who has a walking stick. So *man* is the head noun in this phrase. Similarly, the phrase in NP2 is not about soup but about tins which contain soup. So the head noun in this phrase is *tins*. We can perform a further check on the head noun in these phrases by using the phrase alongside a present tense verb. (The past tense verb *bought* will not work, as it has the same form regardless of the number of the subject.) If the verb has to change its form to reflect the plural number of the noun we identify to be the head, then we can be sure we have identified the head noun correctly. Let us perform this check for NP1:

(1) *The elderly man with the walking sticks leaves early.*
(2) *The elderly men with the walking stick leave early.*

If *stick* were the head noun in NP1, then the verb in (1) should be *leave* (plural) and not *leaves* (singular). The verb is singular *leaves* because it is agreeing with *man*, the singular head noun of the phrase. When we turn the noun we believe to be the head into the plural, as in *men* in (2), the verb must become plural *leave*. So we can have confidence that we have correctly identified *man* to be the head of NP1.

To give you further practice in identifying the heads in noun phrases, you should now attempt Exercise 5.1.

The head noun in a noun phrase is an obligatory part of the phrase. (This statement should be qualified by saying that a pronoun can also be a noun phrase, so some noun phrases do not have a noun as their head.) If we remove the head nouns in NP1 and NP2, an ungrammatical sentence is the result:

*The elderly [...] with the walking stick bought three [...] of organic soup.

However, there are a number of other components in NP1 and NP2. Some of these components are obligatory while others are optional. We can identify these components by selectively removing them from the phrases in NP1 and NP2 and seeing if their removal affects the grammaticality of the sentence. Let's begin by removing the definite article before the head noun in NP1:

*Elderly man with the walking stick bought three tins of organic soup.

Clearly, the result is an ungrammatical sentence. So the definite article is an obligatory component of NP1 where the head noun is a count noun. A definite article is not necessary, however, if the head noun is a plural count noun or if the head noun is a non-count noun. We can have sentences such as the following:

<u>Men</u> attended the show in large numbers. [Plural count noun]
<u>Wine</u> is not good for your health. [Non-count noun]

EXERCISE 5.1 HEADS IN NOUN PHRASES
The following phrases are all noun phrases. Identify the head noun of each phrase:

(a) wonderfully simple solution to the problem
(b) three quick ways to prepare a quiche
(c) the antique vase in the hallway
(d) children who never leave home
(e) valuable crops destroyed by disease
(f) damp clothes blowing in the wind
(g) eager fans besotted by the famous singer
(h) many complex issues to overcome
(i) fraudulent transactions at the bank
(j) quite ridiculous charges against the defendant

So the definite article is an obligatory component of NP1 because the head of this phrase is a singular count noun.

What about the other components of NP1? Are they also obligatory? Let's remove the only other component which stands in front of the head noun *man*. That component is the adjective *elderly*:

The man with the walking stick bought three tins of organic soup.

The adjective can be removed from NP1, and we still end up with a grammatical sentence. Let's remove the words that occur after the head noun in NP1 and see what happens. These words are the prepositional phrase *with the walking stick*:

The elderly man bought three tins of organic soup.

Once again, the result is a perfectly grammatical sentence. The optional adjective *elderly* in front of the head noun and the optional prepositional phrase *with the walking stick* after the head noun are called the pre-modifier and post-modifier, respectively. These are not the only possible pre-modifiers and post-modifiers in noun phrases.

5.2.2 Pre-Modifiers in Noun Phrases

As well as adjectives, nouns can also be pre-modifiers in a noun phrase. Consider the noun phrases below:

the best solution
the really old car
the church warden
the infamous train robbery

In the noun phrase *the best solution* the pre-modifier is the superlative adjective *best*. We can expand the adjective before the head noun into an adjective phrase and this adjective phrase is also a pre-modifier. This can be seen in *the really old car* where the adjective has been expanded by the addition of an adverb into the adjective phrase *really old*. In the noun phrase *the church warden* the noun *church* is the pre-modifier. But is it possible, as it was with adjectives, to expand a noun into a full noun phrase, so that a noun phrase can be a pre-modifier of a head noun? If we look at the final example above, it looks as if a noun phrase *infamous train* is a pre-modifier of *robbery*. However, this is not actually the case, as the adjective *infamous* is a modifier of *train robbery* and not just of *train*. So what we have so far are three pre-modifiers in noun phrases: stand-alone adjectives (these are, in fact, adjective phrases); adjectives which are expanded by adverbs into adjective phrases; and stand-alone nouns.

There appear to be other words that can stand in front of head nouns but which we have not included among the pre-modifiers we have already identified. Consider the following noun phrases:

> *the threatening husband*
> *the mesmerising performance*
> *the promising development*

In Chapter 3, we described words with the form of *threatening* and *promising* as present participles of verbs. Should we, therefore, identify a verbal pre-modifier that is separate from an adjectival pre-modifier and a nominal pre-modifier? The answer is that words like *threatening* and *promising* have sufficient similarity to adjectives to be treated as an adjectival pre-modifier. These words describe attributes of the nouns that follow them. Also, they can take an adjective modifier like *very* so that *the very threatening husband* is a grammatical noun phrase. They also have **comparative** and superlative forms as in *the more threatening husband* and *the most threatening husband*. The three noun phrases above can also be compared to the other noun phrase which we identified in NP1. That noun phrase was:

> *the walking stick*

Is *walking* an adjectival pre-modifier in the way that *threatening* and *promising* appear to be adjectival pre-modifiers? Certainly, *walking* describes an attribute of the stick – it is a stick that is used for walking. However, unlike the other adjectival pre-modifiers, *walking* cannot take an adjective pre-modifier like *very*: **the very walking stick.* Also, we cannot generate comparative and superlative forms of *walking* in the way that we can for other adjectives:

> *the more elderly man – the most elderly man*
> **the more walking stick – *the most walking stick*

The reason *walking* does not appear to qualify as an adjectival pre-modifier is because *walking stick* is a **compound noun**. So what we have in the noun phrase *the walking stick* is a determiner followed by a compound noun, and not a determiner followed by a modifier and then a head noun.

5.2.3 Post-Modifiers in Noun Phrases

In terms of post-modification in the noun phrase, we have already seen in NP1 and NP2 that prepositional phrases are possible post-modifiers:

> *the elderly man with the walking stick*
> *three tins of organic soup*

Because all prepositions are followed by a noun phrase, the use of a prepositional phrase as a post-modifier automatically introduces another noun phrase into the phrase. There are several other types of post-modifiers in noun phrases. They are illustrated by the following examples:

> *the war to end all wars* [To-infinitive]
> *the crisis emerging in the region* [Present participle]

> *the woman withered by criticism* [Past participle]
> *the result which leaves no room for doubt* [Relative clause]
> *boys keen on cricket* [Adjective phrase]

The first three post-modifiers are all types of verb phrase which are introduced by the *to*-infinitive, the present participle and the past participle. A relative clause may also be a post-modifier in a noun phrase. In the example above, the relative clause is introduced by the word *which*. However, relative clauses may also be introduced by *that* and *who*:

> *the girl <u>who</u> lives across the road*
> *the parcel <u>that</u> went astray*

What is the post-modifier of the noun *desire* in the following sentence?

> Taylor's desire to remain in New Zealand means the All Blacks should have
> a deep pool of front rowers to call upon ahead of the global tournament in
> Japan. (*The Dominion Post*, New Zealand, 2017)

Finally, as well as being pre-modifiers in noun phrases, adjective phrases may also be post-modifiers. There are two types of situation where this occurs. In Chapter 3, we described a group of adjectives called post-positive adjectives. These were adjectives that always followed the head noun that they modified such as in *princess royal* and *governor general*. However, where an adjective itself has post-modification as in *keen <u>on cricket</u>*, the adjective phrase also follows the head noun in a noun phrase. This allows us to avoid the second noun phrase in each of the following pairs:

> *boys keen on cricket – *keen on cricket boys*
> *girls fond of chocolate – *fond of chocolate girls*

5.2.4 Noun Phrases in Lara and Ella

To give you practice in identifying and describing pre-modifiers and post-modifiers in noun phrases, let us turn to examine how our two typically developing children, Lara and Ella, use these modifiers in noun phrases. Several of these children's utterances are displayed in Table 5.1. The utterances are presented in chronological age order. Square parentheses include omitted words which have been filled in to help you assess the utterance.

Let us take each child in turn. Lara uses both adjectival and nominal pre-modifiers in her noun phrases. Noun phrases with an adjectival pre-modifier include the following:

> *I got [a] <u>big</u> bread stick.*
> *This is a <u>little</u> part of [the] climbing frame.*
> *I like to buy this <u>lovely</u> hairband.*

TABLE 5.1 Use of noun phrases by two typically developing children

Lara's utterances	Ella's utterances
I made a butterfly song (3;01)	There's a piece for daddy bear (2;11)
I got [a] big bread stick (3;01)	It's time to go home now (3;00)
This is a little part of [the] climbing frame (3;01)	There's a camel on the ceiling (3;00)
I like to buy this lovely hairband (3;01)	And a box which was so big (3;00)
It's baby's time [to] go to sleep (3;02)	I want to have nutella on soft white bread (3;03)
They had a pretend dog in they garden (3;02)	There's a big tree in the plane (3;05)
I found a ball at seaside (3;02)	There was no wavy grass (3;05)
Do you want be the door sitter? (3;02)	There's a brush blowing in the wind (3;05)
I put this dolly in it (3;02)	That's not real food (3;05)
It's type of car black (3;03)	It's meant to be a splodge painting (3;07)
We got two picnic blankets (3;03)	I dipped some water on my finger (3;07)
This is a all fall down tree (3;03)	That's my favourite colour (3;07)
She's looking a horrid face at me (3;03)	I draw a picture with you (3;07)
Not the Emily [who] comes to my nursery (3;03)	That's a wave on the sea (3;07)

> They had a _pretend_ dog in the garden.
> It's type of car _black_.
> She's looking a _horrid_ face at me.

The adjectival pre-modifiers _big_, _little_, _lovely_, _pretend_ and _horrid_ are all used correctly by Lara. They stand immediately before the head noun that they modify. The adjective _big_ is an exception as the noun phrase in which it appears also contains a nominal pre-modifier _bread_. Occasionally, adjectival pre-modifiers appear in the wrong location in the noun phrase. This can be seen in _type of car black_ where the adjective _black_ appears at the very end of the noun phrase instead of before the noun _car_. Lara also uses several nominal pre-modifiers. These are underlined in the phrases below:

> I made a _butterfly_ song.
> I got [a] big _bread_ stick.
> It's _baby's_ time [to] go to sleep.
> Do you want be the _door_ sitter?
> We got two _picnic_ blankets.

Lara makes correct use of these nominal pre-modifiers, several of which are preceded by determiners such as definite and indefinite articles and cardinal numerals like _two_. Among these nominal pre-modifiers is the genitive noun _baby's_. For some grammarians, the genitive is a possessive determiner and is not a pre-modifier at all. This is how the genitive was described in Chapter 4 when we examined determiners.

Lara also uses several different types of post-modifiers in noun phrases. They include relative clauses, *to*-infinitives and, most commonly, prepositional phrases:

Prepositional phrase
This is a little part of [the] climbing frame.
They had a pretend dog in they garden.
I found a ball at seaside.
I put this dolly in it.
It's type of car black.
She's looking a horrid face at me.

To-infinitive
It's baby's time [to] go to sleep.

Relative clause
Not the Emily [who] comes to my nursery. [Relative clause]

Among Lara's prepositional phrases were phrases with nouns (*a ball* at seaside) and phrases with pronouns (*this dolly* in it). In one of these prepositional phrases *climbing frame* is used. This has the same status as *walking stick* which we discussed above. *Climbing* cannot be treated as an adjectival pre-modifier of the noun *frame*. This is because we cannot use the modifier *very* with *climbing* as we can with other adjectives (**very climbing frame*). Also, it is not possible to change *climbing* into comparative and superlative forms as we can do with other adjectives: **more climbing frame* (comparative); **most climbing frame* (superlative). Like *walking stick*, the combination *climbing frame* must be treated as a compound noun rather than a head noun which has an adjectival pre-modifier. Finally, it is not unusual for adults to make creative use of pre-modifiers in a noun phrase. Forms such as the following are not uncommon in everyday language use:

Yesterday, I heard the most mind-blowingly stupid and yet unbelievably funny remark.

At just 3 years of age, Lara is also showing signs of making creative use of pre-modifiers in noun phrases when she says:

This is a all fall down tree.

For her part, Ella uses an equally extensive range of pre-modifiers and post-modifiers in her noun phrases. Several adjectival pre-modifiers are used. They are underlined in the examples below:

There's a big tree in the plane.
There was no wavy grass.
That's not real food.
That's my favourite colour.

The adjectives in the noun phrases in these sentences stand immediately before the head noun that they modify. They are preceded by a number of determiners including the indefinite article *a*, the possessive determiner *my*, and the quantity word *no*. In Table 5.1, Ella uses two nominal pre-modifiers in her noun phrases. The second of these pre-modifiers occurs in a post-modifying prepositional phrase:

> It's meant to be a <u>splodge</u> painting.
> There's a piece for <u>daddy</u> bear.

Several different types of post-modifiers are also used by Ella. Like Lara, prepositional phrases are the most common type of post-modifier in Ella's noun phrases:

> There's a piece <u>for daddy bear</u>.
> There's a camel <u>on the ceiling</u>.
> I want to have nutella <u>on soft white bread</u>.
> There's a big tree <u>in the plane</u>.
> I dipped some water <u>on my finger</u>.
> I draw a picture <u>with you</u>.
> That's a wave <u>on the sea</u>.

Only one of these prepositional phrases uses a pronoun instead of a noun (*a picture <u>with you</u>*). If we look at the noun phrases inside these prepositional phrases, we find an adjectival pre-modifier (<u>*soft white*</u> *bread*) and, as we have just mentioned, a nominal pre-modifier (<u>*daddy*</u> *bear*). Ella uses three other types of post-modifiers in her noun phrases. They are a relative clause, the *to*-infinitive and the present participle:

> And a box <u>which was so big</u>. [Relative clause]
> It's time <u>to go home now</u>. [To-infinitive]
> There's a brush <u>blowing in the wind</u>. [Present participle]

It is interesting to observe how skilled Ella is at using noun phrases. Even at a stage in her **language development** when she is displaying phonological and grammatical immaturities, Ella is able to use pre-modifiers and post-modifiers in noun phrases correctly. In the first example below, the adjectival pre-modifier *green* is pronounced as 'geen' but her noun phrase has adult-like structure. In the second example, Ella incorrectly uses the indefinite article with the non-count noun *honey* and the plural count noun *bees*. But once again, the structure of her noun phrase cannot be faulted.

> A geen horse on a big fair (2;07)
> A honey from a bees (3;03)

5.2.5 Functions in Noun Phrases

To conclude our discussion of noun phrases, we have focussed above on the *structure* of the phrase. However, it is also possible to describe the *function* of different parts within the noun phrase. Consider the following noun phrase.

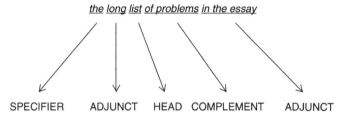

This example can be used to illustrate the function of the parts of a noun phrase. The head of the phrase is clearly *list*. A prepositional phrase *of problems* follows the head and is called a **complement**. The complement completes the meaning expressed by the head and cannot be omitted from the phrase without affecting its meaning. (What is the list a list of? It is a list *of problems*.) Complements have a verbal counterpart as in *they list problems*. This prepositional phrase has a different function from the other prepositional phrase *in the essay*. The latter prepositional phrase is an adjunct in the noun phrase. Adjuncts provide optional, additional information and so they can be omitted from the phrase. Adjuncts can also be stacked. The above phrase can be expanded by the addition of two further adjuncts in the following noun phrase:

> the long list of problems in the essay *about conflict in Eastern Europe*

Adjuncts do not always follow the head of the phrase but may also come before it. In the example above, the adjective phrase *long* is an adjunct which appears before the head. Finally, determiners like the definite article assume the function of a **specifier** in the noun phrase.

The main points in this section are summarised below.

KEY POINTS NOUN PHRASES

- A noun phrase is a sequence of one or more words which consists at a minimum of a head noun (or pronoun). In the sentences *Jack* is ill and *The elderly woman* is ill, the noun phrase is a single word and three words, respectively.
- Determiners are obligatory in some noun phrases. The definite articles in the noun phrases in the sentence *The boy* crossed *the road* cannot be removed without creating an ungrammatical sentence (**Boy crossed road*). In other noun phrases, determiners are optional. For example, the cardinal numeral in the second noun phrase in the sentence *Mary bought *five books** can be removed with no loss of grammaticality (*Mary bought books*).

- Noun phrases can have adjectival pre-modifiers such as _ancient_ church and _unreliable_ witness. The adjectives in these pre-modifiers can also be modified by adverbs to produce phrases like _really ancient_ church and _very unreliable_ witness.
- Noun phrases can also have nominal pre-modifiers in phrases such as _cheese_ sandwich and _almond_ cake. These nominal pre-modifiers are not full noun phrases as is illustrated by the fact that they cannot take a pre-modifier in the way that adjectives can. So in the phrase _stale cheese sandwich,_ the adjective _stale_ does not modify _cheese_ but rather _cheese sandwich._
- Noun phrases can have several post-modifiers. They include prepositional phrases (_members_ _of the choir_), _to_-infinitives (_the place_ _to visit_ _this summer_), past participles (_buildings_ _destroyed_ _by war_), present participles (_protesters_ _throwing_ _stones_), relative clauses (_girl_ _who loves singing_) and adjective phrases (_boys_ _mad_ _about sport_).
- Aside from the structure of a noun phrase, we can also assign function labels such as adjunct, complement and specifier to the parts of a noun phrase.

5.3 Verb Phrases

When we examined the word class of verbs in Chapter 3, we said that verbs could stand on their own in a sentence (so-called lexical or **main verbs**) or they could be preceded by other verbs (auxiliary verbs) in a verb string. The notion of a verb string was simply a convenient way of describing one or more auxiliary verbs followed by a lexical verb. But it has no syntactic status as such. What does have syntactic status is a verb phrase. A verb phrase is a head verb and all of its modifiers. The head verb is a lexical verb like _walk_ and _bought._ We can have no difficulty in identifying _hoping_ as the head verb in the following sentence. But what exactly are the modifiers in this sentence?

    Jack was hoping to leave early.

5.3.1 Pre-Modifiers in Verb Phrases

We can start to address this question by examining the word that immediately precedes the head verb – after all, we looked in front of a head noun to find the pre-modifiers in a noun phrase. The word that precedes _hoping_ is the auxiliary verb _was._ Is this auxiliary verb a modifier of _hoping_ or _hoping_ plus a number of other words in the sentence? To establish just how much of the sentence is modified by _was,_ we can perform a number of tests (see Börjars and Burridge (2010) for further discussion of these so-called constituency tests). The first test is to ask how many of the words following _was_ can be omitted and still result in a grammatical sentence. For the sake of argument, let us test if all the words following the auxiliary verb can be omitted. It turns out that they can:

    Sally wasn't hoping to leave early but Jack was [hoping to leave early].

The bracketed words can be omitted from this sentence with no loss of grammaticality. This suggests that these words are a constituent in the sentence – a unit which has syntactic status in the sentence. So it is beginning to look as if the entire sequence of words *hoping to leave early* is modified by the auxiliary verb. But we are not done yet, as there are other tests which can be performed to help us confirm if this is indeed the case. The second test is to ask if the sequence of words we are examining can be replaced by a single word (a single word, after all, has the status of a constituent in the sentence). It turns out that this is also possible: *Jack was <u>singing</u>*. So there is growing support for the claim that the auxiliary verb is modifying more than just the lexical verb in the sentence. The third test is to ask if the sequence of words *hoping to leave early* can be coordinated with words of similar structure and result in a grammatical sentence. Once again, this appears to be the case:

Jack was hoping to leave early <u>and expecting to hear soon.</u>

A fourth test can also be performed to establish just how much of the original sentence is modified by the auxiliary verb *was*. This test involves the use of the sequence of words *hoping to leave early* in focus position in a **cleft sentence**. It appears that our sequence of words can also pass this test:

What Jack was doing is <u>hoping to leave early</u>.

The sequence of words *hoping to leave early* has passed all four of these tests – it can be omitted with no loss of grammaticality, it can be substituted by a single word, it can be coordinated with a sequence of words of similar structure, and it can be the focus of a cleft sentence. So we can conclude with some certainty that the auxiliary verb *was* is not merely a modifier of the lexical verb *hoping*. Rather, it modifies *hoping* and all the words that follow *hoping*. In effect, the verb phrase in our original sentence is everything other than the noun phrase *Jack*:

Jack <u>was hoping to leave early</u>.

Auxiliary verbs were described in Chapter 3. We noted in that chapter that there could be more than one auxiliary verb before the lexical verb. Verb phrases with two, three and even four auxiliary verbs can occur in English, although the use of four auxiliary verbs is relatively uncommon:

They <u>have been</u> trying to find the keys.
She <u>must have been</u> waiting for several hours.
His taxes <u>must have been being</u> paid by the accountant.

How many auxiliary verbs are there in the following sentence? Underline where they occur:

I feel like it could have been handled more efficiently because this is an international company and it's a big deal. (*Wausau Daily Herald*, Wisconsin, 2017)

TABLE 5.2 The order of auxiliary verbs

	Auxiliary verbs				Main verb	
	modal	perfect	progressive	passive		
They		have	been		trying	to find the keys
She	must	have	been		waiting	for several hours
His taxes	must	have	been	being	paid	by the accountant

In Chapter 3, we said nothing about the order in which auxiliary verbs can occur. The first auxiliary verb slot in a verb phrase is optionally filled by the modal auxiliary verbs *can – could, may – might, shall – should, will – would* and *must*. The second, third and fourth slots are filled by the auxiliary of the perfect *have*, the auxiliary of the progressive *be*, and the auxiliary of the passive *be*, respectively. (Perfect and progressive aspect as well as passive voice were discussed in Chapter 3.) The order of auxiliary verbs in the above sentences is illustrated in Table 5.2.

Auxiliary verbs are not the only modifiers that can occur in front of the main verb. **Negative forms** like *not* and *never* are also pre-modifiers in the verb phrase. As explained in Chapter 3, the use of negation requires that we introduce the dummy auxiliary verb *do*:

> She does <u>not</u> wash the dishes. [Contracted form: *She <u>doesn't</u> wash the dishes*]
> She <u>never</u> washes the dishes.

Negative forms can be used in all sorts of interesting ways in dialects other than Standard British English. Some of these ways are examined in the following Special Topic.

SPECIAL TOPIC 5.1 NEGATIVE FORMS IN NON-STANDARD ENGLISH DIALECTS

In non-standard dialects, the negative form *not* is not always reduced or attached to an auxiliary verb, as it appears above in the sentence *She doesn't wash the dishes*. In Geordie dialect, there are a number of non-standard uses of *not* and the dummy auxiliary verb *do*. The negative form *not* may appear in an unreduced form and attached to an auxiliary verb: '**cannot** speak for other people, really, can you?' Alternatively, Geordie speakers may use a non-standard dummy auxiliary verb with *not* in reduced form attached to it: '**divn't** think they're right now, anyway'. The negative form may be fully articulated but the verb may be reduced. The opposite pattern is observed in Standard English: the negative form is reduced and the verb is fully articulated. Compare the forms in the following examples:

> Standard English: 'I mean, they **aren't** here now'
> Geordie dialect: 'I mean, **they're not** here now'
> Standard English: 'there **isn't** a back door, there's a front door'
> Geordie dialect: '**there's not** a back door, there's a front door'

Both Lara and her grandmother use unreduced *not* in negative tag and other questions. Also, *not* is not attached to the auxiliary verb as it is in Standard English:

> Standard English: '**Aren't** you playing with me?'
> Durham dialect: '**Are** you **not** playing with me?' (Lara)
> Standard English: 'Throw it at me **won't** you?' ('Don't throw it at me won't you?' is ungrammatical in SE)
> Durham dialect: 'Don't throw it at me **will** you **not**?' (Grandmother)

So far, we have discussed the use of a single negative form or particle. There are many English speakers who use more than one negative form. This grammatical feature is known as 'multiple negation'. Geordie speakers and speakers of Belfast English and American English may use two or even three negative forms in a single utterance:

> 'you can**'t** do **nothing** with them'
> 'I'm **not** doing **nothing never** again'

The other group of pre-modifiers in the verb phrase is adverb phrases like the underlined words in the following sentences. Each adverb phrase appears between the auxiliary verb and the lexical verb:

> Jane will <u>almost certainly</u> be late tonight.
> I was <u>just</u> leaving when I heard the phone ring.
> Bill must <u>first</u> discover his strengths.

5.3.2 Pre-Modifiers in Children with Language Disorder

To give you practice in identifying the words that can come before a head verb in a verb phrase, we will examine utterances produced by children with specific language impairment. Several of these children's utterances are presented in chronological age order in Table 5.3. We are interested in these children's use of auxiliary verbs, negative forms and adverb phrases. When an auxiliary verb is used, we need to determine if it as a modal, perfect, progressive or passive auxiliary verb. If you cannot recall these different types of auxiliary verbs, you should revisit the discussion of them in Section 3.3 in Chapter 3.

TABLE 5.3 Verb phrases of children with specific language impairment

Gender (Age)	Utterances of children with SLI
Male (8;04)	And now the rabbit has gone
Female (9;03)	Three bunnies are playing in the sandbox
Female (9;03)	He could not get it
Male (9;04)	And the hare only ated a sandwich
Female (9;07)	The doctor said "could I have a balloon"?
Female (9;07)	The plane was going deeper and deeper
Female (9;07)	The elephant running on the thing and almost fall in
Female (9;07)	The moose was swimming in the water so he can get the ball
Female (9;09)	She accidentally dropped it in the water
Female (9;09)	His stomach really hurted
Female (9;09)	Cookie realised that she should get a doctor because she does not want Carrot to get very sick
Female (9;09)	You have been eating too much
Female (9;09)	She wondering if she could take it off
Female (9;09)	They saw another doctor who was just standing there
Female (9;09)	He ask if he could buy them a balloon

Let us begin by examining how these children use auxiliary verbs. Several modal auxiliary verbs are used by these children. They are underlined in the sentences below:

> He _could_ not get it.
> The doctor said "_could_ I have a balloon"?
> The moose was swimming in the water so he _can_ get the ball.
> She wondering if she _could_ take it off.
> He ask if he _could_ buy them a balloon.
> Cookie realised that she _should_ get a doctor because she does not want Carrot to get very sick.

We described above how modal auxiliary verbs occupy the first of four possible auxiliary verb slots. However, because each of the modal auxiliary verbs in these sentences is the only auxiliary verb to appear before the lexical verb, it is not apparent that this is indeed the position of these verbs. In these sentences, there is use of a modal auxiliary verb with negation (He _could not_ get it). If the contracted form of _not_ had been used, it would attach to the modal auxiliary verb (He _couldn't_ get it). If the modal auxiliary verb _could_ had not been present, the dummy auxiliary verb _do_ would have had to be introduced in order to use negation. This occurs, for example, in the last sentence above where the child says she _does_ not want Carrot. A modal auxiliary verb is also used in an interrogative where it is inverted with a subject pronoun (_Could I_ have a balloon?) as part of direct reported speech.

The perfect auxiliary verb *have* is also evident in these children's utterances. It occurs in the following sentences where it is used to form the present perfect aspect and the present perfect progressive aspect:

> *And now the rabbit has gone.* [Present perfect aspect]
> *You have been eating too much.* [Present perfect progressive aspect]

There are no passive utterances in Table 5.3 with which to illustrate the passive auxiliary *be*. This could be a sign of the grammatical limitations of these children with SLI – the passive voice may be too complex a grammatical construction for these children to produce. Alternatively, it may simply reflect the fact that the narrative production task during which these utterances were produced did not give these children with SLI an opportunity to use the passive voice. However, there are examples of the progressive auxiliary *be*. This auxiliary occurs in the following sentences where it is used in the formation of the present progressive aspect, the past progressive aspect and the present perfect progressive aspect:

> *Three bunnies are playing in the sandbox.* [Present progressive]
> *The plane was going deeper and deeper.* [Past progressive]
> *The moose was swimming in the water so he can get the ball.* [Past progressive]
> *They saw another doctor who was just standing there.* [Past progressive]
> *You have been eating too much.* [Present perfect progressive]

Aside from auxiliary verbs, the children with SLI also use negative forms and adverb phrases before lexical verbs. We have already described the use of *not* alongside a modal auxiliary verb (*could*) and the dummy auxiliary verb *do*. The dummy auxiliary was introduced in order to achieve negation of a sentence with a lexical verb in the absence of another auxiliary verb. Other uses of the dummy auxiliary are shown below:

> *He does not have any money.* [Female; 9;01]
> *They do not know how to swim.* [Female; 9;01]
> *It does not hurt anymore.* [Male; 9;04]
> *The rabbit did not look so well.* [Male; 9;04]

The dummy auxiliary is also used in interrogatives. To form an interrogative, the dummy auxiliary is inverted with a subject noun or pronoun. In the following *wh*– and *yes–no* interrogatives, inversion proceeds correctly for the most part (the first example is an obvious exception). In each interrogative, the dummy auxiliary *do* is underlined:

> *Why do not we go swimming?* [Male; 8;06]
> *Do you like my new airplane?* [Male; 8;06]
> *What did this guy bring to eat?* [Male; 9;04]
> *What did this rabbit do?* [Male; 9;04]
> *Why do you do that?* [Female; 9;09]

The negative form *never* was used less often than *not* by children with SLI. Here are some examples of its use as a pre-modifier in the verb phrase:

> The giraffe <u>never</u> runned. [Female; 8;10]
> They threw all the candy stuff on the ground and <u>never</u> picked it up. [Female;
>   8;11]
> I <u>never</u> seen one of these in ages. [Male; 9;04]

Finally, several adverb phrases are used as pre-modifiers in these children's verb phrases. They occur immediately before the lexical verb in the following sentences from Table 5.3:

> And the hare <u>only</u> ated a sandwich.
> The elephant running on the thing and <u>almost</u> fall in.
> She <u>accidentally</u> dropped it in the water.
> His stomach <u>really</u> hurted.
> They saw another doctor who was <u>just</u> standing there.

To give you further practice in identifying auxiliary and lexical verbs, you should now attempt Exercise 5.2.

5.3.3 Post-Modifiers in Verb Phrases

There are only certain words and constructions which can follow head verbs in a verb phrase. In Chapter 3, we distinguished different types of lexical verbs in accordance with the objects which follow them. Intransitive verbs can stand on their own in the absence of any object or complement. Mono-transitive verbs must be followed by one object. Di-transitive verbs require two objects, one direct and one indirect:

> Sammy <u>laughed</u> throughout the play. [Intransitive verb]
> The teacher <u>thumped</u> the desk. [Mono-transitive verb]
> She <u>showed</u> the picture to her friend. [Di-transitive verb]

EXERCISE 5.2 VERBS IN CHILDREN WITH SPECIFIC LANGUAGE IMPAIRMENT
We described above the use of auxiliary verbs by children with SLI. For the most part, these children were able to use auxiliary verbs correctly. However, there are also occasions when errors in the use of auxiliary and lexical verbs occur. Examine all the utterances from children with SLI which were presented above. Identify any utterance in which there is an error in the use of either an auxiliary verb or a lexical verb. In each case, indicate the type of error that has occurred.

We also described in Chapter 3 two further types of lexical verb: intensive verbs and complex transitive verbs. Also known as **copular verbs**, intensive verbs take a subject complement. This is usually a noun phrase or an adjective phrase which refers to the same entity that is referred to by the subject of the sentence. Complex transitive verbs take a direct object and an object complement. The object complement refers to the same thing as the direct object:

Intensive verbs

Mary is _a special person_. [Subject complement: noun phrase]
They became _difficult_. [Subject complement: adjective phrase]

Complex transitive verbs

She found the class _unfriendly_. [Object complement: adjective]
They elected Donald Trump _president_. [Object complement: noun phrase]
Sally called him _a dishonest man_. [Object complement: noun phrase]

To gain practice in identifying these different types of lexical verb, let us consider how they are used by children with SLI. Table 5.4 contains the utterances of some of these children. These utterances contain examples of the lexical verbs that we have just described. We are interested in the elements (objects and complements) that follow the main verb in each utterance. In some cases, children with SLI use these elements correctly. In other cases, obligatory objects are missing or too many objects are present. It is worth remarking that many of the same difficulties are also observed in the language of typically developing children. However, while the verb errors of these children resolve over time, the errors of children with SLI tend to persist. You should keep the chronological age of the children with SLI in mind when you examine the utterances in Table 5.4.

TABLE 5.4 Use of different types of lexical verbs by children with specific language impairment

Gender (Age)	Utterance	Gender (Age)	Utterance
F (6;08)	Then he makes him better	M (6;05)	He make him more dizzy
M (8;11)	Then she gave it to the toy to the giraffe	M (8;11)	The lifeguard showed her the sign
M (8;11)	The doctor gave them money to the balloon carrier	M (9;07)	The rabbit told the doctor everything
F (9;07)	His mom gived some money	M (8;10)	The elephant is thanking
F (9;07)	The elephant close her eyes	F (9;07)	The moose was finding the plane
M (9;07)	The giraffe was very mad	F (9;07)	The doctor bunny came
F (9;07)	The bunny was running	F (9;03)	She likes the horse
F (9;03)	They saw a diving board	F (9;03)	The balloons is fifty cents
F (9;09)	She was so sad	F (9;09)	So he gave them the last two balloons

For the most part, children with SLI used intransitive verbs and mono-transitive verbs correctly. Examples of utterances which contain these verbs are:

Intransitive verb
The doctor bunny _came_.
The bunny was _running_.

Mono-transitive verb
The elephant close _her eyes_.
The moose was finding _the plane_.
She likes _the horse_.
They saw a _diving board_.

Occasionally, a mono-transitive verb was treated as if it were an intransitive verb and used without an object. This can be seen in the following example:

The elephant is thanking. [Omission of direct object]

These children also used intensive verbs with both noun phrases and adjective phrases as subject complements. Examples of intensive verbs in the utterances in Table 5.4 are:

The giraffe was _very mad_. [Subject complement: adjective phrase]
She was _so sad_. [Subject complement: adjective phrase]
The balloons is _fifty cents_. [Subject complement: noun phrase]

Occasionally, these children also used complex transitive verbs. In the following examples, the direct object is the pronoun *him* and the object complement is an adjective phrase:

Then he makes _him better_. [Object complement: adjective phrase]
He make _him more dizzy_. [Object complement: adjective phrase]

However, when we turn to the use of a more complex group of lexical verbs, di-transitive verbs, difficulties begin to emerge for children with SLI. Certainly, some di-transitive verbs are used correctly by these children. This can be seen in the following utterances from Table 5.4. In these examples, the di-transitive verbs *show, tell* and *give* are followed by an **indirect object** and a direct object:

The lifeguard showed _her the sign_.
The rabbit told _the doctor everything_.
So he gave _them the last two balloons_.

However, children with SLI frequently made erroneous use of the di-transitive verb *give*. Incorrect use of this verb resulted in the following ungrammatical sentences:

His mom gived _some money_.
Then she gave _it to the toy to the giraffe_.
The doctor gave _them money to the balloon carrier_.

In the first example, a direct object, *some money*, is used in the absence of an indirect object, even though the latter is not recoverable from context. In the second example, a direct object pronoun (*it*) is followed by two indirect object noun phrases (*to the toy* and *to the giraffe*). In the third example, the verb *gave* is followed by an indirect object pronoun (*them*), a direct object noun phrase (*money*), and an indirect object noun phrase (*to the balloon carrier*). It seems that children with SLI can misuse the verb *give* in several different ways!

The other post-modifiers in verb phrases are adverbs, prepositions and clauses. As well as being pre-modifiers in a verb phrase, adverb phrases can also be post-modifiers:

> Michael has *just* arrived. *[Adverb phrase as pre-modifier]*
> She drives *very quickly*. *[Adverb phrase as post-modifier]*

Prepositional phrases are used commonly as post-modifiers in verb phrases. These phrases convey spatial, temporal and other meanings:

> They sat *under the tree*. *[Space]*
> Sue waited *for five minutes*. *[Time]*
> He walked *with a limp*. *[Manner]*

Finally, clauses can be post-modifiers in a verb phrase. This includes ***that*-clauses** and *to*-infinitive clauses:

> She hoped *that they would not return*.
> Fran wanted *to return the goods*.

It is now your turn to identify different post-modifiers in verb phrases by attempting Exercise 5.3.

5.3.4 Functions in Verb Phrases

To conclude discussion of verb phrases, we turn to the function of different parts of the verb phrase. We have seen that several different structures can follow the head verb in a verb phrase. They include noun phrases, adjective phrases, prepositional phrases and clauses. Where these structures serve to complete the meaning of the head verb, their function is that of a complement. The underlined elements of the following sentences are all complements. In the second sentence, the di-transitive verb *gives* is followed by a direct object (*a cake*) and an indirect object (*Sue*), both of which are complements. The noun, adjective and prepositional phrases which follow the copular verb *be* are **copular complements**:

> Jack bought *the newspaper*.
> Mary gives *Sue a cake*. [Two complements]
> John is *a priest*. [Copular complement]
> She is *brilliant*. [Copular complement]

EXERCISE 5.3 POST-MODIFIERS IN THE VERB PHRASE

We have seen that a number of different elements can follow a head verb in a verb phrase. These elements may be noun phrases, adjectives, adverbs, prepositions and clauses. The following utterances are from children with SLI. Examine each utterance and identify the element(s) that follow(s) the head verb:

(a) The giraffe is getting the water (Male; 5;09)
(b) The elephant wants to swim (Male; 5;09)
(c) The girl sit on the bench (Male; 5;09)
(d) It flied away (Male; 5;09)
(e) They can run faster (Male; 5;07)
(f) He said you are not big enough (Male; 5;07)
(g) He looks so angry (Male; 5;07)
(h) He is the doctor (Male; 5;05)
(i) The giraffe gives him the ball (Female; 6;08)
(j) Then she hurt her knee (Female; 6;08)
(k) Then the lifeguard came (Male; 6;05)
(l) The guy was still laying on the grass (Male; 7;03)
(m) And then he was sweating (Male; 6;06)
(n) The bubbles are making him sick (Female; 7;10)
(o) And then her run so fast (Male; 6;05)
(p) He has a airplane in his hand (Female; 6;08)
(q) Zebra was getting mad (Male; 7;03)
(r) He is hugging his airplane (Female; 7;10)
(s) Give me a balloon (Male; 6;05)
(t) Mister rabbit wanted to have the balloon (Male; 6;06)

> Bill is *in the living room*. [Copular complement]
> Samantha became *distressed*.
> They thought *that he had left*.
> He looked *through the keyhole*.

It may appear that everything we have described as following a head verb in a verb phrase is a complement. However, this is not the case. Not every element that follows a head verb completes the meaning of that verb. This can be seen if we compare the last example above to the following example:

> He ran *through the woods*.

Although both verbs in these sentences are followed by prepositional phrases, *through the keyhole* is a complement while *through the woods* is an adjunct. This is because *through the keyhole* is required to complete the meaning of *looked* while *through the woods* is merely adding optional, additional information. The complement cannot be omitted (**He looked*) while the adjunct can be omitted (*He ran*). Adjuncts like *through the woods* do not just follow the head verb, but can also appear in front of it. The adverb phrase in the following sentence is an adjunct:

> The car <u>really quickly</u> accelerated.

The only other structures in the verb phrase which we have not given function labels to are the negative forms *not* and *never*. These forms are specifiers in the verb phrase:

> She <u>never</u> pays her bills.
> Mike does <u>not</u> want dinner.

As you might expect, the use of verb phrases varies across varieties and dialects of English. In the following Special Topic, we examine the use of verb phrases in, as well as other grammatical features of, New Zealand English (NZE).

SPECIAL TOPIC 5.2 GRAMMATICAL FEATURES OF NEW ZEALAND ENGLISH

Several grammatical features of NZE have been discussed previously in relation to other varieties and dialects of English. For example, the use of second person plural pronouns other than *you* (e.g. *Are youse going out later?*) and past participles as past tense verbs (e.g. *I seen him yesterday*) was described in Sections 3.2.5 and 3.3.1 as features of Belfast English. They are also features of NZE, as the following example illustrates:

> 'We used to drive in from the coast in a van and have a few beers and I
> remember I <u>seen</u> him after a game' (*The Dominion Post*, New Zealand, 2017)

In Section 2.3.2, the Geordie dialect was shown to use adverbs with the same form as adjectives (e.g. *You used to just do it automatic*). This same feature is observed in NZE. Speakers of NZE also use a related feature in which modifier degree adverbs have the same form as adjectives:

> 'There's not too much success with concussion and guys coming back so
> it was good to see a guy like Charlie back and <u>real positive</u> about it' (*The
> Dominion Post*, New Zealand, 2017)

Other grammatical features of NZE include the use of *was* for conditional *were*:

> 'If the love of your life <u>was</u> dying in hospital there is a chance that you would
> not be able to see them' (*Tearaway: The Voice of NZ Youth*, 2017)

A verb–particle combination which is a feature of NZE is *front up*. This form, which means to make an appearance or to turn up, is not found in British English:

> 'You could <u>front up</u> for that week against the Hurricanes and just chip away at it, or you have the break' (*The Dominion Post*, New Zealand, 2017)
> 'My challenge to the minister is why doesn't he <u>front up</u>, as the champion of this system, and hold a meeting with the people who are going to be a part of it?' (*The Southland Times*, New Zealand, 2017)

Another grammatical feature of NZE is the use of singular verb agreement in *there* existential constructions with plural noun phrases. This feature is found in the Niuean speech community in New Zealand but is also in widespread use in most varieties of spoken NZE:

> There'<u>s</u> not <u>many Niueans</u> (Starks and Thompson, 2009)

Double comparatives also occur in NZE, although the frequency of their use is somewhat unclear. The following example is the only double comparative in the Wellington Corpus of Written New Zealand English (Bauer, 1993):

> The title goes halfway to summing up this record, you certainly won't find anything <u>more rarer</u> than this. (CO8 178f)

Finally, NZE speakers can also use *me* instead of *I* in coordinate subjects, as the following example from the International Corpus of English illustrates:

> <u>Me and Carl</u> kind of looked at it (ICE-NZ S1A-010: 116)

Other grammatical features of New Zealand English can be found in the Electronic World Atlas of Varieties of English at: http://ewave-atlas.org

---

How would you characterise the underlined words in the following sentence from a teenage magazine in New Zealand?

> 'And because Hosier Lane is so renowned, the signature artists (the ones who just tag with their initials or sign) move in <u>real quick</u>!' (*Tearaway: The Voice of NZ Youth*, 2017)

The main points in this section are summarised below.

KEY POINTS VERB PHRASES

• A verb phrase consists of a head verb and all of its modifiers. The head verb is a main or lexical verb.

- Auxiliary verbs can stand in front of head verbs. A maximum of four auxiliary verbs can appear before the head verb, although this number of verbs is not commonly used. The first auxiliary slot is filled by modal auxiliary verbs like *can* and *should*. The second and third slots are filled by the perfect auxiliary *have* and the progressive auxiliary *be*, respectively. The fourth slot is filled by the passive auxiliary *be*. The dummy auxiliary verb *do* is introduced into a sentence with a main verb for the purpose of negation (*She does not know*) and to form an interrogative (*Does she like crisps?*).
- Adverb phrases (*She really dislikes him*) and negative forms (*He never talks*) can be pre-modifiers in a verb phrase.
- There are several post-modifiers in verb phrases. They include noun phrases (*John hit the wall*), adjective phrases (*His proposal sounds great*), clauses (*Mary realised that the situation was hopeless*), prepositions (*They sat beside the piano*) and adverb phrases (*She behaved really recklessly*).
- The lexical verb that forms the head of a verb phrase determines the structures that follow the head. Lexical verbs may be intransitive (no object), mono-transitive (one direct object), di-transitive (one direct and one indirect object), intensive (a subject complement) or complex transitive (a direct object and object complement).
- Many structures that follow the head verb have the function of complement. A complement completes the meaning of the head verb (*Mike likes chocolate*). Other structures that follow the head verb have an adjunct function. An adjunct provides optional, additional information (*She unwinds in the evening*). The negative forms *not* and *never* have the function of specifier in the verb phrase.

5.4 Adjective Phrases

The head of an adjective phrase is an adjective. Each of the underlined words in the following sentences is the head of an adjective phrase:

> Jonathan was *wise* to leave early.
> She was *unhappy* with his suggestion.
> He was *unpopular* at work.

5.4.1 Pre-Modifiers in Adjective Phrases

Adjectives can be pre-modified by adverb phrases. These phrases are most typically degree adverbs or intensifying expressions like *very, really* and *extremely*. Adverbs such as *really* intensify the attribute that is expressed by the adjective. This can be seen in the sentence:

> Jane was *really tired* yesterday.

A pre-modified adjective in an adjective phrase can itself be a pre-modifier in a noun phrase. This occurs in the following sentence where the adjective phrase *really tired* is a pre-modifier of the noun *woman*:

> Jack helped the *really tired* woman.

Not all adjectives can be pre-modified by adverbs like *very* and *really*. Some adjectives capture attributes that cannot be characterised in terms of degrees. Three such adjectives are shown below:

> *very <u>equal</u> angle*
> *really <u>dead</u> animal*
> *extremely <u>illegal</u> action*

5.4.2 Post-Modifiers in Adjective Phrases

There are a number of possible post-modifiers in adjective phrases. Clauses can be post-modifiers. This includes *to*-infinitive clauses, *that*-clauses and **comparative clauses**:

> She was too big <u>to fit into the dress</u>. [*To*-infinitive clause]
> He was angry <u>that his shirt was stained</u>. [*That*-clause]
> The dessert was sweeter <u>than she wanted</u>. [Comparative clause]

As well as being pre-modifiers in an adjective phrase, adverbs can also be post-modifiers. In the second example below, one adverb (*quite*) pre-modifies the adjective *limited* and another adverb (*indeed*) post-modifies it:

> He was not strong <u>enough</u> for the competition.
> The modifiers in an adverb phrase are quite limited <u>indeed</u>.

Prepositional phrases can also be post-modifiers in adjective phrases. These phrases are optional after adjectives like *afraid* or obligatory following adjectives like *fond*:

> June was afraid <u>of the dark</u>.
> June was afraid.
> Kate is fond <u>of chocolate</u>.
> *Kate is fond.

5.4.3 Adjective Phrases in Children with Language Disorder

To give you practice in identifying pre-modifiers and post-modifiers in adjective phrases, we now examine how these phrases are used by children with SLI. Several utterances which contain adjective phrases are displayed in Table 5.5. These children used a number of adverb phrases as pre-modifiers. These phrases are underlined in the utterances below:

> She is <u>really</u> sad.
> She was <u>so</u> happy that she didn't go by the pool no more.
> She was <u>very</u> mad at him.
> One of them were <u>too</u> full.

TABLE 5.5 Use of adjective phrases by children with specific language impairment

Gender (Age)	Utterances
Male (8;06)	She is really sad
Female (8;11)	They both was scared of the airplane
Female (8;09)	The girl is bouncing her favouritest ball
Female (8;09)	She was so happy that she didn't go by the pool no more
Male (8;01)	She was happy to play right now
Female (8;09)	She was very mad at him
Male (9;06)	The giraffe was very angry at her
Male (8;01)	One of them were too full
Female (7;06)	The zebra was happy with his airplane

Table 5.5 also contains an utterance which shows what can go wrong when an adverb is not used to pre-modify an adjective. Here, the superlative form of the adjective *favourite* should be *most favourite* rather than *favouritest*:

> The girl is bouncing her <u>favouritest</u> ball.

Several post-modifiers in adjective phrases can also be illustrated by the utterances in Table 5.5. Prepositional phrases were often used by these children as post-modifiers:

> They both was scared <u>of the airplane</u>.
> She was very mad <u>at him</u>.
> The zebra was happy <u>with his airplane</u>.

Clauses too were used by the children with SLI. Most commonly, they took the form of *to*-infinitive clauses and *that*-clauses:

> She was happy <u>to play right now</u>.
> She was so happy <u>that she didn't go by the pool no more</u>.

5.4.4 Functions in Adjective Phrases

Once again, we conclude with discussion of the functions of the different parts of an adjective phrase. An adjective phrase can consist of a stand-alone adjective or an adjective with other words. The adjective is the head of the phrase. The term 'head' is already a functional label. Adverb phrases can come before the head and are called specifiers. The post-modifiers in adjective phrases – mostly prepositional phrases and clauses – have the function of complement in the phrase. These different functional components of adjective phrases are illustrated below:

HEAD ADJECTIVE	*proud*
SPECIFIER + HEAD ADJECTIVE	*very proud*
HEAD ADJECTIVE + COMPLEMENT	*proud of her achievements*
SPECIFIER + HEAD ADJECTIVE + COMPLEMENT	*very proud of her achievements*

There is no better way to expand your knowledge of adjective phrases than to see them in actual use. The following Special Topic is designed to do just that.

SPECIAL TOPIC 5.3 ADJECTIVE PHRASES IN TALK ABOUT FOOD

Perhaps unsurprisingly, children make extensive use of adjective phrases to describe food. This occurs during and outside of mealtimes. Our typically developing child Ella is no exception. She uses adjective phrases quite often to describe food during interactions with her parents. Ten of Ella's food-related utterances are shown below. Each utterance contains an adjective phrase:

(a) Can I have a little bit of lemonade? (3;00)
(b) I'm not hungry (3;00)
(c) I want to have Nutella on soft white bread (3;03)
(d) This is called scrambled eggs (3;05)
(e) It's getting a bit soft (3;05)
(f) It might be a bit juicy (3;05)
(g) A pears might be not ripe for a minute (3;05)
(h) That not real food (5;00)
(i) I like them spicy (5;00)
(j) They look spicy (5;00)

Ella makes varied use of adjective phrases. These phrases are often used as pre-modifiers in noun phrases: *a little bit of lemonade; soft white bread; scrambled eggs; real food*. Within adjective phrases, Ella uses both pre-modifiers and post-modifiers. In the phrases *a bit soft* and *a bit juicy*, Ella is using *a bit* as a pre-modifying adverb. In the adjective phrase *ripe for a minute*, she uses a prepositional phrase (*for a minute*) as a post-modifier. Some of Ella's adjective phrases are subject complements in a sentence while other phrases are object complements. In the following utterances an adjective phrase is used as a subject complement:

> *I'm not hungry.*
> *They look spicy.*

This is because the lexical verbs in these utterances are intensive or copular verbs. Ella also uses adjective phrases as object complements. This occurs in *I like them spicy* where the adjective phrase *spicy* refers to the same things as the direct object pronoun *them*. The direct object and adjective phrase follow a complex transitive verb in this utterance. Even at the relatively young age of 3 to 5 years, Ella is able to use adjective phrases in a range of quite complex ways.

The main points in this section are summarised below.

> ## KEY POINTS ADJECTIVE PHRASES
>
> - An adjective phrase consists of a head adjective and its modifiers. Some of these modifiers come before the head adjective (pre-modifiers) while others come after the head adjective (post-modifiers).
> - Adverb phrases can be pre-modifiers in an adjective phrase. Typically, they take the form of degree adverbs (intensifying expressions) like *very, really* and *extremely* which intensify the attribute or property expressed by the adjective (*really old, very pretty*).
> - Post-modifiers in an adjective phrase include adverbs (*strong enough*), prepositional phrases (*stressed at work*) and clauses. Clauses may take the form of *to*-infinitive clauses (*fortunate to be rich*) and *that*-clauses (*angry that she left a mess*).
> - Adjective phrases can be used as pre-modifiers and post-modifiers in other phrases. For example, they can appear as a pre-modifier in a noun phrase (*really sick child*) and as a post-modifier in a verb phrase (*sounds really great*).
> - Adjective phrases can also be characterised in terms of the functions of their parts. The pre-modifier in an adjective phrase is the specifier (*very late*). The term 'complement' is used of the prepositional phrases and clauses which are post-modifiers in an adjective phrase.

5.5 Adverb Phrases

Adverb phrases observe the same three-part structure that is seen in other phrases. The head of an adverb phrase is an adverb. An adverb can stand on its own as an adverb phrase as it does in each of the following sentences:

> *They sing beautifully.*
> *Tom left early.*
> *Sue will arrive soon.*
> *They went abroad.*

5.5.1 Pre-Modifiers in Adverb Phrases

Pre-modifiers in an adverb phrase are limited to other adverbs. Pre-modifying adverbs often intensify the meaning expressed by the head adverb. For example, in the sentence *Bill walked very slowly*, Bill did not just walk slowly. Rather, he walked very slowly. Any of the following words can serve as a pre-modifier of the head adverb *slowly* in this sentence:

> *Bill walked very/really/extremely/rather/too/quite slowly.*

These pre-modifiers can all stand before the adverb *slowly* because this adverb is gradable. Adverbs which are not gradable cannot be pre-modified by adverbs like *really* and *very*:

> *Mary travelled very southwards.*
> *Peter looked really skywards.*

Certain other adverbs can modify gradable adverbs like *slowly*. For example, we can use sentences such as the following:

> Bill walked <u>unbelievably</u> slowly.
> Bill walked <u>ridiculously</u> slowly.
> Bill walked <u>infuriatingly</u> slowly.

These lexical adverbs convey additional meaning in the adverb phrase and do not intensify the gradable adverb that is the head of the phrase. The two-word combination of head adverb and adverb pre-modifier can occupy different positions in a sentence. It can occur at the beginning or the end of a sentence. It can also stand immediately before or after the lexical verb:

> <u>Relatively recently,</u> Oscar travelled to Moscow.
> Oscar travelled to Moscow <u>relatively recently</u>.
> Oscar <u>relatively recently</u> travelled to Moscow.
> Oscar travelled <u>relatively recently</u> to Moscow.

The choice of location is often determined by what effect the speaker is trying to create. For example, if the timing of Oscar's trip to Moscow is judged by the speaker to be particularly important, then this can be given prominence by using the first sentence above. Other adverb phrases cannot move around a sentence with such ease. The adverb phrase *very late* can only occur either at the end of the sentence or immediately before the lexical verb. Its use at the beginning of the sentence is stylistically clumsy, as indicated by the '?', while its use immediately after the lexical verb is ungrammatical:

> Sam contacted the office <u>very late</u>.
> Sam <u>very late</u> contacted the office.
> ?<u>Very late</u> Sam contacted the office.
> *Sam contacted <u>very late</u> the office.

Young, typically developing children are remarkably adept at working out the positions that adverb phrases can occupy within a sentence. The utterances below were produced by Lara when she was 3 years and 3 months old. Lara uses adverb phrases in sentence-initial position and in sentence-final position. Other adverb phrases appear before the lexical verb. Even at this relatively young age, Lara appears to have a sufficiently well-developed knowledge of the grammar of English to avoid ungrammatical sentences like *I will together put the ends*:

I will put the ends <u>together</u>.
Pick that bit up <u>quickly</u>.
<u>Now</u> it's ready.
Monster hasn't gone <u>yet</u>.
I'm <u>just</u> riding.
Can we put that way <u>round</u>?

An adverb phrase can be a modifier in another phrase. For example, in the following sentences an adverb phrase is a pre-modifier and a post-modifier in a verb phrase:

June <u>really quickly</u> left the room.
Mike walks <u>really quickly</u>.

An adverb phrase can also be a pre-modifier and a post-modifier in an adjective phrase:

The child is <u>really quite</u> sick.
The fence is tall <u>enough</u>.

An adverb phrase can be a pre-modifier in an adverb phrase. In the sentence below, a pre-modified adverb (*so unbelievably*) is a pre-modifier in an adverb phrase:

They responded <u>so unbelievably</u> slowly.

In the following examples, a pre-modified adverb in an adverb phrase modifies an entire clause:

<u>Rather bizarrely</u> she lept out of her seat.
<u>Quite unexpectedly</u> Fran came through the door.

5.5.2 Post-Modifiers in Adverb Phrases

There is only one possible post-modifier in an adverb phrase, the prepositional phrase. Prepositional phrases tend to be found in sentence-initial adverb phrases:

Unfortunately <u>for Jack</u>, the treatment arrived too late.
Luckily <u>for the woman</u>, her handbag was still on the bus.

5.5.3 Adverb Phrases in Adults with Alzheimer's Dementia

Like other phrases, adverb phrases can best be grasped by examining their use by real language users. Adults with probable **Alzheimer's dementia** produced each of the utterances in Table 5.6. Unlike semantic knowledge, which can deteriorate early in Alzheimer's dementia, grammatical knowledge often remains intact until a late stage of disease. These utterances were used during a narrative production

TABLE 5.6 Use of adverb phrases by adults with Alzheimer's dementia

Gender (Age)	Utterances
Male (57 years)	The water is still flowing
Male (59 years)	It already is starting to fall over
Female (73 years)	There are curtains there
Female (75 years)	I don't quite get that
Female (75 years)	Basically it's kind of a distressing scene
Male (81 years)	And pretty soon it's not gonna be very quiet
Male (67 years)	The mother doesn't seem too affected by it
Male (67 years)	Don't make too much noise
Male (67 years)	She can't reach it apparently
Male (63 years)	One of her feet is obviously in the water
Male (63 years)	It looks like maybe tennis shoes
Male (77 years)	She didn't know it perhaps

task, the Cookie Theft **picture description task** in the Boston Diagnostic Aphasia Examination (Goodglass et al., 2001).

The use of adverb phrases by these adults is noteworthy in several respects. More often than not, adverb phrases are used without either pre-modifiers or post-modifiers. This occurs in utterances such as the following:

> The water is _still_ flowing.
> It _already_ is starting to fall over.
> There are curtains _there_.
> I don't _quite_ get that.
> She can't reach it _apparently_.

But even in the absence of their own modifiers, these adverb phrases serve as pre-modifiers and post-modifiers in other types of phrases. In the first example below, the adverb phrase *too* is a pre-modifier in an adjective phrase. In the second example, the adverb phrase *apparently* is a post-modifier in a verb phrase. In the third example, the adverb phrase *too* is a pre-modifier in a noun phrase. In the fourth example, the adverb phrase *basically* appears to modify the entire clause:

> The mother doesn't seem _too affected by it_. *[Adjective phrase]*
> She _can't reach it apparently_. *[Verb phrase]*
> Don't make _too much noise_. *[Noun phrase]*
> Basically _it's kind of a distressing scene_. *[Clause]*

These adults do, however, also use adverb phrases which contain pre-modifiers and post-modifiers. The adverb phrase in the first utterance below has an adverb (*pretty*) as a pre-modifier. The adverb phrase in the second utterance has a prepositional phrase (*in the water*) as a post-modifier:

> And <u>pretty soon</u> it's not gonna be very quiet.
> One of her feet is <u>obviously in the water</u>.

The adverb phrases used by these adults convey a range of meanings. Several express a lack of certainty on the part of the speaker. They include *perhaps* and *maybe* in these examples:

> She didn't know it <u>perhaps</u>.
> It looks like <u>maybe</u> tennis shoes.

Other adverb phrases express spatial and temporal meanings, as the following examples illustrate:

> There are curtains <u>there</u>. [Space]
> The water is <u>still</u> flowing. [Time]
> It <u>already</u> is starting to fall over. [Time]

Finally, there are certain words in these utterances which we would not so readily identify as being adverb phrases. We tend to think of the word *pretty* as being an adjective (e.g. *Sally is pretty*). However, in the first utterance below *pretty* is a pre-modifying adverb in an adverb phrase. Other words in English which can be both adjectives and adverbs are *early* and *late*, e.g. *Chomsky's <u>early</u> writing is fascinating* (adjective) and *He arrived <u>early</u>* (adverb). The informal expression *kind of* in the second example below is also an adverb. In the last example, the word *over* is an adverb. It is part of the verb–particle combination *fall over*. So-called intransitive phrasal verbs are described in Section 3.3 in Chapter 3:

> And <u>pretty soon</u> it's not gonna be very quiet.
> Basically it's <u>kind of</u> a distressing scene.
> It already is starting to fall <u>over</u>.

How would you characterise the word *pretty* in the following sentences?

> 'So we're pretty sure what we're going to face'. (*Waikato Times*, New Zealand, 2017)
>   'Tech and us know each other pretty well'. (*The Southland Times*, New Zealand, 2017)
>   'It's pretty hard. Just watching the lads go about their work and being on the sideline'. (*The Dominion Post*, New Zealand, 2017)

It is now time for you to get practice at identifying and describing adverb phrases for yourself. Either individually or in a group, you should attempt the task in Exercise 5.4.

EXERCISE 5.4 ADVERB PHRASES IN ALZHEIMER'S DEMENTIA

The following utterances have been produced by adults who are exhibiting early-stage Alzheimer's dementia. Each utterance contains one or more adverb phrases. For the utterances in Part A, you should identify the adverb phrase. Also, indicate if a pre-modifier and/or a post-modifier is/are present in the phrase. For the utterances in Part B, you should identify the adverb phrase. Also, indicate if the adverb phrase is a pre-modifier or a post-modifier in another type of phrase.

Part A
 (a) I see it very clearly (male; 66 years)
 (b) The mother is washing dishes absentmindedly (female; 74 years)
 (c) I see the little boy's down here (female; 70 years)
 (d) The cookies must be pretty good (male; 77 years)
 (e) Here's a little boy high up on the ladder (male; 83 years)
 (f) I'm looking outside but that yard is okay (male; 50 years)
 (g) The place is very pretty (female; 66 years)
 (h) She also spilled the water (female; 73 years)
 (i) She's inside drying the clothes (male; 66 years)
 (j) The little girl has her finger right up to her mouth (male; 72 years)

Part B
 (a) The curtains are very distinct (male; 57 years)
 (b) The boy is also falling off the stool (male; 59 years)
 (c) The stool's about ready to fall (female; 65 years)
 (d) They've already eaten (male; 68 years)
 (e) I have not so much trouble (male; 66 years)
 (f) Let's see now (male; 68 years)
 (g) The other is somewhat obliterated (male; 63 years)
 (h) The mother is apparently washing or drying the dishes (male; 51 years)
 (i) His sister is telling him to be very quiet (male; 51 years)
 (j) There are a number of cabinets on the sink counter as it stretches around (male; 63 years)

5.5.4 Functions in Adverb Phrases

Finally, we conclude discussion of adverb phrases by examining the functions of the parts of the phrase. We have seen how an adverb can be a pre-modifier in an adverb phrase. The function of the adverb pre-modifier is an adjunct. The only possible post-modifier in an adverb phrase is a prepositional phrase. The function of the prepositional phrase is a complement. Adjuncts and complements in adverb phrases are illustrated in the examples below:

This works <u>really</u> [Adjunct] *well* [Head] *<u>for its size</u>* [Complement].
He moves <u>quite</u> [Adjunct] *gracefully* [Head] *<u>for a man</u>* [Complement].

The main points in this section are summarised below.

KEY POINTS ADVERB PHRASES

- An adverb phrase is a head adverb and its modifiers. An adverb on its own without a pre-modifier or a post-modifier is also an adverb phrase.
- An adverb can be a pre-modifier in an adverb phrase (*<u>really</u> quickly, <u>quite</u> stupidly*). The only possible post-modifier in an adverb phrase is a prepositional phrase (*effortlessly <u>for an amateur</u>*).
- Adverb phrases can be pre-modifiers and post-modifiers in other phrases. They can be pre-modifiers in adjective phrases (*<u>quite unbelievably</u> stupid*) and post-modifiers in verb phrases (*sings <u>rather beautifully</u>*).
- Adverb phrases can occupy a range of positions in the sentence. They may appear in sentence-initial position (*<u>Happily</u> I do not need to worry*) and in sentence-final position (*Sue walked along the street <u>quite happily</u>*). They can occur directly before a lexical verb (*She was <u>just</u> singing*) or directly after a lexical verb (*They might leave <u>early</u>*).
- The pre-modifier in an adverb phrase has the function of an adjunct. The post-modifier in an adverb phrase has the function of a complement, e.g. *He works <u>very</u>* [Adjunct] *hard* [Head] *<u>for a junior partner</u>* [Complement].

5.6 Prepositional Phrases

The final type of phrase we need to examine is the prepositional phrase. As one might expect by this stage, a prepositional phrase consists of a head preposition and its modifiers. However, we must already note a feature which sets prepositional phrases apart from other phrases. Whereas in other phrases the head can stand on its own without modifiers, this is not possible in a prepositional phrase. This is because a preposition which occurs on its own results in an ungrammatical sentence:

The house is <u>next to the lake</u>. [Prepositional phrase]
*The house is next to.
They live in Portugal <u>during the winter</u>. [Prepositional phrase]
*They live in Portugal during.

We merely note this feature of prepositional phrases, but continue to describe prepositions as the head of prepositional phrases in exactly the same way that we describe nouns and verbs as the heads of noun phrases and verb phrases, respectively.

The following sentences each contain a prepositional phrase. These sentences illustrate that, like adverb phrases, prepositional phrases can occupy a range of positions in the sentence. This includes sentence-initial and sentence-final positions as in the first two examples below. Prepositional phrases can also follow a lexical verb as in the final example:

Following the incident, she contacted the police.
They returned home after dark.
Sally walked for two hours yesterday.

A sentence may contain one, two, three or more prepositional phrases. Of course, a sentence may also contain no prepositional phrases:

She sat on the bench. [One prepositional phrase]
Billy lay on the sofa for an hour. [Two prepositional phrases]
He put the flowers in the vase on the table next to the door. [Three prepositional phrases]
After midnight she heard steps on the concrete pavement beside her house in York. [Four prepositional phrases]

5.6.1 Post-Modifiers in Prepositional Phrases

Each of the prepositional phrases in the above sentences contains the same post-modifier: a noun phrase. Pronouns may take the place of noun phrases in the post-modifier of a prepositional phrase:

We walked towards the ancient church ~ We walked towards it.
The men talked about the country's politicians ~ The men talked about them.
Fran lives above George ~ Fran lives above him.

In some non-standard dialects, the pronoun becomes separated from the preposition. This can be seen in the following utterance of Lara's grandmother, who is a speaker of Durham dialect:

*'I'm gonna put **him** a red coat **on** because he's a red coat'*

Prepositional phrases can also be post-modifiers in prepositional phrases. The first preposition in each of the following underlined phrases is the head preposition:

Do not disturb me until after the meeting.
They appeared from behind the wall.

Occasionally, adjectives can occur as post-modifiers in prepositional phrases. In the following sentences, the prepositions *as* and *for* are post-modified by adjectives:

This strikes me as ridiculous.
We took him for dead.

Adverbs can also be post-modifiers in prepositional phrases. The first word in the underlined phrases is a head preposition:

She was chairwoman until recently.
We can't stay for long.

The final group of post-modifiers in prepositional phrases is clauses. In the sentences below, clauses are headed by the prepositions *on* and *for*:

> It depends <u>on how you approach it</u>.
> He is asking <u>for what he is entitled to</u>.

5.6.2 Pre-Modifiers in Prepositional Phrases

Adverbs are the only possible pre-modifier in a prepositional phrase. The first word in each of the underlined phrases below is an adverb:

> It was <u>just after midnight</u>.
> They crept <u>back through the tunnel</u>.
> Jack lept <u>right over the bar</u>.

5.6.3 Other Phrases and the Prepositional Phrase

Prepositional phrases are often post-modifiers in other types of phrases. Noun phrases may contain a prepositional phrase as a post-modifier. The bracketed words in the sentences below are noun phrases. Within these noun phrases, the prepositional phrase as post-modifier is underlined:

> Pete bought [a book <u>about the French revolution</u>].
> The pupil had [a lesson <u>on volcanoes</u>].
> Mike sold [his Vienna wall clock <u>with roman numerals</u>].

Each of these noun phrases can be expanded by the addition of further prepositional phrases. The following sentence contains a noun phrase (NP2) within a noun phrase (NP1), each with a prepositional phrase as a post-modifier:

> The pupil had a lesson on the formation of volcanoes.
>   a <u>lesson on the formation of volcanoes</u> [NP1: Head noun + prep. phrase]
>   the <u>formation of volcanoes</u> [NP2: Head noun + prep. phrase]

Prepositional phrases can also be post-modifiers in verb phrases. More than one prepositional phrase may appear in the post-modifier of a verb phrase:

> Joan stood <u>on the front lawn</u>.
> Mary walked <u>through the doorway into brilliant sunshine</u>.

Adjective phrases may have a prepositional phrase as a post-modifier. The bracketed words in the following sentences are adjective phrases. The prepositional phrases within them are underlined:

> Oscar was [so afraid <u>of the dark</u>].
> The teenage boys were [really mad <u>about football</u>].

Finally, prepositional phrases may also be post-modifiers in adverb phrases. In these contexts, the head preposition in the phrase is often the word *for*:

> [Unfortunately <u>for Sue</u>], her guests arrived late.
> Jack sang [really well <u>for an amateur</u>].

5.6.4 Prepositional Phrases in Lara and Ella

You can only become skilled at identifying and describing prepositional phrases in sentences by examining their use in actual language. To this end, we now examine utterances produced by the two typically developing children we started the chapter with: Lara and Ella. Each utterance in Table 5.7 contains one or more prepositional phrases. Lara was 3 years and 3 months old when these utterances were produced. Ella was 3 years and 7 months old.

Let us begin by examining how Lara uses prepositional phrases. Lara's prepositional phrases contain both pre-modifiers and post-modifiers. She uses the only possible pre-modifier in a prepositional phrase – an adverb phrase – in the following utterances. The prepositional phrase is indicated in brackets. The adverb pre-modifier in each phrase is underlined:

> I'm getting [<u>right</u> in pirate ship].
> I'm [<u>right up</u> to there].

Several post-modifiers in prepositional phrases can also be illustrated by means of Lara's utterances in Table 5.7. As one might expect, a noun phrase was most commonly used as a post-modifier:

> I'm getting [right in <u>pirate ship</u>].

TABLE 5.7 Use of prepositional phrases by Lara and Ella

Lara's utterances	Ella's utterances
I'm getting right in pirate ship	Get another bowl for Jennifer
Is Amy scared of something?	I dipped some water on my finger
I'm running to the shops	Her pram is coloured in different colours
Can you look after my bag?	I think it's pointing at the radio
It was a bit of my hoover	I'm drawing on the table
The chair's too heavy for me	A pears might be not ripe for a minute
I'm right up to there	I think he's staring at something
I can wait until after Christmas	Can have a look in there
Can I have a drink of your apple juice?	She wants up on there
I need to stick the tea towel on there	You're straight in the flowerbeds
Doesn't she want to sit on here?	Don't sit next to me
You're a great big pain in the bum	I want salt on mine

I'm running [to <u>the shops</u>].
Can you look [after <u>my bag</u>]?
It was a bit [of <u>my hoover</u>].
Can I have a drink [of <u>your apple juice</u>]?
You're a great big pain [in <u>the bum</u>].

Lara also uses prepositional phrases in which a pronoun takes the place of a noun phrase as a post-modifier in the phrase. In the following examples, the indefinite pronoun *something* and the personal pronoun *me* are used:

Is Amy scared [of <u>something</u>]?
The chair's too heavy [for <u>me</u>].

As well as noun phrases, Lara also uses adverb phrases and prepositional phrases as post-modifiers in prepositional phrases:

Adverb phrase
I'm right up [to <u>there</u>].
I need to stick the tea towel [on <u>there</u>].
Doesn't she want to sit [on <u>here</u>].

Prepositional phrase
I can wait [until <u>after Christmas</u>].

Lara's prepositional phrases can be further analysed in terms of their role as post-modifiers in other types of phrases. Often, her prepositional phrases assume the role of post-modifier in a noun phrase. In the following utterances, noun phrases are bracketed. The post-modifying prepositional phrases within these phrases are underlined:

It was [a bit <u>of my hoover</u>].
Can I have [a drink <u>of your apple juice</u>]?

Lara also uses prepositional phrases as post-modifiers in verb phrases. The bracketed verb phrases in the following utterances each contain a prepositional phrase as a post-modifier:

I'm [running <u>to the shops</u>].
Can you [look <u>after my bag</u>]?

In Section 3.3 in Chapter 3, the verb–particle combination *look after* in the example above was described as a prepositional verb – a verb which takes a prepositional phrase as an object. Prepositional verbs were distinguished from transitive phrasal verbs like *turn on* by virtue of the fact that the preposition could not be separated from the rest of the phrase. So while the sentence *She turned the radio on* is grammatical, the sentence **She looked the children after* is clearly not.

To a lesser degree, Lara uses prepositional phrases as a post-modifier in both adjective phrases and adverb phrases. In the following utterances, two adjective phrases contain a prepositional phrase as a post-modifier:

> Is Amy [scared _of something_]?
> The chair's [too heavy _for me_].

A prepositional phrase is used as a post-modifier in the adverb phrase in this utterance:

> I'm [right up _to there_].

Like Lara, Ella uses pre-modifiers and post-modifiers in her prepositional phrases. In the following utterances, an adverb phrase is used as a pre-modifier in a prepositional phrase:

> She wants [_up_ on there].
> You're [_straight_ in the flowerbeds].

Noun phrases are also the most commonly used post-modifier in Ella's prepositional phrases. The noun phrase post-modifiers in the following prepositional phrases include proper nouns (_Jennifer_), common nouns (_table_) and compound nouns (_flowerbeds_). Determiners including the definite and indefinite article and the possessive determiner (_my_) precede the nouns in these phrases:

> Get another bowl [for _Jennifer_].
> I dipped some water [on _my finger_].
> Her pram is coloured [in _different colours_].
> I think it's pointing [at _the radio_].
> I'm drawing [on _the table_].
> A pears might be not ripe [for _a minute_].
> You're straight [in _the flowerbeds_].

Pronouns sometimes take the place of noun phrases as post-modifiers in prepositional phrases. In the following utterances, pronouns include the indefinite pronoun (_something_), the personal pronoun (_me_), and the possessive pronoun (_mine_):

> I think he's staring [at _something_].
> Don't sit [next to _me_].
> I want salt [on _mine_].

Ella uses one other post-modifier in her prepositional phrases. The adverb phrase _there_ is a post-modifier in the prepositional phrases in the following utterances:

> Can have a look [in _there_].
> She wants up [on _there_].

Like Lara, Ella's prepositional phrases appear as post-modifiers in a number of other types of phrase. The noun phrases in these utterances have prepositional phrases as post-modifiers:

> Get [another bowl _for Jennifer_].
> I dipped [some water _on my finger_].
> Can have [a look _in there_].
> I want [salt _on mine_].

Most of Ella's prepositional phrases are used as post-modifiers in verb phrases, as in the following examples:

> I think it's [pointing _at the radio_].
> I'm [drawing _on the table_].
> I think he's [staring _at something_].
> You [are _straight in the flowerbeds_].
> Don't [sit _next to me_].

Less commonly, Ella uses prepositional phrases as post-modifiers in adjective phrases and adverb phrases. The following utterances contain adjective phrases with post-modifying prepositional phrases:

> Her pram is [coloured _in different colours_].
> A pears might be not [ripe _for a minute_].

A prepositional phrase is a post-modifier in an adverb phrase in the following example:

> She wants [up _on there_].

This discussion has demonstrated that long before typically developing children reach their fourth birthday, they are competent in using prepositional phrases with a range of pre- and post-modifiers. They are also able to use these phrases as post-modifiers in noun, verb, adjective and adverb phrases. For our typically developing children at least, the acquisition of prepositional phrases appears to pose few challenges during language development. In Exercise 5.5, we will see if the same is true of children with specific language impairment.

5.6.5 Functions in Prepositional Phrases

We conclude discussion of prepositional phrases by examining the functions of the parts of these phrases. The bracketed prepositional phrases in the sentences below contain a noun phrase and a prepositional phrase as post-modifiers. They complete the meaning of the head preposition – constructions such as *Sally is sitting in* and *The man appeared from* are ungrammatical. As such, they are called 'complements':

EXERCISE 5.5 PREPOSITIONAL PHRASES IN CHILDREN WITH SPECIFIC LANGUAGE IMPAIRMENT

The following utterances were produced by children with specific language impairment during a narrative production task. Each utterance contains a prepositional phrase. You should (i) identify the prepositional phrase including any pre-modifiers and/or post-modifiers, and (ii) indicate if the prepositional phrase is a post-modifier in another type of phrase. How does the use of prepositional phrases by these children with SLI compare to the use of these same phrases by typically developing children like Lara and Ella? The gender and chronological age of each child are indicated in brackets:

(a) April was like so mad at Sally (male; 9;4 years)
(b) Sit on this bench for a while (male; 8;6 years)
(c) Longnose was running toward the water (female; 9;9 years)
(d) The ball fell right into the pool (male; 9;7 years)
(e) The bunny put some more sand on the castle (female; 9;7 years)
(f) There was an elephant playing with a ball near the pool (male; 9;7 years)
(g) An elephant with a net came (male; 9;7 years)
(h) The bunny is full of food (female; 9;3 years)
(i) The elephant felled in love with the zebra (male; 9;8 years)
(j) The moose was swimming in the water (female; 9;7 years)

> Sally is sitting [in the room].
> The man appeared [from behind the wall].

Pre-modifying adverbs like almost, nearly, right and just assume the functional label of 'specifier' in prepositional phrases. Each of the bracketed prepositional phrases in the following sentences contains a specifier:

> Jack was [almost next to the chairman].
> She was [nearly in front of the camera].
> They arrived [right before the accident].
> It was [just after midnight].

The main points in this section are summarised below.

KEY POINTS PREPOSITIONAL PHRASES

- A prepositional phrase consists of a head preposition and all of its modifiers. Unlike other phrases, the head in a prepositional phrase cannot stand on its own. Constructions such as *Mary lives next to and *Tom likes the vase with, which contain head prepositions with no post-modifier, are ungrammatical.

- There is only one possible pre-modifier in a prepositional phrase: the adverb phrase. In the sentence *Jim lives <u>right</u> above the shop*, the adverb phrase *right* pre-modifies the preposition *above*.
- Post-modifiers in a prepositional phrase are more numerous than pre-modifiers. They include noun phrases as in the bracketed prepositional phrase in the sentence *They cut the tree [in <u>the garden</u>]*. Pronouns may replace noun phrases as post-modifiers in prepositional phrases. This occurs in the second of these sentences: *Mary put icing [on <u>the cake</u>]* and *Mary put icing [on <u>it</u>]*.
- Less commonly, head prepositions may be post-modified by prepositional phrases: *They postponed the decision [until <u>after Christmas</u>]*. Adjective phrases may also be post-modifiers in prepositional phrases: *We took him [for <u>insane</u>]*.
- Adverb phrases are also possible post-modifiers in prepositional phrases. In the sentence *She has opposed the plans [until <u>now</u>]*, the adverb phrase *now* is post-modifying the head preposition *until*. Clauses, too, can be post-modifiers in prepositional phrases. The underlined words in the following sentence form a post-modifying clause: *She longed [for <u>what the government had promised</u>]*.
- Prepositional phrases can also be post-modifiers in a range of other phrases. This includes noun phrases (*the man <u>with a hat</u>*), verb phrases (*walked <u>through the door</u>*), adjective phrases (*anxious <u>about the situation</u>*) and adverb phrases (*really well <u>for a novice</u>*).
- Phrases can become very complex indeed when other phrases are embedded within them. For example, there are three prepositional phrases embedded within the complex noun phrase *the tree next to the lake at the end of the garden*. These phrases are *next to the lake at the end of the garden* (PP1), *at the end of the garden* (PP2), and *of the garden* (PP3).
- Prepositional phrases can also be examined in terms of the functions of their parts. Post-modifiers like noun phrases (*in <u>tears</u>*) and prepositional phrases (*until <u>after the holidays</u>*) complete the meaning of the head preposition and are complements in the phrase. Pre-modifying adverb phrases (*<u>right</u> above his head*) are specifiers in prepositional phrases.

SUMMARY

In this chapter you have seen the following:

- Phrases have an internal structure that consists at a minimum of a head and either a pre-modifier or a post-modifier, or both.
- The structures that may be pre-modifiers in phrases vary with phrase type. The pre-modifier in the noun phrase *cold weather* is an adjective and in the verb phrase *nearly missed the bus* is an adverb phrase.
- The structures that may be post-modifiers in phrases also vary with phrase type. The post-modifier in the adjective phrase *afraid of the dark* is a prepositional phrase and in the adverb phrase *unfortunately for the boy* is a prepositional phrase.
- The internal structure of phrases can be highly complex. The prepositional phrase *beside the ancient church with two spires* contains a noun phrase *the ancient church with two spires* as a post-modifier. This noun phrase contains a

prepositional phrase *with two spires* as a post-modifier. This prepositional phrase contains a noun phrase *two spires* as a post-modifier.

- The internal parts of a phrase may also be given functional labels. In the prepositional phrase *right next to the tree*, the pre-modifying adverb *right* is a specifier while the post-modifying noun phrase *the tree* is a complement.

WEBSITE PHRASES

After reading the chapter, visit the website and test your knowledge of phrases by answering the multiple-choice questions for this topic.

HOMEWORK ASSIGNMENT

The British Council offers advice on English grammar to British teachers who are planning to teach American students. Some of this advice is shown in the box below. Using your knowledge of verbs, how would you characterise these grammatical differences between British and American English? Are these grammatical features found only in Standard American English, or are they also features of non-standard dialects of American English?

BRITISH COUNCIL: BRITISH ENGLISH AND AMERICAN ENGLISH

Americans use certain verb forms less than speakers of British English, and a British teacher might mark wrong some things that an American teacher would say are correct:

> **American English:** *Did you do your homework yet?*
> **British English:** *Have you done your homework yet?*
> **American English:** *I already ate.*
> **British English:** *I've already eaten.*

In British English, 'have got' is often used for the possessive sense of 'have' and 'have got to' is informally used for 'have to'. This is much less common in American English:

> **British English:** *I've got two sisters.*
> **American English:** *I have two sisters.*
> **British English:** *I've got to go now.*
> **American English:** *I have to go now.*

SUGGESTIONS FOR FURTHER READING

(1) Börjars, K. and Burridge, K. (2010) *Introducing English Grammar*, Second Edition. New York and Abingdon: Routledge.

For extended discussion of verb phrases and noun phrases, you should consult chapters 6 and 7 in this volume. In chapter 6, different classes of lexical verbs and the post-verbal elements that accompany them are addressed. The discussion in chapter 7 on noun phrases asks how a noun phrase can be spotted and guides you on how to locate the head of the phrase. There is also examination of pre-modifiers and post-modifiers in noun phrases.

(2) Ballard, K. (2013) *The Frameworks of English*, Third Edition. Houndmills, Basingstoke: Palgrave Macmillan.

In chapter 5 of this volume, there is a clear, accessible examination of the five phrase types which are discussed in this chapter: noun phrases; verb phrases; adjective phrases; adverb phrases; and prepositional phrases. The chapter also addresses the embedding of phrases.

(3) Altenberg, E. P. and Vago, R. M. (2010) *English Grammar: Understanding the Basics*. Cambridge: Cambridge University Press.

Part II: Kinds of Phrases in this volume contains several units which address the phrase types that are examined in this chapter. These units are Noun Phrases (unit 9), Prepositional Phrases (unit 10), Verb Phrases (unit 11) and Auxiliary Phrases (unit 12). Each of these units contains Test Yourself questions and answers.

QUESTIONS PHRASES

(1) The following utterances were produced by Lara, a child with normal language development. In each utterance, a noun phrase is underlined. Identify the pre-modifier and/or post-modifier in each of the underlined phrases.

(a) I'm going to get <u>food for the horse</u> (3;00)

(b) She's <u>a horrid people</u> (3;00)

(c) I making <u>some little prickles</u> (3;00)

(d) I want <u>the little boy to go</u> (3;00)

(e) I think it's up in <u>my attic room</u> now (2;11)

(f) That's <u>a bit of green plasticine</u> (2;11)

(g) I want you to make <u>pretend tea for me</u> (3;00)

(h) We're going to <u>that pretend animal farm</u> (3;00)

(i) This is <u>a very good place</u> (3;00)

(j) That's not <u>a lovely book</u> (3;00)

(2) Only certain words can stand before and after head verbs in verb phrases. The following utterances are produced by children with SLI. Identify the pre-modifiers in the utterances in Part A and the post-modifiers in the utterances in Part B.

Part A

(a) He didn't got it back (Male; 5;02)

(b) The doctor cannot get it from the water (Male; 5;02)

(c) And he still has a tummy ache (Female; 5;07)

(d) The other elephant will get the airplane (Female; 6;01)

(e) I just drop it (Male; 6;07)

Part B

(a) Then the manager gets impossible (Female; 6;08)

(b) So he pick a balloon first (Female; 6;08)

(c) The giraffe gave the ball to missus elephant (Male; 6;06)

(d) He pretended it was flying (Male; 6;06)

(e) Missus rabbit was very embarrassed (Male; 6;06)

(3) The following utterances are produced by children with SLI. Each utterance contains an adjective phrase. Identify the head of the phrase along with any pre-modifiers and post-modifiers.

(a) The giraffe is mad at the elephant (Male; 8;10)

(b) She was happy that she got a bandaid (Female; 8;11)

(c) The giraffe was so happy (Male; 8;05)

(d) She was happy that he got it for the elephant (Male; 9;06)

(e) She was responsible for it (Female; 6;08)

(f) He was really sad that he lost his friend balloon (Male; 9;06)

(g) I am sorry about that (Female; 6;11)

(h) Then elephant is very shy with giraffe (Female; 6;11)

(i) The rabbit is so sorry to get the balloon up there (Female; 6;11)

(j) She was nice to the giraffe (Male; 7;04)

(4) Young, typically developing children can use adverb phrases to express a range of meanings. Some of these meanings are *manner, direction, degree, frequency, place* and *time.* The following utterances were produced by Lara when she was 3 years and 3 months old. Identify the adverb phrase in each utterance. Also, indicate the type of meaning that is expressed by the adverb phrase.

(a) Can I see in there?

(b) Monster hasn't gone yet.

(c) I do mine quickly.

(d) Amy go away.

(e) Amy can play with my field now.

(f) I've nearly finished mine.

(g) Didn't rain tonight.

(h) Why is that helmet too small for me?

(i) Are they too busy now?

(j) I don't want to play it today.

(k) There's lots and lots of things here.

(l) I always bring high chairs.

(m) You are nearer the kitchen.

(n) Can you read that again?

(o) I need to get through.

(p) I want her to come straight back.

(q) Nearly bigger than you.

(r) She's gone away now.

(s) It still hurts.

(t) My daddy's upstairs.

(5) The following utterances were produced by children with specific language impairment. Each utterance contains a prepositional phrase. Either individually or in a group, you should undertake the following: (i) underline the prepositional phrase in each utterance, (ii) indicate if the phrase contains pre- and/or post-modifiers, and (iii) state if the prepositional phrase is a post-modifier in a noun, verb, adjective, or adverb phrase.

(a) She runned towards here (female; 8;10 years)

(b) The elephant was going on the diving board (male; 9;7 years)

(c) The giraffe got very angry at the elephant (female; 9;6 years)

(d) She forgot about that (female; 9;9 years)

(e) Moose was mad at the elephant (female; 9;7 years)

(f) Three bunnies are playing in the sandbox (female; 9;3 years)

(g) A elephant is bouncing a ball by the pool (female; 9;3 years)

(h) Longnose was walking toward him (female; 9;9 years)

(i) He gets sick of the food (female; 9;3 years)

(j) The giraffe was mad at her (female; 9;3 years)

REVISION PHRASES

(1) For each of the following noun phrases, (i) identify the pre-modifier, head and post-modifier, and (ii) describe the word classes and constructions that make up each of the categories under (i).

(a) the old house beside the lake

(b) a council estate that Jack vandalised

(c) his threatening demands to pay the ransom

(d) that first child throwing stones

(e) the club's girls keen on sport

(2) For each of the following sentences, (i) locate the head of the noun phrase in the sentence, and (ii) describe the pre-modifier and/or post-modifier in each phrase.

(a) A brilliant idea came to her.

(b) The branches of the tree were alight.

(c) They saw a bright yellow light.

(d) I know the answer.

(e) I met several interesting people.

(f) There's a knife with a red handle.

(g) That's the person I was expecting.

(h) We fell over on the slippery wet path.

(i) Who's the king of the castle?

(j) Each entry won something.

(3) Identify the function of the noun phrase in each of the following sentences. The terms you should use are *subject, object, complement* and *adverbial*.
   (a) We hid the treasure.
   (b) The old building is attractive.
   (c) He waited five minutes.
   (d) The irate customer complained.
   (e) This is the house.
   (f) He called last week.
   (g) I bought a book.
   (h) This must be the spot.
   (i) The elderly man sat pensively.
   (j) They arrive next week.
   (k) He gave her the report.

(4) *True or false:* For some grammarians, genitives like *man's* in *man's car* is a possessive determiner and is not a nominal pre-modifier.

(5) For each of the following sentences, (i) identify the pre-modifier, head and post-modifier of the verb phrase, and (ii) describe the word classes and constructions that make up each of the categories under (i).
   (a) He didn't give the gift to the teacher.
   (b) She quickly became angry.
   (c) We never walk in the park.
   (d) They have been living dangerously.
   (e) He didn't realise that the child had disappeared.
   (f) The team must win next week.
   (g) I've often travelled abroad.
   (h) They are leaving tomorrow.
   (i) John and Mary have forgotten their keys.
   (j) They must have been waiting for hours.
   (k) I would definitely vote for her.
   (l) The children are destroying the park.
   (m) We are going by bus.
   (n) The rabbits jumped across the road.
   (o) He hoped that she would return.

(6) *True or false:* Modal auxiliary verbs precede all other auxiliary verbs in the pre-modifier of verbs.

(7) For each of the following sentences, (i) identify the phrase in italics as an adjective, adverb or prepositional phrase, and (ii) identify the pre-modifier, head, and post-modifier in each phrase.
   (a) The judge decided that the poodle was *excessively large for the breed.*
   (b) He wanted to live *right beside the forest.*
   (c) After the assault the young girl was *too distressed to leave the house.*
   (d) He recovered *more rapidly than we had expected.*
   (e) *Unfortunately for the patient,* the new drug arrived too late.

(f) The wild horse charged *straight into the crowd.*

(g) The thief was clearly visible *from behind the wall.*

(h) The man was *furious that his son had lied.*

(i) For many the prisoner's release had occurred *too quickly for comfort.*

(j) She was *extremely fond of ice cream.*

(k) *Following the match* they travelled home together.

(l) The show was *too long for the children.*

(m) He reacted *more calmly than she had expected.*

(n) The elderly man was *too frail to walk.*

(o) The nasty boy watched her *with a grin.*

(p) The patient's condition was *worse than the doctor had imagined.*

(q) He responded *very favourably* to the plans.

(r) The children jumped *straight over the fence.*

(8) Most adjectives can be pre-modified by adverbs such as *very* and *really* (e.g. *very tired*). Give *three* adjectives where this type of pre-modification is not possible.

(9) Identify the function of the adjective, prepositional and adverb phrases in each of the following sentences. The terms you should use are *complement* and *adverbial*.

(a) The play was postponed because of illness.

(b) She is very fond of animals.

(c) They are in Italy for one month.

(d) His death happened rather quickly.

(e) Fran likes her salads really fresh.

(f) He travels rather often.

(10) How would you characterise the word *pretty* in the sentence *He arrived pretty late*?

(11) For each of the following sentences, (i) identify the phrase in italics, and (ii) describe the function of the phrase within the sentence.

(a) His sandwiches were *stale.*

(b) Play was suspended *on account of poor light.*

(c) The construction work was completed *by October.*

(d) He lived *in London because of his job.*

(e) He hoped to be away *for six weeks.*

(f) She approached the problem *very calmly.*

(g) Jill found her meal *very salty.*

(h) They left the party *rather abruptly.*

(i) The children were attacked *by the dog.*

(j) He drove *quite carelessly* on the day of his test.

(12) *True or false:* A pronoun can be a post-modifier in a prepositional phrase.

6 Clauses

LEARNING OBJECTIVES

By the end of this chapter you will be able to do the following:

- Give a definition of a clause.
- Understand that a clause may be a full sentence or may be part of a sentence.
- Recognise a range of clause patterns based on the functions of phrases within clauses.
- Be able to identify when clauses are linked by means of coordinating conjunctions and subordinating conjunctions and to state what this indicates about the relative syntactic standing of clauses in a sentence.
- Understand the structure and function of different types of finite subordinate clause: declarative subordinate clauses; interrogative subordinate clauses; and relative clauses.
- Understand the structure and function of different types of non-finite subordinate clause: *to*-infinitive clauses; bare infinitive clauses; *–ing* participle clauses; and *–ed* participle clauses.

6.1 Introduction to Clauses

The phrases examined in the last chapter are the building blocks of clauses. A clause consists of a main or lexical verb, any elements required by the main verb and any optional elements that a speaker or writer may decide to include. When a clause is not part of a larger clause, it is known as a **main clause** or sentence. In the following clauses (and sentences), the subject is the only obligatory element in the first example. In the second example, a direct object and subject are both obligatory. In the third example, a subject, direct object and indirect object are obligatory. All three clauses contain an optional element, which is known as an adverbial. It can be omitted without resulting in an ungrammatical clause or sentence:

> *She sings beautifully.*
> (SUBJECT + LEXICAL VERB + ADVERBIAL)
> *Jack hit the table with full force.*
> (SUBJECT + LEXICAL VERB + DIRECT OBJECT + ADVERBIAL)
> *Sally gave her sister the book without hesitation.*
> (SUBJECT + LEXICAL VERB + INDIRECT OBJECT + DIRECT OBJECT + ADVERBIAL)

It can be seen that in each of these clauses (and sentences), certain types of phrases assume the role of subject, adverbial and so on. The subject is a noun phrase (*Jack, Sally*) or a pronoun (*she*). The adverbial is an adjective phrase (*beautifully*) or a prepositional phrase (*with full force*). In Section 6.2, we will examine the different functions of phrases within clauses and the clause patterns that combinations of phrases make possible. Each of the above clauses (and sentences) can be conjoined with other clauses by means of the coordinating conjunctions *and, but* and *or*. In the following examples, *she sings beautifully* is now a clause within a larger sentence which contains a second clause of equal syntactic status:

> She sings beautifully <u>and</u> he writes skilfully.
> She sings beautifully <u>but</u> he sings terribly.
> She sings beautifully <u>or</u> she chants beautifully.

However, it is also possible for *she sings beautifully* to appear as a clause in a sentence and for this clause not to have the same syntactic standing as a second clause in the sentence. In each of the following sentences, *she sings beautifully* is a subordinate clause which depends on a main clause or the full sentence:

> Peter thinks <u>that she sings beautifully</u>.
> Sue hopes <u>that she sings beautifully</u>.
> June decided <u>that she sings beautifully</u>.

Each of the subordinate clauses in these sentences is introduced by the subordinating conjunction *that*. (If you are unsure about the differences between coordinating and subordinating conjunctions, you should revisit Section 4.4 in Chapter 4.) The clause that each subordinate clause depends on is the main clause or sentence and not just *Peter thinks, Sue hopes* and *June decided*. It is not uncommon for subordinate clauses to be used in the absence of the subordinating conjunction *that*:

> Peter thinks <u>she sings beautifully</u>.

In Sections 6.3 and 6.4, the structure and function of different types of subordinate clause will be examined. Subordinate clauses are distinguished on the basis of whether they contain a finite verb (finite subordinate clauses) or a non-finite verb (non-finite subordinate clauses). Three **finite subordinate clauses** will be examined in Section 6.3: declarative clauses; interrogative clauses; and relative clauses. In Section 6.4, subordinate clauses based on the four non-finite verb forms will be examined: *to*-infinitive; bare infinitive; –*ing* participle; and –*ed* participle. (You might want to refresh your memory of the difference between finite and non-finite verbs by revisiting Section 3.3 in Chapter 3.) Following earlier chapters, clause structure and function will be illustrated by considering examples of clause use in typically developing children, individuals with language disorders, and speakers of non-standard dialects. In the meantime, to get you thinking about the relation and standing of one clause to another clause in a sentence, you should attempt Exercise 6.1.

6.2 Functions in Clauses

In Chapter 5, the functions of different parts of phrases were examined. Phrases can also assume different functions within a clause. We began this chapter by examining three clauses (or sentences). Each of these clauses contained obligatory functions like subject and direct object (the latter is obligatory following a transitive verb) and optional functions like adverbial. It was also noted that certain types of phrases fulfilled these functions. So while noun phrases could be subjects and objects in a clause, adverb phrases and prepositional phrases often have an adverbial function. In this section, the functions of different parts of clauses will be examined in more detail. These functions give rise to a number of clause patterns. Clauses too can have functions like subject and object in a sentence. The functions of different types of subordinate clauses in sentences will be examined in Sections 6.3 and 6.4.

Arguably, the most important grammatical function of any phrase in a clause is that of subject. This is because without a subject it is not possible for a clause or sentence to say anything at all. The subject can be variously characterised but in general is the person or thing that undertakes the action of the verb. (This is said with the qualification that there are many clauses where the subject is undertaking no action whatsoever, e.g. *Jane has a cold.*) The subject role in a clause is most often fulfilled by a noun phrase or a pronoun. Less often, a prepositional phrase may also be a subject. Less easily identified subjects in clauses are the **existential** ***there*** and the **dummy subject** *it*:

The aggressive dog attacked the child. [Noun phrase]
She likes foreign holidays. [Pronoun]
After six is the quietest time of the day. [Prepositional phrase]
There is an accident at the end of the road. [Existential *there*]
It is raining again. [Dummy subject *it*]

The subjects in the above examples all appear at the beginning of the clause or sentence. However, this is not always the case. As the examples below illustrate, a subject may appear after an auxiliary verb in **yes–no interrogatives** and **wh-interrogatives**. Subjects can also appear at the end of a clause or sentence when a passive voice construction is used. Subjects may also appear after an adverb phrase:

Is *Sue* helping her mother? [*yes–no* interrogative]
What is *John* doing in the shed? [*wh*-interrogative]
The child was attacked by *the dog*. [Passive voice]
Tomorrow *Peter* departs for Rome. [Adverb phrase]

The rest of the clause or sentence tells us about the subject and is called the **predicate**. Verb phrases function as predicates. A predicate may be one word as in the example below which contains an intransitive verb:

Tom *smiled*.

Alternatively, a predicate may be quite lengthy and complex as the following example illustrates:

Bobby *made Jack his national campaign director during the hard-fought election*.

Within this complex predicate, there are a number of phrases each of which has a certain grammatical function in the clause or sentence. The verb *made* is a **predicator**. The noun phrases *Jack* and *his national campaign director* are a direct object and an object complement, respectively. The clause ends with the prepositional phrase *during the hard-fought election* which is an adverbial. So while the noun phrase *Bobby* in this clause has only a single grammatical function (i.e. subject), four further functions – predicator, direct object, object complement and adverbial – are contained in the predicate.

So far, we have illustrated five functions in a clause. To recap, these functions are subject, direct object, predicator, object complement and adverbial. It is important to point out that in the same way that pronouns can be subjects in clauses, pronouns can also be direct objects in clauses (*Mike thumped him*). The function of object complement may also be realised by structures other than a noun phrase, as in the example above. Adjective phrases and prepositional phrases may also be object complements in clauses:

The hot weather made Suzy *very ill*. [Adjective phrase]
The announcement threw her plans *into disarray*. [Prepositional phrase]

There are two other functions of phrases in clauses. They can also be indirect objects and subject complements. We saw these functions at work in Chapter 3 when we discussed different classes of lexical verbs. An indirect object typically occurs alongside a direct object after a di-transitive verb. It can be a noun phrase as in the first example below or a pronoun as in the second example:

> Paula showed <u>Bill</u> the oil painting.
> Mike told <u>her</u> the truth.

A subject complement was also described in Chapter 3. It appears after intensive verbs like *be, get* and *sound*. A subject complement may be realised by a noun phrase or an adjective phrase:

> George is <u>*a professional footballer*</u>. [Noun phrase]
> The concerto sounds <u>*wonderful*</u>. [Adjective phrase]

Having introduced the functions of phrases in clauses, we can now summarise a number of different clause patterns. Eight patterns are exemplified by the clauses in Table 6.1. These patterns are not exhaustive. It is possible, for example, for a prepositional phrase to function as an adverbial complement in a clause which contains an intensive verb, e.g. *Mary is <u>in a state of distress</u>*. Nonetheless, the eight patterns on display are some of the most common that you will encounter.

Of particular note is the fact that most grammatical functions can be realised by different types of phrases. For example, the adverbial function in Table 6.1 is realised by a noun phrase (*next week*), an adverb phrase (*quickly*) and a prepositional phrase (*to London*). Subject complements are realised by noun phrases (*an employment lawyer*) and adjective phrases (*complacent*). Object complements are also realised by noun phrases (*chief executive*) and adjective phrases (*dizzy*). What this demonstrates is that it is not possible to 'read off' the function of a phrase in a clause based on the form or structure of a phrase. Identifying the functions of different parts of a clause demands more work than that!

TABLE 6.1 Eight clause patterns

SUBJECT + PREDICATOR	SUBJECT + PREDICATOR + OBJECT$_D$
e.g.: The children are singing. Tom laughs.	*e.g.:* Sarah bought an expensive book. Mandy dropped the porcelain cup.
SUBJECT + PREDICATOR + OBJECT$_I$	**SUBJECT + PREDICATOR + OBJECT$_I$ + OBJECT$_D$**
e.g.: The girl told him. She showed him.	*e.g.:* Sue gave John a classic watch. He showed the police the burial plot.
SUBJECT + PREDICATOR + COMP$_{SUB}$	**SUBJECT + PREDICATOR + OBJECT$_D$ + COMP$_{OBJ}$**
e.g.: Sue is an employment lawyer. Bob is getting complacent.	*e.g.:* They elected him chief executive. The fumes made Pat dizzy.
SUBJECT + PREDICATOR + ADVERBIAL	**SUBJECT + PREDICATOR + OBJECT$_D$ + ADVERB.**
e.g.: They arrive next week. He runs quickly.	*e.g.:* She wrapped the gift hastily. They took the train to London.

From a relatively early age, typically developing children are able to use utterances with a range of clause patterns. Several of Lara's utterances are displayed in Table 6.2. These utterances were used by Lara during interactions at home with her mother, father and grandmother. She was 3 years and 3 months old at the time of recording. You should spend some time examining these utterances and thinking about their clause patterns before we discuss them below.

Lara's use of clause patterns is noteworthy in several respects. Firstly, certain clause patterns appeared in abundance in the data while others were relatively scarce. As one might expect, the simplest clause pattern of all – SUBJECT + PREDICATOR – was used quite extensively. However, patterns that involve the use of indirect objects and object complements were present only infrequently in the data. We can speculate about the reasons for this difference in frequency of use. However, one plausible explanation might be the greater conceptual and

TABLE 6.2 Clause patterns in Lara's utterances

Clause pattern	Lara's utterances
$S + P$	I'm hiding He's running It hurts I'm hoovering My doggy's going
$S + P + O_D$	I want it I want that You save that rocking thing I need these little ducklings I've found the sheep
$S + P + O_I$	I told her I will show you
$S + P + O_D + O_I$	I gave it to you I'm reading a book to you
$S + P + C_{SUB}$	Amy's getting wet Amy's horrid This is lovely water You're the monster I'm a ghost
$S + P + O_D + C_{OBJ}$	I call it bum I will get the pram ready
$S + P + A$	You stay there You sit on the egg Monster hasn't gone yet Amy go away She can't go on mummy's knee
$S + P + O_D + A$	She's not sharing that with me I got nobody in the house I will put the ends together I do mine quickly I said it first

grammatical complexity of indirect objects over direct objects, and object complements over subject complements. Secondly, Lara realises these clause patterns in various ways. Let us consider the pattern SUBJECT + PREDICATOR + DIRECT OBJECT + ADVERBIAL. In the following examples from Table 6.2, the direct object is realised by a demonstrative pronoun (*that*), an indefinite pronoun (*nobody*), a noun phrase (*the ends*), a possessive pronoun (*mine*) and a personal pronoun (*it*). Meanwhile, the adverbial is realised by prepositional phrases (*with me, in the house*) and adverb phrases (*together, quickly, first*):

> *She's not sharing that with me.*
> *I got nobody in the house.*
> *I will put the ends together.*
> *I do mine quickly.*
> *I said it first.*

The same is true of the other clause patterns that Lara uses. The following examples from Table 6.2 exemplify the clause pattern SUBJECT + PREDICATOR + SUBJECT COMPLEMENT. The subject function in these sentences is variously realised by a proper noun (*Amy*), a demonstrative pronoun (*this*) and personal pronouns (*you, I*). The subject complement is realised by adjective phrases (*wet, horrid*) and noun phrases (*lovely water, the monster, a ghost*). At just over 3 years of age, Lara is already skilled at using a range of structures for each of the grammatical functions:

> *Amy's getting wet.*
> *Amy's horrid.*
> *This is lovely water.*
> *You're the monster.*
> *I'm a ghost.*

Thirdly, the examples in Table 6.2 are also noteworthy on account of the completeness of their clause patterns. Lara also used utterances in which one or more functions were omitted:

> *[...] sitting by egg.*
> *[...] not doing me.*
> *Amy [...] horrid.*
> *She's had it [...] long time.*

In the first two utterances above, Lara omitted a subject. In the third utterance, a predicator is omitted. In the final utterance, part of the adverbial *for a long time* is omitted. Lara also omitted more than one function on occasion. In the following utterances, the subject and predicator are both omitted:

> *[...] bit sticky.* [Omitted: *It is*]
> *[...] not Lara.* [Omitted: *I am*]

However, the fact that omissions of this type were relatively uncommon suggests that by 3 years of age, Lara is already adept at using a range of different clause patterns.

It is now time for you to get practice in identifying the clause patterns of some of Lara's utterances by attempting Exercise 6.2.

EXERCISE 6.2 CLAUSE PATTERNS

Either individually or in a group, you should examine the following utterances. Then, you should attempt to characterise each utterance according to one of the clause patterns displayed in Table 6.2:

(a) She's too little.
(b) He's gone to bed.
(c) You missed a bit.
(d) Amy's doing it.
(e) I'm a bird.
(f) I win first.
(g) You shut that gate.
(h) You're not doing yours quickly.
(i) Amy's shouting.
(j) I'm playing properly.
(k) I'm driving.
(l) I'm mummy's friend.
(m) I can't see it anywhere.
(n) You can come in my bed.
(o) You can have that.
(p) I'm going home.
(q) Amy hasn't got a duvet.
(r) I want a lolly.
(s) I'm running to the shops.
(t) This is my house.

Now that you have knowledge of clause patterns, you can examine the use of clauses by adults with Alzheimer's dementia in the following Special Topic.

SPECIAL TOPIC 6.1 CLAUSE PATTERNS IN ALZHEIMER'S DEMENTIA

The grammatical terminology that has been introduced so far also allows us to describe clause patterns that are used by adults with Alzheimer's dementia. The cognitive deficits of these adults, and particularly their problems with memory, are evident in the following task. Adults with probable Alzheimer's dementia were given three words and were asked to use these words to form a sentence. The words could occur in any order in the sentences that the adults produced. The clause patterns of these adults' sentences are shown below:

Target words: *bureau; open; drawer*
(a) *She opened the drawer* (Male; 77 years) **[S + P + O$_D$]**
(b) *The drawer was in the bureau* (Male; 77 years) **[S + P + C$_{ADV}$]**
(c) *The bureau drawer was open* (Female; 65 years) **[S + P + C$_{SUB}$]**
(d) *Open the bureau drawer* (Female; 69 years) **[P + O$_D$]**
(e) *I open the drawer of the bureau* (Male; 58 years) **[S + P + O$_D$ + A]**
(f) *The bureau has an open drawer* (Male; 78 years) **[S + P + O$_D$]**
(g) *I cleaned the bureau drawer* (Female; 60 years) **[S + P + O$_D$]**
(h) *You could open the drawer* (Female; 83 years) **[S + P + O$_D$]**
(i) *The little girl opened the door drawer* (Female; 76 years) **[S + P + O$_D$]**
(j) *Open the door* (Female; 79 years) **[P + O$_D$]**

Target words: *chair; doctor; sit*
(a) *I sat two hours in the doctor's office* (Female; 74 years) **[S + P + A + A]**
(b) *Sit on a chair* (Female; 79 years) **[P + A]**
(c) *I sat in the doctor's chair* (Male; 78 years) **[S + P + A]**
(d) *The doctor checks my health* (Male; 58 years) **[S + P + O$_D$]**
(e) *The doctor sits in the chair* (Male; 74 years) **[S + P + A]**
(f) *Doctor sit in chair* (Female; 79 years) **[S + P + A]**
(g) *I sit in the chair at the doctor's office* (Male; 63 years) **[S + P + A + A]**
(h) *The doctor will sit on the chair* (Male; 78 years) **[S + P + A]**
(i) *This is a chair* (Male; 56 years) **[S + P + C$_{SUB}$]**
(j) *The sick man sat in the chair* (Male; 78 years) **[S + P + A]**

It is not uncommon for these adults to produce sentences which do not contain all three target words. Examples include: *she opened the drawer; I cleaned the bureau drawer; sit on a chair;* and *the sick man sat in the chair*. The omission of one or more target words is explained by the fact that these adults are unable to keep all three words in working memory long enough in order to construct a sentence based on them. For the most part, clause patterns involve three functions, the most common of which is S + P + O$_D$ and S + P + A. These adults occasionally produce sentences that contain four functions. These clause patterns are S + P + A + A and S + P + O$_D$ + A. There is also some evidence of lexical disturbances in these adults. For example, the word *door* is used in place of *bureau* and *drawer*. This is to be expected as lexical problems are also a feature of language in adults with Alzheimer's dementia.

The main points in this section are summarised below.

> **KEY POINTS CLAUSE PATTERNS**
>
> - Phrases in clauses can be assigned different grammatical functions. These functions are subject, predicator, direct object, indirect object, subject complement, object complement and adverbial.
> - At a minimum, a sentence must contain a subject and a predicator (e.g. *The man ran*). The subject appears at the beginning of a declarative sentence. However, in other types of sentences such as interrogatives and passives, the subject appears after an auxiliary verb (e.g. *Are you going to the party?*) and at the end of a sentence (e.g. *The boy was bitten by the dog*).
> - Other grammatical functions in a sentence are determined by the type of lexical verb which is used. For example, a mono-transitive verb must be followed by a direct object (e.g. *Bob hit the wall*) and a di-transitive verb must be followed by a direct object and an indirect object (e.g. *John gave the apple to Suzy*).
> - There are two complement functions: subject complement and object complement. The subject complement refers to the same person or thing as the subject of a sentence and is used with intensive verbs (e.g. *Sally is a teacher*). The object complement refers to the same person or thing as the direct object of a sentence and is used with complex transitive verbs (e.g. *She called Mark a twit*).
> - The adverbial function adds additional, optional information to a sentence. This information often relates to place and time (e.g. *They flew to Rome last week*).
> - Grammatical functions can be realised by different structures or forms. For example, the subject function can be realised by noun phrases (*The dogs are barking*), personal pronouns (*They are noisy*) and demonstrative pronouns (*That is interesting*). Adjective phrases and noun phrases can both be object complements (*She called him stupid*; *They elected Trump president*).

6.3 Finite Subordinate Clauses

The clause patterns that were examined in Section 6.2 were built around a single lexical verb. However, many sentences contain two or three lexical verbs and each of these verbs is the basis of a clause. The question then arises of how these clauses are linked to each other. In Section 6.1, coordination was described as the linking of clauses of equal syntactic status (e.g. *Tom is wise and John is foolish*). Clauses which are linked by means of the coordinating conjunctions *and, but* and *or* are not dependent on other clauses and are not above (superordinate to) or below (subordinate to) other clauses in a sentence. However, clauses which are linked by means of **subordination** do not have equal syntactic status. One clause is always dependent on, or subordinate to, another clause (hence, the term 'subordinate clause'). If the latter clause is not dependent on any other clause, it is called a main clause or sentence. This dependency relation between clauses can allow several subordinate clauses to occur within a single sentence. These different levels of clause can be illustrated by the sentence in Figure 6.1.

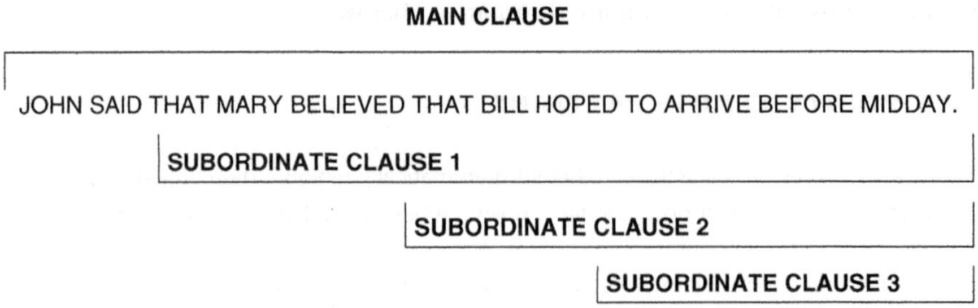

MAIN CLAUSE

JOHN SAID THAT MARY BELIEVED THAT BILL HOPED TO ARRIVE BEFORE MIDDAY.

SUBORDINATE CLAUSE 1

SUBORDINATE CLAUSE 2

SUBORDINATE CLAUSE 3

Figure 6.1 A main clause and its subordinate clauses

This sentence or main clause contains three subordinate clauses. As speakers and writers, we tend to avoid the use of sentences with so many clauses – these sentences push our memory and linguistic decoding skills to their absolute limits! However, this sentence with its multiple clauses can be used to illustrate an important distinction in our discussion of subordinate clauses. Each of these four clauses is distinguished according to whether its lexical verb is a tensed verb form (i.e. a finite verb) or is a verb form that is not marked for tense (i.e. a non-finite verb). (If you are unsure of the difference between finite and non-finite verbs, you should revisit Section 3.3 in Chapter 3.) If a lexical verb is a finite verb, then the clause which contains it is a finite subordinate clause. If a lexical verb is a non-finite verb, then the clause which contains it is a **non-finite subordinate clause**. Let us apply this distinction to each of the four clauses in the sentence in Figure 6.1. The lexical verbs in the main clause and each of its subordinate clauses are as follows:

Main clause: *said*
Subordinate clause 1: *believed*
Subordinate clause 2: *hoped*
Subordinate clause 3: *to arrive*

The verbs *said, believed* and *hoped* are marked for past tense and are finite verbs. The clauses which contain these verbs (the main clause and subordinate clauses 1 and 2) are finite clauses. The lexical verb in subordinate clause 3 is a *to*-infinitive. The *to*-infinitive is a non-finite verb, and the clause which contains it is a non-finite clause. The sentence in Figure 6.1 therefore consists of three finite clauses and one non-finite clause.

Subordinate clauses 1 and 2 in Figure 6.1 are introduced by the subordinating conjunction (or **complementiser**) *that. That*-clauses are one of two types of **declarative subordinate clause**. The other type is an **adverbial subordinate clause**. Aside from declarative clauses, the second main category of finite subordinate clause is interrogative clauses. Declarative and interrogative clauses will be examined in this section. In Section 6.4, non-finite subordinate clauses will be examined. These clauses are based on the four non-finite verb forms introduced in Chapter 3: bare infinitive; *to*-infinitive; *–ing* participle; and *–ed* participle. For each clause type, structural features of the clause will be addressed first followed by an examination of the functions that the clause can play in a sentence. To illustrate these clauses, examples of their use by typically developing children and children and adults with language disorders will be included in the discussion below.

6.3.1 Declarative Subordinate Clauses

Let us return to the two *that*-clauses in the sentence in Figure 6.1, which is reproduced below:

> John said [**SC1** that Mary believed [**SC2** that Bill hoped to arrive before midday]].

These clauses can be characterised in terms of both structure and function. In terms of structure, each of these *that*-clauses is a declarative sentence with *that* added to the front of it. These clauses are direct objects of the verbs *said* (SC1) and *believed* (SC2) in the above sentence. *That*-clauses can also function in sentences as subjects and subject complements. Let us take SC2 and turn it into a subject and a subject complement in the following sentences:

> <u>That Bill hoped to arrive before midday</u> was wishful thinking. [Subject]
> The most bizarre thing was <u>that Bill hoped to arrive before midday</u>. [Subject
>   complement]

When we examined phrases in Chapter 5, we described how *that*-clauses could also be complements of adjectives and nouns:

> He was angry <u>that his shirt was stained</u>.
> the belief <u>that he would return some day</u>

The subordinating conjunction or complementiser *that* is not always present in *that*-clauses. For example, the sentence in Figure 6.1 is no less grammatical when it appears as follows:

> John said Mary believed Bill hoped to arrive before midday.

That can also be omitted with no loss of grammaticality in the following sentence:

> He was angry his shirt was stained.

Clearly, *that* is optional in a *that*-clause which functions as a direct object or is the complement of an adjective. However, when a *that*-clause has the function of a subject or is the complement of a noun, as in the following examples, the complementiser cannot be so readily omitted:

> *Bill hoped to arrive before midday was wishful thinking.
> *the belief he would return some day

Other declarative subordinate clauses have an adverbial function. They are intro-duced by a range of complementisers other than *that* such as *because, since, although* and *before*. Like adverbials in general, they add additional, optional information which answers questions like *why?* (reason), *when?* (time), *how often?* (frequency) and *where?* (place). Examples of these adverbial subordinate clauses are shown in the sentences below:

> *Because it was very late, they booked into a hotel.* [Reason]
> *His situation improved greatly, since he left home.* [Time]
> *He owned a flat, where the assault occurred.* [Place]

Identify the declarative subordinate clause in the following sentence. What is the function of this clause?

> Don Frank had travelled with his wife from Kaukana to join in the festivities, but the couple also decided it was too much for them to tackle. (*Wausau Daily Herald*, Wisconsin, 2017)

To give you further practice in working with declarative subordinate clauses, you should now attempt Exercise 6.3.

EXERCISE 6.3 LARA AND DECLARATIVE SUBORDINATE CLAUSES
At just 3 years of age, Lara is already using *that*-clauses and declarative subor-dinate clauses introduced by complementisers other than *that*. Several of Lara's utterances are listed below. For each utterance, underline the declarative subor-dinate clause. Then identify the function that the clause fulfils. The terms you should use are *subject, direct object, subject complement* and *adverbial*:

(a) Do you think daddy's home?
(b) Give him some arms so he can hold his hose.
(c) I think it's a jigsaw.
(d) I didn't tell you I didn't like you.
(e) Amy can come in house if she wants.
(f) Can you see I'm holding on very tight?
(g) I think she doesn't want to go to bed.
(h) Can you bring me those because I can't reach them?
(i) I'm cleaning Amy's bottle so she can drink them all again.
(j) Move out of the way because my horsey will go.
(k) I think she's a bit poorly.
(l) If people get sick, I will open it.
(m) I just need to take that out so I can clean the lid.
(n) You get a hoover out of your alcove before I hoover.
(o) Help me make this because I don't like to do it on my own.

6.3.2 Interrogative Subordinate Clauses

A further type of finite subordinate clause is a *yes–no* interrogative clause. It is introduced by one of two complementisers or subordinating conjunctions: *if* and *whether*. These clauses are underlined in the following sentences:

> They asked <u>if I would like to join them for dinner</u>.
> Mike queried <u>if the meal would arrive on time</u>.
> John wondered <u>whether the new plans would be cost effective</u>.

These clauses are direct objects of the verbs *asked, queried* and *wondered*. These same verbs cannot be followed by *that*-clauses (**They asked that I would like to join them for dinner*). However, there are certain verbs which can take *that*-clauses and **if/whether-clauses**. Two such verbs are *know* and *state*:

> He knows <u>that the storm will soon pass</u>.
> Do you know <u>if Bill has arrived yet</u>?
> The announcer stated <u>that the prime minister had resigned</u>.
> The guests stated <u>if they wanted room service</u>.

Like *that*-clauses, interrogative clauses can also be complements of adjectives and nouns:

> He was unsure <u>if they wanted to stay for dinner</u>.
> The decision <u>whether the riot should be contained or dispersed</u> was taken after
>   midnight.

In some positions in a clause or sentence, **interrogative subordinate clauses** can appear with either *if* or *whether* as a complementiser. One position where these complementisers are interchangeable is when the clause is a direct object:

> He asked <u>if they knew the way to Clintock House</u>.
> He asked <u>whether they knew the way to Clintock House</u>.
> Sally wondered <u>if the situation could be retrieved</u>.
> Sally wondered <u>whether the situation could be retrieved</u>.

However, if we try to move one of these clauses from its position as direct object in a sentence to subject in a sentence, what we find is that only the complementiser *whether* can be used with the clause:

> <u>Whether the situation could be retrieved</u> was still very much in doubt.
> *<u>If the situation could be retrieved</u> was still very much in doubt.

If the subject moves to the end of the sentence (i.e. is extraposed), then either *if* or *whether* may be used with the clause again:

> It was still very much in doubt <u>if/whether the situation could be retrieved</u>.

There is another type of interrogative subordinate clause which corresponds to *wh*-interrogatives. Like *if/whether*-clauses, so-called **wh-clauses** can appear as a direct object and as a complement of adjectives and nouns:

> He queried *why this course of action was necessary.* [Direct object]
> He was unclear *why this course of action was necessary.* [Complement of
>   adjective]
> He raised the issue *why this course of action was necessary.* [Complement of
>   noun]

Wh-clauses have a further function over *if/whether*-clauses. That function is an adverbial:

> The baby is very irritable, *when she is hungry and tired.*

In *wh*-subordinate clauses, there is a missing element in the clause. Consider the *wh*-clause in the following sentence:

> I don't know *why he left so early.*

The missing element in this clause is the dummy auxiliary *do*. This becomes apparent when the *wh*-clause is turned into a main clause:

> Why *did* he leave so early?

You should now use your knowledge of interrogative subordinate clauses to attempt Exercise 6.4.

EXERCISE 6.4 USE OF INTERROGATIVE SUBORDINATE CLAUSES BY LARA AND HER PARENTS

At 3 years of age, Lara is using a range of interrogative subordinate clauses. Lara's mother and father also use these clauses in their utterances to her. Several utterances produced by Lara and her parents are listed below. For each utterance, underline the interrogative subordinate clause. Then identify the function that the clause fulfils:

(a) *Lara:* When she's not on it I will go on it.
(b) *Father:* I wouldn't be surprised if you said a whole picnic hamper.
(c) *Lara:* Shall I show you how I make a big long field?
(d) *Mother:* It isn't funny if you do that.
(e) *Lara:* I'm just wondering if we don't want it.
(f) *Father:* I'll show you how you do that.
(g) *Lara:* I'm going to shop when they go to sleep.
(h) *Mother:* Don't know if that'll stay on very well.
(i) *Lara:* Shall I show you how the wind blew it?
(j) *Mother:* There's no reason why you forget things.

6.3.3 Relative Clauses

Another finite subordinate clause which also contains a missing element is the relative clause. The missing element is represented by a *wh*-word. Consider the following examples in which the relative clause is indicated in brackets:

> The man [*who* is crossing the road] works in the bank.
> The house [*which* is next to the river] is for sale.
> They helped the woman [*whose* car had broken down].

The *wh*-word in each sentence is a relative pronoun. The relative pronoun takes the place of the preceding noun phrase (called the 'antecedent') in the relative clause. We can illustrate this as follows:

> *The man* is crossing the road.
> *The house* is next to the river.
> *The woman's car* had broken down.

The purpose of the relative clauses in the above sentences is to restrict the number of people and objects which should be considered in the referent of the noun phrase. There are many men, houses and women which the speaker could be referring to. However, the speaker who uses these sentences intends the hearer to consider *only* the man who is crossing the road, *only* the house which is next to the river, and *only* the woman whose car has broken down. Relative clauses which function in this way are called **restrictive relative clauses**. There are other relative clauses which do not restrict the referent of the noun phrase but which function to convey further information about the noun phrase to the hearer. So-called **non-restrictive relative clauses** are illustrated by the sentences below:

> Tom Brown, who has never taken work seriously, announced his retirement last week.
> The Prime Minister, who wants a quick resolution, held talks into the night.
> His old Ford Escort, which held many fond memories for him, failed its inspection.

The relative clauses in these sentences are not serving to restrict the **reference** of the preceding noun phrases. In fact, these noun phrases already have a very restricted reference by virtue of being proper nouns which name specific people and things. Rather, the function of these relative clauses is to provide incidental information about each of their antecedents.

Relative pronouns like *who* and *which* in the sentences above take the place of subject noun phrases (e.g. *Tom Brown has never taken work seriously*). However, relative pronouns can also take the place of object noun phrases in a relative clause. When this is the case, the relative pronoun *whom* is used:

> The girl *whom* you described sounds very pretty.
> [Direct object NP: *You described the girl*]
> The man to whom you sent the parcel was very grateful.
> [Indirect object NP: *You sent the parcel to the man*]

Although the use of *whom* in these sentences is prescriptively correct, it sounds somewhat formal to most present-day speakers of English. These speakers are much more likely to use a sentence like the following:

> *The man <u>who</u> you sent the parcel <u>to</u> was very grateful.*

This sentence offends prescriptive sensibilities in two ways. Firstly, the sentence contains the subject relative pronoun instead of the object relative pronoun (*who* instead of *whom*). Secondly, the preposition is at the end of the relative clause rather than in front of the relative pronoun *whom* which is its object. However, as we emphasised in Section 1.2 in Chapter 1, our approach to grammar in this book is a descriptive one. Accordingly, no judgement is passed on sentences like the one above (they are not examples of 'bad grammar') or on speakers who use sentences of this type. But even prescriptive grammarians must prefer the first sentence in the following pair of sentences, despite the fact that the preposition in this sentence stands at the end of the relative clause:

> *There's a stool <u>that</u> he is <u>on</u>.* [59-year-old man with Alzheimer's dementia]
> **There's a stool <u>on which</u> he is.* [Preferred form of prescriptive grammarian]

There is a further relative pronoun which we must examine: the use of *whose*. We used an example of *whose* above in the sentence: *They helped the woman <u>whose car had broken down</u>.* As with all relative pronouns, the relative pronoun *whose* is taking the place of a noun phrase in the relative clause. The noun phrase in this case is a genitive:

> *<u>The woman's car</u> had broken down.*

The genitive noun phrase which is replaced by *whose* in each of the sentences on the left is made explicit in the corresponding sentences on the right:

The man <u>whose</u> wife passed away is very lonely.	<u>The man's wife</u> passed away.
They spoke to the woman <u>whose</u> child was missing.	<u>The woman's child</u> was missing.
Frank saw the boy <u>whose</u> dog was lost.	<u>The boy's dog</u> was lost.

In each of the above sentences, *whose* is the subject in the relative clause. The relative pronoun *whose* can also be an object in a relative clause. In each of the following pairs of sentences, the first sentence contains a genitive noun phrase as an object. In the second sentence in each pair, the relative pronoun *whose* replaces this noun phrase and is an object in the relative clause:

> *Joan doesn't like <u>Sally's brother</u>.*
> *Sally, <u>whose</u> brother Joan doesn't like, is unwell.*
> *Bill taught <u>the headmaster's daughter</u>.*
> *The headmaster, <u>whose</u> daughter Bill taught, retires next year.*
> *Alice visits <u>the vicar's wife</u> regularly.*
> *The vicar, <u>whose</u> wife Alice visits regularly, is organising the summer fair.*

There is another noteworthy feature about the use of the relative pronoun *whose*. In each of the above sentences, *whose* replaces an animate noun phrase such as *Sally's brother* and *the vicar's wife*. For prescriptive grammarians, this represents the correct use of this relative pronoun. The use of *whose* to replace inanimate noun phrases is discouraged by prescriptive grammarians and also sounds somewhat unnatural or odd to many native speakers of English:

> *The plan, <u>whose</u> implementation would be costly, was rejected by the directors.*
> *They mended the table, <u>whose</u> legs were broken.*

The solution, in writing at least, is to introduce the rather formal expression *of + which* into the relative clause:

> *The plan, the implementation <u>of which</u> would be costly, was rejected by the directors.*
> *They mended the table, the legs <u>of which</u> were broken.*

We have now described four relative pronouns: *who, which, whom* and *whose*. Table 6.3 summarises the use of these pronouns in relative clauses.

TABLE 6.3 Relative pronouns in English

Relative pronoun	Context of use	Examples
Who	Subject in relative clause Animate noun phrase Restrictive relative clause Non-restrictive relative clause	*The girl <u>who</u> sings is tall.* (restrictive clause) *Pat Smith, <u>who</u> is lazy, is absent again today.* (non-restrictive clause)
Which	Subject in relative clause Object in relative clause Animate noun phrase Inanimate noun phrase Restrictive relative clause Non-restrictive relative clause Preposition + *which*	*The train <u>which</u> travels to York is late.* (restrictive clause) *The dog next door, <u>which</u> barks all day, is at the vet.* (non-restrictive clause) *The book, which you recommended, is great.* (object in relative clause) *The house <u>in which</u> he lives is uninhabitable.* (preposition + which)
Whom	Object in relative clause Animate noun phrase Restrictive relative clause Non-restrictive relative clause Preposition + *whom*	*The girl <u>whom</u> you reported to the police has disappeared.* (restrictive clause) *Mrs Brown <u>whom</u> we admire is an excellent teacher.* (non-restrictive clause) *The man <u>to whom</u> the threat was made is afraid to leave home.* (preposition + whom)
Whose	Genitive noun phrase Animate noun phrase Restrictive relative clause Non-restrictive relative clause Preposition + *whose*	*The man, <u>whose</u> dog attacked us, is very unpleasant.* (restrictive clause) *The high court barrister, <u>whose</u> idiosyncracies are most amusing, asked for an adjournment.* (non-restrictive clause) *The Queen, at <u>whose</u> request you were invited, will attend the banquet.* (preposition + whose)

You should now use your knowledge of relative clauses to complete Exercise 6.5.

EXERCISE 6.5 USE OF RELATIVE CLAUSES BY LARA AND HER FAMILY

Lara, her parents and her grandmother Elsie use relative clauses during their verbal exchanges with each other at home. Several utterances produced by Lara and these members of her family are displayed below. For each utterance, (i) underline the relative clause including the relative pronoun, and (ii) indicate if the relative pronoun is a subject or object in the relative clause:

(a) *Lara:* Pick that bit up that I just dropped.
(b) *Mother:* That's the corn that they eat.
(c) *Lara:* Not the Emily that comes to my nursery.
(d) *Mother:* I'm not playing with naughty girls who have tantrums.
(e) *Lara:* This white one that I had.
(f) *Grandmother:* That's the horse you see.
(g) *Mother:* I think there's a bit that goes in between those two.
(h) *Father:* That's a letter that mummy and daddy got.
(i) *Mother:* What about this jigsaw that's already out?
(j) *Father:* I'm gonna lie down here and I'm gonna try and rock Amy at the same time which is an amazing feat.

We are not quite finished with relative pronouns. It will not have escaped the attentive reader that on one occasion above, the word *that* was used as a relative pronoun. It occurred in an utterance produced by a 59-year-old man with Alzheimer's dementia:

>   There is a stool <u>that</u> he is on.

That can replace any relative pronoun which appears on its own at the front of a restrictive relative clause. To demonstrate that this is the case, let us test the use of *that* in the restrictive relative clauses in Table 6.3. What we find is that *that* works just as well as *who, which* and *whom*, and in some cases (the last example) even better than these other relative pronouns:

>   The girl <u>who</u> sings is tall.
>   The girl <u>that</u> sings is tall.
>   The train <u>which</u> travels to York is late.
>   The train <u>that</u> travels to York is late.
>   The girl <u>whom</u> you reported to the police has disappeared.
>   The girl <u>that</u> you reported to the police has disappeared.

That and the other relative pronouns that it replaces can also be deleted altogether, but only when they appear in object position in the relative clause.

In subject position, the deletion of these pronouns results in ungrammatical sentences:

> *The girl you reported to the police has disappeared.* [*whom/that* is object]
> **The girl sings is tall.* [*who/that* is subject]
> **The train travels to York is late.* [*which/that* is subject]

However, let us not forget that speakers of non-standard dialects like Geordie dialect can delete even relative pronouns in subject position. In Section 3.2 in Chapter 3, we saw the following example in which the subject relative pronoun *who* is omitted:

> 'father had three brothers [**who**] lived round the next street'

Finally, to the extent that *that* can also appear in a relative clause, it is necessary to think about how *that* in a relative clause can be distinguished from the type of *that*-clauses with which we began this section. For most purposes, this distinction can be made in two ways. Firstly, in a relative clause *that* can be replaced by *who* and *which*. This replacement is not possible in a *that*-clause:

> *The flowers <u>that</u> she bought were truly beautiful.* [Relative clause]
> The flowers <u>which</u> she bought were truly beautiful.
> *He challenged the idea <u>that</u> lessons can be learned from history.* [*That*-clause]
> **He challenged the idea <u>which</u> lessons can be learned from history.

Secondly, there is always a missing element or constituent in a relative clause which is represented by the relative pronoun. In a *that*-clause, there is no such missing element – the clause is complete by itself. This can be seen if we return to the examples above. In the relative clause we are missing an object which is represented by *that* (*she bought_____*). However, the clause *lessons can be learned from history* in the second example (a *that*-clause) is essentially complete. You would also do well at this point to remember the different functions of relative clauses and *that*-clauses. In a relative clause, *that* is serving as a modifier which restricts the reference of the noun phrase. In a *that*-clause, the clause is a complement of a noun phrase which it defines:

> *The woman <u>that</u> cleans the church is married to the vicar.*
> [Reference of NP is restricted to a particular woman]
> *They opposed the suggestion <u>that</u> immigration has negative consequences.*
> [Clause defines NP: the suggestion *is* that immigration has negative
>   consequences]

Is the underlined clause in the following sentence a relative clause or a *that*-clause?

> 100 years ago, our founders designed two innovations <u>that changed the world</u>.
> (*Wausau Daily Herald*, Wisconsin, 2017)

The main points in this section are summarised below.

KEY POINTS FINITE SUBORDINATE CLAUSES

- Clauses are built up around the lexical verbs in a sentence. A sentence which contains two or three lexical verbs will also have two or three clauses. The issue then for grammarians is how these clauses are linked to each other.
- Clauses may be linked by means of coordination and subordination. Clauses which are linked by means of coordination have equal syntactic status. The two clauses linked by *and* in the following sentence have the same syntactic status in the sentence: *Bill is a teacher and Sally is a doctor*.
- Clauses may also be linked by means of subordination. In this case, one clause (a subordinate clause) is dependent on another clause (the main clause or sentence). The underlined clause in the following sentence is dependent on the main clause (the full sentence): *I imagined that the extra money would be needed*.
- Subordinate clauses can be distinguished according to whether they contain a tensed verb form (a finite verb) or a verb form that is not marked for tense (a non-finite verb). These verb forms give rise to finite and non-finite subordinate clauses, respectively.
- Finite subordinate clauses include declarative subordinate clauses (e.g. *Sue thinks that the dress is pretty*), interrogative subordinate clauses (e.g. *He asked if there was a shortcut through the park*), and relative clauses (e.g. *They sold the vase which they found in the attic*).
- There are two types of declarative subordinate clause: *that*-clauses (a declarative sentence with *that* in front of it) and declarative sentences introduced by complementisers (or subordinating conjunctions) other than *that*.
- *That*-clauses can be objects of verbs (e.g. *She thought that the painting was valuable*), subjects (e.g. *That the painting was valuable was obvious*), and subject complements (e.g. *The clear evidence was that the painting was valuable*). They can also be complements of adjectives (e.g. *She was afraid that the leak would get worse*) and nouns (e.g. *the hope that the conflict would end*).
- Declarative subordinate clauses with a range of complementisers other than *that* have an adverbial function. These clauses address questions such as *When?* and *Why?* (e.g. *She left the party early because she had to write an essay*).
- There are two types of interrogative subordinate clause: *if/whether*-clauses (correspond to *yes–no* interrogatives) and *wh*-clauses (correspond to *wh*-interrogatives). Both types of clause can be objects of verbs, and complements of adjectives and nouns. Additionally, *whether*-clauses can be a subject in a sentence and *wh*-clauses can have an adverbial function.
- A further finite subordinate clause is the relative clause. In all relative clauses, a relative pronoun replaces a preceding noun phrase known as the 'antecedent'. Relative clauses can be restrictive (narrow the reference of the noun phrase) or non-restrictive (provide incidental information).
- Relative pronouns can be subjects in relative clauses (e.g. *The woman who knits baked cakes for the fair*) and objects (e.g. *The elderly man whom you saw reported the incident*). The relative pronoun *whose* takes the place of a genitive noun phrase in a relative clause (e.g. *The man whose sister is ill attended the meeting*). Prescriptive grammarians object to the use of *whose* to replace an inanimate noun phrase (e.g. *The car whose door was open had been vandalised*).

- Relative pronouns which appear on their own at the front of restrictive relative clauses can be replaced by *that* (e.g. *The tree which/that was planted last year has died*). The use of *that* in a relative clause should not be confused with *that* in a *that*-clause (e.g. *It was his firm belief <u>that his wife had left him</u>*). It is only in relative clauses that *who* or *which* can take the place of *that*. Also, *that* in a relative clause is replacing a missing element or constituent. In a *that*-clause, the clause is essentially complete.

6.4 Non-Finite Subordinate Clauses

The four non-finite verb forms in English are the bare infinitive, the *to*-infinitive, the *–ing* participle and the *–ed* participle. The clauses which are constructed around these verbs are non-finite subordinate clauses. These clauses will be the focus of this section. When these verb forms were introduced in Section 3.3 in Chapter 3, it was in the context of the following sentences. The non-finite subordinate clause is underlined in each sentence:

> *The walker saw the woman <u>enter the park</u>.* [Bare infinitive]
> *They wanted <u>to visit Beijing</u>.* [To-infinitive]
> *<u>Leaving home</u> is a very stressful experience.* [*–ing* participle]
> *<u>Postponed for the second time</u>, the match was about to take place.* [*–ed* participle]

There are two noteworthy features of these clauses. The first is that they are not introduced by complementisers like *that* and *if*. The second feature is that they do not have a subject. We will say more about each of these features as we examine these clauses in more detail.

6.4.1 Bare Infinitive Clauses

The bare infinitive is formed from what was described in Section 3.3 as the **base form** of the verb. There are only certain verbs in English which permit a bare infinitive to follow them. Some of these verbs are *see, let, make* and *help*. The following examples from Lara illustrate the use of bare infinitives after two of these verbs, *let* and *help*:

> *Amy won't <u>let</u> me <u>play</u>.*
> *I'll <u>let</u> her <u>have</u> that.*
> *<u>Let</u> me <u>put</u> it in there.*
> *I will <u>help</u> you <u>tidy</u> up.*
> *Can you <u>help</u> me <u>build</u> a house?*
> *I'll <u>let</u> you <u>have</u> that bit.*
> *<u>Help</u> me <u>make</u> this because I don't like to do it on my own.*

Each of the bare infinitives in these sentences is preceded by an object pronoun. Is this pronoun a subject of the bare infinitive clause? Or is it an object of verbs like *let* and *help*? In grammatical terms, it is difficult to decide. The mere fact that the pronoun has an object form is not sufficient reason to say that it is the object of verbs like *let* and *help*. Object pronouns are used in other sentences where they function as subjects. For example, the question *Who wants chips?* can receive the response *Me* which functions as a subject (compare I *want chips*). Alternatively, pronouns like *me* and *her* appear to be objects of the verb *let* in much the same way as they are objects in sentences like *She hit me* and *They like her*. Börjars and Burridge (2010) take the view that these pronouns have the status of objects of verbs like *let* and *help*, and that the bare infinitive clauses in these sentences are **subjectless clauses**. However, even in the absence of a syntactic subject, a subject is nonetheless understood. For example, the understood subject of the bare infinitive clause in *Amy won't let me play* is clearly the referent of *me*.

In terms of the functions of bare infinitive clauses, the bare infinitive clauses in the sentences above are objects of the verbs *let* and *help*. Beyond these sentences, bare infinitive clauses are relatively uncommon in everyday language use. One further context in which these clauses are used is in **pseudo-cleft sentences**. The bare infinitive clause in this pseudo-cleft sentence is underlined: *What she did was prepare the meal early*. In pseudo-cleft sentences, an entire clause (*what she did*) is topicalised. The constituent represented by *what* in this clause is specified (focalised) by the subject complement, a bare infinitive clause.

Can you identify the bare infinitive clauses in the following sentences?

> The rescheduling of the features from Saturday's abandoned Trentham meeting saw them run on Nelson's home track. (*The Dominion Post*, New Zealand, 2017)
> We fight the idea of man as head of the household, insisting on shared parenting and shared housework and equal rights, but we can't let that vestige go. (*The Sydney Morning Herald*, 2017)

To give you further practice in identifying bare infinitive clauses, you should now attempt Exercise 6.6.

EXERCISE 6.6 BARE INFINITIVE CLAUSES

The following utterances have been produced by adults with probable Alzheimer's dementia during the Cookie Theft picture description task in the Boston Diagnostic Aphasia Examination (Goodglass et al., 2001). For each utterance, you should underline the bare infinitive clause. Name the five verbs in these utterances which permit a bare infinitive clause to follow them:

(a) She's helping him get the cookies (Female; 71 years)

(b) She let the sink run over (Female; 74 years)
(c) Let me scan it a little bit more (Female; 65 years)
(d) The mother is having water run over the sink (Male; 50 years)
(e) She has let the sink overflow (Male; 70 years)
(f) Please let me go (Female; 74 years)
(g) Somebody let the water run over (Female; 66 years)
(h) She's letting the water run out of the faucet onto the floor (Female; 85 years)
(i) The mother's seeing the water run over the sink (Female; 71 years)
(j) She's making the sink run over (Female; 87 years)

6.4.2 *To*-Infinitive Clauses

To-infinitive clauses are more common in everyday language use than bare infinitive clauses. To begin our examination of this non-finite subordinate clause, consider the following utterances of Lara, a typically developing child who was just over 3 years old at the time of production:

> *I want to be elephant.*
> *Do you want to have those?*
> *Bear's going to get you.*
> *We need to come to my house.*
> *Are you trying to get up here?*
> *It's supposed to be that way.*
> *I want to play with it.*

The *to*-infinitive clauses which are underlined in these sentences function as objects of verbs such as *want* and *need*. But these clauses have several other functions beyond object. They can also be a subject in a sentence. To illustrate the subject function of this clause, we turn to another of Lara's utterances:

> *It's easier to catch them.*

The underlined *to*-infinitive is a subject in extraposed position. With slight reworking, this clause can also assume the normal subject position in the sentence:

> *To catch them is easier.*

It might appear that another of Lara's utterances has the same structure as the sentence with the **extraposed subject** above. That utterance is:

> *Elsie is ready to go to the seaside.*

But what we have here is yet another function of *to*-infinitive clauses. That function is a modifier in an adjective phrase. Noun phrases, too, can have *to*-infinitive clauses as modifiers. In Lara's data set, there were no examples of this function of *to*-infinitive clauses, and so the following sentences have been devised:

> The journalist reported on the war <u>to end all wars</u>.
> Molly knew the way <u>to solve the problem</u>.

Lara did, however, use *to*-infinitives with an adverbial function. The adverbial of purpose in this utterance becomes apparent when we ask why the speaker undertook the action captured by the verb in the higher clause. Why did the speaker decide to come out now? It was *in order to get some music*.

> I'm coming out now <u>to get some music</u>.

Lara produced a number of other utterances which contain *to*-infinitive clauses. A question of some interest is the status of the underlined words in these utterances. Are words like *you* and *her* objects of the verbs in the higher clauses of these sentences? Or are they subjects in the *to*-infinitive clauses? You will recall that we asked a similar question of bare infinitive clauses in sentences like *Amy won't let <u>me</u> play*:

> I don't want <u>her</u> to get my field.
> I want <u>you</u> to come up here.
> I need <u>you</u> to help me.
> I don't want <u>you</u> to tidy up.
> I want <u>you</u> to help me make it big.

And in the same way that we described the bare infinitive clause as a subjectless clause, we will say that the *to*-infinitive clauses in these sentences do not have a syntactic subject and that words like *you* and *her* are objects of higher verbs such as *want* and *need*. However, the subject can still be understood in each case. For example, in the first example above, the referent of the pronoun *her* is the subject of the *to*-infinitive clause. Also, even though Lara did not oblige us with examples in her data set, it is easy to introduce a subject into these clauses by means of the complementiser *for*:

> I don't want <u>for her</u> to get my field.

In Section 1.2 in Chapter 1 we described a feature of Northern Irish English which has more than a fleeting similarity to the *to*-infinitive clause with subject in the sentence above. The so-called **for–to infinitive** occurs when the subject is omitted. The British Library attributes this grammatical feature to speakers in East Harting (a hamlet in the Chichester district of West Sussex) and speakers in Bleanish Island (a townland in County Fermanagh in Northern Ireland):

> 'people kept a few hens **for to get** a few eggs'

It should also be mentioned that the understood subject is not always the preceding noun phrase or pronoun as it is in Lara's examples above. In the following devised examples, *the congregation* is the understood subject of the *to*-infinitive clause in the first sentence. However, in the second sentence the understood sub-ject of the *to*-infinitive clause is *the preacher*:

> *The preacher urged the congregation <u>never to take drugs</u>.*
> *The preacher promised the congregation <u>never to take drugs</u>.*

These features of *to*-infinitive clauses can be illustrated further by examining the use of these clauses by adults with probable Alzheimer's dementia. In Table 6.4, the utterances of several of these adults are displayed. Each utterance was pro-duced during the Cookie Theft picture description task of the Boston Diagnostic Aphasia Examination (Goodglass et al., 2001). The gender and age of each subject are also displayed. Examine each of these utterances before reading the detailed discussion of them below.

The *to*-infinitive clauses in these utterances fulfil several grammatical functions and exhibit a range of structural features. The underlined clauses in the following examples are all objects of the lexical verb in the main clause:

> *The little boy's trying <u>to get into the cookie jar</u>.*
> *He's going <u>to break his leg</u>.*
> *I want <u>to kill you</u>.*

TABLE 6.4 Use of *to*-infinitive clauses by adults with dementia

Gender; Age	Utterances of adults with dementia
Female; 74 years	He wants cookies to give to his sister
Female; 65 years	The stool's about ready to fall
Female; 78 years	The girl is telling him what to do
Male; 74 years	He's climbing up to get cookies
Female; 66 years	The little boy is going to get killed if he doesn't get up
Male; 78 years	She seems to be looking out the window at the lawn
Female; 79 years	The little boy's trying to get into the cookie jar
Female; 81 years	You need water in there to wash the dishes
Female; 70 years	Sister's back to try for some more cookies
Female; 83 years	He's going to get hurt when the chair tips over
Male; 79 years	She's asking him to bring some of this down
Male; 78 years	That's dirty to have that on the floor
Female; 70 years	The little girl reaching up to give the jar to her brother
Female; 76 years	So I don't know what to tell you
Male; 78 years	He's gonna [going to] break his leg
Male; 78 years	I wanna [want to] kill ya [you]
Female; 85 years	The girl's got her hand up to get the cookie
Female; 75 years	His stool is starting to fall
Female; 60 years	The boy is going to be hurt
Female; 86 years	She's trying to wipe the plates dry

His stool is starting <u>to fall</u>.
She's trying <u>to wipe the plates dry</u>.

The subject function was relatively uncommon in the utterances of these adults. However, there is one example of an extraposed subject in Table 6.4. By reworking the utterance, the *to*-infinitive clause can also assume the normal subject position in a sentence:

That's dirty <u>to have that on the floor</u>. [Extraposed subject]
<u>To have that on the floor</u> is dirty. [Normal subject position]

In the following utterance, it may appear that we have another extraposed subject. After all, the *to*-infinitive clause follows the adjective *ready* in the same way that it follows the adjective *dirty* in the above utterance. However, in the following utterance the *to*-infinitive clause is a modifier of the adjective *ready*. The test of this clause's modifier status is that it is not possible to rework the sentence so that the *to*-infinitive clause is in the normal subject position:

The stool's about ready <u>to fall</u>.
*<u>To fall</u> the stool is about ready.

In three utterances in Table 6.4, the *to*-infinitive clause has an adverbial function. An adverbial of purpose is indicated by the fact that the *to*-infinitive can be preceded by *in order*:

He's climbing up [in order] <u>to get cookies</u>.
The little girl [is] reaching up [in order] <u>to give the jar to her brother</u>.
The girl's got her hand up [in order] <u>to get the cookie</u>.

What is the function of the *to*-infinitive clauses in the following sentences?

Counsel Charlotte Carr said: 'To treat a police officer differently could lead to ridicule and contempt from the public and to suppress a particular occupation invites a perception that certain classes of persons will be treated differently before the court.' (*New Zealand Herald*, 2017)
    We're still innovating to make a difference in people's lives. (*Wausau Daily Herald*, Wisconsin, 2017)
    Never seemingly short of energy, Smith sat out last week's regular season finale against the Reds in Dunedin to refresh ahead of the playoffs. (*The Southland Times*, New Zealand, 2017)

It was described above how the *to*-infinitive clause is a subjectless clause in which the subject is nevertheless understood. In some cases, the understood subject is the object of the main clause. This can be seen in the following example from Table 6.4. Here, the subject of the *to*-infinitive clause is the referent of the object pronoun *him*:

She's asking <u>him</u> to bring some of this down.

In other cases, the understood subject of the *to*-infinitive clause is the subject of the main clause. In these examples from Table 6.4, the understood subject of the *to*-infinitive clause is the referent of the subject noun or pronoun in the main clause:

> *<u>He</u> wants cookies to give to his sister.*
> *<u>You</u> need water in there to wash the dishes.*
> *<u>Sister</u>'s back to try for some more cookies.*

Some of the *to*-infinitives used by these adults with dementia contain auxiliary verbs. A non-standard auxiliary verb *get* is used in place of *be* in the first two examples below. This is related to the fact that these adults are American English speakers:

> *The little boy is going to <u>get</u> killed if he doesn't get up.*
> *He's going to <u>get</u> hurt when the chair tips over.*
> *The boy is going to <u>be</u> hurt.*
> *She seems to <u>be</u> looking out the window at the lawn.*

Finally, *to*-infinitives may also appear in *wh*-clauses, as the following examples from Table 6.4 illustrate. These are non-finite interrogative subordinate clauses:

> *The girl is telling him <u>what to do</u>.*
> *So I don't know <u>what to tell you</u>.*

You can get further practice in describing the structure and function of *to*-infinitive clauses by attempting question (5) at the end of the chapter. The examples used in this question are also actual utterances of adults with probable Alzheimer's dementia.

6.4.3 *–ing* Participle Clauses

Non-finite subordinate clauses can also be built up around *–ing* participles. As with the other clauses we have examined, clauses based on *–ing* participles have a number of functions. In illustration of these functions, consider the following sentences:

> *<u>Losing a loved one</u> is very distressing.*
> *<u>Frightening young children</u> is not funny.*

In each of these sentences, an *–ing* participle clause assumes the function of a subject which the rest of the sentence (the predicate) describes. The subject can also occur at the end of the sentence (an extraposed subject). This requires the introduction of the expletive *it*:

> *It is very distressing <u>losing a loved one</u>.*
> *It is not funny <u>frightening young children</u>.*

Clauses built around –*ing* participles can also fulfil other functions. In the following sentences, the underlined clauses are objects of the lexical verbs *reported* and *like* in the main clause:

> She reported <u>seeing him in London</u>.
> They like <u>listening to music</u>.

In the following sentences, –*ing* participle clauses are modifiers in noun phrases. Like restrictive relative clauses, participle clauses narrow the referent of the noun phrase. However, unlike restrictive relative clauses, they lack a complementiser (a relative pronoun which functions as a subject):

> Jane stared at the girls <u>talking during the movie</u>. [–*ing* participle clause]
> Jane stared at the girls <u>who were talking during the movie</u>. [Restrictive relative clause]
> Peter mimicked the boy <u>swimming in the pool</u>. [–*ing* participle clause]
> Peter mimicked the boy <u>who is swimming in the pool</u>. [Restrictive relative clause]

The final function of –*ing* participles is as adverbial clauses. In this function, prepositions often precede the participle:

> <u>By viewing the building from the side</u>, she got a different perspective.
> <u>After living alone for years</u>, Jack decided it was time to get married.
> <u>Combing his hair</u>, he got into the car.
> He silenced her <u>by frowning</u>.

Sometimes, an –*ing* participle occurs deep within a number of phrases in a sentence. Consider the following utterance, which was produced by a 66-year-old man with Alzheimer's dementia. The –*ing* participle in this utterance occurs in a prepositional phrase which is a post-modifier in a noun phrase. In its turn, the noun phrase is a post-modifier in a prepositional phrase:

> She's [$_{PP}$ in [$_{NP}$ the process [$_{PP}$ of <u>drying dishes</u>]]].

Identify the –*ing* participle clauses in the following sentences. What is the function of these clauses?

> Brandon Edwards remained on the shuttle bus with his already-weary family, opting to head home. (*Wausau Daily Herald*, Wisconsin, 2017)
> After viewing the daunting wait, half the riders stayed on the bus with the Edwards family. (*Wausau Daily Herald*, Wisconsin, 2017)
> Adopting a diet that is both sustainable and healthy may seem hard. (*Tearaway: The Voice of NZ Youth*, 2016)
> 'Ordering the suppression of Mr Buis' occupation because he is a police officer undermines the principle that all members of society are equal under the law', Gendall said. (*New Zealand Herald*, 2017)

To give you further practice in identifying –*ing* participle clauses, you should now attempt Exercise 6.7.

EXERCISE 6.7 –*ING* PARTICIPLE CLAUSES

Each of the following utterances was produced by an adult with Alzheimer's dementia during a picture description task. For each utterance, you should (i) underline the –*ing* participle clause, and (ii) state its function as a subject, object, adverbial or modifier of a noun:

(a) There's a path leading to a garage (Female; 73 years)
(b) I think that's all I see going on (Male; 51 years)
(c) Here's mama drying the dishes (Female; 74 years)
(d) In looking out the window, she's letting her sink run over (Male; 68 years)
(e) I did mention the water running out of the sink (Female; 87 years)
(f) Stealing cookies is the first bad thing I see (Female; 85 years)
(g) It's another house coming right next door to it (Female; 68 years)
(h) It came splashing down (Female; 74 years)
(i) There's a slight breeze coming in the kitchen window (Male; 66 years)
(j) The little girl was helping the boy to get to the cookie jar but he started stumbling (Female; 57 years)

You may have noticed that the –*ing* participle clauses in the above examples lack complementisers. However, the preposition *for* can function as a complementiser, allowing the realisation of an overt subject in an –*ing* participle clause. Similar use of the preposition *for* also occurs in *to*-infinitive clauses:

> The water's spilling <u>for the woman</u> drying the dishes. [–*ing* participle clause]
> <u>For Mark</u> to hold these views is appalling. [*to*-infinitive clause]

When a syntactic subject is used in an –*ing* participle clause, it has an object form. This can best be illustrated by the use of pronouns which change their form with case (the noun phrase *the woman* in the above example has the same form for subject and object). In the following examples, the object pronouns are subjects of the participle clauses *swimming the channel* and *leaving the club*:

> I imagined <u>him</u> swimming the channel.
> Mike saw <u>her</u> leaving the club.

Subjects in participle clauses may also appear in possessive form, such as *his* and *our* in the following examples:

> <u>His</u> passing the exam surprised his parents.
> <u>Our</u> winning the award created great excitement.

As with bare infinitive and *to*-infinitive clauses, it can sometimes be difficult to decide if a noun phrase or a pronoun is the object of the lexical verb in the main clause or the subject of the non-finite participle clause. In the following sentences, *the man* and *her* may be objects of *heard* and *criticised*, respectively, or subjects of the *–ing* participles *walking* and *leaving*:

> He heard <u>the man</u> walking at a quick pace.
> Mary criticised <u>her</u> leaving so early.

In favour of *the man* and *her* having object status is the simple fact that he heard the man and Mary criticised her – the meaning of these sentences leads us to treat this noun phrase and pronoun as objects. As with the other non-finite subordinate clauses we have examined, *–ing* participle clauses are viewed as subjectless clauses in which a subject is nevertheless understood.

To develop your knowledge of clauses further, you should now read the following Special Topic.

SPECIAL TOPIC 6.2 CLAUSES IN CHILDREN WITH SPECIFIC LANGUAGE IMPAIRMENT

Unlike in earlier chapters, little mention has been made of children with SLI in this chapter. There is a reason for this. Clause structure and function are often compromised in children with SLI as part of their language disorder. The result is that these children tend to use simple sentences which contain a single lexical verb (i.e. one clause). When two or more clauses are used in a sentence, they are typically conjoined by means of coordinating conjunctions such as *but* and *and*. However, children with SLI can also produce finite and non-finite subordinate clauses which warrant examination. The following examples are taken from a narrative production task:

(a) The elephant say the ball is in the swimming pool (Female; 9;7 years)
(b) The lifeguard came to check on the elephant and moose (Female; 9;7 years)
(c) I think that is what he did (Male; 9;7 years)
(d) The lifeguard shows to her on the wall it says no running (Female; 9;3 years)
(e) They tried to fix it (Female; 9;3 years)
(f) There was an elephant playing with a ball near the pool (Male; 9;7 years)
(g) The little elephant told everything what happened (Male; 9;7 years)
(h) The lifeguard pointed to the sign that said no running (Male; 9;7 years)
(i) She was checking if he was alright (Male; 8;10 years)
(j) The giraffe was showing her what it does (Male; 9;4 years)

These children with SLI use a range of finite subordinate clauses, including declarative, interrogative, and relative clauses. Declarative or *that*-clauses are evident in the utterances in (a), (c) and (d). The complementiser *that* is not explicitly present in any of these utterances, although its location is indicated below:

The elephant say [that] <u>the ball is in the swimming pool</u>.
I think [that] <u>that is what he did</u>.
The lifeguard shows to her on the wall [that] <u>it says no running</u>.

The underlined *that*-clauses in these utterances are objects of the lexical verbs *say, think* and *show*. These children with SLI also use interrogative subordinate clauses. The clause introduced by the complementiser *if* in the example below is a direct object of the lexical verb *checking*:

She was checking <u>if he was alright</u>.

Wh-clauses are a further type of interrogative subordinate clause. They were also used by these children. These clauses are underlined in the utterances below:

I think that is <u>what he did</u>.
The giraffe was showing her <u>what it does</u>.

The *wh*-clause in the first utterance is couched within a *that*-clause. In the second example, the *wh*-clause is the direct object of the verb *show*, while the pronoun *her* is an indirect object. Relative clauses were also used by these children. In the first example, a non-standard relative pronoun (*what*) is used in place of *that*. The relative pronouns in these examples replace an indefinite pronoun (*everything*) and a noun phrase (*the sign*) in the relative clause:

The little elephant told everything <u>what happened</u>.
The lifeguard pointed to the sign <u>that said no running</u>.

Two types of non-finite subordinate clause also occurred. *To*-infinitive clauses are underlined in the following examples. Their function in these utterances differs, however. In the first example, the *to*-infinitive clause has an adverbial function. In the second example, the *to*-infinitive clause is an object of the lexical verb *tried*:

The lifeguard came <u>to check on the elephant and moose</u>.
They tried <u>to fix it</u>.

These children also occasionally used *–ing* participle clauses, as in the following example:

There was an elephant <u>playing with a ball near the pool</u>.

Although children with SLI tend to use simple clauses which are linked by means of coordination, these examples clearly demonstrate that they are also capable of using finite and non-finite subordinate clauses like typically developing children.

6.4.4 –ed Participle Clauses

The final non-finite subordinate clause to be examined is built around the –ed participle. Consider the following sentences:

> The developers want <u>the house built before the summer.</u>
> <u>When instructed to leave the building,</u> do not take bags and other possessions.
> <u>Banned by the government,</u> the angry students took to the streets.
> The plans <u>redrawn by an architect</u> were presented to councillors.

The underlined –ed participle clauses in these sentences can be used to illustrate the different functions of these clauses. In the first sentence, the clause is the object of the lexical verb (*want*) in the main clause. The clauses in the next two sentences are both adverbials. Like other adverbial clauses, these clauses address questions relating to time (*When?*) and reason (*Why?*):

> When should you not take bags and other possessions?
> When you are <u>instructed to leave the building.</u>
> Why did the angry students take to the streets?
> Because they were <u>banned by the government.</u>

In the final example above, the –ed participle clause is a modifier of the noun *plans*. Like –ing participle clauses, this function of –ed participle clauses resembles a relative clause. There is nothing to distinguish the meaning of this sentence from the following sentence which contains a relative clause:

> The plans, <u>which were redrawn by an architect,</u> were presented to councillors.

Clauses built around –ed participles can have subjects. In the first example above, it seems clear that *the house* is not an object of the verb *want* but is a subject of the participle clause. After all, it is not the case that the developers want the house. Rather, what they want is for the house to be built before the summer. In the other –ed participle clauses we have examined in this section, there is no overt subject. Nevertheless, a subject can still be understood in each case. For example, we have little difficulty in establishing that it was the angry students who were banned by the government in the third sentence above.

   Both typically developing (TD) children and children with SLI used relatively few –ed participle clauses in their data sets. Some examples of the use of these clauses are shown below:

> There was a little girl <u>named cookie.</u> [SLI: female; 9;9 years]
> He is getting <u>the knot undone.</u> [SLI: male; 8;5 years]
> This guy got <u>it all tangled.</u> [TD: male; 4;7 years]

In the first example, the participle clause *named cookie* is a modifier of the noun *girl*. The participle clauses in the other examples are objects. T*he knot* and *it* are most likely to be subjects in these clauses. To treat this noun phrase and pronoun as objects of the higher verbs *getting* and *got* would require us to say that he is getting the knot and the guy got it, neither of which appears to be part of the meaning of these utterances.

The main points in this section are summarised below.

KEY POINTS NON-FINITE SUBORDINATE CLAUSES

- There are four non-finite verb forms in English: the bare infinitive; *to*-infinitive; *–ing* participle; and *–ed* participle. A non-finite subordinate clause can be constructed around each of these verb forms.
- A bare infinitive clause uses the base form of the verb. Bare infinitives follow certain verbs like *see, let, make* and *help* (e.g. *Oscar saw Sue leave the shop*). Bare infinitive clauses can function as objects, as in the Oscar example. They can also be used in pseudo-cleft sentences (e.g. *What she did was prepare the meal early*). Because it is the case that Oscar saw Sue, we are inclined to say that *Sue* is the object of the higher verb *saw*.
- *To*-infinitive clauses are more common than bare infinitive clauses and fulfil a wider range of grammatical functions. *To*-infinitive clauses can be objects (*They decided to leave early*), subjects (*To oppose the plans is futile*), modifiers in adjective phrases (*Frank is happy to miss the show*) and noun phrases (*Bob found a way to save money*), and adverbials (*She got up early to see the sunrise*). An overt subject can be introduced into a *to*-infinitive clause by means of the preposition *for* which functions as a complementiser (*For Jim to make that allegation was very courageous*). Even when an overt subject is not present, a subject may nonetheless be understood. For example, *Mary* is the understood subject of the *to*-infinitive clause in the sentence *I need Mary to help me*.
- *–ing* participle clauses are also relatively common in written and spoken language. These clauses can be subjects in a sentence, either in normal subject position (*Losing a loved one is very distressing*) or in an extraposed position (*It is very distressing losing a loved one*). They can also function as objects (*I like hearing from Mike*), modifiers in noun phrase (*The kids screaming at their parents ruined the day out*), and adverbials (*By renting the property, you make savings*). An overt subject can be introduced into an *–ing* participle clause by way of the preposition *for* which functions as a complementiser (*For the people organising the event, the bad weather was a disaster*). Object pronouns (*I imagined her squeezing into the dress*) and possessive forms (*Our asking for more cake caused offence*) may be subjects in *–ing* participle clauses.
- *–ed* participles can also be the basis of non-finite subordinate clauses. A passive meaning is always present. These participle clauses can be objects (*She occupied a house inherited from her grandmother*), adverbials (*Exhausted, they retired for the evening*), and modifiers of nouns (*They bought a chair crafted by hand*). Some *–ed* participle clauses have subjects, such as *a house* in the above example. Even when a subject is not present, one can be understood. For example, it is *they* who are exhausted in the sentence: *Exhausted, they retired for the evening*.

SUMMARY

In this chapter you have seen the following:

- A clause contains a main (lexical) verb, any elements required by the main verb as well as one or more optional elements. In the clause *Mike ate the pizza very quickly*, the noun phrases *Mike* (subject) and *the pizza* (direct object) are required by the main verb *ate*, while the adverb phrase *very quickly* (adverbial) is an optional element.
- There are a range of clause patterns. The simplest pattern is SUBJECT + PREDICATOR in clauses like *Tim smiles* and *Oscar winks*. The clause pattern for *Mike ate the pizza very quickly* is SUBJECT + PREDICATOR + DIRECT OBJECT + ADVERBIAL.
- Clauses which are linked by coordinating conjunctions have equal syntactic status (*Bill opened the door and Joe closed the window*). When clauses are linked by subordinating conjunctions, one clause is dependent on another clause (a main clause or sentence). In the sentence *Jack thought the movie was terrible*, the clause *the movie was terrible* is dependent on the full sentence.
- There are different types of finite subordinate clause: a declarative subordinate clause (*Frank wished that the man would leave*); an interrogative subordinate clause (*They asked if the match was postponed*); and a relative clause (*The man, who lives across the road, owns a boat*). These clauses have different functions: *that*-clause (direct object of *wished*) and *if*-clause (direct object of *asked*). Relative clauses are modifiers in noun phrases.
- There are different types of non-finite subordinate clause: bare infinitive clause (*They saw the man bury the treasure*); *to*-infinitive clause (*They decided to visit the zoo*); *–ing* participle clause (*Leaving home is a stressful experience*); and *–ed* participle clause (*Destroyed by conflict, the building was demolished*). These clauses also have functions. For example, the *–ing* participle clause *leaving home* is a subject, while the *to*-infinitive clause *to visit the zoo* is a direct object of the verb *decided*.

WEBSITE CLAUSES

After reading the chapter, visit the website and test your knowledge of clauses by answering the multiple-choice questions for this topic.

HOMEWORK ASSIGNMENT

In this chapter, you have been introduced to the following clauses:

Declarative subordinate clauses	*Bare infinitive clauses*	*–ed participle clauses*
Interrogative subordinate clauses	*To-infinitive clauses*	
Relative clauses	*–ing participle clauses*	

Examine the following extract from an article that appeared on 11 July 2017 in the Australian newspaper *The Sydney Morning Herald*. Use your knowledge of clauses to find one or more examples of the above clauses in this extract.

DONALD TRUMP JNR 'WAS TOLD' LAWYER MEETING WAS PART OF RUSSIAN EFFORT

Donald Trump's son was told prior to meeting a Russian lawyer whom he believed had information damaging to Hillary Clinton that the material was part of a Russian government effort to help his father's presidential campaign, the *New York Times* has reported, citing three people with knowledge of the email.

Publicist Rob Goldstone, who helped broker the June 2016 meeting, sent the email to Donald Trump jnr, the *Times* said. Goldstone's message indicates that the Russian government was the source of the potentially damaging information, according to the *Times*.

Earlier on Monday, the US President's eldest son offered to talk to the Senate committee investigating alleged Russian interference in the presidential election, after he acknowledged meeting the Russian lawyer during the campaign.

"Happy to work with the committee to pass on what I know," Donald Trump jnr wrote on Twitter.

SUGGESTIONS FOR FURTHER READING

(1) Aarts, B. (2011) *Oxford Modern English Grammar*. Oxford: Oxford University Press.

Part III of this volume contains a number of chapters that examine clause patterns and finite and non-finite subordinate clauses. The relevant chapters are chapter 6 (Clause types and negation), chapter 7 (Finite subordinate clauses) and chapter 8 (Non-finite and verbless subordinate clauses). Key points, further reading and numerous examples are provided.

(2) Kroeger, P. R. (2005) *Analyzing Grammar: An Introduction*. Cambridge: Cambridge University Press.

Chapter 12 in this book examines subordinate clauses. Among the clauses examined are coordinate and subordinate clauses, complement clauses, adverbial clauses and relative clauses. Exercises at the end of the chapter provide you with practice in identifying these different clauses.

(3) Huddleston, R. and Pullum, G. K. (2005) *A Student's Introduction to English Grammar*. New York: Cambridge University Press.

There are several chapters in this volume which will extend your understanding of clauses. They are chapter 4 (Clause structure, complements, and adjuncts), chapter 10 (Subordination and content clauses), chapter 11 (Relative clauses) and chapter 13 (Non-finite clauses and clauses without verbs). Further reading and exercises are also provided.

QUESTIONS CLAUSES

(1) Sixty of Lara's utterances are listed in Appendix 2. Go to this appendix and organise these utterances according to the five most common clause patterns that Lara uses:

S + P

$S + P + O_D$

$S + P + C_{SUB}$

S + P + A

$S + P + O_D + A$

(2) Each of the following utterances is produced by an adult with probable Alzheimer's disease during the Cookie Theft picture description task of the Boston Diagnostic Aphasia Examination (Goodglass et al., 2001). Each utterance contains either a declarative subordinate clause or an interrogative subordinate clause (but you should keep on your toes as some contain both types of clause!). You should identify the type of clause in each utterance. For a declarative subordinate clause, you should indicate if the clause is a *that*-clause or a clause introduced by some other type of complementiser. For an interrogative subordinate clause, you should indicate if the clause is an *if/whether*-clause or a *wh*-clause:

(a) I don't know what the heck they're doing here though (Female; 71 years)

(b) I think he's gonna land himself on the floor (Male; 79 years)

(c) He's going to fall because the stool is tilted too much (Male; 83 years)

(d) I don't know what that is (Male; 74 years)

(e) I guess this is breakfast (Female; 68 years)

(f) I thought it looked like a nose and a mouth (Female; 87 years)

(g) I don't know whether it's a ball or a cake (Female; 76 years)

(h) Wonder what my husband is doing (Female; 70 years)

(i) The little boy is gonna fall off the chair if he doesn't be careful (Female; 79 years)

(j) I don't know if there's anything more there or not (Female; 69 years)

(k) The sink's running over the water on the floor while she's drying the dishes (Female; 81 years)

(l) He's gonna fall off since it's tipping over (Female; 75 years)

(m) I don't know why she didn't turn the water off (Female; 49 years)

(n) I guess there's a breeze blowing (Female; 67 years)

(o) He's going to get hurt when the chair tips over (Female; 83 years)

(p) You know he's the one that's trying to get the cookie jar (Female; 72 years)

(q) This boy is almost falling off the chair when he's putting up the picture (Female; 79 years)

(r) The bench is toppling over as the kid is standing on (Male; 71 years)

(s) I don't know what you call them (Female; 78 years)

(t) I don't think she knows what they're up to (Female; 75 years)

(3) The following utterances are produced by adults with probable Alzheimer's dementia during the Cookie Theft picture description task. For each utterance, you should (i) underline the relative clause and relative pronoun, and (ii) indicate if the relative pronoun is a subject or an object of the relative clause in which it appears:

(a) There's a young boy that's getting a cookie jar (Male; 57 years)

(b) He's standing on a stool that's tipping over (Female; 73 years)

(c) Then there's an angle here that is incomplete (Male; 68 years)

(d) A girl laughing at her brother who is taking cookies out of the cookie jar (Male; 69 years)

(e) There's a tree which you can see through the half open window (Male; 67 years)

(f) The little girl wants the cookie that the kid is stealing from the cookie jar (Male; 71 years)

(g) I see a little boy climbed up on a stool that is reaching for a cookie out of the cookie jar (Male; 51 years)

(h) She is reaching for the cookie that he has in his hand (Male; 51 years)

(i) Mama's drying the dishes as usual for mamas if they don't have a husband that dries them or washes them or whatever (Male; 68 years)

(j) The little girl pushed over the chair with the boy that was reaching up to get the cookies (Male; 68 years)

(4) We described in this chapter how *that* can appear in *that*-clauses and in relative clauses. To give you practice in recognising these different uses of *that* in clauses, you should examine the following utterances which have been produced by adults with probable Alzheimer's dementia. Each utterance was used during the Cookie Theft picture description task of the Boston Diagnostic Aphasia Examination (Goodglass et al., 2001). For each utterance, you should underline the clause which contains *that* and indicate if this clause is a *that*-clause or a relative clause. But you need to be careful as some utterances contain both types of clause!

(a) Did I say that the stool was tilted? (Female; 63 years)

(b) The ladder that he's standing on is beginning to fall (Female; 65 years)

(c) I did say that the water's running in the sink and overflowing (Female; 83 years)

(d) She's got the curtain mixed up with the dish that she's drying (Female; 84 years)

(e) She's too busy to see that the sink is overflowing (Female; 88 years)

(f) There's handles that I can see on two sets of cabinets (Female; 57 years)

(g) I guess that's a cookie jar (Female; 79 years)

(h) Here's a lady that's washing the dishes (Male; 83 years)

(i) There's dishes that had been washed and she's drying them (Male; 77 years)

(j) A window outside that I can see (Male; 58 years)

(k) I think that he'll lose his cookies (Female; 70 years)

(l) I assume that these are flowers (Female; 63 years)

(m) A stool that's going to project somebody into a fall (Female; 72 years)

(n) Two cups and a plate that probably are dry (Female; 72 years)

(o) I assume she's already washed the plate that she's drying (Female; 71 years)

(p) I think that's the activity (Female; 71 years)

(q) I did mention that the stool was tilting (Male; 64 years)

(r) Is there a number that there's supposed to be on it? (Female; 80 years)

(s) The mother is washing dishes and forgetting that the water is running (Male; 66 years)

(t) The little boy has a cookie in his hand that he got by climbing the step ladder (Female; 70 years)

(5) Answer the following questions about *to*-infinitive clauses. All clauses occur in utterances produced by adults with probable Alzheimer's dementia during a picture description task:

(a) What is the understood subject of the *to*-infinitive clause in this sentence? *His sister maybe is telling him to be quiet* (Male; 77 years)

(b) What is the function of the *to*-infinitive clause in this sentence? *She's too busy to see that the sink is overflowing* (Female; 88 years)

(c) What is the understood subject of the *to*-infinitive clause in this sentence? *She has allowed the water to overflow on the floor* (Female; 89 years)

(d) What is the function of the *to*-infinitive clause in this sentence? *She forgot to look at the spigots* (Female; 61 years)

(e) What is the understood subject of the *to*-infinitive clause in this sentence? *She still has a couple of cups and a plate to wash* (Female; 89 years)

(f) What is the function of the *to*-infinitive clause in this sentence? *Little girl is reaching up to grab hers* (Female; 72 years)

(g) What is the understood subject of the *to*-infinitive clause in this sentence? *She wants one to eat* (Male; 69 years)

(h) What is the function of the *to*-infinitive clause in this sentence? *That's a good way to break his neck* (Female; 65 years)

(i) What is the understood subject of the *to*-infinitive clause in this sentence? *You want me to tell you the grass is growing* (Female; 72 years)

(j) What is the function of the *to*-infinitive clause in the following sentence? *There is a little boy who has climbed up on a stool to get cookies from the cookie jar* (Female; 63 years)

(k) What is the understood subject of the *to*-infinitive clause in this sentence? *They're getting something to eat here* (Female; 62 years)

(l) What is the auxiliary verb in the *to*-infinitive clause in this sentence? *He's going to be hurt* (Female; 74 years)

(m) What is the understood subject of the *to*-infinitive clause in this sentence? *I think she's telling him to watch it* (Female; 65 years)

(n) What is the function of the *to*-infinitive clause in this sentence? *He's ready to go over* (Female; 59 years)

(o) What is the syntactic subject of the *to*-infinitive clause in this sentence? *That's bad enough for me to do* (Female; 65 years)

(6) The following utterances are produced by adults with Alzheimer's dementia. For each utterance, underline the *–ing* participle clause. Also, identify the overt or understood subject of each participle clause:

(a) The mother's in the kitchen running the water at the sink (Female; 73 years)

(b) A sink that's overrunning with water splashing down onto her shoes (Male; 66 years)

(c) You see the little boy stealing cookies (Male; 80 years)

(d) There's a child reaching in a cookie jar (Male; 63 years)

(e) The mother is at the sink washing a dish (Male; 63 years)

(f) The window is open looking out onto shrubbery and a path to another house (Male; 63 years)

(g) There are three dishes sitting on the sink counter (Male; 63 years)

(h) There's a girl standing in front of the sink and drying a plate (Female; 75 years)

(i) Mother won't hear him getting up there (Female; 68 years)

(j) She saw the little boy falling (Female; 68 years)

(k) There's a boy getting in the cookie jar (Female; 89 years)

(l) The water's spilling for the woman drying the dishes (Female; 90 years)

(m) The first bad thing I see is the water running out of the sink (Female; 85 years)

(7) Each of the following sentences contains an *–ed* participle clause. Underline the participle clause in each sentence. Also, state the function of the clause as an object, adverbial or modifier of a noun:

(a) Security personnel should have the fans searched for alcohol.

(b) Ravaged by war, the city was largely uninhabitable.

(c) They bought the book valued at a thousand pounds.

(d) The couple wanted the property sold as part of the divorce settlement.

(e) The castle built in Roman times was a huge visitor attraction.

(f) When asked to explain herself, the girl began to cry.

(g) They followed the route taken by most pilgrims.

(h) The devastation strewn before them was testimony to the force of the storm.

(i) Postponed on account of bad weather, the match was about to take place.

(j) The publisher needed the proofs checked within one week.

REVISION CLAUSES

(1) For each of the following sentences, identify (i) the main clause, and (ii) the subordinate clause(s):

(a) He said that Fred wanted to travel abroad.

(b) Mary hoped that John would leave the party early.

(c) The suspect claimed that he did not see the woman leave the hotel.

(d) They wished that they had stayed for one more week.

(e) The council decided that all taxes should be increased.

(2) *True or false:* Clauses which are linked by means of subordinating conjunctions have equal syntactic status.

(3) Identify the clause in brackets in each of the following sentences as either a finite clause or a non-finite clause. Where a clause is non-finite, state what type of non-finite clause it is:

(a) [Moving home] is a very stressful experience.

(b) He argued [that the new development destroyed the environment].

(c) [The boy protested his innocence].

(d) He decided [to make a fresh start].

(e) [Beaten for the third time] the distressed woman phoned the police.

(4) Using the terms *subject, predicator, direct object, indirect object, complement* and *adverbial*, describe the functional patterns of the following clauses:

(a) The girls are screaming.

(b) The team achieved success effortlessly.

(c) The soldiers attacked the fortress.

(d) The student performs erratically.

(e) The host spoke to his guests.

(f) He eats his steak rare.

(g) He gave the actor an award.

(h) The students seem friendly.

(5) Describe the type of semantic meaning expressed by the clauses in brackets. The terms that you should use are *temporal, conditional, concessive, comparative, result* and *reason*:

(a) They own a dog [although they have no dog licence].

(b) He was arrested [because he was a government critic].

(c) [After he had a heart attack] he changed his lifestyle considerably.

(d) The weather at home was terrible [so we went abroad].

(e) [If we run quickly] we will get to the lecture on time.

(f) They had less work [than they had imagined].

(6) Describe the functional patterns of the clauses below using the following notation:

S+P   S+P+DO   S+P+IO   S+P+IO+DO

S+P+C   S+P+DO+C   S+P+A   S+P+DO+A

(a) The audience applauded.

(b) We went to Blackpool.

(c) I kicked the ball.

(d) She asked me a question.

(e) The foul was obvious.

(f) I'll wash the dishes tomorrow.

(g) Mary called me a twit.

(h) They spoke to the children.

(i) I love you.

(j) John gave them the message.

(k) Everyone's staring.

(l) The game finished at midday.

(m) You're a fine specimen.

(n) They elected Smith president.

(o) I've walked the dog today.

(p) They told the teacher.

(7) Identify the clause that is (i) subordinate to, and (ii) superordinate to the clause in italics in the following sentence: They thought *that she said that the match was postponed*.

(8) Describe the part of the sentence in italics as a finite clause or a non-finite clause. For non-finite clauses, state their type:

(a) She decided *to leave the restaurant*.

(b) *Losing a loved one* is very distressing.

(c) He enquired *if the parcel had arrived*.

(d) Mary hopes *that the weather will improve*.

(e) *Delayed by the accident*, he missed the play.

(f) The teenager *who lives across the street* is troublesome.

(g) *What he really thinks* is a secret.

(h) Jill saw *Bill attack the boy*.

(i) They planned *to stay in Italy*.

(j) *If the children misbehave*, then we will stay at home.

(k) The pupil *who is bullying the girl* has been expelled.

(l) They intend *to stay at home*.

(m) *Aided by her friends*, she finally achieved success.

(9) The following sentences contain finite subordinate clauses. For each sentence, identify the clause in question and state if it is a declarative or an interrogative subordinate clause:

(a) They enquired if the flight would depart on time.

(b) Mike hoped she would return early.

(c) The tax inspector queried if the full accounts had been submitted.

(d) He believed that the situation was not going to improve.

(e) She wondered whether the road would be impassable.

(10) Each of the following sentences contains a *that*-clause. State the function of this clause. The terms you should use are *subject, subject complement* and *direct object*:

(a) That Bill is a successful business man is a complete surprise to me.

(b) The worst thing was that he left without warning.

(c) She thought his ideas were confused and illogical.

(d) The truth of the matter was that Mark had forged the signature.

(e) The police believed the man posed a risk to public safety.

(f) That the company is going into administration is a certainty.

(11) Each of the following sentences contains a relative clause. For each sentence, indicate if the relative clause is restrictive or non-restrictive:

(a) The man, who lives across the road, has lost his cat.

(b) The cathedral in York, which is in need of refurbishment, is trying to raise funds.

(c) The factory worker, who disturbed the burglar, sustained minor injuries.

(d) The race horse, which fell at the third fence, had to be destroyed.

(e) The Russian president, who is a keen cyclist and swimmer, opened the Olympic Games.

(12) Each of the following sentences contains a *to*-infinitive clause. State the function of this clause. The terms you should use are *subject, object* and *adverbial*:

(a) I want to travel to Paris next year.

(b) The teacher left early to catch the bus.

(c) To retire in good health is all anyone can ask for.

(d) The driver tried to make the delivery before midday.

(e) They sold the house to raise funds.

(f) To lose a loved one is very distressing.

7 Sentences

7.1 Introduction to Sentences

At the top of any grammatical hierarchy is the sentence. While linguistic utterances short of complete sentences are certainly meaningful, it is through sentences that we convey **propositional meaning**. Consider the following exchange between two language users, A and B:

A: *Would you like tea or coffee?*
B: *Tea, please*

B has certainly succeeded in communicating that he or she would like tea, even though an utterance which is short of a complete sentence has been produced. However, if we think a bit further about this exchange, we can see that B's utterance only works as a response to A's question because a full sentence (*I would like tea*) can be assumed in this case. B is using A's prior utterance as background to his or her utterance, and has used grammatical ellipsis in response. The key point to take away from this exchange is that a full sentence can be assumed even though it has not been explicitly stated. The sentence and the **proposition** that it expresses is the unit of significance when it comes to establishing the meaning of B's utterance.

In English, there are four types of sentences which can be distinguished according to their form or structural features. These sentences are declaratives, interrogatives, **imperatives** and **exclamatives**. In this chapter, the structure and function of these different sentence types will be examined. A's utterance in the above exchange has the structure of an interrogative – there is inversion of the subject pronoun (*you*) and auxiliary verb (*would*). Meanwhile, B's sub-sentential response reveals an implicit declarative in which there is subject–verb word order (*I would like tea*). The structural features of sentences certainly go some way to identifying their function. In this way, we know when we encounter a sentence in which there is inversion of the subject noun or pronoun and auxiliary verb that we are dealing with some type of question:

> *Is Tom coming to the party?*
> *Did they leave early?*
> *Are Sally and Sue baking cakes for the fair?*

But the structural properties of sentences are not an unfailingly reliable guide to their function. For example, there are many sentences which succeed in asking questions but which do not display inversion. Rather, these sentences have the structure of declaratives (i.e. subject–verb word order). That a question is posed by way of these sentences is apparent in written language by the presence of a question mark. In spoken language, it is the speaker's use of a certain pattern of **intonation** which indicates that a question is intended:

> *Jack is arriving late tonight?*
> *You put the wine in the fridge?*

By the same token, there are many sentences which have the structure of an interrogative (i.e. subject–auxiliary verb inversion) but which are not used to ask questions. Each of the following interrogatives is used to make a **request**:

> *Can you tell me the time?* (Speaker wants to be told the time)
> *Can you close the door?* (Speaker wants the door to be closed)

That a request (or **directive**) is the intended meaning of each of these interrogatives is amply demonstrated by the reaction that would ensue if the hearer simply responded 'yes' in each case. A response of this type would be taken to indicate a lack of hearer cooperation of the type propounded by **H. P. Grice** in his **cooperative principle**. Other directives occur when speakers issue commands, instructions and permission to hearers to do something.

What these examples and other examples like them demonstrate is that the function of sentences corresponds rather loosely to their structural properties. Sentence function is determined in large part by the goals, purposes and **communicative intentions** of the language users who use spoken and written sentences (or utterances) to convey messages to each other. In the study of sentence function, grammar must rub shoulders very closely indeed with **pragmatics** (the branch of linguistics that studies how these wider aspects of context affect meaning and communication). We will see further examples of this loose correspondence between sentence structure and function in the sections which follow. In the meantime, to get you thinking further about this important relationship, you should attempt Exercise 7.1.

EXERCISE 7.1 LARA AND SENTENCE FUNCTION

The following sentences (utterances) were produced by Lara when she was just over 3 years old. For each sentence, identify its structure as a *declarative* or an *interrogative*. Also, state the function of the sentence. The function may be a *statement, question* or a *directive*. If you identify the function as a directive, you should further indicate if the sentence is a type of *request*, or *permission* to the hearer to do something:

- (a) I'm cleaning you.
- (b) I get down?
- (c) Is Emily not at work?
- (d) Can you get Amy a duvet?
- (e) What did she do?
- (f) You can have that.
- (g) My doggy's going.
- (h) Are they very hard pants?
- (i) Can you put them away?
- (j) This is cards again.
- (k) I hoovering your house with your hoover?
- (l) Can I have that bag?
- (m) Amy can come in my bed.
- (n) I'm reading a book to you.
- (o) Can you pick it up?
- (p) Amy can play with them.
- (q) Can I play with it?
- (r) Can I have more breadstick please?
- (s) You've only got a little bit.
- (t) Can you get one out for me?

7.2 Declaratives

Probably the most common sentence type in English (or indeed any language) is the declarative. It is not difficult to see why this is the case. One of the primary purposes of any language is to produce statements about people, places and events in the world. Declarative sentences are the vehicle by means of which statements are expressed.

7.2.1 Structure of Declaratives

Declaratives have a two-part structure that consists of a subject noun phrase followed by a predicate verb phrase. As the following sentences illustrate, the subject noun phrase may be a personal or demonstrative pronoun, a proper or common noun, or a dummy subject like *it* and *there*:

> *She is leaving her job.* [Personal pronoun]
> *This is an amazing painting.* [Demonstrative pronoun]
> *Mike grows pumpkins.* [Proper noun]
> *The boy sat under the tree.* [Common noun]
> *It is very cold in here.* [Dummy subject]
> *There is little chance of success.* [Dummy subject]

The predicate verb phrase may contain a lexical verb on its own (*grows* pumpkins) or a lexical verb with an auxiliary verb (*is leaving* her job). There may also be other elements in the predicate including noun phrases (*her job*), prepositional phrases (*under the tree*) and adjective phrases (*very cold*), which have object, adverbial and complement functions, respectively.

    Declarative sentences are produced by even very young typically developing children. However, the structure of these sentences may not be adult-like in all respects. At just over 2 years of age, Lara occasionally produced declarative sentences in which the subject noun phrase was omitted. However, because the subject could be recovered from context, there was no lack of understanding on the part of the hearer (usually Lara's mother):

> *[I] want my slippers.*
> *[I] want snack.*

In other declarative sentences, Lara included a subject noun phrase only for some element to be omitted from the predicate verb phrase. In the following examples, an auxiliary verb is omitted:

> *You [are] sitting on.*
> *Mummy [is] getting it.*

In the first example above, Lara also omits a noun phrase as the post-modifier of the preposition *on*. In the examples below, the inflectional suffix for third person singular present tense is omitted in each lexical verb:

Mummy sing[s] Rockabye baby.
Mummy take[s] them away.
Mummy go[es] on it.
Mummy get[s] orange.

The predicate in a number of Lara's declarative sentences contained noun phrases in which an indefinite article was omitted:

I've got [a] birthday cake in here.
Mummy get [an] orange.
Want [a] snack.

Notwithstanding these various grammatical immaturities, it is clear that by the start of her second year, Lara already has a sound grasp of declarative sentence structure.

You should now use the knowledge of declarative sentences that you have acquired in this section to read the following Special Topic.

SPECIAL TOPIC 7.1 DECLARATIVE SENTENCES IN CHILDREN WITH SPECIFIC LANGUAGE IMPAIRMENT

We have seen how Lara, a typically developing child, omits grammatical morphemes that carry tense and agreement features in the predicate VP of declarative sentences. This includes the third-person singular present *–s* and the auxiliary *be*. Other grammatical morphemes omitted by typically developing children include the past tense *–ed* and the auxiliary *do*. The period in which these finiteness markers are omitted is prolonged in children with SLI relative to typically developing children. This can be seen in the following declarative sentences which were produced by children with SLI during a narrative production task. Each of these children was over 9 years of age at the time of production:

The girl elephant take[s] it away from him (Female; 9;3 years)
She give[s] it to the giraffe (Female; 9;3 years)
He [is] fixing him (Female; 9;3 years)
And she run [ran] (Male; 9;4 years)
And she fall [fell] down (Male; 9;4 years)
The elephant close[s] her eyes (Female; 9;7 years)
The elephant [is] watching the waves (Female; 9;7 years)

There are other omissions in the predicate VP of declarative sentences used by children with SLI. These omissions also persist well beyond the age at which they normally resolve in typically developing children. In the following declaratives, a prepositional phrase and a noun phrase are omitted. These phrases have the function of an adverbial and an indirect object, respectively. The omitted phrases are provided in parentheses in each case:

Then she put a bandaid [on his knee] (Male; 7;4 years)
Then he gave [the rabbit] one (Male; 6;10 years)

Even within phrases, grammatical parts are omitted. In the declaratives below, definite and indefinite articles are omitted in noun phrases and prepositions are omitted in prepositional phrases:

He is meeting [a] new friend (Female; 6;8 years)
Elephant is very shy with [the] giraffe (Male; 6;10 years)
Elephant slip [on] the floor (Male; 6;10 years)

The genitive marker (*'s*) is also omitted in noun phrases, as the following examples illustrate:

The elephant grabbed to the giraffe['s] airplane (Male; 6;10 years)
The rabbit dropped sand in the dog['s] castle (Male; 6;10 years)
The dog pulled on his doctor['s] arm (Male; 6;10 years)

The combination of these various grammatical omissions results in declarative sentences with much simplified structure in children with SLI.

7.2.2 Function of Declaratives

We began this section by saying that the main function of declarative sentences is to make statements about the world around us. And for the most part, this is true. However, speakers also routinely use sentences which have a declarative structure to ask questions. This can be illustrated by examining the following declaratives which were produced by Lara when she was 2 years and 3 months old:

Mummy want an orange?
Mummy have another apple?
Mummy go like this?

Through use of intonation, Lara succeeds in conveying the interrogative intent behind these utterances. That intent can also be expressed by means of explicit interrogative sentences such as the following:

Does mummy want an orange?
Does mummy have another apple?
Does mummy go like this?

The question arises why Lara asks questions by means of declarative sentences when explicit interrogatives can also be used. After all, there would appear to be a reduced risk that a misinterpretation may arise when an explicit interrogative is used. The reason for this linguistic usage relates to the greater grammatical complexity of interrogatives over declaratives. By using declarative sentences to ask questions, Lara can avoid the use of inversion that is required to form an interrogative. When young children first begin to ask questions, they use declarative sentences with the intonation of a question until such times as their developing grammatical skills permit them to form interrogatives. Adult hearers have no difficulty in establishing the interrogative intent of these sentences and, indeed, use many similar sentences when conversing with their children (and other adults). Here are a few sentences of this type that Lara's mother uses:

> *You want your jelly shoes?*
> *That one goes there?*
> *You hurt your toe?*

Other functions of declaratives include issuing warnings and threats, and making requests. These particular functions were not evident in Lara's data set, but are illustrated by means of the following devised examples:

> *Five swimmers died in this river last year.* [Warning]
> *You might want to reconsider giving evidence in this case.* [Threat]
> *You can pay your bill at the reception desk.* [Request]

Appendix 3 contains other declarative sentences produced by Lara. Either individually or in a group, you should describe the structure and function of these sentences.

The main points in this section are summarised below.

KEY POINTS DECLARATIVES

- Declaratives are one of four types of sentence in English. Declarative sentences can be characterised in terms of their structure and function.
- In structural terms, declaratives consist of a subject noun phrase followed by a predicate verb phrase. The subject noun phrase can be occupied by demonstrative and personal pronoun (*this, you*), by common and proper nouns (*man, Bill*) and by dummy subjects (*it, there*).
- The predicate verb phrase in a declarative can consist of a single lexical verb (*Jack smiles*) or a lexical verb with auxiliary verbs (*Tom is screaming*). It may also contain a range of phrases which function as objects (*Ann drinks milk*), adverbials (*He works next to the bank*) and complements (*Her meal was very tasty*).
- For the most part, the function of declaratives is to make statements. Declaratives are informative in that they can convey information about people, places and things in the world around us.
- Declaratives also have other functions. When used with a certain pattern of intonation, declaratives can be used to ask questions (*The dinner is ready?*). Declaratives may also be used to issue warnings (*The river has burst its banks*), threats (*Big Jim will be at the match tonight*) and make requests (*It is very warm in here* may be a request to have the heating turned down).

7.3 Interrogatives

Like declaratives, interrogatives are a very common type of sentence in language. The use of sentences to ask questions and glean information from others is, after all, one of the primary purposes of any language. There are several different types of interrogatives which will be examined in this section. What unites them all, and distinguishes them from declaratives, is that part of the predicate stands *before* the subject. In declaratives, the entire predicate comes *after* the subject:

> Declarative: Tom *is painting the fence*.
> Interrogative: I̲s̲ Tom *painting the fence?*

The part of the predicate that stands in front of the subject is always a finite auxiliary verb. The grammatical movement which places the auxiliary verb before the subject is called **subject–operator inversion** (the auxiliary verb functions as an operator). If an auxiliary verb is not present, the dummy auxiliary verb *do* is introduced to make inversion possible:

> Declarative: *Mike wants chips.*
> Interrogative: *D̲o̲e̲s̲ Mike want chips?*

7.3.1 *Yes–No* Interrogatives

What we have above is the basic structure of a *yes–no* interrogative (so-called because it invites a *yes* or *no* response). A finite auxiliary verb, which is either present or introduced, leaves its position after the subject in a declarative and moves in front of the subject in an interrogative. Here is a selection of the *yes–no* interrogatives that Lara produced at just over 3 years of age:

> *Shall I pass this to you?*
> *Is it five o'clock?*
> *Do you want this flower?*
> *Can I go on the doggy?*
> *Have you got a hoover?*

Lara uses a range of auxiliary verbs in these *yes–no* interrogatives. There are the modal auxiliary verbs *shall* and *can*. She also uses the **primary auxiliary verbs** *is, do* and *have*. The dummy auxiliary verb *do* was used extensively by Lara at 3 years of age, both in interrogatives and in sentences with negation. Here are further examples of its use in *yes–no* interrogatives at the same age:

> *Does Looby [eat plastic bags]?*
> *Doesn't she want to sit on here?*
> *Did you do that one first?*

In the first example, the predicate is omitted in grammatical ellipsis. However, in the context in which this interrogative was used, the predicate was nevertheless understood by Lara's mother. The dummy auxiliary appears with contracted *not* in the second interrogative. In the third example, the dummy auxiliary is past tense (*did*) and not present tense (*does*) as it is in the first two examples.

Even by 3 years of age, Lara is using *yes–no* interrogatives to perform a range of functions. Interrogatives such as the following are questions which solicit information from the hearer:

> *Is it five o'clock?*
> *Have you got a hoover?*

The following interrogative is not a request for information. Rather, it is posed with a view to getting permission from the hearer to do something, in this case 'have a go' on the doggy:

> *Can I go on the doggy?*

Interrogatives with the same modal auxiliary verb (*Can I … ?*) are also used by Lara to get the hearer to do something. Several of Lara's *yes–no* interrogatives with a directive function are shown below:

> *Can you come and sit on my nest?*
> *Can you look after my bag?*
> *Can you help me?*

So, there are at least three functions of *yes–no* interrogatives. These interrogatives can be information-seeking and permission-seeking. Alternatively, they may be used by the speaker to get a hearer to do something.

On occasion, Lara used a type of *yes–no* interrogative in which the hearer is presented with an alternative. So-called **alternative questions** display the inversion of *yes–no* interrogatives. In addition, however, they force the hearer to choose one of two possibilities. This may prove to be an undesirable choice for a hearer to make, especially when the alternatives are equally unpalatable:

> *Are you sexist or homophobic?*

A hearer might rightly object to the **presupposition** of this question – that the hearer is either sexist or homophobic – by refusing to answer the question at all. Lara posed the following alternative questions to her mother. Fortunately, her mother was not in the position of our hypothetical hearer who was presented with an unpalatable forced choice. When Lara's mother wished to overturn the presupposition of one of Lara's alternative questions, her response made this very clear. This can be seen in the response to the second example below:

> *Is this a helicopter or aeroplane?*
> *Do lions live far away or near us?*
> Mother: *They live near us in the zoo or far away in Africa.*

Lara's mother posed many alternative questions to her. The following examples are a small selection of them:

> Is it the South or the North Pole?
> Is it the black ones or the red ones?
> Is it a Nova like mummy's or a Peugeot like grandad's?

It can be beneficial to use alternative questions with young children. By presenting them with possible responses, these questions reduce the linguistic and cognitive demands on young children. Children do not need to formulate a response and hold it in memory as they would to other types of questions. Instead, the response is formulated for them and must only be held in memory long enough for one of two possibilities to be chosen.

Lara's mother also made extensive use of another type of *yes–no* interrogative known as **tag questions**. Typically, these questions appear at the end of declarative sentences. They can have various functions, but mostly they seek confirmation from the hearer of the speaker's statement. Two key functions of tag questions during interactions with young children is to check understanding of what has been said and to encourage active listening and participation in the exchange on the part of the child. Several examples of tag questions used by Lara's mother are shown below:

> That's a good place to hide, isn't it?
> Amy's there, isn't she?
> You did that, didn't you?
> You don't want that, do you?
> She was being a pain, wasn't she?

There are a number of other features of tag questions which can be illustrated by means of these examples. The subject in the tag question matches the subject in the declarative. If the subject in the declarative is a proper noun like *Amy*, the subject in the tag must be the corresponding personal pronoun (*she*). A demonstrative pronoun like *that* as subject of the declarative is replaced by *it* in the tag. Negatives always appear in contracted form in tag questions. A tag question such as the following is ungrammatical:

> *Amy's there, is <u>not</u> she?

The tag displays the **reverse polarity** of the preceding declarative sentence. If the declarative is positive, the tag question will be negative:

> You <u>did</u> that, <u>didn't</u> you?

If the declarative is negative, the tag question will be positive:

> You <u>don't</u> want that, <u>do</u> you?

Less often, a declarative and its tag may display **constant polarity**. This is where the declarative and tag are both positive. Lara's mother used a number of constant polarity tags like the following examples:

> *It fell down there, did it?*
> *I was holding something, was I?*

Lara's mother does not appear to use these tag questions to seek confirmation from the hearer (in this case, Lara). In the first example, we can imagine her using this sentence to convey an attitude of disbelief or blame to someone for the fact that something had fallen down. In the second example, there is some doubt on the part of the speaker that she did in fact hold something which the tag question is intended to resolve. This is quite unlike the declarative in the following example where the speaker is certain that 'she' was a pain and merely wants the hearer to agree with this view:

> *She was being a pain, wasn't she?*

So, constant polarity appears to confer a different function on tag questions. It also only works when both the declarative and tag are positive. Constant polarity that involves a negative declarative and a negative tag leads to an ungrammatical sentence:

> **I wasn't holding something, wasn't I?*

To get further practice of working with tag questions, you should now attempt Exercise 7.2.

Of course, the tags that have been described so far are typical of British Standard English. But there are also tag questions in non-standard dialects of British English and varieties of English other than British English which do not conform to the grammatical features described above. They include *innit?* and *ain't it?*. The invariant tag *innit?* is typical of the language of London teenagers (Martínez, 2015) and is also found in urban **African American Vernacular English**. As the following examples demonstrate, *innit?* can be used in place of standard tags like *doesn't she?* and *wasn't it?*:

> *She love her chocolate <u>innit</u>?*
> *It was good <u>innit</u>?*

Ain't plus pronoun occurs in American English and British English (Tottie and Hoffmann, 2006). The following examples are from the Longman Spoken American Corpus (LSAC) and the spoken component of the British National Corpus (BNC):

> *Hey, that's Bill Cosby <u>ain't it</u>? (LSAC)*
> *And you've got a pair of black shoes <u>ain't you</u>? (BNC)*

EXERCISE 7.2 TAG QUESTIONS

The following utterances were produced by Lara's mother during verbal exchanges with her daughter at home. Each utterance contains a tag question. Examine the utterances in detail. Indicate if the tags are reverse or constant polarity tags:

(a) It's nice when you share, isn't it?
(b) I think that's a made up name, isn't it?
(c) She's going to pull all those clothes off that shelf, isn't she?
(d) You gave it to me, didn't you?
(e) We don't kick cups, do we?
(f) You can do the round one, can't you?
(g) You can wait until I come back, can't you?
(h) You're off now, are you?
(i) If he's only over there, I'm safe for a bit, aren't I?
(j) You are in a state, aren't you?
(k) You are in a pickle this afternoon, aren't you?
(l) Fish are up there, aren't they?
(m) You like that little chair, don't you?
(n) We'll give Looby a ring, shall we?
(o) You've got the big duck and you've got the little ducklings over there, haven't you?

Some of our adults with Alzheimer's dementia, who are speakers of American English, used particles and words in **colloquial speech** that functioned as tag questions. They included the following forms:

> That's about it, _huh_? (Male; 56 years)
> They're grabbing the cookie jar, _right_? (Female; 70 years)

7.3.2 *Wh*-Interrogatives

Another sub-class of interrogatives is *wh*-interrogatives. Like *yes–no* interrogatives, *wh*-interrogatives involve inversion of the subject and finite auxiliary verb. Additionally, a *wh*-word stands in front of the inverted subject and auxiliary verb in a *wh*-interrogative. The following are all candidates for the *wh*-word slot:

> *What:* What car do you drive? What are you doing?
> *Where:* Where is the wedding to be held?
> *Why:* Why do you want to move house?
> *Who:* Who left the dishes in the sink?
> *Which:* Which dress did you buy?

How: How did she pay for it?
When: When is the train leaving the platform?
Whose: Whose jumper is this?
Whom: To whom did he leave his stamp collection?

Some of these words are adverbs (*when, how, why, where*) while others are pronouns (*who, whom*). Some *wh*-words can be a pronoun in one interrogative and a determiner in another interrogative:

Which: Which do you want? (pronoun); Which desk is yours? (determiner)
What: What did you say? (pronoun); What school did you attend?
    (determiner)
Whose: Whose is this umbrella? (pronoun); Whose class did you attend?
    (determiner)

Each *wh*-word allows a questioner to focus on a particular part of a proposition about which information is lacking. For example, if the questioner wants to identify the person or thing that is responsible for an action (i.e. the subject), then the *wh*-word *who* is used. If the questioner wants to identify the person or thing that is affected by an action (i.e. the object) then the *wh*-words *what* or *which* are used. If the questioner wants information about the location of an action or event (i.e. the adverbial), then the *wh*-word *where* is used. We can fill in these bits of missing information in responses to the *who, what, which* and *where* interrogatives above:

Who left the dishes in the sink? Sally left the dishes in the sink. [Subject]
What car do you drive? I drive a Toyota Yaris. [Object]
Which dress did you buy? I bought the purple one. [Object]
Where is the wedding to be held? The wedding is to be held in church. [Adverbial]

The formation of each of the above *wh*-interrogatives starts with a declarative sentence. By way of illustration, consider the following declarative sentence:

Jack is cutting the grass.

If the questioner wants to know what Jack is cutting, then this is the missing bit of information in the proposition which must be interrogated. Let us underline this part of the declarative sentence and replace it with an appropriate *wh*-word:

Jack is cutting the grass. → *Jack is cutting what.*

The *wh*-word is then moved to the front of the sentence:

What Jack is cutting.

Finally, the subject and auxiliary verb are inverted:

What is Jack cutting?

This basic procedure for the formation of *wh*-interrogatives cannot be followed in all cases. If the declarative sentence does not contain an auxiliary verb, then the dummy auxiliary *do* must be inserted before the *wh*-word is moved to the front of the sentence. This occurs in stage (4) below:

(1) *Jack cleans the car*
(2) *Jack cleans the car*
(3) *Jack cleans what*
(4) *Jack does clean what*
(5) *What Jack does clean*
(6) *What does Jack clean?*

Also, if the *wh*-word is the subject in the sentence, no inversion can occur. The formation procedure in this case has the following stages:

(1) *Mike felled the large tree.*
(2) *Mike felled the large tree.*
(3) *Who felled the large tree?*

If the *wh*-word is part of a noun phrase, then it is the full noun phrase which must move to the front of the sentence. The formation procedure then has the following stages:

(1) *She is mending Oscar's sweater.*
(2) *She is mending Oscar's sweater.*
(3) *She is mending whose sweater.*
(4) *Whose sweater she is mending.*
(5) *Whose sweater is she mending?*

Finally, if the *wh*-word occurs as part of a prepositional phrase, then the preposition may either move with the *wh*-word to the front of the sentence or it may be left behind at the end of the sentence. Let us look at the first of these formation procedures. This is the procedure favoured by the prescriptive grammarian:

(1) *Mary is writing a letter to George.*
(2) *Mary is writing a letter to George.*
(3) *Mary is writing a letter to whom.*
(4) *To whom Mary is writing a letter.*
(5) *To whom is Mary writing a letter?*

The second formation procedure results in an interrogative which prescriptive grammarians judge to be unacceptable, but which is nonetheless part of everyday language use:

(1) *Bill is repairing the boat with wood.*
(2) *Bill is repairing the boat with wood.*
(3) *Bill is repairing the boat with what.*

(4) *What Bill is repairing the boat with.*
(5) *What is Bill repairing the boat with?*

For adults, these formation procedures are part of their internalised knowledge of the grammar of their native language. However, these procedures can cause considerable difficulties for young children who are acquiring their first language. The result is a range of errors in the formation of *wh*-interrogatives. To appreciate these children's difficulties, we consider a number of the errors that Lara made when she produced *wh*-interrogatives for the first time between 2;07 and 3;03 years. Lara produced a number of *wh*-interrogatives in which an incorrect *wh*-word was used. This suggests that at this early stage in her language development, full understanding of the meaning of these words had not been achieved. In the examples below, the *wh*-words *who, where, whose* and *when* are problematic for Lara:

Lara at 2;07 years
Where is that behind that lady? (Target: *Who*)
Where is next to the lady? (Target: *Who*)
What is that little girl? (Target: *Who*)
What you did go? (Target: *Where*)
What they just sitting on the cup? (Target: *Where*)

Lara at 3;00 years
Who is it? (Target: *Whose*)
Where is Grandad going home? (Target: *When*)

Even when the correct *wh*-word is used, other errors occur in Lara's interrogatives. In some cases, a subject noun or pronoun is omitted altogether:

What did look at? (2;07)

Sometimes, subject omission occurred alongside the omission of the auxiliary verb. This resulted in a very simplified *wh*-interrogative structure:

What say? (2;10)
What doing? (2;10)
Where gone? (2;10)
What going to do? (2;10)
What have? (2;10)

More commonly, when an auxiliary verb was omitted, the subject of the interrogative was present, as the following examples illustrate:

What you nicked? (2;07)
What elephant eat? (2;10)
Where they gone? (3;00)
Why you feeding Amy? (3;00)
When Georgie and Abi coming? (3;00)

On some occasions, incorrect auxiliary verbs were used. Most of these errors involved the use of a singular auxiliary verb with a plural subject, although the wrong auxiliary verb was sometimes selected (*be* instead of *have* in the final two examples below):

> *Where has the bike and the car gone?* (2;07)
> *Why has the lights gone?* (3;00)
> *Where is my new shoes?* (3;03)
> *Why is daddy not got a fork?* (3;03)
> *Why are you got your trainers on?* (3;00)

On other occasions, correct auxiliary verbs were present but they did not undergo inversion with the subject in the interrogative:

> *What Mummy did do?* (2;07)
> *What you did look at?* (2;07)
> *What you did do?* (2;07)

On still other occasions, both the auxiliary verb and the lexical verb were marked for tense when tense marking should only be present on the auxiliary verb:

> *What did Daddy forgot?* (3;00)
> *What did you spilt?* (3;00)
> *When did we went to Amy's house?* (3;00)
> *Who did broke it?* (3;03)

Occasionally, Lara also omitted inflectional suffixes such as *–ing* and *–s* from the lexical verbs in her *wh*-interrogatives:

> *Why are we go to doctor's?* (2;07)
> *Why are you do this?* (2;10)
> *Who want to take these?* (2;10)
> *Who want this nut?* (2;10)

Some of Lara's *wh*-interrogatives had obligatory elements missing from the predicate. For example, the object is omitted in the predicate of this *wh*-interrogative:

> *Why did they put in there?* (3;03)

Finally, Lara also produced interrogative errors which displayed such a violation of syntactic structure that they defied explanation. Here are a couple of examples:

> *Where is the pricked her finger?* (2;07)
> *What me you called?* (3;03)

It is now time for you to get further practice in working with *wh*-interrogatives by completing Exercise 7.3.

EXERCISE 7.3 LARA'S USE OF *WH*-INTERROGATIVES

A detailed description of Lara's use of *wh*-interrogatives has been given above. You should make sure you understand the points which were raised in that description before attempting this exercise. Either individually or in a group, you should examine the following *wh*-interrogatives produced by Lara during interactions with her parents at home. For each interrogative, you should describe how it deviates from the adult form in Lara's language community:

(a) What you forget? (2;10)
(b) Why you rubbing your eyes? (3;00)
(c) Who want to play with me? (2;10)
(d) Where does blue has to go? (3;00)
(e) What you got on your scarf? (2;07)
(f) What is these? (3;00)
(g) Why has Amy aten this? (3;03)
(h) Which one else did we went to? (3;03)
(i) What you done? (2;07)
(j) Where is you two mats? (3;03)
(k) Where did they got that book from? (3;03)
(l) What you dry? (2;10)
(m) Who did move my house? (3;00)
(n) Where has Daddy and Amy gone? (3;00)
(o) Why you got pen in car? (2;07)
(p) What you doing with my clothes? (2;07)
(q) Where was you gone? (3;00)
(r) Where is it gone? (2;10)
(s) Why Postman Pat going out the door? (3;03)
(t) Where is two ladies? (2;10)
(u) What is these two called? (2;07)
(v) Why did he lost his leg? (3;00)
(w) How we going to go under there? (2;10)
(x) Why she missed the bus? (3;03)
(y) Why haven't got my teletubbies on? (3;03)
(z) Where the horsie? (2;07)

7.3.3 Function of Interrogatives

We have described in this section how interrogatives may be used to solicit information from the hearer, to secure permission from the hearer to do something or to get someone to do something. However, interrogatives can have other functions as well. Some interrogatives can be posed without the speaker entertaining a genuine belief that they will result in a meaningful response. In the following exchange between Lara and her father, it is clear that Lara's father cannot have high expectations that Lara will be able to understand the question, let alone formulate a competent response. After all, Lara is only 1;11 years at the time of this exchange:

DAD: Are Coventry going to win today?
LARA: mmhm
DAD: Yes
DAD: Good

That Lara's father intends his interrogative to function as a form of **humour** in this exchange is indicated by the fact that he takes her indecisive *mmhm* to be a positive response. This is, presumably, the football result that Lara's father would like to happen – Coventry is clearly his favourite football team. But the point is that this interrogative fulfils none of the functions of interrogatives that we identified earlier. And yet it is playing an important role in this exchange between Lara and her father.

In the example above, there was at least an expectation that Lara would attempt to make a response, just not a particularly competent one. But there is another type of interrogative where the questioner has no expectation at all that a response will be forthcoming. So-called **rhetorical questions** have the same structure as *yes–no* interrogatives and *wh*-interrogatives. But their function is quite different from these other interrogatives. The answers to rhetorical questions are assumed to be so obvious that they obviate any need for a response. They can be illustrated by means of the following utterances of two adults with Alzheimer's dementia during a picture description task:

Female (69 years)
It could be a boy or a girl. Who can tell these days?

Male (75 years)
The children are creating havoc behind their mother's back. Aren't kids really adorable?

Rhetorical questions are as much a pragmatic device as they are an aspect of grammar. For a speaker to succeed in using a rhetorical question, he or she must have knowledge of the ideas and views that are likely to be generally accepted by other language users. For example, the speakers above must know that many people will take the view that boys and girls today dress so similarly that they are almost indistinguishable in appearance, and that most people do not consider mischievous children to be adorable. Considerable world knowledge is bound up in these speaker expectations. The cultural learning that is needed to make these expectations possible places rhetorical questions beyond the linguistic repertoire of young children like Lara. It is for this reason that there were no rhetorical questions in Lara's data set.

The main points in this section are summarised below.

KEY POINTS INTERROGATIVES

- There are two sub-classes of interrogatives in English: *yes–no* interrogatives and *wh-*interrogatives. Both types of interrogative involve subject–operator inversion. If an auxiliary verb is not present, the dummy auxiliary verb *do* must be introduced in order to make inversion possible.
- Most *yes–no* interrogatives have an information-seeking function. However, *yes–no* interrogatives can also be used to secure permission from someone or to get someone to do something.
- The alternative question is a type of *yes–no* interrogative. It involves presenting a hearer with a forced choice between two possibilities.
- Tag questions are a type of *yes–no* interrogative. They are found at the end of a declarative sentence and are mostly used to secure confirmation of a speaker's statement from the hearer.
- Tag questions can display reverse and constant polarity. Reverse polarity, such as a negative tag used with a positive statement (e.g. *She will come, won't she?*), is more common than constant polarity.
- *Wh-*interrogatives are formed by means of inversion. A *wh-*word like *who* and *what* stands in front of the inverted auxiliary verb and subject.
- Another type of interrogative is the rhetorical question. These questions have the same structure as *yes–no* interrogatives and *wh-*interrogatives. However, their function differs from other interrogatives in that a response is not expected.

7.4 Imperatives

7.4.1 Structure of Imperatives

Another type of sentence in English is the imperative. To understand the structural features of imperative sentences, let us consider the following examples produced by Lara at 3;03 years of age:

> *Sit on my nest.*
> *Go to sleep.*
> *Pick that bit up quickly.*
> *Run into the kitchen.*

Imperatives are unlike declaratives and interrogatives in that there is no explicit or overt subject in the sentence. But in each of the above imperatives, it is clear that the hearer (Lara's mother for the most part) is the understood subject. When speakers want to issue a more forceful imperative, the subject is made explicit by the inclusion of the second person pronoun *you*. Lara occasionally used imperatives with an explicit subject as the following examples illustrate:

> *You shut that gate.*
> *You stay there.*

Imperatives with an explicit pronoun *you* as subject should be distinguished from imperatives where the same pronoun is used as a **vocative**. The vocative status of *you* in the following examples is indicated by **punctuation** in written English and by an intonation break in spoken English:

> *You, help me lift this.*
> *Help me lift this, you.*

Aside from the pronoun *you*, expressions like *everyone, somebody* and *all of you* can also be overt subjects in imperatives:

> *Somebody turn that music off.*
> *Everyone leave the building promptly when the alarm sounds.*
> *All of you stop talking.*

In Belfast English, the pronoun *you* can also be used as an overt subject in imperatives. However, unlike Standard English, where *you* stands in pre-verbal position, in Belfast English *you* occurs in post-verbal position:

> *Be you quiet.*
> *Go you away.*
> *Stop you shouting.*

Often, the non-standard second person plural pronouns *youse* and *yousuns* are used in place of *you* in imperatives in Belfast English:

> *Stay youse there.*
> *Leave yousuns quietly.*

Post-verbal subjects other than *you* can also be used in imperatives in Belfast English. The overt subjects in the following imperatives are *somebody* and *everybody*:

> *Run somebody to the shop.*
> *Go everybody home.*

Lara also uses **negative imperatives** during conversations with her mother. The dummy auxiliary verb *do* is needed to form a negative imperative, as illustrated by these utterances of Lara:

> *Don't eat it!*
> *Don't put them away!*
> *Don't get my cards wet!*

The dummy auxiliary *do* is also needed to form a negative imperative of verbs like *be* and *have* which, unlike other verbs, do not require this auxiliary verb to form a negative:

> *Don't be so foolish!*
> *She isn't happy about this decision.*

Don't have such a negative attitude!
They haven't spare change.

In Standard English, if an overt subject is used in a negative imperative, it can only appear after *don't*:

Don't you eat it!

Each of Lara's negative imperatives contains contracted *not*. However, *not* can also appear in full form in negative imperatives, as these adaptations of Lara's utterances illustrate:

Do not eat it!
Do not put them away!
Do not get my cards wet!

There is one context, however, in which *not* can only appear in contracted form, and that is when an overt subject is used in a negative imperative. So while the first example below is acceptable, the second example is ungrammatical:

Don't you eat it!
*Do not you eat it!

Finally, there is a group of imperatives in English which contain an especially forceful command. So-called **emphatic imperatives** are formed with the use of *do*:

Do go away!
Do leave me alone!

Whereas an overt subject can occur in other imperatives, its inclusion in an emphatic imperative is ungrammatical:

Do go away!
*Do you go away!
*You do go away!

7.4.2 Function of Imperatives

We have talked a lot so far about the structure of imperatives. But the function of these sentences is equally interesting. The statement that imperatives function as commands or directives is too simplistic as it stands. Certainly, many imperative sentences do command hearers to execute a range of tasks and activities, as illustrated by the following examples:

Put away the dishes!
Finish your homework!
Run much faster next time!

However, imperatives may also be used to perform other functions such as conveying permission to someone, prohibiting a particular action, giving advice to a hearer, and pleading with or imploring someone to act in a certain way. These functions of imperatives are illustrated by the following examples:

> *Have as much chocolate as you want!* [Permission]
> *Don't swim in these waters!* [Prohibition]
> *Get the best legal representation possible!* [Advice]
> *Do stay a little longer!* [Imploration]

Perhaps unexpectedly, imperatives may also be used to ask questions. This is a function which we most commonly identify with interrogatives (*Are you leaving now?*) and declaratives (*The train is leaving on time?*). But imagine a context in which a father is trying to get his lazy son to do a number of tasks. The father may say to his son *Take these bottles to the recycling centre!* The son might defiantly respond: *Take these bottles to the recycling centre? You must be kidding!* In the son's response, the father's imperative utterance is recast as a question: *You want me to take these bottles to the recycling centre?* That the imperative has the function of a question in this case is indicated by the fact that the son feels compelled to produce a response (*You must be kidding!*), albeit one which will not be favourable to his father.

Another function of imperatives can be illustrated by examining the utterances of Ella, one of our typically developing children. At 3 years and 7 months of age, Ella was recorded during an interaction with her father in which she was showing him how to paint pictures. Three imperatives were produced during this interaction:

> *Make the face first.*
> *Lift my hands.*
> *Write my name.*

None of these imperatives is functioning as a command or directive. This is particularly evident in the final two imperatives. If these utterances were true commands, Ella would be instructing her father to lift her hands and to write her name, which she is definitely not doing. Instead, each of these utterances is serving as commentary on Ella's own actions. It is as if Ella is using these utterances to emphasise for her father the different stages in her painting of a picture, so that he can easily follow these stages, should he wish to paint a picture for himself. Once again, the imperative demonstrates its linguistic versatility by performing a function which is not in any sense a command or directive.

You can now put your knowledge of imperatives into practice by completing Exercise 7.4.

To conclude our discussion of imperatives, we should mention another type of imperative that is used by Lara. These are imperatives which contain *let's*:

> *Let's go out of that way, donkey.*
> *Let's play this.*
> *Let's get in the car.*

EXERCISE 7.4 IMPERATIVES

Both Lara and Ella used imperatives during interactions with their parents at home. Several of these imperatives are displayed below alongside these children's ages. Examine these sentences and then answer the questions that follow them:

Lara's imperatives
Make a field (2;03)
Come on then (3;03)
Do nothing (3;03)
Move out of the way because my horsey will go (3;03)

Ella's imperatives
Wipe that bit off (3;03)
Have a look in the teezer [freezer] (3;05)
Count, daddy (3;05)
Don't sit next to me! (3;05)
And then I say "get out wee man" (3;05)
Get another bowl for Jennifer (3;07)

(a) Identify the imperative in which a vocative occurs.
(b) In which imperative is the dummy auxiliary verb *do* used?
(c) Identify the utterance in which an imperative occurs in direct reported speech.
(d) What is the function of the imperative *Get another bowl for Jennifer*?
(e) Which of the above imperatives occurs in a sentence with more than one clause?

In the other imperatives we have examined, the overt and understood subjects have been the second person (singular or plural) *you*. However, in Lara's imperatives above, the subject is the first person plural *us*. This subject includes the speaker and one or more others. This can be clearly illustrated if we look at the first example above. Here, the subject includes Lara as the speaker of the imperative. But it also includes the donkey that Lara is playing with, and which she explicitly acknowledges by means of the vocative at the end of the utterance. These first-person imperatives are called **imperative particles**. They are used extensively by Lara and her mother as a means of directing play and other activities between them. In the following exchange, Lara and her mother are trying to open a box which contains a Barbie doll:

MOTHER: *These scissors are rubbish, aren't they? Let's try and tear it.*
LARA: *Just tear it.*

The main points in this section are summarised below.

KEY POINTS IMPERATIVES

- Imperatives are formed from the base form of the verb. They differ from declaratives and interrogatives in that there does not need to be an overt subject, although a subject (singular or plural *you*) is nevertheless understood.
- In Standard English, when an overt subject is present, it occupies pre-verbal position (*You stand still*). Other overt subjects in imperatives include *everyone, somebody* and *all of you*.
- The dummy auxiliary verb *do* is used to form negative imperatives (*Don't leave the cupboard open!*). If an overt subject is used in a negative imperative, it can only occur after *don't* (*Don't you scream!*).
- Emphatic imperatives are formed by using *do* (*Do quieten down!*). They cannot take an overt subject.
- Most imperatives have the function of a command or directive. However, they can also perform other functions including granting permission to a hearer to do something and deterring or prohibiting an action on the part of the hearer.
- First-person imperatives or imperative particles are sentences like *Let's take a taxi home*. In imperative particles, the subject includes the speaker and one or more others.

7.5 Exclamatives

7.5.1 Structure and Function of Exclamatives

Exclamatives are the final type of sentence that we will examine. The structure of an exclamative sentence is illustrated by the examples below:

> *What a nightmare the trip turned out to be!*
> *How lovely it was to see him again!*

In an exclamative sentence, a *what*- or *how*-phrase is followed by a subject and a predicate. We saw in Section 7.3 that *what* and *how* may be used to introduce a *wh*-interrogative. That an interrogative is not at issue in these sentences is indicated by the fact that there is no subject–operator inversion in an exclamative. As their name suggests, exclamatives are used to make an exclamation. Typically, these sentences are emotionally charged and are produced by speakers when they are angry, upset or frustrated. In written English, an exclamative is often indicated through the use of an exclamation mark at the end of the sentence. In spoken English, intonation conveys to a hearer than a sentence is used to make an exclamation. The exclamative structure illustrated by the examples above is often reduced in various ways by speakers. The subject and predicate may be omitted altogether, as these examples from Lara's mother and grandmother illustrate:

MOTHER: *What a surprise!*
GRANDMOTHER: *How odd!*

In fact, exclamatives with a reduced form such as these sentences are more common in English than sentences which exhibit the full exclamative structure (Siemund, 2015). Also, there are many other sentences in English which express exclamatory meaning, but which do not have the structure of an exclamative. In the following examples, declaratives and interrogatives (both *yes–no* and *wh*-interrogatives) are used to make exclamations:

> *He has been a complete idiot all his life!*
> *I have had enough of your nonsense!*
> *Are you ever going to grow up!*
> *Who the hell do you think you are!*

Sentences with the full structure of exclamatives were not found in Lara's data set. This is to be expected given the fact that sentences with the structure of exclamatives are rare in any event, and that Lara is a young child who uses a limited range of sentence types (mostly declaratives and interrogatives). Nonetheless, Lara succeeds in conveying exclamatory meaning in other ways. The following sentences are a few of the ways in which this was achieved:

> *A good idea to make a roundabout!*
> *My hair keeps going in my eye!*
> *Monkey can go there!*

In the first example, Lara uses a noun phrase to express strong approval of her mother's suggestion during play to build a roundabout. In the second example, a declarative sentence is used by Lara to express irritation at the fact that her hair, which is not tied back, keeps going into her eye. The third example occurs at the end of a short dispute between Lara and her mother about whether a toy monkey can stand up or sit down. A declarative sentence is used by Lara to make a strong exclamation to the effect that the monkey will be positioned in a certain way.

Although Lara did not produce exclamatives, they were used by members of her family. Lara's mother in particular used exclamative sentences quite often during interaction with her daughter. For the most part, these sentences were uttered with marked intonation. They fulfilled a number of functions including keeping Lara engaged in a range of activities and conveying praise to her when she had completed a task (e.g. *What a great big tower!*). Several of the exclamatives used by Lara's mother, father and grandfather are displayed in Table 7.1. Examine these sentences in detail before reading the discussion of them below.

The sentences displayed in Table 7.1 are certainly not exhaustive of the full range of exclamatives used by Lara's parents and grandfather. But they do illustrate certain features of this type of sentence. The first point to make is that very few – in fact only two – of these sentences exhibit the full structure of an exclamative. These sentences are:

> *What a pity <u>you didn't have the lion one</u>!*
> *How beautiful <u>she is</u>!*

TABLE 7.1 Exclamatives used by Lara's mother, father and grandfather

Speaker	Exclamative
Mother	What a heavy lot!
	What a bad cough!
	What a noise!
	What a lovely bracelet!
	What a mess on the floor!
	What a greedy cat!
	What a greedy baby!
	What a good idea! (*during narrative production*)
	What a calamity!
	What a pity you didn't have the lion one!
	How dare you do something when I told you not to!
	How beautiful she is! (*during narrative production*)
	How silly of daddy!
	How come I'm the one that always has to move!
Father	What a relief!
	What a tower!
Grandfather	What a disaster!
	What a great big tower!

In both examples, a *what-* and *how*-phrase is followed by a subject pronoun (*you, she*) and a predicate (just the single word *is* in the second example). However, in most of the exclamatives in Table 7.1, the subject and predicate are omitted. The reduced grammatical structure of these sentences is typical of the use of exclamatives in English (Siemund, 2015). However, we can easily devise ways in which the full structure of an exclamative can be imposed on these sentences. Let us do just that by introducing a subject and predicate into three of the sentences in Table 7.1:

> *What a greedy baby [Amy is]!*
> *What a great big tower [Lara has made]!*
> *What a heavy lot [daddy is carrying]!*

There are other sentences in Table 7.1 which function as exclamations but which deviate from the rather narrow structural characteristics of an exclamative. The first of these sentences is shown below:

> *How dare you do something when I told you not to!*

In the *how*-exclamatives we have examined so far, the *how*-phrase has contained adjectives like *odd, lovely* and *beautiful*. In this case, the *how*-phrase contains the verb *dare*. However, the subject-predicate structure of the rest of the sentence is consistent with the form of an exclamative. In the following example, it is difficult to see how any expansion of the sentence is possible *without* the use of a *to*-infinitive:

> *How silly of daddy [to leave the car open]!*

Yet, the standard structure of an exclamative permits only a predicate which contains a finite verb, while the *to*-infinitive is a non-finite verb form. The *how*-phrase in this example does at least contain an adjective (*silly*) which is a feature of standard *how*-exclamatives. The following sentence in Table 7.1 also deviates from the structural characteristics of an exclamative:

> *How come I'm the one that always has to move!*

This sentence has the structural characteristics of a *wh*-interrogative, namely, subject–operator inversion. This becomes clear when the sentence is expanded as follows:

> *How <u>does it</u> come about that I'm the one that always has to move?*

Like the sentences before it, this sentence conveys exclamatory meaning using grammatical structure that deviates from the standard structure of the exclamative in English.

Finally, a number of words and phrases can contribute to the exclamatory meaning of a sentence, even sentences which do not have the grammatical structure of exclamatives. The following utterances were produced by adults with Alzheimer's dementia during a picture description task. In the first example, *wowie* occurs in a declarative sentence where it conveys exclamatory meaning. The phrase *the hell* in the second example has a similar exclamatory function:

> *Wowie the boy's going up on a cookie jar [stool] to get cookies!* (Male; 66 years)
> *What the hell else!* (Male; 69 years)

Expressions such as *Oh boy!*, *Oh my!* and *Oh gosh!* were also used by these adults to convey exclamatory meaning. These expressions were used on their own and alongside other types of sentences (e.g. declarative sentences):

> *Oh my, poor kids, he's gonna fall off that cookie jar!* (Male; 68 years)
> *Oh boy! And then in here what happens? Where all that water's coming out of there? Oh gosh!* (Female; 58 years)

The main points in this section are summarised below.

KEY POINTS EXCLAMATIVES

- Exclamatives are sentences like *What little tootsies you have!* and *How ancient this building is!* These sentences are formed when a *what-* or *how*-phrase is followed by a subject and predicate. Exclamatives are not as common as other sentence types in English, particularly declaratives and interrogatives.
- The words *what* and *how* in exclamatives are not information-seeking as they are in *wh*-interrogatives. For example, compare *How old you are!* (exclamative) to *How old are you?* (interrogative). The presence of subject–operator inversion distinguishes interrogatives from exclamatives.

- Often, speakers produce exclamatives with reduced grammatical structure. The subject and predicate may be omitted altogether as in *What a disaster!* and *How horrible!*
- Unlike other sentence types, exclamatives have only one function and that is to produce exclamations. The exclamatory meaning of these sentences is indicated in written English by the presence of an exclamation mark and by intonation in spoken English.
- Other sentence types may also be used to produce exclamations. This includes declaratives (*He's a bloody fool!*) and interrogatives (*What the hell are you doing?!*).

You should now use your knowledge of sentence structure and function to read about echo sentences in the following Special Topic.

SPECIAL TOPIC 7.2 ECHO SENTENCES

Lara's mother also made use of another type of sentence called an echo sentence. When we discussed the formation of *wh*-interrogatives in Section 7.3, we described how *wh*-words such as *what* and *where* were moved to the front of a sentence to produce interrogatives such as *What are you doing?* and *Where is Jack living?* In echo sentences, *wh*-words do not undergo movement to the front of a sentence, but occupy a range of positions within the different types of sentences in which they occur. By way of illustration, consider the following echo sentences which were used by Lara's mother:

> *Can you have some what?*
> *You want what for your birthday?*
> *Don't what?*

These three echo sentences are constructed from a *yes–no* interrogative, a declarative and an imperative. The *wh*-word takes the place of noun phrases in the first two examples and a verb phrase in the last example.

Yes–no interrogative:	*Echo sentence:*
Can you have some <u>chips</u>?	Can you have some <u>what</u>?
Declarative:	*Echo sentence:*
You want <u>a car</u> for your birthday.	You want <u>what</u> for your birthday?
Imperative:	*Echo sentence:*
Don't <u>scream</u>!	Don't <u>what</u>?

In fact, an echo sentence can be formed from any sentence which contains a constituent that can be replaced by a *wh*-word. The following examples were also used by Lara's mother. The *wh*-words in these echo sentences are *whose* and *who*. They replace the genitive form *Jack's* and the proper noun *Brown*, respectively:

> *Got to have <u>whose</u> dinner?*
> *Got to have <u>Jack's</u> dinner.*

Sarah <u>who</u>?
Sarah <u>Brown</u>

Aside from the structure of echo sentences, we must also consider their function. Echo sentences mostly convey exclamatory meaning such as in the following example:

Molly urinated in the street.
Molly did what in the street?!

Echo sentences perform a quite different function in Lara's interactions with her mother. Here, these sentences do not function as exclamations but are used to achieve clarification. This can be seen in the following exchanges between Lara and her mother:

LARA: *Shall I show you where lady's house is?*
MOTHER: *Where who?*
MOTHER: *This is for the who?*
LARA: *This is for the fish.*

Further echo sentences are contained in Appendix 5. Provide a grammatical description of each of these sentences along the lines discussed above. Your description should address the structure *and* function of these sentences.

SUMMARY

In this chapter you have seen the following:

- There are four types of sentence in English which can be distinguished on the basis of their structure. In declaratives, a subject noun phrase precedes a predicate verb phrase (*The woman is singing*). In interrogatives, an operator (a finite auxiliary verb) is followed by a subject and then the rest of the predicate (*Are you sleeping?*). In imperatives, a predicate is used on its own (*Eat your dinner!*) or with the subject pronoun *you* (*You eat your dinner!*). In exclamatives, a *what-* or *how*-phrase is followed by a subject and then a predicate (*What a farce this situation has become!*).
- There is some degree of correspondence between the structure of a sentence and its function. In this way, most declaratives are used to make statements and most interrogatives are used to ask questions. Similarly, most imperatives are used to issue commands and most exclamatives are used to convey exclamatory meaning.
- However, there are many instances where this correspondence between structure and function does not hold. For example, an interrogative sentence may

be used to make a request (*Can you close the door?*). And a declarative sentence may be used to issue threats (*Big Jim will be at the party tonight*) and warnings (*The gunman is on the first floor*), make promises (*I will see you at 9pm*) and ask questions (*Jane is leaving tomorrow morning?*).

WEBSITE SENTENCES

After reading the chapter, visit the website and test your knowledge of sentences by answering the multiple-choice questions for this topic.

HOMEWORK ASSIGNMENT

This assignment has two parts and will require you to access the Electronic World Atlas of Varieties of English at: http://ewave-atlas.org

Part A: In Standard British English, what distinguishes interrogatives from declaratives is that part of the predicate stands before the subject (e.g. <u>Are</u> you *travelling alone?*). However, in **Asian English**, there is declarative word order in interrogative constructions, e.g. 'you know, when we see all these white people, you think, "Oh my God – who they are?"'. Find other examples of varieties which follow the pattern of Asian English.

Part B: In Standard British English, auxiliary verbs are used to form *wh*-interrogatives (e.g. *What <u>is</u> he saying?*). However, in Colloquial American English, a common grammatical pattern is the use of no auxiliaries in *wh*-interrogatives (e.g. *What you doing? What he wants?*). Find other examples of varieties which follow the pattern of Colloquial American English.

SUGGESTIONS FOR FURTHER READING

(1) Kroeger, P. R. (2005) *Analyzing Grammar: An Introduction*. Cambridge: Cambridge University Press.
Chapter 11 in this book is entitled 'Special Sentence Types'. The chapter examines direct and indirect speech acts (an interrogative which functions as a request is an indirect speech act). It also discusses basic word order in sentences, imperative and interrogative sentences, and negation. The chapter contains exercises which will give you practice in identifying different types of sentences.

(2) Huddleston, R. and Pullum, G. K. (2005) *A Student's Introduction to English Grammar*. New York: Cambridge University Press.
Chapter 9 in this volume (Clause type: Asking, exclaiming and directing) provides further discussion of the sentence types examined in this chapter. There are suggestions for further reading and exercises (but no answers). A series of questions (with answers) on sentences in the accompanying website will give

you an opportunity to put your knowledge of different sentence types into practice.

(3) Crystal, D. (2004) *Rediscover Grammar*, Third Edition. Harlow: Pearson Education.

Crystal presents a very accessible discussion of different types of sentences in four short chapters: chapter 4 (Clause types), chapter 5 (Statements and questions), chapter 6 (Directives) and chapter 7 (Exclamatives and echoes). Further readings are provided.

QUESTIONS SENTENCES

(1) In a declarative sentence, the subject NP may be occupied by personal and demonstrative pronouns, by common and proper nouns, and by so-called dummy subjects. The predicate VP may be occupied by a lexical verb without other verbs or by a lexical verb that is preceded by one or more auxiliary verbs. Several of Lara's declarative utterances at 3 years of age are presented below. Identify the constituents in the subject NP and predicate VP in each example:

(a) This is how you do it.

(b) Bear's going to get you.

(c) Amy go away.

(d) There's a pram.

(e) I can do them up.

(f) These are the chairs.

(g) It's not the same.

(h) Monster's gonna get in the kitchen.

(i) He's not over there.

(j) Rosie's got this one.

(2) The following utterances were produced by adults with Alzheimer's dementia during a picture description task. Each utterance contains a tag question. Examine the utterances in detail. Then answer the questions below:

> *Kind of homely girl, isn't she?* (Female; 64 years)
> *I did say the sink's overflowing, didn't I?* (Male; 76 years)
> *It's a kind of calamity, isn't it?* (Female; 67 years)
> *They're busy, aren't they?* (Female; 84 years)
> *It has to be his sister, doesn't it?* (Female; 73 years)
> *This string is not on this, is it?* (Female; 60 years)
> *He survived anyway, huh?* (Female; 70 years)
> *It looks like somebody's laying out in the grass, doesn't it?* (Female; 73 years)
> *And a young girl seems to whisper to him about making noise, doesn't it?* (Female; 87 years)

(a) Give *one* example of a negative tag that contains the dummy auxiliary verb *do*.

(b) Give *one* example of a tag that is found in colloquial speech.

(c) Give *one* example of a tag that contains an incorrect personal pronoun.

(d) Give *one* example of a positive tag.

(e) Give *one* example of a negative tag which follows an elliptical declarative.

(3) A list of *wh*-interrogatives produced by Lara is displayed in Appendix 4. The interrogatives were recorded at four ages: 2;07 years; 2;10 years; 3;00 years; and 3;03 years. You should examine the list in detail and then answer the following questions:

Lara at 2;07 years

(a) In which *wh*-interrogative is a lexical verb omitted?

(b) In which *wh*-interrogative is a singular lexical verb used with a plural subject?

(c) Describe the linguistic features which set the following *wh*-interrogative apart from the adult form: *Why we going Sainsburys?*

(d) In which *wh*-interrogative has an incorrect auxiliary verb been used?

(e) What type of error has occurred in the following *wh*-interrogative? *What that called?*

Lara at 2;10 years

(f) In which *wh*-interrogative has one of two auxiliary verbs been correctly produced?

(g) In which *wh*-interrogative is the dummy auxiliary verb *do* omitted?

(h) In which *wh*-interrogative is an inflectional suffix omitted in a lexical verb?

(i) In which *wh*-interrogative is an auxiliary verb and subject omitted?

(j) In which *wh*-interrogative is there no inversion of the subject and auxiliary verb?

Lara at 3;00 years

(k) In which *wh*-interrogative is an auxiliary verb used unnecessarily?

(l) In which *wh*-interrogative is the dummy auxiliary verb *do* omitted?

(m) In which *wh*-interrogative is an object omitted from the predicate?

(n) Describe the linguistic feature which sets the following *wh*-interrogative apart from the adult form: *Where has the other people gone?*

(o) In which *wh*-interrogative does the *wh*-word appear to have been used with the wrong meaning?

Lara at 3;03 years

(p) In which *wh*-interrogative is past tense marked on both the lexical and the auxiliary verb?

(q) How would the following *wh*-interrogative normally appear in adult form? *Why has she not got her clothes on?*

(r) In which *wh*-interrogative is a singular lexical verb used with a plural subject?

(s) In which *wh*-interrogative does a verb appear as an auxiliary verb before the subject and as a lexical verb after the subject?

(t) Describe the linguistic features which set the following *wh*-interrogative apart from the adult form: *Why did he be on his own?*

(4) Some of the imperatives used by Lara and Ella, two typically developing children, are displayed below. Examine these sentences and then answer the questions below:

Lara's imperatives
Ring Elly (3;03)
Lift me down (3;03)
Put it up in the sky (3;03)
Kick it (3;03)

Ella's imperatives
Give the mousy one tick on it (3;03)
Look at this tulips (3;05)
Just wait there (3;05)
Don't tickle me (3;05)
Dad, look! (3;07)
Do that (3;07)
Try to do that (3;07)
Keep it a little rainbow (3;07)

(a) Two of these imperatives involve the use of the verb *do*. However, in only one of these imperatives is *do* a dummy auxiliary verb. Identify the imperative in question.

(b) What is the status of *Dad* in the imperative *Dad, look!*?

(c) What is the function of each of Lara's imperatives?

(d) Which word used by Ella reduces the force of one of her imperatives?

(e) Give a grammatical description of the imperative *Keep it a little rainbow*.

(5) Each of the following sentences conveys exclamatory meaning. However, only some of these sentences have the grammatical structure of an exclamative. For each sentence, indicate if it has the structure of an exclamative or some other type of sentence:

(a) How silly you were to leave the child alone!

(b) What do you expect from a pig but a grunt!

(c) Is your middle name 'asshole' by any chance!

(d) That bloody idiot will not stop playing his guitar!

(e) What a twit that man is!

(f) Could you be any more annoying!

(g) How wonderful!

(h) Your attitude really stinks!

(i) What a stupid arse you are!

(j) This cheesecake is simply sublime!

REVISION SENTENCES

(1) Sentences are simple when they contain one clause and multiple when they contain more than one clause. Identify each of the following sentences as either *simple* or *multiple*:

(a) John hates red wine but loves white wine.

(b) Sally is working from home.

(c) The children are running through the wood.

(d) Peter and Paul are touring in France.

(e) If we work hard, we will finish early.

(2) Multiple sentences can be further categorised as compound, complex or compound-complex. A compound sentence contains clauses which are linked by coordinating conjunctions. A complex sentence contains clauses which are linked by subordinating conjunctions. A compound-complex sentence contains clauses which are linked by coordinating and subordinating conjunctions. Identify the following sentences as compound, complex or compound-complex:

(a) The thieves emptied the house while the occupants were sleeping.

(b) He liked the house but his wife hated it.

(c) She bought a dress after she went to town but before she met her friends.

(d) If the weather is good, we will extend our stay.

(e) She looks after the children and she does all the cooking.

(3) Identify the function of the following sentences. For each sentence, state whether or not its function corresponds to its grammatical form:

(a) Are you going to the party?

(b) He's in his room?

(c) Fred is in town this week.

(d) Can you make your payment at the desk?

(e) Eat your vegetables!

(f) Would you mind opening the window?

(4) Describe the following sentences as *simple, complex, compound* or *compound-complex*:

(a) Jan works in town.

(b) Sue is making a starter and Fran is making the main meal.

(c) She wants to buy the flat but she hasn't enough money.

(d) She had not left her house since the bomb exploded.

(e) The thug attacked the elderly man.

(f) She cleaned the house after she returned from town but before she made the meal.

(g) Fred loathed the film.

(h) If Oscar comes to the party, Sue will stay at home.

(i) Since he crashed the car and because he returned late from the party, he was grounded.

(j) She will travel to Spain or she will visit her sister.

(k) After he completed his exams, he went on a tour of Europe.

(l) If he washes the car and if he cuts the grass, he will get £20.

(5) The following extract contains different types of sentences. For each underlined sentence, (i) identify its function, and (ii) state if its function corresponds to the grammatical form of the sentence:

> The robbers sped through the streets. Several police vehicles were in pursuit.
> A car emerged suddenly from the right. It stalled in front of the police cars.
> 'Move your car!', shouted one of the officers. 'Hurry it up, you idiot!' screamed
> a second officer. 'Can you help me start it?' replied the frightened motorist. A
> pedestrian asked 'Do you need some help? I am a trained mechanic'. 'Help me,
> please! I can't seem to start it up again', responded the motorist. 'Push it to the
> side of the road. I'll sort it out for you', shouted the mechanic.

(6) *Yes–no* interrogatives can be information-seeking and permission-seeking. Assign one of these functions to each of the following interrogatives:

(a) Can you tell me the time?

(b) Can I use your car this weekend?

(c) Can I stay with you for another week?

(d) Is John leaving today?

(e) Does Mary still live with Frank?

(7) *True or false:* Exclamatives in English are most often produced with reduced grammatical structure.

(8) For each of the following sentences, (i) state the function that is performed by the sentence, and (ii) state if the function corresponds to the grammatical form of the sentence:

(a) Stay in that room!

(b) He is taking his car?

(c) Are they playing in the park?

(d) Leave me, please.

(e) Can you open the window?

(f) The river has burst its banks.

(9) Declarative sentences can be used to issue warnings and threats. They can also be used to make predictions, requests and promises. Assign one of these functions to each of the following declarative sentences:

(a) She will be an Olympic champion one day.

(b) The forest fire is rapidly spreading in this direction.

(c) I will arrive at your party on time.

(d) Smart men don't testify in court.

(e) It's very warm in here.

(10) Each of the following statements is about tag questions. Respond with *true* or *false* to each statement:

(a) The subject in a tag question matches the subject in the preceding declarative.

(b) Tag questions always display reverse polarity.

(c) Negatives always appear in contracted form in tag questions.

(d) Tag questions always seek confirmation from the hearer.

(e) Tag questions are a type of *yes–no* interrogative.

(11) The pronoun *you* can be used as an overt subject in imperative sentences. However, its position in imperative sentences in Standard English differs from its position in non-standard dialects like Belfast English. Describe the use of *you* in the imperatives of Standard English and Belfast English.

(12) Exclamatory meaning can be expressed by sentences which do not have the grammatical structure of an exclamative. Give an example of how a declarative sentence and an interrogative sentence may be used to make exclamations.

ANSWERS

Chapter 1

(1) (a) syntax – the adverb *bitterly* is in the wrong position in the sentence. It should be *She complained bitterly about her boss* or *She complained about her boss bitterly*.

(b) morphology – the prefix in <u>un</u>*heartened* is incorrect. It should be <u>dis</u>*heartened*.

(c) morphology – the prefix in <u>dis</u>*persuaded* is incorrect. It should be <u>un</u>*persuaded*.

(d) syntax – the order of determiners in *his elderly two aunts* is incorrect. It should be *his two elderly aunts*.

(e) morphology – the prefix in <u>de</u>*robed* is incorrect. It should be <u>dis</u>*robed*.

(f) syntax – the adverb *again* is in the wrong position in the sentence. It should be *John played the record again*.

(2) Prescriptive attitudes about language have a considerable influence on the reactions of adult viewers to this children's television programme. There were more than one hundred complaints to the BBC about the programme, with 95 of these complaints relating specifically to the language used by the characters in the show. The characters speak Jamaican Patois which is negatively characterised as 'slang' in the complaints to the BBC. The report includes instances of non-standard English at the levels of pronunciation ('make a bad ting good'), lexical semantics ('irie'), and grammar ('me wan go'). The mother who is worried that her white child will be attacked for using language from the programme to a black child is probably couching her own negative perceptions of Jamaican Patois in a concern about her child's safety.

(3) Knowledge of grammar is beneficial in the following contexts:

(a) Assessment, diagnosis and treatment of children and adults with language disorders: Speech and language therapists (speech-language pathologists in the USA) need to have a sound knowledge of grammar in order to assess, diagnose and treat language disorders such as specific language impairment and aphasia in children and adults.

(b) Teaching English language and linguistics: Knowledge of the structure of the English language is essential to a range of different teachers and lecturers. This includes teachers of English language to school pupils, teachers of English to learners who speak other languages, and lecturers of English language and linguistics at colleges and universities.

(c) Translation services: All forms of translation work require a sound working knowledge of grammar.

(d) Learning foreign languages: Knowledge of grammatical categories (nouns, adjectives, etc.) and constructions (relative clauses, passive voice, etc.) can facilitate the learning of foreign languages.

(e) Medical, health and educational professionals: Language disorders are often detected late with adverse implications for their remediation. Professionals who work with children in the early years are best placed to detect these disorders. They include general practitioners, health visitors, paediatricians, school teachers and psychologists. Knowledge of basic grammatical categories can help these professionals identify language delay in children and make early referrals to speech and language therapy.

(4) (a) Immature language: The child has added the regular past tense suffix –ed to the irregular past tense form (*went*) of the verb 'to go'. Also, the child has used 'did have' in place of the simple past tense 'had'.

(b) Non-standard dialect: The speaker has used a non-standard past participle. In Standard English, the past participle of the verb 'to ring' is 'rung'. In this case, the speaker uses 'rang'.

(c) Non-standard dialect: The speaker has used a non-standard noun. In Standard English, the count noun 'year' takes the suffix –s in the plural. In this case, it is unmarked for plural.

(d) Immature language: The child has produced an overregularisation error by applying the past tense suffix –ed to the infinitive form of the verb 'drink'.

(e) Disordered language: The individual with language disorder is attempting to say 'The girl is skipping'. The definite article (*the*) and auxiliary verb (*is*) are both omitted. This pattern is typical of agrammatism.

(f) Immature language: The child is using the comparative form (*better*) of the irregular adjective 'good'. The degree adverb 'more', which is used to form the comparative of certain adjectives (e.g. *more horrible*) is not needed in this case.

(g) Disordered language: The individual with language disorder omits the inflectional suffix –s from the verb 'need' and uses an incorrect past tense form (*catched*) in place of the infinitive 'to catch'.

(h) Non-standard dialect: A speaker of Standard English would use a relative pronoun (*who*). There is zero relative pronoun in this speaker's utterance.

Revision Questions

(1) Part (b).

(2) Parts (c) and (d).

(3) Latin.

(4) Five aspects of speaker identity: social class; age; ethnicity; gender; and geographical region.

(5) British Broadcasting Corporation (BBC).

(6) Specific language impairment; dyslexia; aphasia.

(7) Speakers of Belfast English are using the past participle form of the verb (*seen, done*) in place of the simple past tense (*saw, did*).

(8) This child has omitted inflectional suffixes from the verbs *want* (*want-s*) and *drop* (*drop-s*). He or she has also omitted determiners in front of the nouns *car* and *dolly* (e.g. *this car, my dolly*).

(9) True.

(10) The use of double negation (*not … nothing*) is unacceptable to a prescriptive grammarian.

(11) (a) syntax; (b) syntax; (c) morphology; (d) syntax; (e) morphology; (f) morphology.

(12) **(a)** Infinitive *to please* must not be split by the adverb *really*.

    (b) A sentence should not contain double negation (*not … nothing*).

    (c) A sentence should not end in a preposition (*with*).

    (d) The preposition *between* must be followed by the object pronoun *me* and not *I*.

    (e) The sentence contains a non-standard personal pronoun *youse*.

Chapter 2

Exercise 2.1

walk: [t] because of preceding voiceless consonant [k]
pretend: [ɪd] because of preceding voiced consonant [d]
believe: [d] because of preceding voiced consonant [v]
strip: [t] because of preceding voiceless consonant [p]
plant: [ɪd] because of preceding voiceless consonant [t]
apply: [d] because of preceding vowel [aɪ]

Exercise 2.2

(a) omission of –*s*; [z]

(b) use of –*s* on noun where there is no change in form

(c) use of –*es* on noun where there is no change in form

(d) omission of –*s*; [z]

(e) use of –s on noun where there is a vowel change

(f) noun has not undergone vowel change for plural

(g) omission of –s and no change of [f] to [v]; [z]

(h) use of –s on incorrect noun (*tea* instead of *cup*); [s]

(i) use of –*ses* instead of –s on *mouth*; [s]

(j) use of plural noun *children* instead of singular noun *child*

(k) noun has not undergone vowel change for plural

(l) omission of –*es*; [z]

Exercise 2.3

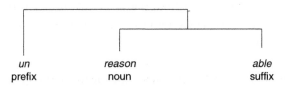

un	*reason*	*able*
prefix	noun	suffix

Formation history: *reason → reasonable → unreasonable*

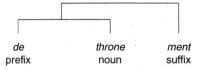

de	*throne*	*ment*
prefix	noun	suffix

Formation history: *throne → dethrone → dethronement*

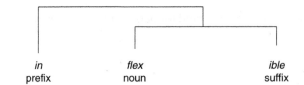

in	*flex*	*ible*
prefix	noun	suffix

Formation history: *flex → flexible → inflexible*

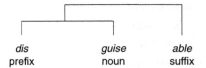

dis	*guise*	*able*
prefix	noun	suffix

Formation history: *guise → disguise → disguisable*

Exercise 2.4

DE's errors in the use of derivational suffixes can be categorised as follows:

(1) *Omission of derivational suffix:*

cabbie → cab

zipper → zip

election → elect

meanness → mean

childish → child

arsonist → arson

killer → kill

tallish → tall

(2) *Use of incorrect derivational suffix:*

swimmer → swimm<u>ing</u>

madly → mad<u>ness</u>

arsonist → arson<u>er</u>

childish → child<u>ly</u>

swiftly → swift<u>y</u>

(3) *Use of inflectional suffix:*

willowy → willow<u>s</u>

chilly → chill<u>s</u>

tallish → tall<u>er</u>

smoothly → smooth<u>er</u>

grower → grown (irregular past participle)

(4) *Other errors:*

blandly → blankly (correct derivational suffix, incorrect base)

smoothly → smootly (correct derivational suffix, incorrect base)

meanness → meaning (incorrect derivational suffix or different word)

talker → talking (incorrect derivational suffix or use of inflectional suffix)

buffer → bluff (omission of derivational suffix and base change or different word)

Exercise 2.5

Part A:

(a) dogleg: root compound; nominal compound (N + N)

(b) angelfish: root compound; nominal compound (N + N)

(c) gun-shy: root compound; adjectival compound (N + ADJ)

(d) housing benefit: synthetic compound; nominal compound (N + N)

(e) lone-wolf: root compound; nominal compound (ADJ + N)

(f) loose-leaf: root compound; adjectival compound (ADJ + N)

(g) make believe: root compound; verbal compound (V + V)

(h) oil painting: synthetic compound; nominal compound (N + N)

Part B:

(a) fighter-bomber: coordinative compound

(b) foxglove: exocentric compound

(c) lovebird: endocentric compound

(d) folk-rock: coordinative compound

(e) newcomer: exocentric compound

(f) nightingale: exocentric compound

(g) playtime: endocentric compound

(h) nursery school: endocentric compound

Exercise 2.6

(a) buttered: de-nominal verb

(b) emptied: de-adjectival verb

(c) cry: de-verbal noun

(d) jetted: de-nominal verb

(e) e-mailed: de-nominal verb

(f) walk: de-verbal noun

(g) carpeted: de-nominal verb

(h) signed: de-nominal verb

(i) humbled: de-adjectival verb

(j) blossomed: de-nominal verb

(k) bared: de-adjectival verb

Exercise 2.7

(a) nutricious + pharmaceutical → nutriceutical

(b) blizzard + disaster → blizzaster

(c) affluent + influenza → affluenza

(d) Channel + tunnel → Chunnel

(e) kitchen + paraphernalia → kitchenalia

(f) motor automobile + memorabilia → motormobilia

(g) gay + radar → gaydar

(h) sky + hijacking → skyjacking

(i) man + bikini → mankini

(j) Britpop + literati → Britpoperati

End-of-Chapter Questions

(1) happy – unhappy; reasonable – unreasonable (prefix *un–*)
    precise – imprecise; possible – impossible (prefix *im–*)
    distinct – indistinct; determinate – indeterminate (prefix *in–*)
    responsible – irresponsible (prefix *ir–*)
    legitimate – illegitimate (prefix *il–*)
    courteous – discourteous; similar – dissimilar (prefix *dis–*)
    fruitful – fruitless; painful – painless (suffixes *–ful* and *–less*)
    Note: *im–*, *ir–* and *il–* are considered to be variants or allomorphs of the prefix *in–* which vary with the first sound of the lexical stem to which they are attached.

(2) (a) put; sit; sterilise
(b) Your flowers are deading
(c) Keep fallinged over
(d) throwed; catched; blowed (overregularisation error)
(e) It camed off; I nearly broked yours; She sawed it
Lara is marking the verb twice for past tense.
(f) Have you broke Sellotape? What have you forgot? She's ate teddy all up now
(g) Lara has added the past tense morpheme –*ed* to the past participle of the verbs.
(h) In *Now she's aten it all up*, Lara has added –*en* from the past participle *eaten* to the past tense form *ate*. This morphological error is the opposite of that identified in the response to question (g) where the past tense morpheme –*ed* was added to the past participle.
(i) Use of –*s* on third-person plural verb: And Amy and Lara sits at the back
Omission of –*s* on third-person singular verb: I think he look like a giraffe!
(j) Use of –*s* on a second-person verb: Can you makes her talk?
Morpheme –*s* attached to pronoun *she* instead of verb *want*: She's want to toddle round

(3) Suffix –*less* is substituted by:
–*ly* (brain<u>less</u> → brain<u>ly</u>)
–*ery* (worth<u>less</u> → worth<u>ery</u>)
Suffix –*ness* is substituted by:
–*y* (ill<u>ness</u> → ill<u>y</u>)
–*ery* (ill<u>ness</u> → ill<u>ery</u>)
–*ing* (mean<u>ness</u> → mean<u>ing</u>)
–*ly* (good<u>ness</u> → good<u>ly</u>)
Suffix –*ist* is substituted by:
–*ing* (stock<u>ist</u> → stock<u>ing</u>)
–*y* (sex<u>ist</u> → sex<u>y</u>)
–*er* (arson<u>ist</u> → arson<u>er</u>)
Suffix –*ly* is substituted by:
–*ed* (part<u>ly</u> → part<u>ed</u>)
–*en* (thick<u>ly</u> → thick<u>en</u>)
–*ness* (mad<u>ly</u> → mad<u>ness</u>)
–*er* (smooth<u>ly</u> → smooth<u>er</u>)
–*y* (swift<u>ly</u> → swift<u>y</u>)

(4) (a) function
(b) containment
(c) time
(d) location
(e) function
(f) comparison

(g) containment
(h) material
(i) source
(j) part-whole

(5) (a) voicing modification [θ] → [ð]
(b) stress modification: ¹insult → in¹sult
(c) no modification
(d) voicing modification [f] → [v]
(e) stress modification: ¹torment → tor¹ment
(f) voicing modification [θ] → [ð]
(g) no modification
(h) voicing modification [f] → [v]
(i) stress modification: ¹decrease → de¹crease
(j) voicing modification [f] → [v]

(6) (a) liaison
(b) enthusiasm
(c) fundraising
(d) emotion
(e) combustion
(f) benchpressing
(g) redaction
(h) vacuum-cleaner
(i) airconditioning
(j) copy-editing

(7) (a) acronym-formation
(b) reduplication
(c) clipping
(d) blending
(e) blending
(f) initialism
(g) clipping
(h) reduplication
(i) blending
(j) initialism

Revision Questions

(1) Stems = domesticate; mistrust; joyful
Roots = domestic; trust; joy

(2) Walked [t]; Played [d]; Trusted [ɪd]; Blinded [ɪd]; Smoked [t]; Longed [d]; Relayed [d]

(3) Houses – number (–s); Travels – person (–s); Managed – tense (–ed); Bill's boat – case ('s); Friendliest – gradation (–est); Sleeping – aspect (–ing)

(4) Vowel change (*louse – lice*)

No change in form (*fish – fish*)

Forms of Greek and Latin origin (Greek: *schema – schemata*; Latin: *curriculum – curricula*)

Addition of suffix *–en* (*ox – oxen*)

Vowel change and use of suffix [ɹən] (*child – children*)

(5) <u>Un</u>sustain<u>able</u> (verb → adjective)

Piti<u>ful</u> (noun → adjective)

Distract<u>able</u> (verb → adjective)

Play<u>ful</u> (verb → adjective)

<u>Mis</u>communication (remains a noun)

Wish<u>ful</u> (verb → adjective)

<u>Dis</u>engage (remains a verb)

<u>Dis</u>loyal (remains an adjective)

<u>Un</u>manage<u>able</u> (verb → adjective)

<u>Un</u>wise (remains an adjective)

(6) country club (N + N); ashtray (N + N); greenhouse (ADJ + N); windbreak (N + V); make-believe (V + V); sea breeze (N + N); killjoy (V + N); waterwheel (N + N); fishpond (N + N); redhot (ADJ + ADJ)

(7) True

(8) Back-formation

(9) CAT scan: acronym (computerised axial tomography)

AIDS: acronym (acquired immune deficiency syndrome)

MRI: initialism (magnetic resonance imaging)

HIV: initialism (human immunodeficiency virus)

ECG: initialism (electrocardiogram)

HRT: initialism (hormone replacement therapy)

STI: initialism (sexually transmitted infection)

TBI: initialism (traumatic brain injury)

PET scan: acronym (positron emission tomography)

ICU: initialism (intensive care unit)

(10) False

(11) Blending

(12) True

Chapter 3

Exercise 3.1

Herd:

The herd has stampeded across the field.

The herd have stampeded across the field.

Staff:

The staff is taking industrial action.
The staff are taking industrial action.
Team:
The team wins all home games.
The team win all home games.
Crew:
The crew is abandoning the race.
The crew are abandoning the race.
Government:
The government has cut public spending.
The government have cut public spending.

Exercise 3.2

(a) Use of contracted *is* with third person singular subject pronoun *it*.
(b) Use of first person singular object pronoun *me* instead of first person singular subject pronoun *I*.
(c) Omission of third person singular subject pronoun *it*.
(d) Omission of third person singular object pronoun *it*.
(e) Use of first person singular object pronoun *me* and *is* instead of first person singular subject pronoun *I* and *am*.
(f) Use of contracted *is* with third person singular subject pronoun *he*.
(g) Use of third person singular object pronoun *her* instead of third person singular subject pronoun *she*.
(h) Use of second person subject pronoun *you* instead of third person singular subject pronoun *he*.
(i) Use of first person singular object pronoun *me* instead of first person singular subject pronoun *I*.
(j) Use of contracted *is* with third person singular subject pronoun *he*.

Exercise 3.3

(a) auxiliary *have*
(b) auxiliary *is*
(c) lexical *are*
(d) auxiliary *has*
(e) lexical *am*
(f) auxiliary *have*
(g) lexical *is*
(h) lexical *is*
(i) auxiliary *am*
(j) auxiliary *is*
(k) auxiliary *am*
(l) lexical *is*

(m) auxiliary *has*
(n) lexical *is*
(o) auxiliary *are*
(p) auxiliary *am*

Exercise 3.4

Part A:
(a) him – obligatory
(b) it – obligatory
(c) mine – obligatory; the tea – obligatory; on the afternoon – optional
(d) a dice – obligatory
(e) it – obligatory; now – optional
(f) something – obligatory
(g) door – obligatory; for me – optional
(h) over gate – optional
(i) the marbles – obligatory; in here – obligatory
(j) in back – optional

Part B:
throwed – mono-transitive
gave – di-transitive
see – intransitive
holded – mono-transitive
sit – intransitive

Exercise 3.5

(a) horrid (adjective phrase)
(b) in the sea (prepositional phrase)
(c) the helicopter (noun phrase)
(d) lovely water (noun phrase)
(e) mummy's friend (noun phrase)
(f) ready (adjective phrase)
(g) a ghost (noun phrase)
(h) the elephant (noun phrase)
(i) in the rain (prepositional phrase)
(j) our bed (noun phrase)

Exercise 3.6

(a) got – past tense verb; got – auxiliary verb
(b) gotten – past participle
(c) got – auxiliary verb

(d) gotten – past participle
(e) got – past participle
(f) got – auxiliary verb
(g) got – past participle; got – past participle
(h) gotten – past participle
(i) got – past participle
(j) got – past participle; got – auxiliary verb

Exercise 3.7

(a) *big* is a pre-modifier in a noun phrase; it is preceded by the determiner *the*
(b) intensifier *very* is not required; *big* should only be followed by the adverb *enough*
(c) *big* is preceded by the intensifier *too*
(d) *big* is one of two adjectives which modify the noun *pain*; Lara gets the order of the adjectives correct (compare *?You're a big great pain*)
(e) Lara omits a noun that *really big* can modify
(f) Lara omits a noun that the adjectives *big bouncy* can modify; on an alternative interpretation, *bouncy* may be used by Lara and her family as a noun to denote a bouncing movement
(g) *big* appears with *long* as a pre-modifier in a noun phrase; Lara uses the adjectives in the correct order (compare *?long big field*)
(h) Lara uses the comparative *bigger*; part of the sentence is implicit or understood, e.g. *Is the blue one bigger [than the red one]?*
(i) *big* is the pre-modifier of a noun phrase; it is preceded by *all* (a quantificational determiner) and the definite article
(j) *big* is one of three adjectives to modify the noun *chair*; Lara orders the adjectives correctly (compare *?big nice strong chair* and *?strong nice big chair*)

Exercise 3.8

(a) proper + *–ly* → properly
(b) out + *–wards* → outwards
(c) other + *–wise* → otherwise
(d) hopeful + *–ly* → hopefully
(e) sky + *–wards* → skywards
(f) happy + *–ly* → happily
(g) left + *–wards* → leftwards
(h) south + *–wards* → southwards
(i) length + *–ways* → lengthways; length + *–wise* → lengthwise
(j) like + *–wise* → likewise
(k) special + *–ly* → specially

(l) end + –*ways* → endways; end + –*wise* → endwise

(m) pleasant + –*ly* → pleasantly

(n) back + –*wards* →backwards

(o) edge + –*ways* → edgeways; edge + –*wise* → edgewise

(p) ready + –*ly* → readily

(q) clock + –*wise* → clockwise

(r) front + –*wards* → frontwards

(s) after + –*wards* → afterwards

(t) crab + –*wise* →crabwise

End-of-Chapter Questions

(1) (a) John – proper noun; love – abstract, non-count noun

(b) horticulturalist – common noun; grass – concrete, count noun

(c) France – proper noun; wines – concrete, count noun

(d) grass – concrete, non-count noun; weekend – common noun

(e) bread – concrete, non-count noun; Smith – proper noun

(f) men – common noun; trust – abstract, non-count noun

(g) Spain – proper noun; wine – concrete, non-count noun

(h) stall – common noun; breads – concrete, count noun

(i) Bill – proper noun; loves – concrete, count noun

(j) trusts – concrete, count noun; name – common noun

(2) (a) Third person plural subject pronoun *they* used in place of possessive determiner *their*.

(b) Possessive determiner *my* used in place of first person singular subject pronoun *I*.

(c) First person singular object pronoun *me* used in place of possessive determiner *my*.

(d) Personal pronoun *you* used in place of possessive determiner *your*.

(e) First person singular object pronoun *me* used in place of possessive determiner *my*.

(f) First person singular object pronoun *me* used in place of possessive determiner *my*.

(g) Personal pronoun *you* used in place of possessive determiner *your*.

(h) First person singular object pronoun *me* used in place of possessive determiner *my*.

(i) Third person singular subject pronoun *he* used in place of possessive determiner *his*.

(j) Third person plural subject pronoun *they* used in place of possessive determiner *their*.

Use of the first person singular object pronoun *me* in place of the possessive determiner *my* may be a feature of Lara's dialect.

(3) (a) I will need these (*that*-clause)

  (b) to see some donkeys at the zoo (*to*-infinitive)

  (c) she can play with it (*that*-clause)

  (d) to stay still (*to*-infinitive)

  (e) your baby's still hungry (*that*-clause)

  (f) to do a wee wee (*to*-infinitive)

  (g) to have a hat on (*to*-infinitive)

  (h) that goes there (*that*-clause)

  (i) you have to tell daddy (*that*-clause)

  (j) to come to our picnic one day (*to*-infinitive)

(4) Part A:

  (a) road + –*worthy* → roadworthy

  (b) sheep + –*ish* → sheepish

  (c) poet + –*ic* → poetic

  (d) loathe + –*some* → loathsome

  (e) coward + –*ly* → cowardly

  (f) care + –*ful* → careful; care + –*less* → careless

  (g) shock + –*ing* → shocking

  (h) professor + –*ial* → professorial

  (i) curl + –*y* → curly

  (j) harm + –*ful* → harmful; harm + –*less* →harmless

  (k) sea + –*worthy* → seaworthy

  (l) psychology + –*ical* → psychological

  Part B:

  (a) old – attributive

  (b) graceful – predicative

  (c) classical – attributive

  (d) unsafe – predicative

  (e) opportunistic – attributive

(5) (a) adjective

  (b) adjective

  (c) adverb

  (d) adverb

  (e) adjective

  (f) adverb

  (g) adjective

  (h) adverb

  (i) adjective

  (j) adverb

  These sentences demonstrate that one and the same word can be an adjective in one sentence and an adverb in another sentence.

(6) (a) home

(b) together

(c) up; quickly

(d) yet

(e) just

(f) round

(g) now

(h) up

(i) down; there

(j) here

Direction: up; down

Place: here; there

Time: now; yet

Manner: quickly; together

Revision Questions

(1) (a) wallet (thing); (b) pen (thing); (c) children (person); (d) happiness (concept); (e) town (place); (f) home (concept); (g) problem (concept); (h) girls (person); (i) horror (concept); (j) house (thing)

(2) (a) auxiliary verbs = *has, been*; main verb = *running*

(b) auxiliary verbs = *will, be*; main verb = *going*

(c) main verb = *anticipate*

(d) auxiliary verbs = *must, have*; main verb = *left*

(e) auxiliary verb = *shall*; main verb = *have*

(f) main verb = *is*

(g) auxiliary verb = *could*; main verb = *fix*

(h) auxiliary verbs = *do, would*; main verbs = *wish, stay*

(i) auxiliary verb = *do*; main verbs = *know, said*

(j) auxiliary verb = *have*; main verb = *found*

(3) *had* (auxiliary verb) *known* (main verb)

could (auxiliary verb) *change* (main verb)

had been (auxiliary verbs) *working* (main verb)

opened (main verb)

were (auxiliary verb) *disappearing* (main verb)

was (main verb)

had (auxiliary verb) *met* (main verb)

was (main verb)

had (auxiliary verb) *been* (main verb)

cultivate (main verb)

would (auxiliary verb) *improve* (main verb)

(4) (a) *frantically* (manner); (b) *now* (time); (c) *there* (place); (d) *home* (direction); (e) *aimlessly* (manner)

(5) (a) lexical verb (*was, went, using*)

(b) auxiliary verb (*are*)

(c) proper noun (*Bill*)

(d) common noun (*boy, school, students, butter*)

(e) concrete noun (*boy, school, students, butter*)

(6) (a) *tastier – tastiest*; (b) *worse – worst*; (c) *more reliable – most reliable*; (d) *smaller – smallest*; (e) *better – best*

(7) (a) *most diligently* (manner); (b) *where* (place); (c) *already* (time); (d) *when* (time); (e) *locally* (place); (f) *how* (manner)

(8) (a) *endless* (attributive); (b) *unforeseen* (attributive); (c) *irreparable* (predicative); (d) *historical* (attributive); (e) *precocious* (predicative)

(9) (a) *yours* (possessive); (b) *this* (demonstrative); (c) *she* (personal); *herself* (reflexive); (d) *anyone* (indefinite); (e) *each other* (reciprocal); (f) *who* (interrogative); (g) *something* (indefinite); (h) *who* (relative); (i) *nobody* (indefinite); (j) *they* (personal); *one another* (reciprocal)

(10) (a) *gave* (di-transitive verb); (b) *smiled* (intransitive verb); (c) *thumped* (mono-transitive verb); (d) *elected* (complex transitive verb); (e) *choked* (intransitive verb)

(11) (a) *quicklier – quickliest*; (b) *more forcefully – most forcefully*; (c) *faster – fastest*; (d) *more recently – most recently*; (e) *further – furthest*

(12) Part A:

(a) present progressive

(b) past perfect

(c) past perfect progressive

(d) present perfect

(e) past progressive

(f) present perfect progressive

(g) present perfect progressive

(h) past progressive

(i) present perfect

(j) past perfect

(k) present progressive

(l) past progressive

(m) present perfect progressive

(n) present progressive

(o) past perfect

(p) present perfect

Part B:

(a) active voice

(b) passive voice

(c) passive voice

(d) active voice

(e) passive voice

(f) active voice

(g) passive voice

(h) active voice

Chapter 4

Exercise 4.1

(a) her two children
(b) her – possessive determiner; two – cardinal numeral
(c) possessive determiner
(d) definite article
(e) some trees; some shrub

Exercise 4.2

(a) <u>for</u> the elephant → <u>to</u> the elephant
(b) <u>on</u> the elephant → <u>at</u> the elephant
(c) <u>on</u> a balloon → <u>onto</u> a balloon
(d) a plane → <u>with</u> a plane
(e) <u>on</u> his hands → <u>in</u> his hands
(f) <u>over</u> the ground → <u>on</u> the ground
(g) <u>on</u> the giraffe hand → <u>in</u> the giraffe hand
(h) the elephant → <u>to</u> the elephant
(i) <u>in the side</u> the water → <u>inside</u> the water
(j) <u>in</u> the sandbox → <u>into</u> the sandbox

Exercise 4.3

(a) but; clauses
(b) or; nouns
(c) and; adjectives
(d) and; clauses
(e) or; clauses
(f) but; clauses
(g) and; adverbs
(h) and; clauses
(i) or; nouns
(j) and; nouns
(k) or; clauses
(l) and; clauses
(m) or; nouns
(n) but; clauses
(o) or; clauses

Exercise 4.4

(a) that: The stool <u>that the boy is standing on</u> is tipping over.

(b) if: She's standing in water <u>if that's action</u>.

(c) so: She's asking him for one <u>so he's handing one down to her</u>.

(d) because: The little girl's crying <u>because he ain't giving her no cookies</u>.

(e) so that: His sister is sushing <u>so that the mother won't turn around</u>.

(f) while: She seems to be looking out the window <u>while she's drying her dish</u>.

(g) as: The mother is washing the dishes <u>as the sink is running over</u>.

(h) that: I did say <u>[that] she was letting the water run over the sink</u>.

(i) while: She is washing dishes <u>while her sink is overflowing with water onto the floor</u>.

(j) that: The stool is turning over on him <u>that he's standing on</u>.

End-of-Chapter Questions

(1) (a) the – definite article – central determiner
some – quantifying expression – post-determiner
more – quantifying expression – post-determiner

(b) the – definite article – central determiner
no – quantifying expression – post-determiner

(c) one – cardinal numeral – post-determiner

(d) her – possessive determiner – central determiner

(e) the – definite article – central determiner
last – general ordinal – post-determiner
two – cardinal numeral – post-determiner

(f) all – quantifying expression – pre-determiner
his – possessive determiner – central determiner

(g) no – quantifying expression – post-determiner

(h) three – cardinal numeral – post-determiner
the – definite article – central determiner

(i) the – definite article – central determiner
his – possessive determiner – central determiner

(j) the – definite article – central determiner
two – cardinal numeral – post-determiner

(k) all – quantifying expression – pre-determiner
her – possessive determiner – central determiner

(l) all – quantifying expression – pre-determiner

(m) no – quantifying expression – post-determiner

(n) the – definite article – central determiner
fifty – cardinal numeral – post-determiner

(o) another – quantifying expression – post-determiner

(2) Ben's room was one <u>of</u> the best <u>in</u> the block. <u>In addition to</u> a wash-basin there was a wardrobe <u>with</u> two shelves and, <u>next to</u> that, a large cupboard. <u>In front of</u> the cupboard was a small table <u>with</u> a drawer, and <u>inside</u> the drawer was a booklet <u>of</u> information <u>about</u> the town, <u>along with</u> some notepaper. <u>On top</u>

<u>of</u> the wardrobe there were some extra pillows and, <u>underneath</u> those, some extra blankets. <u>At</u> the other end <u>of</u> the room was a small fridge. He looked hopefully <u>inside</u> the fridge, but <u>instead of</u> the expected cans <u>of</u> juice he found only a piece <u>of</u> mouldy cheese, <u>together with</u> some stale bread. He drew the curtains and looked <u>out of</u> the window. <u>Across</u> the street was a café, <u>with</u> tables <u>outside</u> the door. A group <u>of</u> men were sitting <u>around</u> one <u>of</u> the tables, arguing intently <u>about</u> something.

(3) (a) and: coordinating
  (b) and: coordinating; since: subordinating
  (c) if: subordinating; or: coordinating
  (d) after: subordinating
  (e) but: coordinating
  (f) so that: subordinating
  (g) either...or: coordinating
  (h) unless: subordinating
  (i) not only...but also: coordinating
  (j) when: subordinating
(4) (a) and: adverbs
  (b) until: clauses
  (c) and: nouns
  (d) or: adjectives
  (e) while: clauses
  (f) but: clauses
  (g) but: clauses
  (h) and: adjectives
  (i) or: nouns
  (j) if: clauses; or: nouns

Revision Questions

(1) (a) *half the* (fraction + definite article); *her* (possessive determiner)
  (b) *twice a* (multiplying expression + indefinite article)
  (c) *the* (definite article); *every* (quantity word)
  (d) *this* (demonstrative determiner); *your* (possessive determiner); *the* (definite article)
  (e) *all five* (all + cardinal numeral); *the* (definite article)
(2) (a) definite article; (b) demonstrative; (c) quantity word; (d) possessive; (e) quantity word; (f) indefinite article; (g) ordinal numeral; (h) cardinal numeral; (i) indefinite article; (j) cardinal numeral; (k) possessive; (l) demonstrative
(3) (a) preposition; *He was considering his future* (verb)
  (b) verb; *Following the incident, procedures were revised* (preposition)

(c) verb; *Regarding your complaint, we have decided to provide a refund* (preposition)

(d) preposition; *I am including you on the guest list* (verb)

(e) verb; *Excluding the driver, there were twenty people on the bus* (preposition)

(4) (a) *of* (preposition); *as* (subordinating conjunction)

    (b) *although* (subordinating conjunction); *on* (preposition)

    (c) *if* (subordinating conjunction); *in* (preposition)

    (d) *that* (subordinating conjunction); *when* (subordinating conjunction); *on* (preposition)

    (e) *before* (subordinating conjunction); *into* (preposition)

    (f) *even though* (subordinating conjunction); *before* (preposition)

(5) (a) *if;* (b) *because;* (c) *in order that; so that;* (d) *unless;* (e) *while;* (f) *until*

(6) (a) time; (b) cause; (c) place; (d) means; (e) place

(7) (a) *above* (place); (b) *for* (time); (c) *on account of* (cause); (d) *with* (means); (e) *between* (place)

(8) (a) *and* (coordinating conjunction); adjectives

    (b) *but* (coordinating conjunction); clauses

    (c) *after* (subordinating conjunction); clauses

    (d) *or* (coordinating conjunction); nouns

    (e) *if* (subordinating conjunction); clauses

    (f) *since* (subordinating conjunction); clauses

(9) (a) a lake; (b) that third fence; (c) the five books; (d) my room; (e) half her salary

(10) (a) *ten;* (b) *many;* (c) *our;* (d) *half;* (e) *first;* (f) *twice;* (g) *the;* (h) *an;* (i) *previous/last;* (j) *this*

(11) (a) *while;* (b) *but;* (c) *and;* (d) *if;* (e) *since;* (f) *or;* (g) *because;* (h) *although;* (i) *but;* (j) *because*

(12) Central determiner

Chapter 5

Exercise 5.1

(a) solution

(b) ways

(c) vase

(d) children

(e) crops

(f) clothes

(g) fans

(h) issues

(i) transactions

(j) charges

Exercise 5.2

Omission of auxiliary verb:
The elephant [is/was] running on the thing and almost fall in.
She [is/was] wondering if she could take it off.
I [have] never seen one of these in ages.
Incorrect lexical verb:
The giraffe never <u>runned</u>. [Overregularisation error: target form *ran*]
His stomach really <u>hurted</u>. [Overregularisation error: target form *hurt*]
He <u>ask</u> if he could buy them a balloon. [Omission of –ed: target form *asked*]
And the hare only <u>ated</u> a sandwich. ['Double' past tense: *ate* + *-ed*]
The elephant running on the thing and almost <u>fall</u> in. [Target form either *falls* or *fell*]

Exercise 5.3

(a) direct object: noun phrase (*the water*)
(b) *to*-infinitive clause (*to swim*)
(c) prepositional phrase (*on the bench*)
(d) adverb phrase (*away*)
(e) adverb phrase (*faster*)
(f) *that*-clause (*you are not big enough*)
(g) subject complement: adjective phrase (*so angry*)
(h) subject complement: noun phrase (*the doctor*)
(i) indirect object: pronoun (*him*); direct object: noun phrase (*the ball*)
(j) direct object: noun phrase (*her knee*)
(k) no post-modifier: intransitive verb (*came*)
(l) prepositional phrase (*on the grass*)
(m) no post-modifier: intransitive verb (*sweating*)
(n) direct object: pronoun (*him*); object complement: adjective phrase (*sick*)
(o) adverb phrase (*so fast*)
(p) direct object: noun phrase (*a airplane in his hand*)
(q) subject complement: adjective phrase (*mad*)
(r) direct object: noun phrase (*his airplane*)
(s) indirect object: pronoun (*me*); direct object: noun phrase (*a balloon*)
(t) *to*-infinitive clause (*to have the balloon*)

Exercise 5.4

Part A:
(a) very clearly – adverb pre-modifier (*very*)
(b) absentmindedly – no pre-modification or post-modification
(c) down here – adverb pre-modifier (*down*)

(d) pretty – no pre-modification or post-modification

(e) high up on the ladder – adverb pre-modifier (*high*); prepositional phrase post-modifier (*on the ladder*)

(f) outside – no pre-modification or post-modification

(g) very – no pre-modification or post-modification

(h) also – no pre-modification or post-modification

(i) inside – no pre-modification or post-modification

(j) right up to her mouth – adverb pre-modifier (*right*); prepositional phrase post-modifier (*to her mouth*)

Part B:

(a) very – pre-modifier in an adjective phrase (*very distinct*)

(b) also – pre-modifier in a verb phrase (*also falling off the stool*); Note: *off* is an adverb in a verb-particle combination (*falling off*)

(c) about – pre-modifier in an adjective phrase (*about ready*)

(d) already – pre-modifier in a verb phrase (*already eaten*)

(e) so – pre-modifier in a noun phrase (*so much trouble*)

(f) now – post-modifier in a verb phrase (*see now*)

(g) somewhat – pre-modifier in an adjective phrase (*somewhat obliterated*)

(h) apparently – pre-modifier in a verb phrase (*apparently washing or drying the dishes*)

(i) very – pre-modifier in an adjective phrase (*very quiet*)

(j) around – post-modifier in a verb phrase (*stretches around*)

Exercise 5.5

(a) *at Sally*; post-modifier noun phrase (*Sally*); prepositional phrase is a post-modifier in an adjective phrase (*so mad at Sally*)

(b) *on this bench for a while*; post-modifier noun phrase (*this bench for a while*); prepositional phrase is a post-modifier in a verb phrase (*sit on this bench for a while*)

(c) *toward the water*; post-modifier noun phrase (*the water*); prepositional phrase is a post-modifier in a verb phrase (*running toward the water*)

(d) *right into the pool*; pre-modifier adverb (*right*) and post-modifier noun phrase (*the pool*); prepositional phrase is a post-modifier in a verb phrase (*fell right into the pool*)

(e) *on the castle*; post-modifier noun phrase (*the castle*); prepositional phrase is a post-modifier in a noun phrase (*some more sand on the castle*)

(f) prepositional phrase (1): *with a ball near the pool* and prepositional phrase (2): *near the pool*; prepositional phrase (1) has a noun phrase as a post-modifier (*a ball near the pool*) and prepositional phrase (2) has a noun phrase as a post-modifier (*the pool*); prepositional phrase (1) is a post-modifier in a verb phrase (*playing with a ball near the pool*) and prepositional phrase (2) is a post-modifier in a noun phrase (*a ball near the pool*)

(g) *with a net*; post-modifier noun phrase (*a net*); prepositional phrase is a post-modifier in a noun phrase (*an elephant with a net*)

(h) *of food*; post-modifier noun phrase (*food*); prepositional phrase is a post-modifier in an adjective phrase (*full of food*)

(i) prepositional phrase (1): *in love with the zebra* and prepositional phrase (2): *with the zebra*; prepositional phrase (1) has a noun phrase as a post-modifier (*love with the zebra*) and prepositional phrase (2) has a noun phrase as a post-modifier (*the zebra*); prepositional phrase (1) is a post-modifier in a verb phrase (*felled in love with the zebra*) and prepositional phrase (2) is a post-modifier in a noun phrase (*love with the zebra*)

(j) *in the water*; post-modifier noun phrase (*the water*); prepositional phrase is a post-modifier in a verb phrase (*swimming in the water*)

There are a number of differences in the use of prepositional phrases by these children with SLI and the typically developing children Lara and Ella. Lara and Ella used a greater range of post-modifiers in their prepositional phrases. These post-modifiers are noun phrases, adverb phrases and prepositional phrases. Children with SLI only used noun phrases as post-modifiers in prepositional phrases. Another difference between these children can be seen in the types of phrases in which prepositional phrases are used as post-modifiers. For the typically developing children Lara and Ella, prepositional phrases are used as post-modifiers in noun, verb, adjective and adverb phrases. For children with SLI, prepositional phrases are only used as post-modifiers in noun, verb and adjective phrases.

End-of-Chapter Questions

(1) (a) pre-modifier: none; post-modifier: prepositional phrase (*for the horse*)
   (b) pre-modifier: adjective (*horrid*); post-modifier: none
   (c) pre-modifier: adjective (*little*); post-modifier: none
   (d) pre-modifier: adjective (*little*); post-modifier: *to*-infinitive (*to go*)
   (e) pre-modifier: noun (*attic*); post-modifier: none
   (f) pre-modifier: none; post-modifier: prepositional phrase (*of green plasticine*)
   (g) pre-modifier: adjective (*pretend*); post-modifier: prepositional phrase (*for me*)
   (h) pre-modifier: adjective (*pretend*) and noun (*animal*); post-modifier: none
   (i) pre-modifier: adjective phrase (*very good*); post-modifier: none
   (j) pre-modifier: adjective (*lovely*); post-modifier: none
(2) Part A:
   (a) dummy auxiliary (*did*) and negative form (*n't*)
   (b) modal auxiliary (*can*) and negative form (*not*)
   (c) adverb phrase (*still*)
   (d) modal auxiliary (*will*)
   (e) adverb phrase (*just*)

Part B:

(a) subject complement: adjective phrase (*impossible*)

(b) direct object: noun phrase (*a balloon*); adverb phrase (*first*)

(c) direct object: noun phrase (*the ball*); indirect object: prepositional phrase (*to missus elephant*)

(d) *that*-clause (*[that] it was flying*)

(e) subject complement: adjective phrase (*very embarrassed*)

(3) (a) head: *mad*; pre-modifier: none; post-modifier: prepositional phrase (*at the elephant*)

(b) head: *happy*; pre-modifier: none; post-modifier: *that*-clause (*that she got a bandaid*)

(c) head: *happy*; pre-modifier: adverb phrase (*so*); post-modifier: none

(d) head: *happy*; pre-modifier: none; post-modifier: *that*-clause (*that he got it for the elephant*)

(e) head: *responsible*; pre-modifier: none; post-modifier: prepositional phrase (*for it*)

(f) head: *sad*; pre-modifier: adverb phrase (*really*); post-modifier: *that*-clause (*that he lost his friend balloon*)

(g) head: *sorry*; pre-modifier: none; post-modifier: prepositional phrase (*about that*)

(h) head: *shy*; pre-modifier: adverb phrase (*very*); post-modifier: prepositional phrase (*with giraffe*)

(i) head: *sorry*; pre-modifier: adverb phrase (*so*); post-modifier: *to*-infinitive (*to get the balloon up there*)

(j) head: *nice*; pre-modifier: none; post-modifier: prepositional phrase (*to the giraffe*)

(4) (a) there – place

(b) yet – time

(c) quickly – manner

(d) away – direction

(e) now – time

(f) nearly – degree

(g) tonight – time

(h) too – degree

(i) too – degree; now – time

(j) today – time

(k) here – place

(l) always – frequency

(m) nearer – place

(n) again – frequency

(o) through – place

(p) straight back – direction

(q) nearly – degree

(r) away – direction; now – time

(s) still – time

(t) upstairs – place

(5) (a) *She runned <u>towards here</u>*; post-modifier adverb (*here*); prepositional phrase is a post-modifier in a verb phrase (*runned towards here*)

(b) *The elephant was going <u>on the diving board</u>*; post-modifier noun phrase (*the diving board*); prepositional phrase is a post-modifier in a verb phrase (*going on the diving board*)

(c) *The giraffe got very angry <u>at the elephant</u>*; post-modifier noun phrase (*the elephant*); prepositional phrase is a post-modifier in an adjective phrase (*very angry at the elephant*)

(d) *She forgot <u>about that</u>*; post-modifier demonstrative pronoun (*that*); prepositional phrase is a post-modifier in a verb phrase (*forgot about that*)

(e) *Moose was mad <u>at the elephant</u>*; post-modifier noun phrase (*the elephant*); prepositional phrase is a post-modifier in an adjective phrase (*mad at the elephant*)

(f) *Three bunnies are playing <u>in the sandbox</u>*; post-modifier noun phrase (*the sandbox*); prepositional phrase is a post-modifier in a verb phrase (*playing in the sandbox*)

(g) *A elephant is bouncing a ball <u>by the pool</u>*; post-modifier noun phrase (*the pool*); prepositional phrase is a post-modifier in a noun phrase (*a ball by the pool*)

(h) *Longnose was walking <u>toward him</u>*; post-modifier personal pronoun (*him*); prepositional phrase is a post-modifier in a verb phrase (*walking toward him*)

(i) *He gets sick <u>of the food</u>*; post-modifier noun phrase (*the food*); prepositional phrase is a post-modifier in an adjective phrase (*sick of the food*)

(j) *The giraffe was mad <u>at her</u>*; post-modifier personal pronoun (*her*); prepositional phrase is a post-modifier in an adjective phrase (*mad at her*)

Revision Questions

(1) (a) head = noun *house*; pre-modifier = adjective *old*; post-modifier = prepositional phrase *beside the lake*

(b) head = noun *estate*; pre-modifier = noun *council*; post-modifier = relative clause *that Jack vandalised*

(c) head = noun *demands*; pre-modifier = participle *threatening*; post-modifier = infinitive clause *to pay the ransom*

(d) head = noun *child*; pre-modifier = none; post-modifier = participle *throwing stones*

(e) head = noun *girls*; pre-modifier = none (*club's* is a possessive determiner); post-modifier = adjective phrase *keen on sport*

(2) (a) head = noun *idea*; pre-modifier = adjective *brilliant*; post-modifier = none

(b) head = noun *branches*; pre-modifier = none; post-modifier = prepositional phrase *of the tree*

(c) head = noun *light*; pre-modifier = adjectives *bright, yellow*; post-modifier = none

(d) head = noun *answer*; pre-modifier = none; post-modifier = none

(e) head = noun *people*; pre-modifier = adjective *interesting*; post-modifier = none

(f) head = noun *knife*; pre-modifier = none; post-modifier = prepositional phrase *with a red handle*

(g) head = noun *person*; pre-modifier = none; post-modifier = relative clause *[whom] I was expecting*

(h) head = noun *path*; pre-modifier = adjectives *slippery, wet*; post-modifier = none

(i) head = noun *king*; pre-modifier = none; post-modifier = prepositional phrase *of the castle*

(j) head = noun *entry*; pre-modifier = none; post-modifier = none

(3) (a) *the treasure* (object); (b) *the old building* (subject); (c) *five minutes* (adverbial); (d) *the irate customer* (subject); (e) *the house* (complement); (f) *last week* (adverbial); (g) *a book* (object); (h) *the spot* (complement); (i) *the elderly man* (subject); (j) *next week* (adverbial); (k) *the report* (object)

(4) True.

(5) (a) head = verb *give*; pre-modifier = auxiliary verb *did* and negative form *not*; post-modifier = noun phrase *the gift to the teacher*

(b) head = verb *became*; pre-modifier = adverb *quickly*; post-modifier = adjective *angry*

(c) head = verb *walk*; pre-modifier = negative form *never*; post-modifier = prepositional phrase *in the park*

(d) head = verb *living*; pre-modifier = auxiliary verbs *have been*; post-modifier = adverb *dangerously*

(e) head = verb *realise*; pre-modifier = auxiliary verb *did* and negative form *not*; post-modifier = subordinate clause *that the child had disappeared*

(f) head = verb *win*; pre-modifier = auxiliary verb *must*; post-modifier = noun phrase *next week*

(g) head = verb *travelled*; pre-modifier = adverb *often*; post-modifier = adverb *abroad*

(h) head = verb *leaving*; pre-modifier = auxiliary verb *are*; post-modifier = adverb *tomorrow*

(i) head = verb *forgotten*; pre-modifier = auxiliary verb *have*; post-modifier = noun phrase *their keys*

(j) head = verb *waiting*; pre-modifier = auxiliary verbs *must have been*; post-modifier = prepositional phrase *for hours*

(k) head = verb *vote*; pre-modifier = auxiliary verb *would* and adverb *definitely*; post-modifier = prepositional phrase *for her*

(l) head = verb *destroying*; pre-modifier = auxiliary verb *are*; post-modifier = noun phrase *the park*

(m) head = verb *going*; pre-modifier = auxiliary verb *are*; post-modifier = prepositional phrase *by bus*

(n) head = verb *jumped*; pre-modifier = none; post-modifier = prepositional phrase *across the road*

(o) head = verb *hoped*; pre-modifier = none; post-modifier = subordinate clause *that she would return*

(6) True.

(7) (a) adjective phrase: head = adjective *large*; pre-modifier = adverb *excessively*; post-modifier = prepositional phrase *for the breed*

(b) prepositional phrase: head = preposition *beside*; pre-modifier = adverb *right*; post-modifier = noun phrase *the forest*

(c) adjective phrase: head = adjective *distressed*; pre-modifier = adverb *too*; post-modifier = infinitive clause *to leave the house*

(d) adverb phrase: head = adverb *rapidly*; pre-modifier = adverb *more*; post-modifier = comparative clause *than we had expected*

(e) adverb phrase: head = adverb *unfortunately*; pre-modifier = none; post-modifier = prepositional phrase *for the patient*

(f) prepositional phrase: head = preposition *into*; pre-modifier = adverb *straight*; post-modifier = noun phrase *the crowd*

(g) prepositional phrase: head = preposition *from*; pre-modifier = none; post-modifier = prepositional phrase *behind the wall*

(h) adjective phrase: head = adjective *furious*; pre-modifier = none; post-modifier = subordinate clause *that his son had lied*

(i) adverb phrase: head = adverb *quickly*; pre-modifier = adverb *too*; post-modifier = prepositional phrase *for comfort*

(j) adjective phrase: head = adjective *fond*; pre-modifier = adverb *extremely*; post-modifier = prepositional phrase *of ice cream*

(k) prepositional phrase: head = preposition *following*; pre-modifier = none; post-modifier = noun phrase *the match*

(l) adjective phrase: head = adjective *long*; pre-modifier = adverb *too*; post-modifier = prepositional phrase *for the children*

(m) adverb phrase: head = adverb *calmly*; pre-modifier = adverb *more*; post-modifier = comparative clause *than she had expected*

(n) adjective phrase: head = adjective *frail*; pre-modifier = adverb *too*; post-modifier = infinitive clause *to walk*

(o) prepositional phrase: head = preposition *with*; pre-modifier = none; post-modifier = noun phrase *a grin*

(p) adjective phrase: head = adjective *worse*; pre-modifier = none; post-modifier = comparative clause *than the doctor had imagined*

(q) adverb phrase: head = adverb *favourably*; pre-modifier = adverb *very*; post-modifier = none

(r) prepositional phrase: head = preposition *over*; pre-modifier = adverb *straight*; post-modifier = noun phrase *the fence*

(8) Equal; dead; illegal

(9) **(a)** prepositional phrase *because of illness* (function = adverbial)

(b) adjective phrase *very fond of animals* (function = complement)

(c) prepositional phrases *in Italy* and *for one month* (function = adverbial)

(d) adverb phrase *rather quickly* (function = adverbial)

(e) adjective phrase *really fresh* (function = complement)

(f) adverb phrase *rather often* (function = adverbial)

(10) The word *pretty* is a pre-modifying adverb in an adverb phrase.

(11) **(a)** adjective phrase *stale* (function = complement)

(b) prepositional phrase *on account of poor light* (function = adverbial)

(c) prepositional phrase *by October* (function = adverbial)

(d) prepositional phrases *in London* and *because of his job* (function = adverbial)

(e) prepositional phrase *for six weeks* (function = adverbial)

(f) adverb phrase *very calmly* (function = adverbial)

(g) adjective phrase *very salty* (function = complement)

(h) adverb phrase *rather abruptly* (function = adverbial)

(i) prepositional phrase *by the dog* (function = adverbial)

(j) adverb phrase *quite carelessly* (function = adverbial)

(12) True.

Chapter 6

Exercise 6.1

(a) Two clauses linked by coordination (*but*); clauses have equal syntactic status.

(b) Two clauses linked by subordination (relative pronoun *who*); clauses do not have equal syntactic status: relative clause (*who arranges flowers in church*) depends on the main clause (*The woman, who arranges flowers in church, is very ill*).

(c) Two clauses linked by subordination (*that*); clauses do not have equal syntactic status: subordinate clause (*he would arrive on time*) depends on the main clause (*They hoped that he would arrive on time*).

(d) One clause with no coordination or subordination.

(e) Three clauses linked by coordination (*and, but*); clauses have equal syntactic status.

(f) Two clauses linked by coordination (*and*); clauses have equal syntactic status.

(g) Two clauses linked by subordination (*that* is understood but not present); clauses do not have equal syntactic status: subordinate clause (*the film will last two hours*) depends on the main clause (*I imagine that the film will last two hours*).

(h) Two clauses linked by subordination (relative pronoun *which*); clauses do not have equal syntactic status: relative clause (*which were validated by the board*) depends on the main clause (*The plans, which were validated by the board, were very costly*).

(i) One clause with no coordination or subordination.

(j) Two clauses linked by coordination (*or*); clauses have equal syntactic status.

Exercise 6.2

(a) $S + P + C_{SUB}$

(b) $S + P + A$

(c) $S + P + O_D$

(d) $S + P + O_D$

(e) $S + P + C_{SUB}$

(f) $S + P + A$

(g) $S + P + O_D$

(h) $S + P + O_D + A$

(i) $S + P$

(j) $S + P + A$

(k) $S + P$

(l) $S + P + C_{SUB}$

(m) $S + P + O_D + A$

(n) $S + P + A$

(o) $S + P + O_D$

(p) $S + P + A$

(q) $S + P + O_D$

(r) $S + P + O_D$

(s) $S + P + A$

(t) $S + P + C_{SUB}$

Exercise 6.3

(a) Do you think <u>daddy's home</u>? (Function: *direct object*)

(b) Give him some arms <u>so he can hold his hose</u>. (Function: *adverbial*)

(c) I think <u>it's a jigsaw</u>. (Function: *direct object*)

(d) I didn't tell you <u>I didn't like you</u>. (Function: *direct object*)

(e) Amy can come in house <u>if she wants</u>. (Function: *adverbial*)

(f) Can you see <u>I'm holding on very tight</u>? (Function: *direct object*)

(g) I think <u>she doesn't want to go to bed</u>. (Function: *direct object*)

(h) Can you bring me those <u>because I can't reach them</u>? (Function: *adverbial*)

(i) I'm cleaning Amy's bottle <u>so she can drink them all again</u>. (Function: *adverbial*)

(j) Move out of the way <u>because my horsey will go</u>. (Function: *adverbial*)

(k) I think <u>she's a bit poorly</u>. (Function: *direct object*)

(l) <u>If people get sick</u>, I will open it. (Function: *adverbial*)

(m) I just need to take that out <u>so I can clean the lid</u>. (Function: *adverbial*)

(n) You get a hoover out of your alcove <u>before I hoover</u>. (Function: *adverbial*)

(o) Help me make this <u>because I don't like to do it on my own</u>. (Function: *adverbial*)

Exercise 6.4

(a) <u>When she's not on it</u> I will go on it. (Function: *adverbial*)

(b) I wouldn't be surprised <u>if you said a whole picnic hamper</u>. (Function: *complement of adjective*)

(c) Shall I show you <u>how I make a big long field</u>? (Function: *direct object*)

(d) It isn't funny <u>if you do that</u>. (Function: *complement of adjective*)
(e) I'm just wondering <u>if we don't want it</u>. (Function: *direct object*)
(f) I'll show you <u>how you do that</u>. (Function: *direct object*)
(g) I'm going to shop <u>when they go to sleep</u>. (Function: *adverbial*)
(h) Don't know <u>if that'll stay on very well</u>. (Function: *direct object*)
(i) Shall I show you <u>how the wind blew it</u>? (Function: *direct object*)
(j) There's no reason <u>why you forget things</u>. (Function: *complement of noun*)

Exercise 6.5

(a) Pick that bit up <u>that I just dropped</u>. (Relative pronoun: *direct object*)
(b) That's the corn <u>that they eat</u>. (Relative pronoun: *direct object*)
(c) Not the Emily <u>that comes to my nursery</u>. (Relative pronoun: *subject*)
(d) I'm not playing with naughty girls <u>who have tantrums</u>. (Relative pronoun: *subject*)
(e) This white one <u>that I had</u>. (Relative pronoun: *direct object*)
(f) That's the horse <u>you see</u>. (Implicit relative pronoun: *direct object*)
(g) I think there's a bit <u>that goes in between those two</u>. (Relative pronoun: *subject*)
(h) That's a letter <u>that mummy and daddy got</u>. (Relative pronoun: *direct object*)
(i) What about this jigsaw <u>that's already out</u>? (Relative pronoun: *subject*)
(j) I'm gonna lie down here and I'm gonna try and rock Amy at the same time <u>which is an amazing feat</u>. (Relative pronoun: *subject*)

Exercise 6.6

(a) She's helping him <u>get the cookies</u>.
(b) She let the sink <u>run over</u>.
(c) Let me <u>scan it a little bit more</u>.
(d) The mother is having water <u>run over the sink</u>.
(e) She has let the sink <u>overflow</u>.
(f) Please let me <u>go</u>.
(g) Somebody let the water <u>run over</u>.
(h) She's letting the water <u>run out of the faucet onto the floor</u>.
(i) The mother's seeing the water <u>run over the sink</u>.
(j) She's making the sink <u>run over</u>.
The five verbs which permit a bare infinitive clause to follow them are *help, let, have, see* and *make*.

Exercise 6.7

(a) There's a path <u>leading to a garage</u>. (Function: *modifier of noun*)
(b) I think that's all I see <u>going on</u>. (Function: *object*)
(c) Here's mama <u>drying the dishes</u>. (Function: *modifier of noun*)

(d) <u>In looking out the window</u>, she's letting her sink run over. (Function: *adverbial*)

(e) I did mention the water <u>running out of the sink</u>. (Function: *modifier of noun*)

(f) <u>Stealing cookies</u> is the first bad thing I see. (Function: *subject*)

(g) It's another house <u>coming right next door to it</u>. (Function: *modifier of noun*)

(h) It came <u>splashing down</u>. (Function: *adverbial*)

(i) There's a slight breeze <u>coming in the kitchen window</u>. (Function: *modifier of noun*)

(j) The little girl was helping the boy to get to the cookie jar but he started <u>stumbling</u>. (Function: *object*)

End-of-Chapter Questions

(1) $S + P + O_D$	(16) $S + P + A$	(31) $S + P + O_D$	(46) $S + P + C_{SUB}$
(2) $S + P + O_D$	(17) $S + P + O_D$	(32) $S + P$	(47) $S + P + O_D$
(3) $S + P + O_D$	(18) $S + P + O_D + A$	(33) $S + P + C_{SUB}$	(48) $S + P + C_{SUB}$
(4) $S + P + O_D + A$	(19) $S + P + A$	(34) $S + P + O_D + A$	(49) $S + P + O_D$
(5) $S + P + O_D$	(20) $S + P + C_{SUB}$	(35) $S + P + O_D$	(50) $S + P + C_{SUB}$
(6) $S + P + O_D + A$	(21) $S + P + O_D$	(36) $S + P + O_D$	(51) $S + P + O_D$
(7) $S + P + O_D$	(22) $S + P + C_{SUB}$	(37) $S + P + C_{SUB}$	(52) $S + P + O_D + A$
(8) $S + P + O_D + A$	(23) $S + P + O_D$	(38) $S + P + C_{SUB}$	(53) $S + P + C_{SUB}$
(9) $S + P + C_{SUB}$	(24) $S + P + C_{SUB}$	(39) $S + P + O_D$	(54) $S + P + O_D$
(10) $S + P + O_D$	(25) $S + P$	(40) $S + P + C_{SUB}$	(55) $S + P + C_{SUB}$
(11) $S + P + C_{SUB}$	(26) $S + P + O_D$	(41) $S + P + O_D$	(56) $S + P + C_{SUB}$
(12) $S + P + O_D$	(27) $S + P + C_{SUB}$	(42) $S + P + O_D$	(57) $S + P$
(13) $S + P + O_D$	(28) $S + P + O_D$	(43) $S + P + O_D + A$	(58) $S + P + O_D$
(14) $S + P + A$	(29) $S + P + O_D$	(44) $S + P + A$	(59) $S + P + O_D$
(15) $S + P$	(30) $S + P + O_D$	(45) $S + P + O_D$	(60) $S + P + C_{SUB}$

(2)(a) I don't know <u>what the heck they're doing here though</u>.
(Interrogative subordinate clause: *wh*-clause)

(b) I think <u>he's gonna land himself on the floor</u>.
(Declarative subordinate clause: *that*-clause)

(c) He's going to fall <u>because the stool is tilted too much</u>.
(Declarative subordinate clause: *because*-complementiser)

(d) I don't know <u>what that is</u>.
(Interrogative subordinate clause: *wh*-clause)

(e) I guess <u>this is breakfast</u>.
(Declarative subordinate clause: *that*-clause)

(f) I thought <u>it looked like a nose and a mouth</u>.
(Declarative subordinate clause: *that*-clause)

(g) I don't know <u>whether it's a ball or a cake</u>.
(Interrogative subordinate clause: *whether*-clause)

(h) Wonder <u>what my husband is doing</u>.
(Interrogative subordinate clause: *wh*-clause)

   (i) The little boy is gonna fall off the chair <u>if he doesn't be careful</u>.
      (Declarative subordinate clause: *if*-complementiser)

   (j) I don't know <u>if there's anything more there or not</u>.
      (Interrogative subordinate clause: *if*-clause)

   (k) The sink's running over the water on the floor <u>while she's drying the dishes</u>.
      (Declarative subordinate clause: *while*-complementiser)

   (l) He's gonna fall off <u>since it's tipping over</u>.
      (Declarative subordinate clause: *since*-complementiser)

  (m) I don't know <u>why she didn't turn the water off</u>.
      (Interrogative subordinate clause: *wh*-clause)

   (n) I guess <u>there's a breeze blowing</u>.
      (Declarative subordinate clause: *that*-clause)

         (o) He's going to get hurt <u>when the chair tips over</u>.
      (Interrogative subordinate clause: *wh*-clause)

   (p) You know <u>he's the one that's trying to get the cookie jar</u>.
      (Declarative subordinate clause: *that*-clause)
      Note: This sentence also contains a relative clause (*that's trying to get the cookie jar*)

   (q) This boy is almost falling off the chair <u>when he's putting up the picture</u>.
      (Interrogative subordinate clause: *wh*-clause)

   (r) The bench is toppling over <u>as the kid is standing on</u>.
      (Declarative subordinate clause: *as*-complementiser)

   (s) I don't know <u>what you call them</u>.
      (Interrogative subordinate clause: *wh*-clause)

   (t) I don't think <u>she knows what they're up to</u>.
      (Declarative subordinate clause: *that*-clause)
      Note: This sentence also contains an interrogative *wh*-clause (*what they're up to*)

(3) (a) There's a young boy <u>that's getting a cookie jar</u>. (Function: *subject*)

   (b) He's standing on a stool <u>that's tipping over</u>. (Function: *subject*)

   (c) Then there's an angle here <u>that is incomplete</u>. (Function: *subject*)

   (d) A girl laughing at her brother <u>who is taking cookies out of the cookie jar</u>. (Function: *subject*)

   (e) There's a tree <u>which you can see through the half open window</u>. (Function: *direct object*)

   (f) The little girl wants the cookie <u>that the kid is stealing from the cookie jar</u>. (Function: *direct object*)

   (g) I see a little boy climbed up on a stool <u>that is reaching for a cookie out of the cookie jar</u>. (Function: *subject*)

   (h) She is reaching for the cookie <u>that he has in his hand</u>. (Function: *direct object*)

   (i) Mama's drying the dishes as usual for mamas if they don't have a husband <u>that dries them or washes them or whatever</u>. (Function: *subject*)

(j) The little girl pushed over the chair with the boy <u>that was reaching up to get the cookies</u>. (Function: *subject*)

(4) (a) Did I say <u>that the stool was tilted</u>? (*that*-clause)

(b) The ladder <u>that he's standing on</u> is beginning to fall. (relative clause)

(c) I did say <u>that the water's running in the sink and overflowing</u>. (*that*-clause)

(d) She's got the curtain mixed up with the dish <u>that she's drying</u>. (relative clause)

(e) She's too busy to see <u>that the sink is overflowing</u>. (*that*-clause)

(f) There's handles <u>that I can see on two sets of cabinets</u>. (relative clause)

(g) I guess <u>that's a cookie jar</u>. (*that*-clause)

(h) Here's a lady <u>that's washing the dishes</u>. (relative clause)

(i) There's dishes <u>that had been washed</u> and she's drying them. (relative clause)

(j) A window outside <u>that I can see</u>. (relative clause)

(k) I think <u>that he'll lose his cookies</u>. (*that*-clause)

(l) I assume <u>that these are flowers</u>. (*that*-clause)

(m) A stool <u>that's going to project somebody into a fall</u>. (relative clause)

(n) Two cups and a plate <u>that probably are dry</u>. (relative clause)

(o) I assume <u>she's already washed the plate that she's drying</u>. (*that*-clause: *she's already washed the plate that she's drying*; relative clause: *that she's drying*)

(p) I think <u>that's the activity</u>. (*that*-clause)

(q) I did mention <u>that the stool was tilting</u>. (*that*-clause)

(r) Is there a number <u>that there's supposed to be on it</u>? (relative clause)

(s) The mother is washing dishes and forgetting <u>that the water is running</u>. (*that*-clause)

(t) The little boy has a cookie in his hand <u>that he got by climbing the step ladder</u>. (relative clause)

(5) (a) The referent of the object pronoun *him* in the main clause is the understood subject.

(b) The function of the *to*-infinitive clause is modifier of the adjective *busy*.

(c) The referent of the object noun phrase *the water* in the main clause is the understood subject.

(d) The function of the *to*-infinitive clause is object of the lexical verb *forgot*.

(e) The referent of the subject pronoun *she* in the main clause is the understood subject.

(f) The function of the *to*-infinitive clause is adverbial.

(g) The referent of the subject pronoun *she* in the main clause is the understood subject.

(h) The function of the *to*-infinitive clause is modifier of the noun *way*.

(i) The referent of the object pronoun *me* in the main clause is the understood subject.

(j) The function of the *to*-infinitive clause is adverbial.

(k) The referent of the subject pronoun *they* in the main clause is the understood subject.

(l) *Be* is the auxiliary verb in the *to*-infinitive clause.

(m) The referent of the object pronoun *him* in the main clause is the understood subject.

(n) The function of the *to*-infinitive clause is modifier of the adjective *ready*.

(o) The syntactic subject of the *to*-infinitive clause is the object pronoun *me* which is preceded by the complementiser *for*.

(6) (a) The mother's in the kitchen <u>running the water at the sink</u>. (Subject: *the mother*)

(b) A sink that's overrunning with water <u>splashing down onto her shoes</u>. (Subject: *water*)

(c) You see the little boy <u>stealing cookies</u>. (Subject: *the little boy*)

(d) There's a child <u>reaching in a cookie jar</u>. (Subject: *a child*)

(e) The mother is at the sink <u>washing a dish</u>. (Subject: *the mother*)

(f) The window is open <u>looking out onto shrubbery and a path to another house</u>. (Subject: *the window*)

(g) There are three dishes <u>sitting on the sink counter</u>. (Subject: *three dishes*)

(h) There's a girl <u>standing in front of the sink and drying a plate</u>. (Subject: *a girl*)

(i) Mother won't hear him <u>getting up there</u>. (Subject: referent of *him*)

(j) She saw the little boy <u>falling</u>. (Subject: *the little boy*)

(k) There's a boy <u>getting in the cookie jar</u>. (Subject: *a boy*)

(l) The water's spilling for the woman <u>drying the dishes</u>. (Subject: *the woman*)

(m) The first bad thing I see is the water <u>running out of the sink</u>. (Subject: *the water*)

(7) (a) Security personnel should have <u>the fans searched for alcohol</u>. (Function: *object*)

(b) <u>Ravaged by war</u>, the city was largely uninhabitable. (Function: *adverbial*)

(c) They bought the book <u>valued at a thousand pounds</u>. (Function: *modifier of noun*)

(d) The couple wanted <u>the property sold as part of the divorce settlement</u>. (Function: *object*)

(e) The castle <u>built in Roman times</u> was a huge visitor attraction. (Function: *modifier of noun*)

(f) <u>When asked to explain herself</u>, the girl began to cry. (Function: *adverbial*)

(g) They followed the route <u>taken by most pilgrims</u>. (Function: *modifier of noun*)

(h) The devastation <u>strewn before them</u> was testimony to the force of the storm. (Function: *modifier of noun*)

(i) <u>Postponed on account of bad weather</u>, the match was about to take place. (Function: *adverbial*)

(j) The publisher needed <u>the proofs checked within one week</u>. (Function: *object*)

Revision Questions

(1) (a) main clause = *He said that Fred wanted to travel abroad;* subordinate clause 1 = *that Fred wanted to travel abroad;* subordinate clause 2 = *to travel abroad*

(b) main clause = *Mary hoped that John would leave the party early;* subordinate clause = *that John would leave the party early*

(c) main clause = *The suspect claimed that he did not see the woman leave the hotel;* subordinate clause 1 = *that he did not see the woman leave the hotel;* subordinate clause 2 = *the woman leave the hotel*

(d) main clause = *They wished that they had stayed for one more week;* subordinate clause = *that they had stayed for one more week*

(e) main clause = *The council decided that all taxes should be increased;* subordinate clause = *that all taxes should be increased*

(2) False.

(3) (a) non-finite clause (*–ing* participle clause); (b) finite clause; (c) finite clause; (d) non-finite clause (*to*-infinitive clause); (e) non-finite clause (*–ed* participle clause)

(4) (a) subject + predicator

(b) subject + predicator + direct object + adverbial

(c) subject + predicator + direct object

(d) subject + predicator + adverbial

(e) subject + predicator + indirect object

(f) subject + predicator + direct object + complement

(g) subject + predicator + indirect object + direct object

(h) subject + predicator + complement

(5) (a) concessive; (b) reason; (c) temporal; (d) result; (e) conditional; (f) comparative

(6) (a) S+P; (b) S+P+A; (c) S+P+DO; (d) S+P+IO+DO; (e) S+P+C; (f) S+P+DO+A; (g) S+P+DO+C; (h) S+P+IO; (i) S+P+DO; (j) S+P+IO+DO; (k) S+P; (l) S+P+A; (m) S+P+C; (n) S+P+DO+C; (o) S+P+DO+A; (p) S+P+IO

(7) Clause subordinate to clause in italics: *that the match was postponed*
Clause superordinate to clause in italics: *They thought that she said that the match was postponed*

(8) (a) non-finite clause (*to*-infinitive clause); (b) non-finite clause (*–ing* participle clause); (c) finite clause; (d) finite clause; (e) non-finite clause (*–ed* participle clause); (f) finite clause; (g) finite clause; (h) non-finite clause (bare infinitive clause); (i) non-finite clause (*to*-infinitive clause); (j) finite clause; (k) finite clause; (l) non-finite clause (*to*-infinitive clause); (m) non-finite clause (*–ed* participle clause)

(9) (a) interrogative subordinate clause = *if the flight would depart on time*

(b) declarative subordinate clause = *she would return early*
(c) interrogative subordinate clause = *if the full accounts had been submitted*
(d) declarative subordinate clause = *that the situation was not going to improve*
(e) interrogative subordinate clause = *whether the road would be impassable*

(10) (a) *that Bill is a successful business man* = subject
(b) *that he left without warning* = subject complement
(c) *[that] his ideas were confused and illogical* = direct object
(d) *that Mark had forged the signature* = subject complement
(e) *[that] the man posed a risk to public safety* = direct object
(f) *that the company is going into administration* = subject

(11) (a) *who lives across the road* = restrictive relative clause
(b) *which is in need of refurbishment* = non-restrictive relative clause
(c) *who disturbed the burglar* = restrictive relative clause
(d) *which fell at the third fence* = restrictive relative clause
(e) *who is a keen cyclist and swimmer* = non-restrictive relative clause

(12) (a) *to travel to Paris next year* = object
(b) *to catch the bus* = adverbial
(c) *to retire in good health* = subject
(d) *to make the delivery before midday* = object
(e) *to raise funds* = adverbial
(f) *to lose a loved one* = subject

Chapter 7

Exercise 7.1

(a) Structure: *declarative*; Function: *statement*
(b) Structure: *declarative*; Function: *question*
(c) Structure: *interrogative*; Function: *question*
(d) Structure: *interrogative*; Function: *directive (request)*
(e) Structure: *interrogative*; Function: *question*
(f) Structure: *declarative*; Function: *directive (permission)*
(g) Structure: *declarative*; Function: *statement*
(h) Structure: *interrogative*; Function: *question*
(i) Structure: *interrogative*; Function: *directive (request)*
(j) Structure: *declarative*; Function: *statement*
(k) Structure: *declarative*; Function: *question*
(l) Structure: *interrogative*; Function: *question*
(m) Structure: *declarative*; Function: *directive (permission)*
(n) Structure: *declarative*; Function: *statement*
(o) Structure: *interrogative*; Function: *directive (request)*
(p) Structure: *declarative*; Function: *directive (permission)*
(q) Structure: *interrogative*; Function: *question*

(r) Structure: *interrogative*; Function: *directive (request)*
(s) Structure: *declarative*; Function: *statement*
(t) Structure: *interrogative*; Function: *directive (request)*

Exercise 7.2

(a) reverse
(b) reverse
(c) reverse
(d) reverse
(e) reverse
(f) reverse
(g) reverse
(h) constant
(i) reverse
(j) reverse
(k) reverse
(l) reverse
(m) reverse
(n) constant
(o) reverse

Exercise 7.3

(a) Omission of auxiliary verb *did*
(b) Omission of auxiliary verb *are*
(c) Omission of inflectional suffix *-s*
(d) Incorrect lexical verb (*has* instead of *have*)
(e) Omission of auxiliary verb *have*
(f) Incorrect lexical verb (*is* instead of *are*)
(g) Incorrect past participle (*aten* instead of *eaten*)
(h) Incorrect lexical verb (*went* instead of *go*); *one else* could be replaced by *other one*
(i) Omission of auxiliary verb *have*
(j) Incorrect lexical verb (*is* instead of *are*); personal pronoun *you* should be replaced by possessive determiner *your*
(k) Incorrect lexical verb (*got* instead of *get*)
(l) Omission of auxiliary verb *did*
(m) Unnecessary auxiliary verb (<u>did</u> *move*) instead of main verb alone (*moved*)
(n) Incorrect auxiliary verb (*has* instead of *have*)
(o) Omission of auxiliary verb *have*; omission of articles in *a pen* and *the car*
(p) Omission of auxiliary verb *are*
(q) Incorrect auxiliary verb (*was* instead of *have*)

(r) Incorrect auxiliary verb (*is* instead of *has*)
(s) Omission of auxiliary verb *is*
(t) Incorrect lexical verb (*is* instead of *are*); omission of article in *the two ladies*
(u) Incorrect auxiliary verb (*is* instead of *are*)
(v) Incorrect lexical verb (*lost* instead of *lose*)
(w) Omission of auxiliary verb *are*
(x) Omission of auxiliary verb *did*; incorrect lexical verb (*missed* instead of *miss*)
(y) Omission of subject *you*
(z) Omission of lexical verb *is*

Exercise 7.4

(a) Count, daddy
(b) Don't sit next to me!
(c) And then I say "get out wee man".
(d) directive
(e) Move out of the way because my horsey will go.

End-of-Chapter Questions

(1) (a) Subject NP = demonstrative pronoun; Predicate VP = lexical verb
  (b) Subject NP = common noun; Predicate VP = auxiliary and lexical verb
  (c) Subject NP = proper noun; Predicate VP = lexical verb
  (d) Subject NP = dummy subject; Predicate VP = lexical verb
  (e) Subject NP = personal pronoun; Predicate VP = auxiliary and lexical verb
  (f) Subject NP = demonstrative pronoun; Predicate VP = lexical verb
  (g) Subject NP = dummy subject; Predicate VP = lexical verb
  (h) Subject NP = common noun; Predicate VP = auxiliary and lexical verb
  (i) Subject NP = personal pronoun; Predicate VP = lexical verb
  (j) Subject NP = proper noun; Predicate VP = auxiliary and lexical verb
(2) (a) Choose from:
    And a young girl seems to whisper to him about making noise, <u>doesn't it</u>?
    It has to be his sister, <u>doesn't it</u>?
    It looks like somebody's laying out in the grass, <u>doesn't it</u>?
  (b) *He survived anyway,* <u>huh</u>*?*
  (c) *And* <u>a young girl</u> *seems to whisper to him about making noise, doesn't* <u>it</u>*?*
  (d) *The string is not on this,* <u>is it</u>*?*
  (e) *[She's a] kind of homely girl, isn't she?*
(3) (a) Choose from: *What that? Where all other ones?*
  (b) Choose from: *What is these? Where is my pyjamas? Where is our shadows?*
  (c) Omission of auxiliary verb *are* and preposition *to*
  (d) Choose from: *Where is it come from? Where has my two ladies gone? Where has the other ones gone? What is all those called?*

(e) Omission of passive auxiliary verb *is*

(f) *What you been doing?*

(g) Choose from: *What mummy said? What you had?*

(h) *What you look at?*

(i) *Where going?*

(j) *Where they were gone?*

(k) Choose from: *Who did do that? Who did take this lid off?*

(l) Choose from: *What she want me for? Where you put your glasses? Why you put that on here?*

(m) *Why have you got?*

(n) Use of singular auxiliary verb (*has*) instead of plural auxiliary verb (*have*)

(o) *Where is daddy going to get?*

(p) *Why did I lost it?*

(q) *Why hasn't she got her clothes on?*

(r) *Where is the other ones?*

(s) *Why is Sally isn't there?*

(t) A single lexical verb (*was*) can be used in place of the auxiliary verb and main verb *did ... be*.

(4) (a) Don't tickle me.

(b) vocative

(c) directive

(d) <u>Just</u> wait there.

(e) This imperative contains a verb in base form (*keep*) followed by a direct object pronoun (*it*) and a noun phrase which has an object complement function (*a little rainbow*).

(5) (a) exclamative

(b) *wh*-interrogative

(c) *yes–no* interrogative

(d) declarative

(e) exclamative

(f) *yes–no* interrogative

(g) exclamative (subject and predicate omitted)

(h) declarative

(i) exclamative

(j) declarative

Revision Questions

(1) (a) multiple; (b) simple; (c) simple; (d) simple; (e) multiple

(2) (a) complex; (b) compound; (c) compound-complex; (d) complex; (e) compound

(3) (a) grammatical form = interrogative; function = question; function corresponds to form

(b) grammatical form = declarative; function = question; function does not correspond to form

(c) grammatical form = declarative; function = statement; function corresponds to form

(d) grammatical form = interrogative; function = request (directive); function does not correspond to form

(e) grammatical form = imperative; function = command (directive); function corresponds to form

(f) grammatical form = interrogative; function = request (directive); function does not correspond to form

(4) (a) simple; (b) compound; (c) compound; (d) complex; (e) simple; (f) compound-complex; (g) simple; (h) complex; (i) compound-complex; (j) compound; (k) complex; (l) compound-complex

(5) *The robbers sped through the streets:*
Grammatical form = declarative; function = statement; function corresponds to form
Several police vehicles were in pursuit:
Grammatical form = declarative; function = statement; function corresponds to form
A car emerged suddenly from the right:
Grammatical form = declarative; function = statement; function corresponds to form
It stalled in front of the police cars:
Grammatical form = declarative; function = statement; function corresponds to form
Move your car!:
Grammatical form = imperative; function = command; function corresponds to form
Hurry it up, you idiot!:
Grammatical form = imperative; function = command; function corresponds to form
Can you help me start it?:
Grammatical form = interrogative; function = request; function does not correspond to form
Do you need some help?:
Grammatical form = interrogative; function = question; function corresponds to form
I am a trained mechanic:
Grammatical form = declarative; function = statement; function corresponds to form
Help me, please!:
Grammatical form = imperative; function = imploration; function does not correspond to form

I can't seem to start it up again:
Grammatical form = declarative; function = statement; function corresponds to form
Push it to the side of the road:
Grammatical form = imperative; function = command; function corresponds to form
I'll sort it out for you:
Grammatical form = declarative; function = promise; function does not correspond to form

(6) (a) information-seeking; (b) permission-seeking; (c) permission-seeking; (d) information-seeking; (e) information-seeking

(7) True.

(8) **(a)** grammatical form = imperative; function = command; function corresponds to form

(b) grammatical form = declarative; function = question; function does not correspond to form

(c) grammatical form = interrogative; function = question; function corresponds to form

(d) grammatical form = imperative; function = imploration; function does not correspond to form

(e) grammatical form = interrogative; function = request; function does not correspond to form

(f) grammatical form = declarative; function = statement; function corresponds to form

(9) (a) prediction; (b) warning; (c) promise; (d) threat; (e) request

(10) (a) true; (b) false; (c) true; (d) false; (e) true

(11) In Standard English, the pronoun *you* occurs in pre-verbal position (e.g. *You be quiet!*). In Belfast English, the pronoun *you* occurs in post-verbal position (e.g. *Be you quiet!*).

(12) Declarative sentence: *You are a complete bloody idiot!*
Interrogative sentence: *Can you piss off!*

APPENDICES
Appendix 1

Data set 1: progressive –*ing*
I'm just put them in a little bit okay? (2;09)
I'm sterilise (2;10)
Keep fallinged over (2;10)
I'm sit on the floor (2;10)
Because I'm drink daddy's drink (2;11)
Shall I be tickle you? (3;00)
You are break it (3;00)
Shall I colouring in the lines for you? (3;02)
Your flowers are deading (3;03)

Data set 2: past tense, irregular
It camed off (2;09)
She throwed it (2;10)
Her own toys what we buyed (2;10)
Little girl falled off (2;10)
I nearly broked yours (2;10)
I maked the pretty plant (2;10)
I catched it (2;11)
I runned away (2;11)
He blowed them up (3;00)
But I taked that off (3;00)
I didn't get it off when I shaked it (3;00)
I winned that jigsaw (3;02)
She sawed it (3;02)
I taked it off (3;02)
You holded something (3;03)

Data set 3: past participle, irregular
Have you broke Sellotape? (2;09)
He's fallened over (2;10)
Because it's eatened all up (2;10)
Now she's aten it all up (3;00)

What have you forgot? (3;01)
I think daddy has hide them (3;02)
She's ate teddy all up now (3;02)

Data set 4: third-person singular –*s*
And Amy and Lara sits at the back (2;09)
I think he look like a giraffe! (2;10)
I think she want to lie on her mat (2;10)
Can you makes her talk? (2;10)
Off you go says the mummies (3;00)
Put it in the corner [for] when he come home (3;00)
She's want to toddle round (3;02)

Appendix 2

Lara's utterances
 (1) She will break it.
 (2) You hurt me.
 (3) Amy's not sharing it.
 (4) She won't share anything with me.
 (5) You can have those bricks.
 (6) I got it in my drill.
 (7) They haven't got any stairs.
 (8) I need another gate for that bit.
 (9) It's the helicopter.
(10) I will mend it.
(11) It's Fireman Sam.
(12) I'm getting three.
(13) I wanted you.
(14) I'm getting on the horsie.
(15) Monkey is swinging.
(16) My donkey's there.
(17) I throwed him.
(18) I did a big jump down.
(19) Donkey go there.
(20) She looks a bit poorly.
(21) I want that.
(22) I'm your farmer.
(23) They have a rest.
(24) This is mine.
(25) It's hiding.
(26) I'm closing my eyes.
(27) That's my candle.
(28) I see it.
(29) I'm making a gun.
(30) I need another gate.
(31) I'm doing this.

(32) He's woofing.
(33) These are the chairs.
(34) I put mine down.
(35) I want a skipping rope.
(36) I found one.
(37) This is the paddling pool.
(38) This is our bed.
(39) You hoovering my house.
(40) It's very noisy.
(41) I don't want that.
(42) You holded something.
(43) I can put it there.
(44) We'll hoover together.
(45) I'm cleaning you.
(46) This is bendy.
(47) We got a dice.
(48) You're the mummy.
(49) You can have that.
(50) That's my hoover.
(51) They don't like you.
(52) I've got some animals in that one.
(53) That's a lady.
(54) I want a red one.
(55) This is my bag.
(56) It's goblin.
(57) She forgot.
(58) I'm making one.
(59) I play this.
(60) This is my donkey.

Appendix 3

Lara at 2;03 years
This can't fit on.
I put them in the fridge.
They are too big.
It is coming out!
Grandma's bringing a bigger one.
I got my slippers.
You got one there.

Lara at 3;03 years
I'm a bird.
I will put the ends together.
You're not doing yours quickly.
Amy won't let me play.
He wants to go on here.
We'll hoover together.
I didn't tell you I didn't like you.
I told her.
I want a skipping rope.
This is the paddling pool.
That hit you.
I don't want you to tidy up.
This is not a helicopter.
We've got to wash it then.
That's my hoover.
I put mine down.
It's not snap.
You're allowed to do that.
I got lots of cards now.
You have only got a few.
I'm just having a look for more books.
There's a badge here.
You are taking the things off me.

That's for you.
I'm getting on the horsey.
It's very noisy this hoover.
It was a bit of my hoover.
I can't see it anywhere.
I'm going to share them out.
I'm not going to have any.
You holded something.
You hoovering my house.
I have these cards.
You get a hoover out of your alcove.
I don't want her to get my field.
You can't go on mummy's knee.
This is our bed.
I want to sit next to you.
I'm sitting here too.
I said it first.
I'm holding on very tight.
I want to put them away.
I'm hiding.
I'm playing properly.
I haven't had any go.
I'll let her have that.
Amy hasn't got a duvet.
You can come in my bed.
She can sleep on that one.

Appendix 4

Lara at 2;07 years
What you got?
What they doing?
What that called?
What is all those called?
What that?
What you gonna buy next time?
What is these?
Mummy, what you doing?
What you got under your robe?
What you got on today?
What you doing with them?
Where is pricked her finger over there?
Where is pricked her finger?
Where all other ones?
Where has the other ones gone?
Where is my pyjamas?
Where has my two ladies gone?
Where is our shadows?
Where is it come from?
Why we going Sainsburys?

Lara at 2;10 years
What you doing?
What you done?
What you taking?
What you got?
What you going to do?
What mummy said?
What is these?
What you making?
What you been doing?
What you had?

What we gonna have to do?
What you looking at?
What you look at?
Where has Lara and Mummy gone?
Where is my tights?
Where is my biscuits?
Where they gone?
Where we going?
Where going?
Where my yoghurt?
Where has your nuts gone?
Where is the bin men?
Where has the wiggly worms gone?
Where they were gone?
Where you gone then?
Why will it mucked up with my hands?

Lara at 3;00 years
What she want me for?
What you looking at?
What you watching?
What you doing?
Where are you gone?
Where has Grandad and Amy gone?
Where has your wellies gone?
Where daddy playing?
Where has the cows gone?
Where has the wheels gone?
Where has you got a plaster?
Where has Mummy and Daddy gone?
Where has the other people gone?
Where is Abi's bobble things?
Where is your keys?
Where you put your glasses?
Where is daddy going to get?
Why are you got a snotty nose?
Why have you got?
Why you put that on here?
Who did do that?
Who did take this lid off?

Lara at 3;03 years
What you doing?
Where is the other ones?

Where is it gone?
Where daddy gone?
Why has she not got her clothes on?
Why did he be on his own?
Why you going downstairs like that?
Why did you already get dressed?
Why you got to keep it?
Why did I lost it?
Why is Sally isn't there?

Appendix 5

The following echo sentences were produced by Lara's parents during interactions with her in the family home.

Lara's father:

What:	He's what?	*Whose:*	On the way to whose house?
	His what?		For whose bedroom?
	Baby what?		
	You're what?	*Who:*	Where's who gone?
	It's got what in it?		Next time who comes?
	Daddy what?		
	Daddy's what?		
	Amy's what?		

Lara's mother:

What:	Forgot what?	You what?	She what?	Do what?	Need what?
	See what?	Down what?	Baby what?	Get what?	One what?
	No what?	That what?	Abi what?	Humpty what?	
	Mummy what?	Everybody what?			
	Bit of what?	She's what?	Bye bye what?	That's what?	
	You get what?	They're what?	Mummy's what?	Is daddy what?	
	It's what?	Daddy did what?	That Floyd what?	Two three what?	
	Mummy hair what?	Postman Pat what?			
	Now come on what?	You're gonna play what?		You didn't get the what?	
	You haven't had what?	We're not playing what?		Mummy to play what?	
	Lara what Postman Pat book?				
Who:	Mummy's being nasty to who?		Mummy feed who?		
	Let who do it?		Where's who gone?		

GLOSSARY

absolute: The base form of an adjective or adverb on a scale of comparison. For regular adjectives and adverbs, this is the form which takes the suffixes *–er* and *–est* to form the comparative and superlative (e.g. *taller – tallest; quicklier – quickliest*).

abstract noun: A noun which denotes an intangible entity. Abstract nouns may refer to emotions (*happiness*), concepts or ideas (*Marxism*), values (*honesty*) and virtues (*patience*).

accusative case The case of the direct object of the sentence. In Latin, words change their endings according to their case. In the sentence *servus sedet* (the slave is sitting) the noun 'servus' is the subject of the sentence and is in the nominative case, hence the *–us* ending. However, in the sentence *dominus servum salūtat* (the master is greeting the slave) the noun 'servum' is the direct object of the sentence and is in the accusative case, hence the *–um* ending.

acronym-formation: In morphology, a non-morphemic word-formation process in which a word is generated from the initial letters of words in a compound or phrase. It is possible to pronounce acronyms as a word (e.g. UNESCO). Where the letters are spelled out (e.g. BBC, WTO), it is called an initialism.

active sentence: See **voice**.

adjective: An open word class that expresses an attribute. Adjectives are attributive when they appear in front of a noun (e.g. *The blue sweater was on the shelf*) and are predicative when they appear after a verb (e.g. *The sweater was blue*).

adjective phrase: A phrase which contains a head adjective and its modifiers. Adverb phrases can be pre-modifiers in an adjective phrase (<u>*really*</u> *unhappy*). Post-modifiers in adjective phrases include clauses (*keen* <u>*to leave early*</u>), adverbs (*strong* <u>*enough*</u>), and prepositional phrases (*anxious* <u>*about her problem*</u>). Adjective phrases can be a modifier in another type of phrase. For example, the adjective phrase *really unhappy* is a pre-modifier in the noun phrase *really unhappy woman*.

adjunct: A type of adverbial. Adjuncts are optional and provide information relating to time, manner, degree, instrument, location and attitude. For example, the underlined words in the following sentence form an adjunct which provides information about the instrument that was used, e.g. *They chopped the tree* <u>*with an axe*</u>.

adverb: An open word class that can modify adjectives (e.g. <u>*very*</u> *pretty*), adverbs (e.g. <u>*rather*</u> *quickly*) and verbs (*walked* <u>*quickly*</u>). Many adverbs are formed by adding the suffix *–ly* to an adjective (e.g. *loud* → *loudly*). However, there are many adverbs in English where this pattern does not apply (e.g. *soon, very*).

adverb phrase: A phrase which contains a head adverb and its modifiers. An adverb phrase can be a pre-modifier in an adverb phrase (_so very_ quickly). Only a prepositional phrase can be a post-modifier in an adverb phrase (_effortlessly_ _for an amateur_). An adverb phrase can be a pre-modifier in an adjective phrase (_really very_ sick) and a post-modifier in a verb phrase (_paints_ _so exquisitely_).

adverbial: Part of the predicate which can be removed without affecting the grammaticality of a sentence. The underlined adverbial in the following sentence can be removed without resulting in an ungrammatical sentence, e.g. _Liz travelled to the United States_ _by plane_. Adverbials answer questions such as _When?_ and _How?_ (in this case, by plane), and can assume different positions in the sentence. The sentence above could read, for example, _Liz travelled_ _by plane_ _to the United States_.

adverbial complement: An adverbial complement conveys the same information as an adverb and must be present for a sentence to be complete. For example, in the sentence _Jack was on the train_, the adverbial complement _on the train_ tells us where Jack was and cannot be omitted without resulting in an ungrammatical sentence *_Jack was_.

adverbial subordinate clause: A type of declarative subordinate clause that is introduced by complementisers like _because, since, although_ and _before_. These clauses provide information relating to the time, place, and manner (among other meanings) of an action or event. For example, in the sentence _John left the theatre early_ _because the play was terrible_, the adverbial subordinate clause presents the reason why John left the theatre early.

affix: A general term to capture morphemes which are added to the front of a base (so-called prefixes like _disagree_) and morphemes which are added to the end of a base (so-called suffixes like _agreement_). Affixation includes prefixation and suffixation.

African American Vernacular English (AAVE): A variety of American English which is spoken by urban working-class and middle-class African Americans. AAVE is also referred to as African American English, Black English, and Ebonics.

agent: A semantic or participant role which describes the initiator of some action. An agent is typically capable of acting with volition (e.g. _The boy_ broke the window).

agrammatic aphasia: A form of non-fluent aphasia in which the speaker retains content words but omits function words and inflectional morphemes from his or her speech. The speaker's verbal output has the appearance of a telegram, e.g. 'Man ... walk ... dog' for _The man is walking the dog_. See also **aphasia**.

agrammatism: A feature of non-fluent aphasia in which the speaker retains content words but omits function words and inflectional morphemes from his or her speech. The retention of content words means that language can still be meaningful even though it is structurally limited. See also **agrammatic aphasia**.

allomorph: A variant of a morpheme, the precise form of which is determined by the sound at the end of the base to which a suffix is added. In English, there are different allomorphs of the plural suffix _–s_ and the past tense suffix _–ed_.

alternative question: A type of interrogative in which a hearer is presented with two or more possible answers (e.g. _Do you live in Chicago or New York?_). Alternative questions contain a presupposition that at least one of the answers is true. See also **interrogative**.

alveolar consonant: Any consonant speech sound the articulation of which involves approximation or closure of the tongue tip (an active articulator) with the alveolar ridge (a passive articulator).

Alzheimer's dementia: Alzheimer's dementia is the most common type of dementia. It is caused by Alzheimer's disease, a neurodegenerative condition. The cognitive deterioration in Alzheimer's disease has implications for an individual's language skills.

American English: A variety of the English language that is used in the United States of America. The pronunciation, lexemes and grammatical constructions of American English distinguish it from British English and other national varieties. There are many different dialects of American English.

anaphoric reference: A form of cohesion in which there is reference to a preceding textual unit (known as the antedecent). In the following example, the pronoun *it* in the second sentence refers to the noun phrase *a red dress* in the first sentence: *Mary bought a red dress. It was very expensive.*

antecedent: A noun phrase which may be referred to by a personal pronoun (*Sally saw the red dress and liked it*), a reflexive pronoun (*Brian washed himself*), or a relative pronoun (*the vase which you dropped*) which appear after it in the sentence.

aphasia: An acquired language disorder in which the expression and/or reception of language (spoken, written and signed) is compromised. Aphasia can be broadly classified as fluent and non-fluent types. It is most commonly caused by a cerebrovascular accident or stroke.

article: A closed word class that consists of the definite article (e.g. *the man*) and the indefinite article (e.g. *a house; an operation*). Articles are a type of determiner. Use of the definite article implies that a hearer knows who or what the speaker is referring to (e.g. *The tall building collapsed*). The indefinite article introduces a person or thing which is not known to the hearer (e.g. *A woman entered the room*).

Asian English: A variety of the English language which is used in the Indian subcontinent where it co-exists alongside thousands of local languages. The English language arrived in South Asia as a result of colonisation.

aspect: The way in which an action denoted by a verb should be viewed with respect to time. There are two aspects in English, so-called perfect aspect and progressive aspect: present perfect (e.g. *They have been on holiday*), past perfect (e.g. *She had been on holiday*), present progressive (e.g. *John is repairing the fence*), past progressive (e.g. *Jill was driving at the time of the accident*), and present perfect progressive (e.g. *They have been eating breakfast*).

attributive adjective: An adjective that comes before the noun to which it relates, e.g. *ancient* church. See also **predicative adjective**.

Australian English: A variety of the English language that is used throughout Australia. The pronunciation, lexemes and grammatical constructions of Australian English distinguish it from British English and other national varieties. There are many different dialects of Australian English.

auxiliary verb: A verb which must occur with a main or lexical verb (e.g. *John was crossing the road*). Modal auxiliary verbs can express a range of meanings including permission (e.g. *You can travel with us*), obligation (e.g. *Sally must attend the lecture*) and ability (e.g. *She can swim ten miles*). See also **lexical verb**.

back-formation: A word-formation process in which forms like *editor* are treated as bases (*edit*) to which a suffix (*–or*) is added. The apparent base is then coined as a verb (*to edit*).

bare infinitive: The infinitive part of the verb less the infinitival marker *to* (*Help me put the chairs away*). The bare infinitive should be distinguished from the *to*-infinitive (*Help me to put the chairs away*).

base form: The form of the verb to which inflections are added. For example, *walk* is a base form to which a range of inflectional suffixes may be added: *walks; walked; walking*.

Belfast English: A dialect of English spoken in Belfast. The pronunciation, lexemes and grammatical constructions of Belfast English distinguish it from Standard English and from other dialects of Northern Irish English.

blending: A non-morphemic word-formation process in which words are merged based on their sound structure. The source words can contribute roughly equally to the blend (e.g. *fantastic* + *fabulous* → *fantabulous*) or one source word can appear in its entirety in the blend (e.g. *Britain* + *exit* → *Brexit*).

bound morpheme: A morpheme which cannot exist independently in language and must be attached to a lexical or free morpheme. Bound morphemes include prefixes such as *un–*, *mis–* and *dis–*, and inflectional and derivational suffixes like *–ness*, *–ed* and *–ing*.

cardinal numeral: A sub-class of numerals which includes *one, thirty* and *a hundred*. Cardinal numerals can be determiners in a noun phrase, e.g. *five flowers*.

Caribbean English: The varieties of English spoken in the West Indies.

case: In some languages morphological inflections indicate the grammatical function (subject, object, etc.) of the word in the sentence. For example, in German the definite article indicates if a noun is the nominative (subject) case (e.g. *Der Hund sitzt neben der Katze*: The dog sits near the cat) or the accusative (direct object) case (e.g. *Der Junge fütterte den Hund*: The boy fed the dog).

central determiner: Four types of determiner which come after pre-determiners in a noun phrase but before post-determiners in a noun phrase. The most common central determiners are the definite article and indefinite article (e.g. *the salary; a career*). Possessives and demonstratives are also central determiners (e.g. *my aspiration; those tools*).

child language acquisition: Also known as first language acquisition. This is the study of the stages that young children pass through on their way to acquiring the phonology, morphology, syntax, semantics and pragmatics of their native language. Different theoretical approaches to language acquisition (e.g. nativism, social interactionism) are also studied in child language acquisition.

Chomsky, Noam: An American academic, born in 1928, who is best known for his contribution to linguistics (transformational grammar) but also for his political views. Chomsky has been a faculty member of the Massachusetts Institute of Technology (MIT) since 1955.

clause: See **comparative clause; infinitive clause; subordinate clause**.

cleft sentence: A type of sentence in which a single message is divided (cleft) into two clauses. There are two types of cleft sentence: *Wh*-cleft (or pseudo-cleft) sentences

(*What I need is a break*) and *It*-cleft sentences (*It was the teenager who vandalised the bus shelter*). Cleft sentences allow speakers to give focus to new information in a sentence. In the sentence *What I need is a break*, that the speaker needs something is old information while what he needs, a break, is new information. In the sentence *It was the teenager who vandalised the bus shelter*, that the bus shelter was vandalised is old information while the individual who committed this act, the teenager, is new information.

clipping: A non-morphemic word-formation process in which a word is shortened through the elision of material at the front of the word (e.g. *telephone* → *phone*), at the end of the word (e.g. *gasoline* → *gas*), or at the front and the end of the word (e.g. *influenza* → *flu*).

collective noun: A noun which denotes a group of people or animals (e.g. *staff*, *herd*). Collective nouns have both singular and plural forms (*herd* – *herds*). They can be used with plural verbs even in the singular form (*The staff are on holiday next week*).

colloquial speech: Spoken language which is used in informal conversational contexts. Colloquial speech contains slang and grammatical and lexical forms which are less likely to occur in formal contexts.

common noun: A noun which is a general name for people (*woman*), places (*town*) and things (*chair*). Common nouns can form a phrase with the definite article (*the woman*). See also **proper noun**.

communicative intention: A mental state which has particular significance in utterance interpretation. A hearer cannot be said to have understood a speaker's utterance unless he is able to establish the communicative intention which motivated the speaker to produce it.

comparative: An adjective or an adverb that is on the mid-point of a scale of comparison. For most adjectives in English, the comparative is formed by adding the suffix –*er* to the absolute form of the adjective (e.g. *Paul is taller than John*), although irregular comparative forms are quite common (e.g. *Sue is better than Mary*). In English, the suffix –*(i)er* (e.g. *Paula runs faster than Fred*) or the word 'more' is used to form the comparative of adverbs (e.g. *He drives more carelessly out of town*).

comparative clause: A clause that is introduced by a comparative adjective or adverb. In the sentence *She is more attractive than you think*, the underlined clause is preceded by a comparative adjective (*more attractive*). In the sentence *Jack drives more slowly than you might imagine*, the underlined clause is preceded by a comparative adverb (*more slowly*).

complement: In a phrase, the complement completes the meaning expressed by the head. In the noun phrase *man with a walking stick*, the prepositional phrase completes the meaning of the head noun *man* and is the complement of the phrase. The term 'complement' can also be used to describe the function of a phrase within a clause. In the sentence *They elected Trump president*, the noun phrase *president* is an object complement because it refers to the same person as the direct object *Trump*. See also **object complement; subject complement**.

complementiser: Another term for subordinating conjunctions such as *although, since* and *after*. Complementisers introduce declarative and interrogative subordinate clauses such as *that*-clauses (*I believe that they will visit*) and *if/whether*-clauses (*She asked if they had left*).

complex intransitive verb: See **intensive verb**.

complex preposition: See **preposition**.

complex transitive verb: A verb which requires a direct object and an object complement. The object complement refers to the same thing as the direct object, e.g. *The teacher called <u>the class lazy</u>*.

compound noun: See **compounding**.

compounding: When two or more roots come together, a compound is formed. Compounds can contain bound morphemes (e.g. *democrat*) or free morphemes (e.g. *greenhouse*), and may be written as a single word (e.g. *birthday*), as two separate words (e.g. *black economy*) or as a hyphenated word (e.g. *pearl-grey*).

concrete noun: A noun which denotes a tangible entity such as a person (*boy*), object (*book*), event (*party*), or place (*town*).

confrontation naming: The presentation of an object or picture of an object which a subject is required to name. Confrontation naming is used to assess lexical retrieval.

conjunction: A closed word class that includes coordinating conjunctions (e.g. *and, or, but*) and subordinating conjunctions (e.g. *because, since*). Coordinating conjunctions can link nouns (e.g. *cheese <u>and</u> wine*), adjectives (e.g. *black <u>or</u> white*), adverbs (e.g. *quickly <u>and</u> easily*), and clauses (e.g. *Bill likes French wine <u>but</u> Sally likes German wine*), while subordinating conjunctions can only link clauses (e.g. *It was raining <u>so</u> we took a taxi to the restaurant*).

constant polarity: A grammatical feature of tag questions in which a positive tag question is used with a positive declarative (e.g. *You wash the dishes, will you?*). Constant polarity leads to an ungrammatical sentence when the declarative and tag question are both negative (e.g. **You didn't clean it, didn't you?*). See also **tag question**.

content word: Words that convey most meaning in a sentence. Content words belong to open classes like noun (e.g. *table, holiday*), verb (e.g. *play, run*), adjective (e.g. *tasty, solid*) and adverb (e.g. *fast, hastily*). See also **function word**.

context: Any aspect of a language user's knowledge, physical environment and social relationships to others may shape the production and interpretation of utterances and form part of their context. These aspects include physical context (e.g. setting of a conversation), social context (e.g. social standing of speaker and hearer), epistemic context (background knowledge of speaker and hearer), and linguistic context (e.g. preceding utterances in a conversation).

conversion: A word-formation process which changes the word class of a lexeme but does not add morphological material. Conversion is a source of many verbs in language, e.g. *jet → to jet*.

cooperative principle: A principle proposed by H. P. Grice to capture certain rational expectations between participants in verbal and non-verbal exchanges. This principle is the basis upon which speakers and hearers can derive implied meanings from utterances in conversation.

coordinating conjunction: The conjoining of two or more elements of equal syntactic status using the coordinating conjunctions *and, or* and *but*. The elements so conjoined may be nouns (e.g. *John likes wine <u>and</u> cheese*), adjectives (e.g. *The dog is* wet _and_ dirty), adverbs (e.g. _They worked quickly _and_ competently_) or clauses (e.g. _Fran likes Spain _but_ Paul likes France_).

coordination: See **coordinating conjunction**.

coordinative compound: This is a compound which contains two heads rather than a head and a modifier (e.g. _teacher – researcher_). The heads contribute equally to the meaning of the compound.

copular complement: See **copular verb**.

copular verb: A group of verbs which do not take a direct object or an indirect object. Instead, these verbs take a copular complement. The verb _be_ is a copular verb. In each of these sentences, a form of _be_ is followed by a copular complement: _She is _angry_; He is _a doctor_; They are _in a bad situation__. As these examples illustrate, a copular complement can be an adjective phrase, a noun phrase or a prepositional phrase. The following verbs are also copular verbs: _She _became_ enraged; They _seem_ happy; It _felt_ strange; It _sounds_ fantastic_.

correlative conjunction: A two-part conjunction that joins sentence elements of equal syntactic status. For example, _not only ... but also_ joins two nouns in the sentence _Bill is _not only_ a lawyer _but also_ a lecturer_.

count noun: Any noun which can have a plural form and can be preceded by the indefinite article _a_ or _an_, e.g. a table/tables; an eye/eyes. See also **non-count noun**.

declarative: A type of sentence in which a subject noun phrase precedes the predicate verb phrase, e.g. _The boy is running_ (the boy = subject; is running = predicate).

declarative subordinate clause: A type of finite subordinate clause. There are two types of declarative subordinate clause: _that_-clauses (_We hoped _that they would return_) and adverbial subordinate clauses (_She chose red wine _although she really wanted white wine__).

definite article: See **article**.

demonstrative determiner: The use of a singular demonstrative (_this/that_) or a plural demonstrative (_these/those_) as a determiner in a noun phrase (_this kite, those children_). _This kite_ indicates a kite close to the speaker. The noun phrase _those children_ indicates children at a distance from the speaker.

demonstrative pronoun: The words _this/that_ and _these/those_ can also stand alone as pronouns in a sentence, e.g. _This_ is tastier than _that_. Some uses of demonstrative pronouns refer to non-linguistic context (e.g. _This_ is bright red where _this_ may refer to a dress). Other uses can refer to preceding text (e.g. _That was a clear explanation_) and are known as anaphoric pronouns.

derivational morphology: A type of morphemic word-formation which includes prefixation and suffixation. Whereas inflectional morphemes generate word-forms (e.g. _walks, walking, walked_), derivational morphemes generate new words (e.g. _discover, discovery, discoverable_).

descriptive approach: An approach to the study of grammar which characterises the actual use of grammar. Descriptive approaches to grammar and language generally are consistent with the modern study of linguistics. See also **prescriptive approach**.

descriptive grammarian: A grammarian who pursues a descriptive approach to the study of grammar. See also **descriptive approach**.

determiner: A class of words that occur before nouns and indicate the type of reference nouns have. Determiners include definite and indefinite articles (e.g. *the train, a mountain*), 'quantity' words (e.g. *many people, several books*), cardinal and ordinal numerals (e.g. *one bus, first prize*), possessives (e.g. *my plan, our hopes*) and demonstratives (e.g. *that way, those men*).

developmental disorder: Any disorder which has its onset in the developmental period and can compromise motor, cognitive, linguistic and social development. Autism spectrum disorder and specific language impairment are common developmental disorders which have implications for language and communication amongst other domains.

developmental period: A period of time during which cognitive, linguistic and other abilities are acquired by infants, children and young people. The developmental period can extend for many years according to certain definitions.

dialect: The pronunciation, lexemes, grammatical structures and discourse features of a particular variety of a language. Some dialects have high prestige (e.g. Standard English) while others have low prestige.

direct object: See **object**.

directive: A type of utterance which aims to get the hearer to do something. Directives include commands (e.g. *Shut that door!*) and requests (e.g. *Can you tell me the time?*). Directives were one of five types of speech act proposed by the philosopher of language John Searle.

discourse: In terms of linguistic analysis, discourse is the level of language above individual sentences. The focus of study is on extended extracts of language in spoken and written texts.

di-transitive verb: A verb which requires a direct object and an indirect object. The indirect object precedes the direct object (e.g. *He gave me the book*). If the order is reversed and the direct object precedes the indirect object, then *to* or *for* must appear before the indirect object (e.g. *He gave the book to me*).

dummy auxiliary: The dummy auxiliary *do* is used to negate declarative sentences which do not contain an auxiliary and to turn them into interrogatives. For example, the sentence *The man parked the car* can be negated as in *The man didn't park the car* and can become an interrogative as in *Did the man park the car?* Some auxiliary is needed in these sentences and the semantically empty auxiliary *do* fulfils this purpose.

dummy subject: Where a clause must have a subject but there is no person or thing which can assume this function, a dummy subject is used. Dummy subjects are semantically empty. In English there are two dummy subjects: *it* and *there*. Examples of these subjects in use are *It is very warm today* and *There will be a bus in five minutes*.

dyslexia: A reading impairment which has its onset in childhood (developmental dyslexia) or in adulthood (acquired dyslexia). Adult-onset dyslexia may occur as part of aphasia.

East Anglia dialect: A dialect of British English which is associated with the English counties of Norfolk and Suffolk. Historically, East Anglian English played an important role in the formation of British Standard English, in the development of colonial Englishes (e.g. American English of New England), and in the formation of the Englishes of Australia and New Zealand.

elision: The omission of sounds, syllables, morphemes or words in spoken and written discourse.

ellipsis: This occurs when a speaker omits a clause, phrase or word from a sentence which is recoverable from context. This can be seen in the exchange between A and B below:

A: Would you like a large whiskey?

B: *I would [like a large whiskey]*

emphatic imperative: An imperative which can be formed with *do* if there is a null subject (e.g. *Do keep the noise down!*). Overt subjects cannot occur in an emphatic imperative (e.g. **Do you stop that!*). See also **imperative**.

encephalitis: An inflammation of the brain. Encephalitis is most often caused by a viral infection (e.g. herpes simplex virus) but it can also be caused by bacterial infections (e.g. tuberculosis).

endocentric compound: A compound in which the modifier is a sub-type of whatever is expressed by the head. A *playroom* is a type of room that is used for playing.

exclamative: A type of sentence which has the structure: *what-* or *how*-phrase followed by a subject and then a predicate (e.g. *What a headache you have caused!*). More often than not, exclamatives appear in a reduced form in which the subject and predicate are omitted (e.g. *What a headache!*). Exclamatory meaning can also be conveyed by sentences which do not have the structure of an exclamative. These sentences include declaratives (e.g. *He is a bloody idiot!*) and interrogatives (e.g. *What on earth are you doing?!*).

existential *there*: The word *there* is most often used as an adverb in sentences (e.g. *She lives <u>there</u>*). However, the word *there* also has an existential use where it may be followed by or preceded by a part of the verb *be* (e.g. *<u>There</u> is a beautiful painting; Is <u>there</u> some milk in the fridge?*).

exocentric compound: A compound which is a sub-type of something outside of the compound itself. A *bluebottle* is a type of insect. Because 'insect' exists outside of the compound, *bluebottle* is an exocentric compound.

extraposed subject: In a declarative sentence, the subject stands before the verb (*<u>Michael Phelps</u> is the new world champion*). However, in a sentence where extraposition has occurred, the subject follows the verb and is postponed until the end of the sentence (*The new world champion is <u>Michael Phelps</u>*). Extraposed subjects are often used for stylistic effect.

FG syndrome: An X-linked recessive disorder which is predominantly found in males. The disorder is characterised by physical and cognitive abnormalities including cardiac defects, short stature, mental retardation and unusual facial features (e.g. prominent forehead).

finite subordinate clause: A subordinate clause that contains a tensed verb form (e.g. a finite verb). There are three types of finite subordinate clause: declarative subordinate clauses; interrogative subordinate clauses; and relative clauses.

finite verb: A finite verb form carries tense, that is, it is morphologically marked as present (*she walk<u>s</u>*) or past (*she walk<u>ed</u>*).

first language acquisition: See **child language acquisition**.

***for–to* infinitive:** A variant of the *to*-infinitive clause in Standard English. The '*for–to*' infinitive is a feature of Northern Irish English as well as other non-standard dialects of English (e.g. *She went into town <u>for to do the shopping</u>*).

fraction: Fraction words are a type of pre-determiner in a noun phrase. Fractions are underlined in the following noun phrases: <u>*a third of*</u> *his salary;* <u>*two-fifths of*</u> *the work;* <u>*half of*</u> *his driveway.*

free morpheme: A free or lexical morpheme can exist on its own in language without other morphemes. Lexemes like *car* and *house* are free morphemes.

function word: Words which have a grammatical function and belong to closed classes like preposition (e.g. *through, during*), conjunction (e.g. *but, since*) and pronoun (e.g. *we, they, that*). See also **content word**.

gender: Grammatical gender is a feature of a language like German which has masculine, feminine and neuter nouns, definite and indefinite articles and adjectival endings. In English, grammatical gender has been lost, with masculine and feminine pronouns like *he/him* and *she/her* relating to biological sex.

general ordinal: A sub-class of ordinal numerals that expresses sequence but does not correspond to numbers. General ordinals include *next, previous, last* and *subsequent*. This group of ordinals are post-determiners in the noun phrase, e.g. *all his* <u>*previous*</u> *achievements*.

generative grammar: A term used to describe a number of different theories of syntax which originate in the work of Noam Chomsky and his colleagues in the mid-1950s. The central thesis of generative grammar is that sentences are generated by a subconscious set of procedures which are a feature of the human mind. The goal of syntactic theory is to model these procedures.

genitive: A form of the noun which is used in writing to indicate a range of meanings including possession or ownership. The genitive differs for singular nouns (e.g. *dog's bone*) and plural nouns (e.g. *cats' home*). These forms are indistinguishable in speech.

Geordie dialect: A variety of English that is spoken by people who live in Newcastle-upon-Tyne and the surrounding urban area of Tyneside. The Geordie dialect has distinctive phonetic, grammatical and lexical features.

gradable adjective: An adjective which can have comparative and superlative forms. Many adjectives in English inflect for grade (*small – smaller – smallest*). Other adjectives use the adverbs *more* and *most* to form the comparative and superlative (*horrible – more horrible – most horrible*). Some adjectives in English describe properties or attributes which do not permit of degrees. An intensifying adverb like *very* cannot be used with these non-gradable adjectives (**The angles are very equal*).

gradable adverb: An adverb which can have comparative and superlative forms. Many adverbs in English inflect for grade (*quickly – quicklier – quickliest*). Other adverbs use the adverbs *more* and *most* to form the comparative and superlative (*recently – more recently – most recently*). There are many adverbs in English which do not have comparative and superlative forms. They include words like *south-wards* in **They travelled most southwards.*

gradation: A grammatical category that applies to adjectives and adverbs in English. See also **gradable adjective**, **gradable adverb**.

grammar: The branch of linguistics that examines word structure (morphology) and sentence structure (syntax). For Chomsky, the grammar of language also contains phonological and semantic aspects.

grammatical development: The aspect of language development that relates to the acquisition of grammatical structures. Grammatical development includes the acquisition of inflectional morphemes (e.g. *–s, –ed, –ing*) and derivational morphemes (e.g. *–ness, –ful, –ion*) as well as the structures required to form *yes–no* and *wh*-interrogatives, relative and subordinate clauses and active and passive voice constructions.

grammatical disorder: A disorder of the production (expression) and reception (understanding) of the grammatical structures of language. A grammatical disorder may occur in isolation or alongside disorders of other aspects of language (e.g. phonology, semantics). A grammatical disorder may have its onset in the developmental period or in adulthood. These disorders are assessed and treated by speech and language therapists.

grammatical immaturity: A grammatical feature of language which is characteristic of young, typically developing children and which differs from adult-like grammar.

Grice, Herbert Paul: Grice (1913–1988) was an English philosopher of language. He is widely acknowledged to have been the father of modern pragmatics.

head injury: Also known as a traumatic brain injury (TBI). There are two main types of head injury. In an open or penetrating head injury, the skull is fractured or otherwise breached by a missile. In a closed head injury, the brain is damaged while the skull remains intact.

head: The central, obligatory element in a phrase. The head varies with phrase type. For example, the head in a noun phrase is a noun. This noun may be pre-modified (e.g. *black horse*) and/or post-modified (*house beside the river*).

herpes simplex encephalitis: See **encephalitis**.

humour: A technical expression which is intended to cover all pre-theoretical notions of comical, ridiculous or laughable language. Humour is a high-level language skill that is still being acquired into adolescence and young adulthood.

***if/whether*-clause:** See **interrogative subordinate clause**.

imperative: A type of sentence which is formed from the base form of the verb and which lacks a subject (e.g. *Hurry up!*). When an overt subject is used, it occurs in pre-verbal position (e.g. *You stand up!*). In Belfast English, an overt subject occurs in post-verbal position (e.g. *Stand you up!*).

imperative particle: In most imperatives, the overt or understood subject is represented by the (singular or plural) personal pronoun *you*. However, in an imperative particle or first-person imperative, the subject includes the speaker and one or more others (e.g. *Let's clean up this room!*). See also **imperative**.

indefinite article: See **article**.

indefinite pronoun: Pronouns that express notions of definiteness or quantity such as *everything* and *somebody*. Unlike other pronouns, indefinite pronouns do not stand in place of previously occurring noun phrases.

indirect object: See **object**.

infinitive: The 'to' part of the verb (e.g. *to eat, to sleep*). Infinitives may also be used in the absence of 'to'. This is the case in bare infinitives (e.g. *She saw the man leave the club*). Subordinate clauses may be built around the *to*-infinitive form of the verb (e.g. *He intends to leave early*). See also **infinitive clause**.

infinitive clause: A subordinate clause that contains a *to*-infinitive, e.g. *Sally wants to leave early*. In this example, the *to*-infinitive clause functions as the object of the verb *wants*. However, *to*-infinitive clauses can also be the subject in a sentence, e.g. *To climb Mount Everest would be a truly amazing experience*.

inflectional morphology: The branch of morphology which examines the use of bound inflectional morphemes like *–s, –ed* and *–ing* to generate word-forms such as *walks, walked* and *walking*.

inflectional suffix: See **suffix**.

initialism: A type of acronym-formation in which the letters of a word must be individually spelled out (e.g. BBC, WTO) rather than pronounced as a phonetic unit (e.g. UNESCO).

intellectual disability: A term used in the fifth edition of the *Diagnostic and Statistical Manual of Mental Disorders* (American Psychiatric Association, 2013) to describe children and adults with an intelligence quotient (IQ) below 70. Intellectual disability is a feature of many syndromes (e.g. Down syndrome) and is found in other clinical conditions (e.g. autism spectrum disorder). Other terms for intellectual disability are 'learning disability' (in the UK) and 'mental retardation' (in the USA).

intensifying expression: Adverbs such as *really* and *very* which modify adjectives without contributing much semantic content. The function of these adverbs is to intensify the property denoted by the adjective, e.g. *very tired*.

intensive verb: A verb which takes a subject complement, e.g. *The choristers were truly inspirational*. The subject complement in this example is an adjective phrase which refers to the same entity as the subject noun phrase *the choristers*.

intercalative blend: A type of blend in which the sounds of one source word are interspersed with the sounds of another source word. This can be seen in *chuckle + snort → chortle*.

interrogative: The interrogative is one of four sentence types in English: declaratives; imperatives; interrogatives; and exclamatives. There are two types of interrogative: *yes–no* interrogatives and *wh*-interrogatives. To form a *yes–no* interrogative, there is inversion of the subject noun or pronoun and auxiliary verb (e.g. *Is Mary going to the bank?; Are you paying the bill?*). To form a *wh*-interrogative, an interrogative pronoun like *who, which, whom, what* and *whose* appears at the start of a question. Some of these pronouns can only be used on their own (e.g. *Who is coming to the party?*). Other interrogative pronouns can be used on their own or with a noun head (e.g. *What are you doing?; What time is it?*).

interrogative pronoun: Words such as *who, which* and *what* that are used to ask questions, e.g. *Who is coming to the party?*

interrogative subordinate clause: A type of finite and non-finite subordinate clause. Finite interrogative subordinate clauses can be subdivided into clauses introduced by the complementisers *if/whether* (e.g. *They asked if she wanted more time*) and *wh*-clauses (e.g. *I wonder why she left*). There are also non-finite interrogative subordinate clauses as in the use of the *to*-infinitive clause in *I didn't know what to do with my time*.

intonation: Intonation describes pitch movements that occur over the domain of a whole prosodic phrase. These movements are related to the function or meaning of the phrase. For example, a falling pitch pattern expressed on the last lexical stress in the phrase indicates to a hearer that the phrase is complete or definite.

intransitive phrasal verb: An intransitive verb which is accompanied by a particle such as *up* or *off*, e.g. *Things are looking up*.

intransitive verb: Verbs which do not permit objects or complements, e.g. *The boat disappeared without trace*. The intransitive verb *disappeared* is followed by an optional adjunct *without trace* but does not require it to be present.

inversion: A property of auxiliary verbs. To form an interrogative, an auxiliary verb is inverted with a subject noun or pronoun, e.g. *Is the guest leaving today?*

language development: See **child language acquisition**.

language disorder: The term used to describe a breakdown in the formulation or production of language (expressive language disorder) and the comprehension or understanding of language (receptive language disorder). A language disorder may be developmental or acquired in nature and may affect any language level (phonology, syntax, etc.).

Latin: The language of ancient Rome and its empire. Latin has been widely used as a language of scholarship and administration and has had considerable influence on the development of English through these uses.

laxing: The process by means of which a tense vowel becomes lax.

lexeme: A semantic word. The lexeme is the basic unit of lexical semantics.

lexical stem: A base morpheme to which other morphemes are added. A stem is simple when it has no more basic part (e.g. *table*) or complex when it contains more basic parts. For example, the stem to which *un–* is added in *unworthy* is a complex stem because it consists of *worth* and the suffix *–y*.

lexical verb: Also known as main verbs. Lexical verbs are content words that can take suffixes like *–ed* (e.g. *walked*), *–s* (e.g. *walks*) and *–ing* (e.g. *walking*). See also **auxiliary verb**.

linguistic competence: Internalised knowledge of the grammar of one's native language, including its sound system (phonology), word order (syntax) and meaning (semantics). According to Chomsky, linguistic competence permits native speakers to determine if a sentence is well-formed or is ungrammatical, and to decide if one sentence is a paraphrase of another sentence.

linguistics: The scientific study of the structure and function of language. The structure and function of language are studied in a number of sub-disciplines including phonetics, phonology, morphology, syntax, semantics and pragmatics. There are also a number of applied disciplines in linguistics including sociolinguistics, psycholinguistics and clinical linguistics.

locative preposition: See **preposition**.

main clause: A clause that is not embedded as a dependent in a larger clause. The main clause is the sentence.

main verb: See **lexical verb**.

mass noun: See **non-count noun**.

mean length of utterance: A measure of grammatical complexity which is frequently used to characterise children's language development or the grammatical competence of adults with language disorders such as aphasia. Mean length of utterance can be measured in words or morphemes.

modal auxiliary verb: See **auxiliary verb**.

modality: Modality captures the attitude of a speaker (or writer) towards the events expressed in a sentence and the certainty or probability with which the speaker believes that these events may actually happen.

Modern English: The English language in the period from around 1500 to the present day.

modifier: The constituent of a compound or phrase which specifies the head. The modifier *dinner* in the compound noun *dinner lady* specifies a lady who works in a school canteen.

mono-transitive verb: Verbs which require one object only, a direct object. The direct object may take the form of a noun phrase or a pronoun, e.g. *The man thumped the table; The boy hit him.*

morpheme: The smallest meaningful unit of a word. Free morphemes can occur on their own and are thus words (e.g. *fly, cat*). Bound morphemes cannot exist in isolation and must be attached to other morphemes (e.g. *unhappy, agreeable*).

morphology: The linguistic discipline that studies the internal structure of words and the patterns and principles that underlie their composition. The morpheme is the unit of analysis.

multiple negation: The use of two or more negative markers, e.g. *I didn't do nothing.* While single negation is a feature of Standard English (e.g. *I didn't do anything*), multiple negation is a feature of African American Vernacular English and other vernacular English dialects.

multiplying expression: Words and phrases like *twice* and *three times*. Multipliers are pre-determiners in the noun phrase, e.g. *twice the price, three times a year.*

narrative: A type of spoken or written discourse in which the events of a story are narrated to a listener or reader. The events so narrated are normally in the past and typically involve one or more actors.

native language: A native language or first language is the language that one is exposed to from birth or during the critical period for language development.

negation: A property of auxiliary verbs whereby a negative marker can be added to them, e.g. *I cannot come to the party; She won't leave the room.*

negative form: Words like *not* and *never* which are pre-modifiers in a verb phrase (*She does not wash dishes; He has never left home*). The negative form *not* is often used in its contracted form, particularly in spoken language. In its contracted form, *not* attaches to the auxiliary verb, e.g. *He doesn't clean the car; They won't be at the party*.

negative imperative: An imperative sentence which contains *not*. To form a negative imperative, the dummy auxiliary verb *do* must be used (e.g. *Don't wash the shirts!*). If an overt subject is used in a negative imperative, it must appear after *don't* (e.g. *Don't you lock me out!*). The negative form *not* must appear in contracted form when an overt subject is used in a negative imperative. Otherwise, it can appear in full form (e.g. *Do not sing!*). See also **imperative**.

non-count noun: Any noun which cannot have a plural form and which cannot be preceded by the indefinite article *a* or *an*, e.g. *courage, butter*. Non-count nouns are also known as mass nouns. See also **count noun**.

non-finite subordinate clause: A subordinate clause that contains a verb which is not marked for tense (i.e. a non-finite verb). There are four types of non-finite subordinate clause: bare infinitive clauses; *to*-infinitive clauses; *–ing* participle clauses; and *–ed* participle clauses.

non-finite verb: A verb which does not carry tense agreement. The present participle (*walking*), past participle (*walked*), infinitive (*to walk*) and bare infinitive (*walk*) are all non-finite verbs.

non-restrictive relative clause: See **relative clause**.

non-standard dialect: A language variety which differs in terms of pronunciation, vocabulary and grammar from a standard variety. Non-standard dialects are often associated with certain geographical regions and social classes. They can have less prestige than standard varieties which are also dialects.

Northern Irish English: A variety of English spoken in Northern Ireland. The pronunciation, lexemes and grammatical constructions of Northern Irish English distinguish it from Standard English. Belfast English is one dialect of Northern Irish English.

noun: An open word class that can inflect for number (e.g. *pen/pens*). Nouns can be the names of things (e.g. *vase*), people (e.g. *Bill, sister*), animals (e.g. *elephant*), places (e.g. *Rome*), processes (e.g. *industrialisation*), and concepts (e.g. *truth, honour*).

noun phrase: A noun and its pre-modifiers and post-modifiers. The pre-modifiers in a noun phrase include other nouns (e.g. *brick walls*) and adjectives (e.g. *black sheep*). The post-modifiers in a noun phrase include prepositional phrases (e.g. *students in taxis*), infinitives (e.g. *war to end all wars*) and relative clauses (e.g. *woman who sings in the choir*).

number: A grammatical property of a number of word classes in English including nouns, verbs and pronouns. The difference between singular and plural nouns in English is marked morphologically, with singular nouns unmarked (*dog*) and plural nouns marked by the suffix *–s* (*dogs*).

numeral: See **cardinal numeral; ordinal numeral**.

object: A clause element that is required by transitive verbs (e.g. *John kicked the ball*). Objects are affected by the action of the verb and can be direct or indirect. In the sentence *Sally gave <u>the keys</u> to <u>the mechanic</u>*, the first noun phrase is the direct object and the second noun phrase is the indirect object.

object complement: A predicative complement which is co-referential with the object in the sentence. The object complement *president* is co-referential with the object *Bill Clinton* in the sentence *They elected <u>Bill Clinton president</u>*.

object pronoun: See **pronoun**.

Old English: The English language in the period starting around AD 450, with the arrival of West Germanic settlers (Angles, Saxons and Jutes) in southern Britain, up to about 1100.

onomatopoeic form: (onomatopoeia) A word which sounds like the action or thing to which it refers (e.g. *hiss, boom*).

ordinal numeral: Numerals like *first, second* and *third* which express sequence or order. Ordinal numerals are post-determiners in the noun phrase, e.g. *the first hurdle*.

orthographic form: The written form of a word. The use of the written symbol system (orthography) of a language to represent a word.

overregularisation error: An error in normal language development where children apply the regular past tense suffix *–ed* to verbs which have irregular past tense forms (e.g. *goed, drawed*) or the plural suffix *–s* to nouns which have irregular plural forms (e.g. *mouses*).

palatal consonant: A consonant sound that is produced by raising the blade of the tongue towards or against the hard palate just behind the alveolar ridge.

palatalisation: The production of consonant sounds with the blade of the tongue drawn further towards the hard palate than in their normal pronunciation.

paraphrase: Sentences or phrases that convey the same meaning using different wording. Some paraphrases exhibit semantic equivalence while others display a broader, approximate equivalence.

passive sentence: See **voice**.

past participle: Part of the verb that is used to form the present perfect aspect (e.g. *They have <u>broken</u> the window*) and the past perfect aspect (e.g. *Mary had <u>endorsed</u> the candidate*). Most past participles in English are formed by adding the suffix *–ed* to the infinitive of the verb. However, there are many past participles which do not follow this pattern (e.g. *been, woken*).

past tense: A tense of verbs which indicates that an event took place in the past. For regular verbs in English, the past tense is formed by adding the suffix *–ed* to the infinitive (e.g. *walked, played*). However, there are many verbs in English which have irregular past tense forms (e.g. *go → went; bring → brought*).

performative verb: A verb which when used in the first person singular present tense constitutes an act of promising, betting, warning, and so on (e.g. *I promise I will arrive on time*).

person: A grammatical category which is used to classify pronouns (e.g. *I, you, he*), possessive determiners (e.g. *my, your, his*), and verbs (e.g. *walk, walks*) according to whether they indicate the speaker (first person), the addressee (second person), or a third party (third person).

personal pronoun: A group of pronouns in English which can take the place of noun phrases. For example, in the sentence *Jack read the book and liked it very much*, the personal pronoun *it* replaces the noun phrase *the book* (the antecedent). Personal pronouns in English exhibit the properties of number (singular and plural), case (subject and object) and person (first, second and third person).

phonological realisation: Phonemes can have different realisations depending on the contexts in which they are used. In morphology, a morpheme like the English past tense morpheme (*–ed*) has different phonological realisations depending on the phonetic context in which this morpheme is used.

phonology: The study of the organisation of speech sounds into systems. Phonologists examine how particular sounds are used to distinguish between words (e.g. *pat – bat*). The phoneme is the unit of analysis.

picture description task: A task in which an examinee is asked to describe a black-and-white line drawing of a familiar scene in the presence of an examiner. Picture description tasks are an effective way to elicit the production of expository discourse.

possessive determiner: Use of a possessive pronoun (e.g. *my, his, her*) as a determiner in a noun phrase (e.g. *our pool, your dreams*). Possessive pronouns can also be used as nouns (e.g. *This is mine*).

possessive pronoun: A group of pronouns in English which can occur independently as noun phrases (e.g. *I want yours instead of mine*) or as determiners in a noun phrase (e.g. *Jill likes to drive my car*).

post-determiner: A group of determiners which stand in front of the head noun in the noun phrase. Post-determiners include cardinal numerals (*one day*), ordinal numerals (*first place*), general ordinals (*previous meeting*), and quantifying expressions (*many issues*).

post-modifier: A phrase or clause which follows and modifies the head of a phrase. For example, in the noun phrase *the vase next to the light*, the post-modifier is a prepositional phrase. In the noun phrase *the girl who sings in the choir*, the post-modifier is a relative clause. See also **pre-modifier**.

post-positive adjective: An adjective which follows the noun that it modifies. Examples include *princess royal* and *times past*.

pragmatics: The branch of linguistics that studies the use of language or how features of context influence meaning and communication. Grammar cannot be studied in isolation of pragmatics. This is because pragmatic factors such as politeness influence the grammatical structure of an utterance. For example, a sentence with interrogative structure (e.g. *Can you tell me the time?*) is a more polite way to ask for something than a sentence with imperative structure (e.g. *Tell me the time!*).

pre-determiner: The first determiner slot in the noun phrase. Pre-determiners include multiplying expressions (*twice, three times*), fractions (*half, two-thirds*) and the quantity words *all* and *both*.

predicate: That part of a sentence in English which stands to the right of a subject and provides information about the subject. Predicates can be a single word (e.g. *Bob blinks*) or many words (e.g. *Sally stormed through the door in a fit of rage*). The function of predicate is always filled by a verb phrase.

predicative adjective: An adjective which follows a verb in a sentence (e.g. *The dog was ferocious*). See also **attributive adjective**.

predicator: This is a functional label which is applied to the head of the predicate of a sentence. In the sentence *Molly knit the sweater*, the predicate is *knit the sweater* while the head verb *knit* is the predicator.

prefix: Prefixation is a word-formation process in morphology that can change the meanings of words through the addition of prefixes like *un–* (e.g. *unstable, unhelpful*), *dis–* (e.g. *dishearten, disagreeable*) and *mis–* (e.g. *misunderstanding, misapprehension*).

prefixation: A morphemic word-formation process in which a morpheme known as a prefix is added to the front of a base morpheme, e.g. *disagree*. Prefixes change word meaning but for the most part maintain the word class of a lexeme.

pre-modifier: The words which precede the head of a phrase and modify it. For example, in the noun phrase *stressful predicament*, the pre-modifier is an adjective. In the verb phrase *never washes the dishes*, the pre-modifier is the negative form *never*. See also **post-modifier**.

preposition: A closed word class which occurs before a noun phrase (e.g. *during the cold weather*). Most prepositions are single words and are known as simple prepositions. Prepositions of more than one word are called 'complex' prepositions and include two-word prepositions (e.g. *due to, along with*) and three-word prepositions (e.g. *in addition to*). Prepositions can express a range of meanings including space (e.g. *next to the church*), time (e.g. *during summer*) and means (e.g. *with an axe*). The term 'locative preposition' describes a preposition which expresses spatial meaning.

prepositional phrase: A preposition and its pre-modifiers and post-modifiers. Adverbs can be pre-modifiers in a prepositional phrase (e.g. *back through the tunnel*). Post-modifiers in prepositional phrases include nouns (e.g. *in spring*) and prepositions (e.g. *from under the bridge*).

prepositional verb: Verbs which are followed by a prepositional phrase (e.g. *She looked at the menu*). The element following the preposition can be the subject in a passive sentence (*The menu was looked at*). Prepositional verbs are a type of mono-transitive verb.

prescriptive approach: An approach to the study of grammar that stipulates the grammatical forms that speakers should use or ought to use. Prescriptive grammarians produce rules against splitting the infinitive form of the verb (e.g. *I want you to really work hard*) and ending sentences with prepositions (e.g. *Is this the mop you cleaned the floor with?*).

prescriptive grammarian: A grammarian who pursues a prescriptive approach to the study of grammar. See also **prescriptive approach**.

present participle: The part of the verb which has an *–ing* ending (*singing, walking*). The present participle is used to form progressive aspect (e.g. *The boy is crossing the road* is present progressive aspect).

present tense: One of two tenses in English (the other tense is past tense). The simple present tense in English consists of just a lexical verb with no auxiliary verb (e.g. *she walks home*). The present tense does not always correspond to present time. For example, the simple present tense may be used to describe a future event (e.g. *Bill flies to Milan next week*).

prestige: Prestige in sociolinguistics refers to the social evaluations that speakers attach to a language, variety or dialect. The prestige of a language, variety or dialect is closely connected to the prestige of its speakers.

presupposition: A presupposition is information which is assumed, taken for granted or in the background of an utterance. Presuppositions reduce the amount of information that a speaker must explicitly state. Their purpose or function is, therefore, to achieve some economy in terms of communication. Presuppositions are triggered by certain lexical items and constructions. For example, the cleft construction in the sentence *It was the teenager who vandalised the car* presupposes that someone vandalised the car.

primary auxiliary verb: English has three primary auxiliary verbs: *do, be* and *have*. These auxiliaries contribute to grammatical constructions such as progressive aspect (e.g. *The boy is crossing the road*) but carry little meaning themselves.

progressive aspect: See **aspect**.

pronoun: A closed word class that occurs in positions typically occupied by nouns (e.g. *Joan/she posted the parcel to the children/them*). Pronouns can be distinguished by case such as subject pronouns (e.g. *she, we*) and object pronouns (e.g. *her, them*). There are several different types of pronouns including personal pronouns (e.g. *I, you*), possessive pronouns (e.g. *my, our*), demonstrative pronouns (e.g. *this, those*) and reflexive pronouns (e.g. *himself, ourselves*).

pronunciation: The way in which the speakers of a dialect produce speech sounds (also known as accent). For many years, Received Pronunciation (RP) has been considered to be the standard for the pronunciation of British English.

proper noun: The name of a person (*Mary*), a city (*Paris*), a country (*Russia*), or a brand (*Lucozade*). Proper nouns have a capital first letter and cannot take the definite article.

proposition: A unit of meaning that is expressed by a sentence and is either true or false, depending on whether or not it corresponds to states of affairs in the world. Two sentences with different grammatical structures can express the same proposition, e.g. *The dog bit the man* (active voice) and *The man was bitten by the dog* (passive voice) convey the same proposition.

propositional meaning: Meaning which is based on the proposition expressed by a sentence. The study of propositional meaning was dominant in linguistics up until the emergence of work by Austin, Searle and Grice in the latter half of the twentieth century.

pseudo-cleft sentence: See **cleft sentence**.

punctuation: A system of symbols used in written language with the purpose of clarifying meaning for the reader. Common forms of punctuation include apostrophes, commas and full stops.

quantifying expression: See **quantity word**.

quantity word: Words such as *all, many, several* and *few* which express the quantity of something. Quantity words are determiners in a noun phrase where they can fill more than one determiner slot. For example, in the noun phrases *all his books* and her _many plans_, quantity words fill the slots of pre-determiner and post-determiner, respectively.

reciprocal pronoun: Pronouns like _each other_ and _one another_ which express a two-way (reciprocal) relationship and require an antecedent in the same clause, e.g. _John and Mary glanced at each other in disbelief._

reduplication: A non-morphemic word-formation process in which a word is repeated (e.g. _bye-bye_) or repeated with a vowel change (e.g. _hip-hop_) or a conso-nant change (e.g. _lovey-dovey_). Reduplication is a feature of children's language in onomatopoeic forms like _choo-choo_.

reference: A semantic relation between expressions in language and individuals and entities in the external world. The individuals and entities to which linguistic expressions refer are called 'referents'. Even though it is a semantic concept, ref-erence is important to grammarians in several ways (e.g. distinguishing restrictive and non-restrictive relative clauses). See also **referent**.

referent: In semantics, a person or thing in the external world that is referred to or denoted by a linguistic expression.

reflexive pronoun: Pronouns which end in _–self_ or _–selves_ and which have an antecedent in the same clause, e.g. _Mike burnt himself on the cooker._

relative clause: A clause which modifies a noun, e.g. _the woman who bakes cakes_. Relative clauses are introduced by relative pronouns like _who, which, whom_ and on occasion _that_ (e.g. _This is the only house that is standing_). Relative clauses can be restrictive and non-restrictive. In a restrictive relative clause, the clause narrows the referent of the preceding noun phrase (e.g. _The boy who is crossing the road is very nasty_). In a non-restrictive relative clause, the relative clause provides inci-dental information about the preceding noun phrase which already has a specific referent (e.g. _Jack Brown who drinks quite heavily mended the fence_). See also **relative pronoun**.

relative pronoun: Pronouns such as _who, whom_ and _which_. Relative pronouns are found at the beginning of a relative clause and relate the clause to a preced-ing noun phrase, e.g. _The girl who left early passed the exam_. See also **relative clause**.

request: A type of directive, one class of speech acts. Speakers can make requests directly by means of declaratives or imperatives (e.g. _I want you to pay your bill at reception_) or indirectly by means of interrogatives (e.g. _Can you pay your bill at reception?_). See also **directive**.

restrictive relative clause: See **relative clause**.

reverse polarity: A grammatical feature of tag questions in which a negative tag follows a positive declarative (e.g. _You will help me with dinner, won't you?_) and a positive tag follows a negative declarative (e.g. _You won't leave the window open, will you?_). See also **tag question**.

rhetorical question: A question which has the same structure as a _yes–no_ interrog-ative or a _wh_-interrogative. However, unlike other interrogatives where an answer is expected (and is usually forthcoming), the answer to a rhetorical question is considered to be so obvious that no response is expected, e.g. _Who needs a lazy, incompetent man in their lives?_

root: The root of a word is the part that is unanalysable morphologically. It differs from the stem which is the root and its affixes. In the word *unhelpful*, the root is *help* and the stem is *helpful*.

root compound: A compound in which the constituents are two simple lexemes (e.g. *wheelchair*).

schizophrenia: A serious mental illness which is diagnosed on the basis of positive and negative symptoms. Positive symptoms include thought disorder, delusions and hallucinations (mostly auditory). Negative symptoms include affective flattening, poverty of speech, apathy, avolition and social withdrawal.

semantics: The study of the linguistic meaning of words (lexical semantics) and sentences.

sentence: A sentence is a string of words that usually expresses a proposition. It consists of at least one clause and is not part of any larger clause. There are four sentence types in English: declaratives; imperatives; interrogatives; and exclamatives.

sibilant sound: A fricative sound like [s, z, ʃ, ʒ] which has more acoustic energy (that is, greater loudness) at a higher pitch than other fricative sounds.

simple preposition: See **preposition**.

specific language impairment: A severe developmental language disorder. Specific language impairment has been described as a diagnosis by exclusion as language impairment occurs in the absence of hearing loss, craniofacial anomaly, intellectual disability, psychiatric disturbance and other factors which are known to cause language disorder.

specifier: A functional label which is used to describe that part of a phrase which occurs before the head. The head determines the type of specifier that is required. For example, no specifier appears before a proper noun while count nouns require an obligatory specifier in the singular. Specifiers vary with different types of phrases. In noun phrases, determiners like the definite and indefinite articles are specifiers. In verb phrases, the negative forms *not* and *never* are specifiers. Adverbs are specifiers in adjective phrases (*quite remarkable*).

speech act: A term used by Austin and later Searle to describe utterances which perform acts or actions. Both Austin and Searle recognised different types of speech acts such as assertives (e.g. statements) and directives (e.g. requests).

speech and language therapist: The health professional who assesses, diagnoses and treats children and adults with communication and swallowing disorders. The term 'speech-language pathologist' is used in the USA.

speech and language therapy: The clinical profession that is responsible for the management of clients with communication and swallowing disorders. The term 'speech-language pathology' is used in the USA.

split infinitive: A grammatical feature in which an adverb is inserted between *to* and the verb in an infinitive (e.g. *John hopes to really excel at sport*). Split infinitives are a prohibited grammatical form according to prescriptive grammarians.

Standard English: A dialect of English which has considerable prestige because of its association with formal education, media and other powerful institutions. All English language teaching, whether to native speakers of English or to native speakers of other languages, uses Standard English.

stress migration: The movement of primary stress from one syllable to another syllable in a word.

stroke: Also known as a cerebrovascular accident (CVA). Strokes may be caused by a blood clot (embolus) in one of the blood vessels in the brain or leading to the brain (embolic stroke), or by a haemorrhage (haemorrhagic stroke) in one of these vessels.

subject: A subject is a constituent that performs the action described by the predicate. In the sentence *Jack baked a cake*, the predicate (*baked a cake*) is performed by Jack. So the noun phrase *Jack* is the subject of this sentence.

subject complement: A predicative complement which is co-referential with the subject in the sentence. The subject complement *teacher* is co-referential with the subject *Sally* in the sentence *Sally is a teacher*.

subject–operator inversion: A type of grammatical movement in which a finite auxiliary verb (operator) is moved in front of a subject noun or pronoun to form an interrogative (e.g. *Is John leaving now?*).

subject pronoun: See **pronoun**.

subjectless clause: Not every clause in English contains a subject. So-called subjectless clauses are found in imperative sentences (e.g. *Get help! Leave me!*). Non-finite subordinate clauses lack a syntactic subject (e.g. *Exhausted by the journey, they went to bed early*). A subject may also be omitted when it can be recovered by the listener from context (e.g. A: *How did you get to the match?* B: *Drove the van*).

subordinate clause: A clause which is at a lower level than (is subordinate to) another clause. In the sentence *I will give you £10 if you wash the car*, the clause *you wash the car* is subordinate to the clause *I will give you £10*. Subordinate clauses include relative, comparative and *to*-infinitive clauses. They are often introduced by subordinating conjunctions such as *if, although* and *because*.

subordinating conjunction: Conjunction words like *because, if* and *although* which link a dependent clause (a subordinate clause) to an independent clause (a main clause or sentence). In the sentence *She missed school because she was ill*, the subordinating conjunction *because* introduces a subordinate clause which is dependent on the full sentence. Subordinating conjunctions can express a range of meanings. In the example just given, the subordinate clause expresses the reason why something happened (Why did she miss school? Reason: She was ill).

subordination: The use of subordinating conjunctions (e.g. *because, since*) or relative pronouns (e.g. *who, which*) to link clauses in such a way that one clause is dependent on (or subordinate to) another clause. In the following examples, the underlined clauses are subordinate to the main clause or sentence: *Jack thought that it must be Friday; She enjoyed her job, although she received a small salary*.

suffix: There are two types of suffixes in English words: inflectional suffixes and derivational suffixes. Inflectional suffixes have a grammatical function and include *–ed* to indicate past tense and *–ing* for progressive aspect. These suffixes create new word-forms (not new words). Derivational suffixes are more numerous than inflectional suffixes. They change the class of words and in doing so create new words. For example, the suffix *–ion* changes 'institute' from a verb to a noun (*institution*). In *fairness* and *agreement*, the suffixes *–ness* and *–ment* change an adjective and a verb, respectively, into nouns.

suffixation: A word-formation process which changes the word class of a lexeme and involves the attachment of a bound morpheme to the end of a base (e.g. *mindful, reasonable*).

superlative: Gradable adjectives and adverbs can have superlative forms. For most adjectives in English, the superlative is formed by adding the suffix *–est* to the absolute form of the adjective (e.g. *Jill is the smartest pupil in the class*), although irregular superlative forms are quite common (e.g. *Sam is the worst boy in the class*). In English, the word 'most' is used to form the superlative of adverbs (e.g. *He drives most carelessly in town*).

syntax: The study of how phrases and sentences are constructed; the study of sentence structure.

synthetic compound: A compound in which at least one of the constituents contains a bound morpheme (e.g. *flying circus*).

tag question: A type of *yes–no* interrogative which occurs at the end of a declarative sentence (e.g. *You will help me with my homework, won't you?*). When speakers use tag questions, it is often with the purpose of seeking confirmation of a statement from a hearer. See also **interrogative**.

tense: A semantic and grammatical system that allows speakers to situate events in time. English has two tenses: present and past. Present tense often does not correspond to present time. For example, in the sentence *Fran visits Moscow in June*, the present tense verb *visits* refers to future time.

that-clause: A type of subordinate clause which is introduced by *that* and which may occur as an independent sentence. *That*-clauses can fulfil different functions in a sentence. They may be subjects (*That you arrived late is a bad sign*), direct objects (*I imagine that the proposals will be accepted*), and subject complements (*The most perplexing thing was that he did not raise an objection*).

transitive phrasal verb: A transitive phrasal verb is a transitive verb followed by a particle, e.g. *They locked the hens up*. The direct object in a transitive phrasal verb can appear before the particle.

transitive verb: A verb which must be followed by a noun phrase which is a direct object (e.g. *He hit the table*).

variety: A neutral term for a language or dialect.

verb: An open word class which contains main or lexical verbs and auxiliary verbs. Verbs can be marked for tense such as present tense (e.g. *walks*) and past tense (e.g. *walked*). Verbs also display agreement with the subject of the sentence, should this be a noun (e.g. *Sally plays the piano*) or a pronoun (e.g. *She likes chocolate*). See also **auxiliary verb; lexical verb**.

verb phrase: A verb and its pre-modifiers and post-modifiers. Auxiliary verbs (e.g. *has been waiting*), negative forms (e.g. *never cleans*), and adverbs (e.g. *purposefully hid*) can be pre-modifiers in verb phrases. Post-modifiers in verb phrases include noun phrases (e.g. *stole the ornament*), adjectives (e.g. *became angry*), adverbs (e.g. *walked slowly*), prepositions (e.g. *stood next to the pillar*) and clauses (e.g. *hoped that she would leave*).

vocative: A vocative is a nominal or a pronominal element in a sentence that refers to the addressee of a sentence. The proper nouns in the following sentences are vocatives: *Mark, what are you doing?* and *Sally, look at that kite!*. Also, the pronoun *you* is a vocative in the sentence *Stop screaming, you!*.

voice: A grammatical relationship between the subject and object in a sentence. In the active voice, the subject precedes the verb in the sentence (e.g. *Mary followed the man*). In the passive voice, the subject *Mary* follows the verb while the object *the man* precedes the verb (e.g. *The man was followed by Mary*). The three parts of the passive are part of the verb *be*, the passive participle and a *by* phrase. The *by* phrase is an optional element.

voiced consonant: Any consonant speech sound the production of which does involve vocal fold vibration.

voiceless consonant: Any consonant speech sound the production of which does not involve vocal fold vibration.

vowel quality: Vowel quality captures the features of a vowel along the three dimensions of high – low (or close – open), front – back and unrounded – rounded. The first two dimensions relate to the tongue and associated jaw position. The third dimension specifies the posture of the lips.

***wh*-clause:** See **interrogative subordinate clause**.

***wh*-interrogative:** See **interrogative**.

word class: Words can be grouped according to morphological and structural characteristics, such as they can take the same inflections or they can occur in the same positions in phrases. These groupings, which include nouns, verbs, determiners and adjectives, are called word classes or syntactic categories.

word-formation: A branch of morphology which studies the morphemic and non-morphemic processes by means of which new words are generated.

***yes–no* interrogative:** See **interrogative**.

BIBLIOGRAPHY

American Psychiatric Association 2013. *Diagnostic and Statistical Manual of Mental Disorders*, Fifth Edition. Washington, DC: American Psychiatric Association.

Barr, W. B., Bilder, R. M., Goldberg, E., Kaplan, E. and Mukherjee, S. 1989. 'The neuropsychology of schizophrenic speech', *Journal of Communication Disorders* 22:5, 327–49.

Bauer, L. 1993. *Manual of Information to Accompany the Wellington Corpus of Written New Zealand English*. Department of Linguistics, Victoria University of Wellington: Wellington, New Zealand.

Becker, J. T., Boiler, F., Lopez, O. L., Saxton, J. and McGonigle, K. L. 1994. 'The natural history of Alzheimer's disease: Description of study cohort and accuracy of diagnosis', *Archives of Neurology* 51:6, 585–94.

Beeke, S., Wilkinson, R. and Maxim, J. 2007. 'Individual variation in agrammatism: A single case study of the influence of interaction', *International Journal of Language & Communication Disorders* 42:6, 629–47.

Börjars, K. and Burridge, K. 2010. *Introducing English Grammar*, Second Edition. Abingdon and New York: Routledge.

British Library 2016a. Sounds familiar? Accents and dialects of the UK. Available at: www.bl.uk/learning/langlit/sounds/regional-voices/grammatical-variation/. Accessed online 3 March 2016.

British Library 2016b. Sounds familiar? Geordie grammar. Available at: http://www.bl.uk/learning/langlit/sounds/case-studies/geordie/grammar/. Accessed online 3 October 2016.

Brown, R. 1973. *A First Language: The Early Stages*. Cambridge, MA: Harvard University Press.

Carnie, A. 2013. *Syntax: A Generative Introduction*, Third Edition. Oxford: Wiley-Blackwell.

Chaika, E. 1982. 'A unified explanation for the diverse structural deviations reported for adult schizophrenics with disrupted speech', *Journal of Communication Disorders* 15:3, 167–89.

Chomsky, N. 1965. *Aspects of the Theory of Syntax*. Cambridge, MA: The MIT Press.

Forrester, M. A. 2002. 'Appropriating cultural conceptions of childhood: Participation in conversation', *Childhood* 9:3, 255–76.

Goodglass, H., Kaplan, E. and Barresi, B. 2001. *Boston Diagnostic Aphasia Examination*, Third Edition. Baltimore, MD: Lippincott Williams & Wilkins.

MacWhinney, B. 2000. *The CHILDES Project: Tools for Analyzing Talk*, Third Edition. Mahwah, NJ: Lawrence Erlbaum Associates.

MacWhinney, B., Fromm, D., Forbes, M. and Holland, A. 2011. 'AphasiaBank: Methods for studying discourse', *Aphasiology* 25:11, 1286–1307.

Martínez, I. P. 2015. 'Variation, development and pragmatic uses of *innit* in the language of British adults and teenagers', *English Language and Linguistics* 19:3, 383–405.

McCardle, P. and Wilson, B. 1993. 'Language and development in FG syndrome with callosal agenesis', *Journal of Communication Disorders* 26:2, 83–100.

McGregor, K. K., Rost, G. C., Guo, L. Y. and Sheng, L. 2010. 'What compound words mean to children with specific language impairment', *Applied Psycholinguistics* 31:3, 463–87.

Moore, M. E. 2001. 'Third person pronoun errors by children with and without language impairment', *Journal of Communication Disorders* 34:3, 207–28.

Peccei, J. S. 1999. *Child Language*, Second Edition. London and New York: Routledge.

Public Broadcasting Service 2005. Do you speak American?. Available at: www.pbs.org/speak/. Accessed online 16 July 2017.

Rastle, K., Tyler, L. K. and Marslen-Wilson, W. 2006. 'New evidence for morphological errors in deep dyslexia', *Brain and Language* 97:2, 189–99.

Rickford, J. R. 1999. *African American Vernacular English*, Oxford and Malden, MA: Blackwell Publishers.

Rickford, J. R. and Théberge Rafal, C. 1996. 'Preterite Had + V-Ed in the narratives of African-American preadolescents', *American Speech* 71:3, 227–54.

Rowland, C. F. and Fletcher, S. L. 2006. 'The effect of sampling on estimates of lexical specificity and error rates', *Journal of Child Language* 33:4, 859–77.

Siemund, P. 2015. 'Exclamative clauses in English and their relevance for theories of clause types', *Studies in Language* 39:3, 698–728.

Smith Doody, R., Hrachovy, R. A. and Feher, E. P. 1992. 'Recurrent fluent aphasia associated with a seizure focus', *Brain and Language* 42:4, 419–30.

Starks, D. and Thompson, L. 2009. 'Agreement patterns in existential constructions in the New Zealand Niuean community', *World Englishes* 28:3, 319–35.

Tomblin, J. B., Records, N. L., Buckwalter, P., et al. 1997. 'Prevalence of specific language impairment in kindergarten children', *Journal of Speech, Language, and Hearing Research* 40:6, 1245–60.

Tottie, G. and Hoffmann, S. 2006. 'Tag questions in British and American English', *Journal of English Linguistics* 34:4, 283–311.

Trudgill, P. 1999. 'Standard English: What it isn't', in T. Bex and R. Watts (eds.), *Standard English: The Widening Debate*. London: Routledge, pp. 117–28.

Warrington, E. K. and Shallice, T. 1984. 'Category specific semantic impairments', *Brain* 10:3, 829–54.

INDEX